The Two-Month Bridge to

"A Course in Miracles"

The Two-Month Bridge to
"A Course in Miracles"

≈ • ≈

A Condensed Edition of
"A Course in Miracles"

Donald James Giacobbe

Miracle Yoga Services

The overall cover design, graphics, and interior layout of the text were created by Donald James Giacobbe.

Published by Miracle Yoga Services
http://www.miracleyoga.org
— miracleyoga@gmail.com —
Cottonwood, Arizona

Printed in the United States of America

BISAC Subject Codes and Headings:

OCC027510 Body, Mind, and Spirit: Spirituality—A Course in Miracles

OCC014000 Body, Mind & Spirit—New Thought

REL012120 Religion: Christian Life—Spiritual Growth

Library of Congress Control Number: 2012907130

Giacobbe, Donald James
The Two-Month Bridge to A Course in Miracles:
A Condensed Edition of A Course in Miracles

ISBN 978-0-9843790-3-3

CONTENTS

~ • ~

PREFACE xiii
ABOUT THE AUTHOR xiv
INTRODUCTION xv
ACKNOWLEDGMENTS xvi
INSTRUCTIONS FOR THE FIRST MONTH xvii
HOW HABITS FORM xxiii

TEXT (Condensed) — Introduction 1

Chapter 1. THE MEANING OF MIRACLES
   I. Principles of Miracles 3
   II. Revelation, Time and Miracles 6
   III. Atonement and Miracles 8
   IV. The Escape from Darkness 8
   V. Wholeness and Spirit 9
   VI. The Illusion of Needs 10
   VII. Distortions of Miracle Impulses 11

Chapter 2.THE SEPARATION AND THE ATONEMENT
   I. The Origins of Separation 13
   II. The Atonement as Defense 14
   III. The Altar of God 15
   IV. Healing as Release from Fear 16
   V. The Function of the Miracle Worker 17
   VI. Fear and Conflict 19
   VII. Cause and Effect 20
   VIII. The Meaning of the Last Judgment 21

Chapter 3. THE INNOCENT PERCEPTION
   I. Atonement without Sacrifice 23
   II. Miracles as True Perception 23
   III. Perception versus Knowledge 24
   IV. Error and the Ego 26
   V. Beyond Perception 28
   VI. Judgment and the Authority Problem 29
   VII. Creating versus the Self-Image 32

Chapter 4. THE ILLUSIONS OF THE EGO
   I. Right Teaching and Right Learning 34
   II. The Ego and False Autonomy 37
   III. Love without Conflict 40
   IV. This Need Not Be 41
   V. The Ego-Body Illusion 43
   VI. The Rewards of God 44
   VII. Creation and Communication 46

Chapter 5. HEALING AND WHOLENESS
  I. The Invitation to the Holy Spirit 49
  II. The Voice for God 50
  III. The Guide to Salvation 51
  IV. Teaching and Healing 53
  V. The Ego's Use of Guilt 54
  VI. Time and Eternity 57
  VII. The Decision for God 57

Chapter 6. THE LESSONS OF LOVE
  Introduction 59
  I. The Message of the Crucifixion 59
  II. The Alternative to Projection 62
  III. The Relinquishment of Attack 65
  IV. The Only Answer 66
  V. The Lessons of the Holy Spirit 67

Chapter 7. THE GIFTS OF THE KINGDOM
  I. The Last Step 68
  II. The Law of the Kingdom 68
  III. The Reality of the Kingdom 69
  IV. Healing as the Recognition of Truth 69
  V. Healing and the Changelessness of Mind 70
  VI. From Vigilance to Peace 72
  VII. The Totality of the Kingdom 73
  VIII. The Unbelievable Belief 75
  IX. The Extension of the Kingdom 76
  X. The Confusion of Pain and Joy 76

Chapter 8. THE JOURNEY BACK
  I. The Direction of the Curriculum 78
  II. The Difference between Imprisonment and Freedom 78
  III. The Holy Encounter 79
  IV. The Gift of Freedom 80
  V. The Undivided Will of the Sonship 82
  VI. The Treasure of God 83
  VII. The Body as a Means of Communication 85
  VIII. The Body as Means or End 86
  IX. Healing as Corrected Perception 87

Chapter 9. THE ACCEPTANCE OF THE ATONEMENT
  I. The Acceptance of Reality 89
  II. The Answer to Prayer 91
  III. The Correction of Error 92
  IV. The Holy Spirit's Plan of Forgiveness 93
  V. The Unhealed Healer 95
  VI. The Acceptance of Your Brother 96
  VII. The Two Evaluations 97

Chapter 10. THE IDOLS OF SICKNESS
    Introduction 99
   I. At Home in God 99
  II. The Decision to Forget 100
 III. The God of Sickness 101
 IV. The End of Sickness 102
  V. The Denial of God 103

Chapter 11. GOD OR THE EGO
    Introduction 104
    I. The Gifts of Fatherhood 104
   II. The Invitation to Healing 106
  III. From Darkness to Light 106
  IV. The Inheritance of God's Son 108
  V. The "Dynamics" of the Ego 109
  VI. Waking to Redemption 110
 VII. The Condition of Reality 112
VIII. The Problem and the Answer 113

Chapter 12. THE HOLY SPIRIT'S CURRICULUM
    I. The Judgment of the Holy Spirit 116
   II. The Way to Remember God 118
  III. The Investment in Reality 120
  IV. Seeking and Finding 121
  V. The Sane Curriculum 122
  VI. The Vision of Christ 123
 VII. Looking Within 125
VIII. The Attraction of Love for Love 126

Chapter 13. THE GUILTLESS WORLD
   II. The Guiltless Son of God 128
  III. The Fear of Redemption 129
  V. The Two Emotions 131
  VI. Finding the Present 132
 VII. Attainment of the Real World 134
VIII. From Perception to Knowledge 135
  IX. The Cloud of Guilt 137
  X. Release from Guilt. 138
  XI. The Peace of Heaven 141

Chapter 14. TEACHING FOR TRUTH
   II. The Happy Learner 142
  III. The Decision for Guiltlessness 142
  IV. Your Function in the Atonement 144
  V. The Circle of Atonement 146
  VI. The Light of Communication 148
 VII. Sharing Perception with the Holy Spirit 148
VIII. The Holy Meeting Place 149
  IX. The Reflection of Holiness 150
  X. The Equality of Miracles 151
  XI. The Test of Truth 153

Chapter 15. THE HOLY INSTANT
  I. The Two Uses of Time 155
  IV. Practicing the Holy Instant 156
  V. The Holy Instant and Special Relationships 157
  VI. The Holy Instant and the Laws of God 159
  VII. The Needless Sacrifice 159
  VIII. The Only Real Relationship 161
  IX. The Holy Instant and the Attraction of God 161

Chapter 16. THE FORGIVENESS OF ILLUSIONS
  II. The Power of Holiness 163
  IV. The Illusion and the Reality of Love 164
  V. The Choice for Completion 164
  VI. The Bridge to the Real World 166
  VII. The End of Illusions 168

Chapter 17. FORGIVENESS AND THE HOLY RELATIONSHIP
  II. The Forgiven World 169
  III. Shadows of the Past 170
  V. The Healed Relationship 172
  VI. Setting the Goal 174
  VII. The Call for Faith 176
  VIII. The Conditions of Peace 176

Chapter 18. THE PASSING OF THE DREAM
  II. The Basis of the Dream 178
  III. Light in the Dream 179
  IV. The Little Willingness 180
  V. The Happy Dream 181
  VI. Beyond the Body 183
  VII. I Need Do Nothing 185
  VIII. The Little Garden 187
  IX. The Two Worlds 190

Chapter 19. THE ATTAINMENT OF PEACE
  I. Healing and Faith 192
  II. Sin versus Error 193
  IV. The Obstacles to Peace 194

Chapter 20. THE VISION OF HOLINESS
  IV. Entering the Ark 203
  VIII. The Vision of Sinlessness 203

Chapter 21. REASON AND PERCEPTION
  Introduction 206
  I. The Forgotten Song 206
  II. The Responsibility for Sight 207
  III. Faith, Belief and Vision 208
  IV. The Fear to Look Within 209

Chapter 22. SALVATION AND THE HOLY RELATIONSHIP
  I. The Message of the Holy Relationship 210
  II. Your Brother's Sinlessness 210
  V. Weakness and Defensiveness 210
  VI. The Light of the Holy Relationship 211

Chapter 24. THE GOAL OF SPECIALNESS
  I. Specialness as a Substitute for Love 212
  II. The Treachery of Specialness 212
  III. The Forgiveness of Specialness 213
  IV. Specialness versus Sinlessness 213
  V. The Christ in You 214
  VI. Salvation from Fear 216

Chapter 25. THE JUSTICE OF GOD
      Introduction 218
    I. The Link to Truth 218
  III. Perception and Choice 219
  VI. The Special Function 221
  VII. The Rock of Salvation 222
 VIII. Justice Returned to Love 223
  IX. The Justice of Heaven 223

Chapter 26. THE TRANSITION
  II. Many Forms; One Correction 225
  III. The Borderland 225
  IV. Where Sin Has Left 226
  V. The Little Hindrance 227
  VII. The Laws of Healing 229
  X. The End of Injustice 230

Chapter 27. THE HEALING OF THE DREAM
  II. The Fear of Healing 231
  IV. The Quiet Answer 231
  V. The Healing Example 232
  VI. The Witnesses to Sin 233
  VII. The Dreamer of the Dream 234
  VIII. The "Hero" of the Dream 235

Chapter 28. THE UNDOING OF FEAR
  I. The Present Memory 239
  II. Reversing Effect and Cause 239
  IV. The Greater Joining 240
  VI. The Secret Vows 242
  VII. The Ark of Safety 242

Chapter 29. THE AWAKENING
  III. God's Witnesses 244
  V. The Changeless Dwelling Place 244
  VI. Forgiveness and the End of Time 246

VII. Seek Not Outside Yourself 247
VIII. The Anti-Christ 248
IX. The Forgiving Dream 249

Chapter 30. THE NEW BEGINNING
III. Beyond All Idols 251
V. The Only Purpose 253
VI. The Justification for Forgiveness 255
VII. The New Interpretation 256
VIII. Changeless Reality 257

Chapter 31. THE FINAL VISION
I. The Simplicity of Salvation 259
II. Walking with Christ 259
V. Self-Concept versus Self 261
VI. Recognizing the Spirit 263
VII. The Savior's Vision 264
VIII. Choose Once Again 267

MANUAL FOR TEACHERS (Condensed) — Introduction 272

1. Who Are God's Teachers? 272
2. Who Are Their Pupils? 273
3. What Are the Levels of Teaching? 273
4. What Are the Characteristics of God's Teachers? 274
5. How Is Healing Accomplished? 280
6. Is Healing Certain? 282
7. Should Healing be Repeated? 283
8. How Can Perception of Order of Difficulties be Avoided? 284
9. Are Changes Required in the Life Situation of God's Teachers? 284
10. How Is Judgment Relinquished? 285
11. How Is Peace Possible in this World? 286
12. How Many Teachers of God Are Needed to Save the World? 287
13. What Is the Real Meaning of Sacrifice? 288
14. How Will the World End? 289
15. Is Each One to be Judged in the End? 289
16. How Should the Teacher of God Spend his Day? 290
17. How Do God's Teachers Deal with Magic Thoughts? 292
18. How Is Correction Made? 293
19. What Is Justice? 295
20. What Is the Peace of God? 295
21. What Is the Role of Words in Healing? 297
22. How Are Healing and Atonement Related? 298
23. Does Jesus Have a Special Place in Healing? 299
24. Is Reincarnation So? 301
25. Are "Psychic" Powers Desirable? 303
26. Can God be Reached Directly? 304
27. What Is Death? 304
28. What Is the Resurrection? 305
29. As For the Rest... 306

INSTRUCTIONS FOR THE SECOND MONTH 309

THIRTY WORKBOOK LESSONS

INTRODUCTION 311

DAY 1 — LESSON 15
My thoughts are images that I have made 313

DAY 2 — LESSSON 28
Above all else I want to see things differently 314

DAY 3 — LESSON 36
My holiness envelops everything I see 316

DAY 4 — LESSON 41
God goes with me wherever I go 317

DAY 5 — LESSON 44
God is the light in which I see 319

DAY 6 — LESSON 46
God is the Love in which I forgive 321

DAY 7 — LESSON 50
I am sustained by the Love of God 323

DAY 8 — LESSON 62
Forgiveness is my function as the light of the world 324

DAY 9 — LESSON 67
Love created me like itself 325

DAY 10 — LESSON 68
Love holds no grievances 327

DAY 11 — LESSON 69
My grievances hide the light of the world in me 329

DAY 12 — LESSON 74
There is no will but God's 331

DAY 13 — LESSON 78
Let miracles replace all grievances 333

DAY 14 — LESSON 94
I am as God created me 335

DAY 15 — LESSON 108
To give and to receive are one in truth 337

DAY 16 — LESSON 109
        I rest in God 339

DAY 17 — LESSON 121
        Forgiveness is the key to happiness 341

DAY 18 — LESSON 122
        Forgiveness offers everything I want 344

DAY 19 — LESSON 124
        Let me remember I am one with God 347

DAY 20 — LESSON 126
        All that I give is given to myself 349

DAY 21 — LESSON 127
        There is no love but God's 351

DAY 22 — LESSON 134
        Let me perceive forgiveness as it is 353

DAY 23 — LESSON 139
        I will accept Atonement for myself 356

DAY 24 — LESSON 155
        I will step back and let Him lead the way 359

DAY 25 — LESSON 157
        Into His Presence would I enter now 362

DAY 26 — LESSON 158
        Today I learn to give as I receive 364

DAY 27 — LESSON 159
        I give the miracles I have received 366

DAY 28 — LESSON 161
        Give me your blessing, holy Son of God 368

DAY 29 — LESSON 183
        I call upon God's Name and on my own 371

DAY 30 — LESSON 189
        I feel the Love of God within me now 373

SIXTY ANSWERS 375

WHAT'S NEXT? 393

THE MISSING BLESSING 395

PREFACE

≈ ○ ≈

A few friends of mine have told me that their encounter with the philosophy of *A Course in Miracles* was an experience of "love at first sight." However, for many students the experience of the Course is an ongoing roller coaster ride of ups and downs. A friend of mine described his long struggle with the Course in this way: "Over the years I have read it and then thrown it in the trash—twice! Yet now it's actually sinking in, and I'm accepting it."

Why is the Course so challenging? For many students it takes a long time to meet the three challenges of the Course. These three challenges are understanding it, accepting it, and applying it. Reading all 1249 pages of the Course can be daunting and overwhelming because so many new and unusual concepts are presented. Besides absorbing new information, the seeker has the difficult task of letting go of his customary way of perceiving his world and himself.

If you are a beginning student, I suggest reading *An Overview of "A Course in Miracles": Introduction to the Course—What Beginners Need to Know*. This hundred-page book allows you to step away from the confusing details of the Course in order to grasp the big picture and see where the Course is leading you. This brief overview shows you how all the seemingly different ideas in the Course are actually totally interrelated and work together toward the single goal of integrating and unifying the mind to bring inner peace.

Another book I suggest is the one you are reading now because it simplifies your studying of the Course. *The Two-Month Bridge to "A Course in Miracles"* is an abbreviated version of the Course. The most essential teachings of the Course are read during the first month of the Two-Month Bridge. Then during the second month, these Course principles are put into practical application by doing thirty daily Workbook lessons. This two-month learning experience is called a "bridge" because it helps to bridge the gap between being a beginner and being a firmly committed Course student. After you complete the Two-Month Bridge, you will have enough experience with the Course to make an informed decision on whether or not you would like to study the Course in more depth. Perhaps this transition period will encourage you to apply the spiritual principles of the Course to your daily experiences and especially to improving your personal relationships.

ABOUT THE AUTHOR

≈ ∘ ≈

Donald James Giacobbe recorded his life story in his autobiography, *Memory Walk in the Light*. He was employed for sixteen years as a case manager serving developmentally disabled clients. The professional nature of his work limited his ability to express his spiritual motivations overtly, so out of necessity he served as an "undercover agent" for God.

A more direct approach to spirituality was facilitated by living with Zen Buddhist seekers and then being part of a yoga community. Later he was the director of the Aquarian Age Yoga Center in Virginia Beach, VA. He served as an instructor of meditation and yoga, teaching college courses and appearing on television. He specialized in providing yoga teacher training certification courses and leading meditation workshops and retreats. Don has attempted in his teaching of meditation to strip away the rituals of Zen Buddhism and yoga practices and transpose only the bare essence into a Christian context. Techniques of meditation inspired by Eastern sources enhance the use of traditional Christian practices, such as the "Jesus Prayer," and lead to the overshadowing of the Holy Spirit that occurs in Christian contemplation. These techniques can be found in Don's book *Christian Meditation Inspired by Yoga and "A Course in Miracles": Opening to Divine Love in Contemplation*.

Don encourages the doing of God's Will, being receptive to the Holy Spirit, and finding Christ within the temple of one's own heart. While respecting all spiritual expressions, he became a monk by making his vow directly to God, without the stamp of approval from any religious organization. For many years Don used the term "Christian yoga" to describe his spiritual path, which combined following Christ with yoga disciplines. But in recent years he has adopted the term "Miracle Yoga" to describe the specific path of Christian yoga he has chosen. This form of spirituality is a synthesis of yoga and the philosophy of "A Course in Miracles," encouraging the seeker to see with "forgiving eyes" and to perceive Christ in everyone. Don's goal is to maintain a balance between opening to divine love inwardly and allowing that love to be extended outwardly to others. You can contact Don at miracleyoga@gmail.com and read his teachings on the following websites:

www.miracleyoga.org
www.christianyoga.org
www.christianmeditation.org

INTRODUCTION

~ o ~

The Two-Month Bridge helps you to make the transition from being a somewhat skeptical beginner to a committed Course student by providing an intermediate level of training. This book is not a replacement for studying the full version of the Course. Rather, it is designed as an encouragement for studying and applying the entire Course. Reading the complete Text and Manual and doing all of the 365 Workbook lessons can be an intimidating task for a beginner. The Course is not for everyone. However, you won't know if it's right for you unless you at least explore some of what it has to say and have some direct experience of applying its principles. This book provides this opportunity to become familiar with the Course in order to help you decide if it's the right philosophy for you to believe, to study in more depth, and to apply to your daily life. The following is a brief summary of the two primary aspects of the Two-Month Bridge:

For the first month, you will read about the Course principles. *A Condensed Edition of "A Course in Miracles"* is the subtitle since this book contains an abbreviated version of the Course. It has the same words used in the full Course, but less essential and repetitious parts have been deleted for the sake of simplicity. This prevents the beginner from being overwhelmed by receiving too much nonessential information all at once.

For the second month, you have the opportunity to put the spiritual principles you have learned in the first month into practical application by doing thirty of the 365 daily Workbook lessons. The thirty lessons selected for this training period will expose you to a variety of spiritual experiences that will help you identify with your true nature as a spiritual being created by God, Who loves you. Some of these lessons encourage you to develop your inner attunement, while most of these lessons are designed to foster healthy personal relationships based on loving forgiveness. This two-month training period will help you to evaluate the challenges and the benefits of incorporating spiritual principles into your daily life.

ACKNOWLEDGMENTS

~ o ~

I am very grateful for the support, suggestions, encouragement, and proofreading of my sister Lillian Blackburn. Also, my thanks go to Nancy Bonfield and Tom Dunn for their proofreading. In addition, I appreciate Tina Hardy for her copy editing work on *The Two-Month Bridge to "A Course in Miracles."*[1]

1. *The Two-Month Bridge to "A Course in Miracles"* is a 396-page version of the Text, Workbook, and Manual of the Course. This book is a condensed edition of the full 1249 pages of the second edition of *A Course in Miracles*, which is currently in public domain. Helen Schucman is recognized as the author of the Course. However, she preferred to call herself the "scribe" of the Course. She considered Jesus Christ to be the true Author of the Course because he dictated the Course to her. The second edition of the Course was originally copyrighted and published by the Foundation of Inner Peace, P. O. Box 598, Mill Valley, CA 94942-0598.

INSTRUCTIONS FOR THE FIRST MONTH

~ ◦ ~

The first thing to do before starting this learning experience is to ask the Holy Spirit to guide you along the way. Having invited divine assistance, you will be ready to read a condensed version of the Course for the first month of the Two-Month Bridge. This will include 270 pages of the Text, condensed from 669 pages. You will also read 38 of the 92 pages of the Manual. The Course itself is a self-study course so there is no commentary supplied as you read about the spiritual principles.

Besides the abbreviated nature of this condensed edition of the Course, there is one other unique aspect of this presentation of the Text and Manual: Questions have been inserted into the Course. These questions are not intended to be a testing device. Instead, they are intended to be a learning aid used to promote thoughtful consideration of spiritual principles.

During the first month of the Two-Month Bridge, each day you will encounter two numbered questions. For example, on the first day, you will encounter the first question—a two-part question—on page 6. The second question is on page 9. Each day when you reach the second question—always an even numbered question—you will stop reading for that day, except if you want to go back to review what you have already read in order to find the answer to a particular question.

There are five options for answering each question. The first is you may determine the answer from your memory of what you have just read. If you choose this option, it is recommended that you write down your answer. The second option is you can go back to what you have just read to look for the answer. In this case you might want to highlight your answer with a yellow magic marker or underline it with a pencil or pen. The third option is that before you read each section, you skip down and read the question for that section. Then when you read the section, you will already know the question and you can be looking for the answer as you read the text. Here too you can highlight or underline the answer as you read it. The fourth option is you can immediately look up the very short answers, which you will find listed at the end of this book on pages 375 through 392. The fifth option is to complete the entire Two-Month Bridge, and then as a follow-up and review, you can read all of the same questions and a more complete presentation of the same answers in the brief book *"A Course in Miracles" Seven Keys to Heaven: A Simple Framework for Understanding the Course.*

The questions can be answered concisely, for example with one-line answers. However, don't be concerned if your answer is somewhat different than the very concise answers at the end of *The Two-Month Bridge to "A Course in Miracles."* The questions in many cases can have a wide variety of correct answers. For instance, one question is, "What is the ego?" There are literally hundreds of possible answers to this question scattered throughout the entire Course. Repetition of one idea, described in numerous ways, is a teaching device used by the Course to help you to better understand a difficult concept.

Learning the philosophy contained in the Course requires the three steps of reading, comprehending, and remembering. The questions are designed to assist you in manifesting this learning process. During the first month of the Two-Month Bridge, bear in mind something previously stated: The questions have not been inserted into the Course to test your understanding. Rather, the questions are just reminders that tell you to pay particular attention to certain ideas needed to help you understand the Course. Also, the answers listed in *"A Course in Miracles" Seven Keys to Heaven* include lengthy quotations that address the question asked followed by answers that summarize the meaning of the quotations. Reading these quotations more than once helps you to remember these spiritual principles. Why is it necessary to reread the text to extract the answers? Answers provided in a summarized paraphrasing cannot replace the words of the Course itself. After all, it is a self-study course, but do not think you are alone in your studying. Please remember to continually ask the Holy Spirit to help you understand what you are reading. Asking help from the Holy Spirit is in itself a demonstration that you are already putting into practice one of the most important spiritual practices recommended in the Course.

The Holy Spirit has been given to you by God the Father as your Teacher to show you the way back Home. But He requires your cooperation in order for you to learn the lessons that would help you grow spiritually. The Holy Spirit has many instruments at His disposal to produce inner transformation. He works at the subconscious level in this transformation process in ways that may never come to your conscious awareness, but He also works at the conscious level. The transformation process used by the Holy Spirit is introduced in the hundred-page book *An Overview of "A Course in Miracles."* This inexpensive introductory book was written as a way of preparing for the Two-Month Bridge. It is certainly recommended reading if you are guided in that direction by the Holy Spirit. Your spiritual transformation is brought about by the Holy Spirit using seven primary keys to transformation, which I call the "tools" of the Holy Spirit. These are elaborated upon in the book *"A Course in Miracles" Seven Keys to Heaven: A Simple Framework for Understanding the Course.* The seven tools of the Holy Spirit are: forgiveness, Christ's vision, miracles, the holy instant, the holy relationship, the quiet time of meditation, and the Atonement. These seven terms are presented to you now so that as you read the Text and Manual, you will pay particular attention to them. I am asking you to set the simple goal for yourself of being able to answer the following seven questions:

1. What is FORGIVENESS?
2. What is CHRIST'S VISION?
3. What is a MIRACLE?
4. What is the HOLY INSTANT?
5. What is the HOLY RELATIONSHIP?
6. What is a QUIET TIME (MEDITATION)?
7. What is ATONEMENT?

Keep these questions in mind as you read the Text and Manual, and even as you do the Workbook lessons in the second month. Being able to provide simple answers to these seven questions is a very modest goal for your Two-Month Bridge. Nevertheless, if you can come up with at least a one-line answer to each of these questions, you will have a minimal framework for understanding the Course, which you can then build upon in your future study. These seven tools of the Holy Spirit—forgiveness, Christ's vision, miracles, the holy instant, the holy relationship, the quiet time of meditation, and Atonement—form the core of the Course spiritual principles. The seven tools of the Holy Spirit will lead you to the "real world," also called the "face of Christ," so these terms are also important to understand.

When I first started studying the Course, I wondered why the Text didn't have seven distinct chapters that said everything there was to say about each one of these forms of transformation. I was confused by how these ideas were scattered throughout the entire book and repeated from numerous different perspectives. After studying the Course over a period of time, I realized why these spiritual principles are not separated off into clearly defined categories. The reason was that the principles themselves are not separate. They are entirely interrelated and interdependent so they work together. That is why they cannot be fully understood separately, but can be understood as part of a tapestry of spiritual growth. You will have a good understanding of these ideas only after studying them in relation to each other and then putting them into practical application, guided by the Holy Spirit.

Studying the Course is similar to taking a long trip to a foreign country. Using this analogy of a trip to an unfamiliar place, let's review the list of three books that have been recommended and the ideal order for reading them:

1. *An Overview of "A Course in Miracles"* offers an easy-to-follow itinerary showing the outline of your whole trip from beginning to end. Seeing this itinerary lets you decide if you want to take this trip.

2. *The Two-Month Bridge to "A Course in Miracles"* allows you to participate in about one fourth of the journey, and this direct experience helps you determine if you want to complete the journey. Sixty questions about the trip are asked and concisely answered.

3. *"A Course in Miracles" Seven Keys to Heaven* shows you a slide show of the journey, including seven slides of the most memorable highlights of the trip. The same sixty questions about the trip are reviewed again and this time answered in a more complete way.

Each individual book can prepare you to study the full 1249 pages of the Course, but all three books read in this order can consolidate your learning and serve as a better preparation. However, what if you read the books in a different order? Just because the books were designed to be read in this ideal order, it is perfectly all right if you happen to read them in any other order. The three books use different formats to describe the Course. As an analogy, you can think of the Course as if it is a sculpture of an elephant. In this analogy, one book is like a photograph showing a frontal view of the elephant. A second book is similar to a picture presenting a side view. A third book can be compared to a photograph showing a three-quarter view. Just as each photograph shows the whole elephant from a different view, each book outlines the whole Course from a different perspective. All three photographs put together give you a better picture of the elephant sculpture than any single view.

Similarly, reading all three books provides a much more complete picture of the Course. The books are complementary, and the repetition and elaboration of the same spiritual principles seen in three different formats assist your memory in its learning process. Reading any one of these three books will provide you with a simple framework for understanding the spiritual principles of the Course, but reading all three will make that simple framework into a very solid foundation. This solid foundation will consist of an understanding of both how these spiritual principles are interrelated and how they can be put into practical application. Of course, you will have to study the full version of the Course, which includes completing the entire year of Workbook lessons in order to build on this foundation established by reading the three books recommended here.

Learning the Course principles can be compared to the way a child learns to speak. First, the child must be receptive to just listening to others as they speak a totally unfamiliar language. The child has the advantage of having no preconceived ideas and judgments so he just takes everything in and rejects nothing. Then the child picks up a word or two and tries speaking it. He learns to associate the word spoken with a meaning associated with it. Next he adds more words and more related meanings. Then he strings a few words together and understands their related meanings. Later he will gradually learn to put together full sentences. He learns more and more about the interrelationships between the words and their meanings. Still later he will learn more and more nuances of the language he is speaking. The big advantage the child has is that he is patient with himself and never says to himself, "I am not learning this stuff fast enough."

Can you learn as a child does? Ideally you will just read the Text and Manual for the first month, and just take it all in. You don't have to be concerned with ideas that you don't understand. You don't even have to be concerned with questions that you cannot answer. Just be patient with yourself and move on. Absorb whatever you can easily absorb and let the rest go for the time being. Whatever you don't understand in your first reading will become increasingly clear in a second or third reading at a later date. That's how every Course student learns, just as a child learns to speak through putting bits and pieces of words together over an extended period of time. No one learns the Course all at once. Initially you will understand Course concepts as separate ideas like children learn separate words. Later you will see how various Course ideas are completely interrelated, which at first will seem like a very complex network of ideas. Even later you will understand how all the interconnections between Course ideas are leading not toward complexity, but rather toward simplicity and oneness. All this takes study and time, but it is worth the effort because this journey leads toward the appreciation of the precious oneness that is within you and indeed *is You*.

In addition, understanding the Course concepts intellectually is only a beginning of a learning process. The next step is to put those ideas into practical application by completing daily Workbook lessons as you will be doing during the second month of the Two-Month Bridge. But first things first. Your biggest challenge will be to establish and to sustain a daily routine of study, especially if you have had poor study habits in the past. Therefore, the next section will give you specific tools to help you meet that challenge. After you read the next four pages, you will have all the instructions you need to start your first day of your first month of the Two-Month Bridge.

Once you get started, remember to continually ask the Holy Spirit to aid your practice and your understanding because He will surely come in an instant each time you renew your invitation. The Holy Spirit walks the fence between Heaven and earth. His job is to prepare you to be lifted over that fence from time to timelessness by helping you navigate through the world of form. There is no help the Holy Spirit cannot provide because He was created by God the Father to be your Helper. There is no question the Holy Spirit cannot answer since He is God's Answer.

HOW HABITS FORM

~ • ~

This condensed version of the Course requires you to establish a daily habit of studying the Course over a two-month period. That's a lot less time and effort than the many days it would take to read the full 1249 pages of the Course, and much less than the full year it would take to do all 365 Workbook lessons. Nevertheless, even establishing a two-month daily habit of study and application can be rather challenging. This challenge is made much more difficult if you view study as a tedious and unpleasant activity. However, you can meet this challenge successfully by having a positive attitude based on a thorough understanding of the true nature of how habits are established and sustained.

Charles Duhigg is an investigative reporter for *The New York Times* who had analyzed scientific studies regarding the nature of habits. He is the author of the book *The Power of Habits: Why We Do What We Do in Life and in Business*. His book emphasizes that neurological research has shown there are three basic components to forming and maintaining positive habits. These three components are: *the cue, the routine, and the reward*. Most people are well aware of the habit as a routine that includes automatic behavior, but are unaware of the importance of the cue and the reward. The cue is the trigger that sets the routine into motion. The reward is the positive reinforcement associated with some form of pleasurable experience as the final outcome of the habitual behavior. The cue and the reward are tools you can use to help you break persistent, bad habits. Or they can help you establish and maintain new, positive habits.

Understanding how habits form in the brain can help you change habits. A shift in activity from one part of the brain to another part happens when habits are established. The decision to start any new routine begins with brain activity in the front part of the brain called the *prefrontal cortex*, which is the place where we make decisions. However, as the decision becomes a repeated behavior pattern, the brain activity moves to the center of the brain called the *basal ganglia*. This part of the brain stores mental patterns and is also involved with memory and other functions.

Basically the prefrontal cortex is for the hard-working tasks that require conscious effort, and that is why new habits are initiated there. The basal ganglia is for the repetitive tasks that can be done without thinking consciously about them, and that is why the formation of habits in the brain involves a shift from the prefrontal cortex to the basal ganglia. This is a shift from a high maintenance part of the brain that requires effort to a low maintenance part of the brain.

The majority of the *unlearned* involuntary functions of the body, such as breathing, blood pressure, and heartbeat, are regulated by the *medulla oblongata* located in the back of the head. But *learned* behavior habits that were originally voluntary muscle movements are assigned to the basal ganglia. The shift from the prefrontal cortex to the basal ganglia occurs as a habit moves from functioning in its initial state of conscious effort to its later stage of effortlessness. The basal ganglia control repetitive behaviors, the experience of learning through rewards, and focusing attention. All three of these functions are crucial for the formation of habits.

What is most significant about this shift to the basal ganglia is that in performing an established habitual behavior, your mind stops working so hard because it is no longer controlled by the prefrontal cortex. Since the already established habit is no longer regulated by the decision-making part of the brain, the habit seems to be totally outside your control. That explains why it is often so hard to change habitual behavior. That's why you need to utilize the tools of the cue and the reward. It may be hard to change the habitual routine of the basal ganglia, but it is much easier to use the prefrontal cortex to make conscious decisions to change the cue and reward, which in turn will have an effect on changing a habit. This understanding is the key to changing habits—both removing old, bad habits and establishing new, good habits.

You must be able to correctly diagnose the cue and the reward to know how to successfully manage your habits. Once you know what is causing or triggering the habit and once you know the craving or desire that is driving the habit, then you can make helpful changes that affect the habit itself. The cue is the mental trigger for automatic behavior to start. It reminds you to initiate the habit. There are five kinds of cues. They are: the time of day, a certain place, the presence of other people, a particular emotion, or a behavior ritual.

The reward can be anything you associate with pleasure or any reinforcing agent that encourages you to continue to manifest the new habitual behavior. A small amount of especially appetizing food is one reinforcing agent because it produces immediate gratification. Or you may enjoy carrying out a habit in coordination with another person, and in this case the social interaction would be your reward that reinforces your efforts.

To lose weight, Charles Duhigg used what he had learned about habits to break his own habit of eating a cookie in the middle of every day. He noticed that the time of day was his cue because the urge for a cookie always happened between 3:15 and 3:45 PM. He tried to change his reward by replacing a cookie with an apple. Then he tried a cup of coffee to replace the cookie. He even tried taking a walk outside because his reward might be getting a break from his work. But none of these new rewards worked because he had failed to correctly identify the actual reward that was driving his craving for the cookie. Finally he realized that when he was going to the cafeteria to get his cookie, he would socialize with his coworkers. He discovered that this socialization was what he was craving as his reward. Having correctly diagnosed the cue as the time of day and the reward as the socialization, he was able to change his habit. Now at about 3:15 PM every day, he seeks out a coworker for a ten-minute conversation. Consequently, the daily habitual urge for a cookie is totally gone.

Behavioral experiments have shown that if you try to change everything all at once, you will likely fail. Charles Duhigg describes "the golden rule of habit change," which focuses on one behavior. First, you identify a cue—perhaps an easy to remember one that has been an effective trigger in the past. Second, you choose a desirable reward that you associate with pleasure. Third, you establish a new routine, and consistently implement the same cue and reward. This combination of a routine with a familiar cue and reward is the magic formula for firmly establishing and sustaining a new habit. Repeated behavioral experiments have shown this pattern of the same cue and reward being perfectly matched with maintaining a new habit. If you use the right tools of the cue and reward, you can break old habits or establish new ones. It does not matter how old you are or how ingrained your habits have become. You can make effective changes simply by wisely adjusting the cue and the reward.

For example, let's say you want to instill a new habit of doing a daily exercise workout as a means of lowering your weight. Let's say you set up a familiar cue, such as the timing of doing your workout in the morning right after your daily routine of brushing your teeth. Or a different cue might be putting on your workout clothes first thing in the morning. Then as your consistent reward after completing your new workout routine, you select a food treat. You choose a food that you already associate with pleasure, perhaps one pastry or a fruit that you enjoy. Because the new routine is regularly triggered by one specific thing and repeatedly delivers a pleasurable reward, the change becomes a permanent habit.

It seems counterintuitive to have a pleasurable food as a reward based on the fact that you want to do the workout to lose weight. Thus you do not anticipate beforehand that you need this reward as a means of losing weight. Nevertheless, a specific series of scientific studies have shown that giving a small piece of chocolate as a reward significantly increases the likelihood that the new workout routine will be firmly maintained as a long-term habit. Why does a bit of chocolate work? Because it tricks the mind into thinking the routine is about obtaining something pleasurable. At first your neurology does not know that you will enjoy exercise. Workouts can bring about the release of endorphins and other neurological chemicals that offer a pleasurable experience, but that only happens after the habit of workouts is firmly established. Initially the idea of doing the new routine of a workout seems to be a tedious and unpleasant activity. But having a chocolate reward directs the mind toward the pleasurable reward—even though it is just a minor reward. Therefore, you learn to associate your exercise with something you enjoy—an immediate reward right at the start of learning the new habit. Then after this initial period of adjustment, you will gain the beneficial effects of endorphins, which will carry forward your association of exercise with a pleasurable experience. When that happens, the workout becomes a firmly established part of your daily life rather than an unpleasant chore.

Hopefully, the information here about the formation of habitual behavior will help you to establish a new study habit to facilitate the completion of the Two-Month Bridge. The basic recommendation that you can put into practical application for this two-month training period is to wisely choose a cue and a reward that will assist you in reading this condensed version of the Course and in doing the thirty Workbook lessons. An example of a cue you might want to use is to identify a specific time of day to do your daily reading or Workbook lesson. You can even use a timer or an alarm clock and set it for the cue time you have chosen to trigger your daily practice. As an added cue you can do these daily tasks in the same place each day. An example of a reward would be a small food treat that you have at the end of each daily practice. Or perhaps you can have your daily practice before one of your daily meals or other activity that you especially enjoy. You want to make sure that you choose a cue that is easy for you to implement as a reminder to start your daily practice and to choose a reward—even a minor reward—that you associate with some form of personal and immediate gratification. What if you complete the Two-Month Bridge, and you discover through this process that you would like to read the entire Course and do the one year of Workbook Lessons? Having already firmly established a study habit for two months, it will be much easier for you to then simply continue your same daily routine with the same cue and the same reward as you further your study of the entire Course.

The condensed version of the Course begins on the next page, and now you have all the tools you need to get started!

TEXT

~ o ~

INTRODUCTION

1. *This is a course in miracles. It is a required course. Only the time you take it is voluntary. Free will does not mean that you can establish the curriculum. It means only that you can elect what you want to take at a given time. The course does not aim at teaching the meaning of love, for that is beyond what can be taught. It does aim, however, at removing the blocks to the awareness of love's presence, which is your natural inheritance. The opposite of love is fear, but what is all-encompassing can have no opposite.*

2. *This course can therefore be summed up very simply in this way:*

> **Nothing real can be threatened.**
> **Nothing unreal exists.**

Herein lies the peace of God.

Chapter 1. THE MEANING OF MIRACLES

I. Principles of Miracles

1. There is no order of difficulty in miracles. One is not "harder" or "bigger" than another. They are all the same. All expressions of love are maximal.
2. Miracles as such do not matter. The only thing that matters is their Source, which is far beyond evaluation.
3. Miracles occur naturally as expressions of love. The real miracle is the love that inspires them. In this sense everything that comes from love is a miracle.
4. All miracles mean life, and God is the Giver of life. His Voice will direct you very specifically. You will be told all you need to know.
5. Miracles are habits, and should be involuntary. They should not be under conscious control. Consciously selected miracles can be misguided.
6. Miracles are natural. When they do not occur something has gone wrong.
7. Miracles are everyone's right, but purification is necessary first.
8. Miracles are healing because they supply a lack; they are performed by those who temporarily have more for those who temporarily have less.
9. Miracles are a kind of exchange. Like all expressions of love, which are always miraculous in the true sense, the exchange reverses the physical laws. They bring more love both to the giver *and* the receiver.
10. The use of miracles as spectacles to induce belief is a misunderstanding of their purpose.
11. Prayer is the medium of miracles. It is a means of communication of the created with the Creator. Through prayer love is received, and through miracles love is expressed.
12. Miracles are thoughts. Thoughts can represent the lower or bodily level of experience, or the higher or spiritual level of experience. One makes the physical, and the other creates the spiritual.
13. Miracles are both beginnings and endings, and so they alter the temporal order. They are always affirmations of rebirth, which seem to go back but really go forward. They undo the past in the present, and thus release the future.
14. Miracles bear witness to truth. They are convincing because they arise from conviction. Without conviction they deteriorate into

magic, which is mindless and therefore destructive; or rather, the uncreative use of mind.

15. Each day should be devoted to miracles. The purpose of time is to enable you to learn how to use time constructively. It is thus a teaching device and a means to an end. Time will cease when it is no longer useful in facilitating learning.

16. Miracles are teaching devices for demonstrating it is as blessed to give as to receive. They simultaneously increase the strength of the giver and supply strength to the receiver.

17. Miracles transcend the body. They are sudden shifts into invisibility, away from the bodily level. That is why they heal.

18. A miracle is a service. It is the maximal service you can render to another. It is a way of loving your neighbor as yourself. You recognize your own and your neighbor's worth simultaneously.

19. Miracles make minds one in God. They depend on cooperation because the Sonship is the sum of all that God created. Miracles therefore reflect the laws of eternity, not of time.

20. Miracles reawaken the awareness that the spirit, not the body, is the altar of truth. This is the recognition that leads to the healing power of the miracle.

21. Miracles are natural signs of forgiveness. Through miracles you accept God's forgiveness by extending it to others.

22. Miracles are associated with fear only because of the belief that darkness can hide. You believe that what your physical eyes cannot see does not exist. This leads to a denial of spiritual sight.

23. Miracles rearrange perception and place all levels in true perspective. This is healing because sickness comes from confusing the levels.

24. Miracles enable you to heal the sick and raise the dead because you made sickness and death yourself, and can therefore abolish both. *You* are a miracle, capable of creating in the likeness of your Creator. Everything else is your own nightmare, and does not exist. Only the creations of light are real.

25. Miracles are part of an interlocking chain of forgiveness which, when completed, is the Atonement. Atonement works all the time and in all the dimensions of time.

26. Miracles represent freedom from fear. "Atoning" means "undoing." The undoing of fear is an essential part of the Atonement value of miracles.

27. A miracle is a universal blessing from God through me to all my brothers. It is the privilege of the forgiven to forgive.

28. Miracles are a way of earning release from fear. Revelation induces a state in which fear has already been abolished. Miracles are thus a means and revelation is an end.

29. Miracles praise God through you. They praise Him by honoring His creations, affirming their perfection. They heal because they deny body-identification and affirm spirit-identification.

30. By recognizing spirit, miracles adjust the levels of perception and show them in proper alignment. This places spirit at the center, where it can communicate directly.

31. Miracles should inspire gratitude, not awe. You should thank God for what you really are. The children of God are holy and the miracle honors their holiness, which can be hidden but never lost.

32. I inspire all miracles, which are really intercessions. They intercede for your holiness and make your perceptions holy. By placing you beyond the physical laws they raise you into the sphere of celestial order. In this order you *are* perfect.

33. Miracles honor you because you are lovable. They dispel illusions about yourself and perceive the light in you. They thus atone for your errors by freeing you from your nightmares. By releasing your mind from the imprisonment of your illusions, they restore your sanity.

34. Miracles restore the mind to its fullness. By atoning for lack they establish perfect protection. The spirit's strength leaves no room for intrusions.

35. Miracles are expressions of love, but they may not always have observable effects.

36. Miracles are examples of right thinking, aligning your perceptions with truth as God created it.

37. A miracle is a correction introduced into false thinking by me. It acts as a catalyst, breaking up erroneous perception and reorganizing it properly. This places you under the Atonement principle, where perception is healed. Until this has occurred, knowledge of the Divine Order is impossible.

38. The Holy Spirit is the mechanism of miracles. He recognizes both God's creations and your illusions. He separates the true from the false by His ability to perceive totally rather than selectively.

39. The miracle dissolves error because the Holy Spirit identifies error as false or unreal. This is the same as saying that by perceiving light, darkness automatically disappears.

40. The miracle acknowledges everyone as your brother and mine. It is a way of perceiving the universal mark of God.

41. Wholeness is the perceptual content of miracles. They thus correct, or atone for, the faulty perception of lack.

42. A major contribution of miracles is their strength in releasing you from your false sense of isolation, deprivation and lack.

43. Miracles arise from a miraculous state of mind, or a state of miracle-readiness.

44. The miracle is an expression of an inner awareness of Christ and the acceptance of His Atonement.

45. A miracle is never lost. It may touch many people you have not even met, and produce undreamed of changes in situations of which you are not even aware.

46. The Holy Spirit is the highest communication medium. Miracles do not involve this type of communication, because they are *temporary* communication devices. When you return to your original form of communication with God by direct revelation, the need for miracles is over.

47. The miracle is a learning device that lessens the need for time. It establishes an out-of-pattern time interval not under the usual laws of time. In this sense it is timeless.

48. The miracle is the only device at your immediate disposal for controlling time. Only revelation transcends it, having nothing to do with time at all.

49. The miracle makes no distinction among degrees of misperception. It is a device for perception correction, effective quite apart from either the degree or the direction of the error. This is its true indiscriminateness.

50. The miracle compares what you have made with creation, accepting what is in accord with it as true, and rejecting what is out of accord as false.

QUESTION 1. Why is the Course summarized by these two lines: "Nothing real can be threatened. Nothing unreal exists," and what is a miracle and who benefits from the expression of a miracle?

II. Revelation, Time and Miracles

1. Revelation induces complete but temporary suspension of doubt and fear. It reflects the original form of communication between God and His creations, involving the extremely personal sense of creation sometimes sought in physical relationships. Physical closeness cannot achieve it. Miracles, however, are genuinely interpersonal, and result in true closeness to others. Revelation unites you directly with God. Miracles unite you directly with your brother. Neither emanates from consciousness, but both are experienced there. Consciousness is the state that induces action, though it does not inspire it. You are free

to believe what you choose, and what you do attests to what you believe.

2. Revelation is intensely personal and cannot be meaningfully translated. That is why any attempt to describe it in words is impossible. Revelation induces only experience. Miracles, on the other hand, induce action. They are more useful now because of their interpersonal nature. In this phase of learning, working miracles is important because freedom from fear cannot be thrust upon you. Revelation is literally unspeakable because it is an experience of unspeakable love.

3. Awe should be reserved for revelation, to which it is perfectly and correctly applicable. It is not appropriate for miracles because a state of awe is worshipful, implying that one of a lesser order stands before his Creator. You are a perfect creation, and should experience awe only in the Presence of the Creator of perfection. The miracle is therefore a sign of love among equals. Equals should not be in awe of one another because awe implies inequality. It is therefore an inappropriate reaction to me. An elder brother is entitled to respect for his greater experience, and obedience for his greater wisdom. He is also entitled to love because he is a brother, and to devotion if he is devoted. It is only my devotion that entitles me to yours. There is nothing about me that you cannot attain. I have nothing that does not come from God. The difference between us now is that I have nothing else. This leaves me in a state which is only potential in you.

4. "No man cometh unto the Father but by me" does not mean that I am in any way separate or different from you except in time, and time does not really exist. The statement is more meaningful in terms of a vertical rather than a horizontal axis. You stand below me and I stand below God. In the process of "rising up," I am higher because without me the distance between God and man would be too great for you to encompass. I bridge the distance as an elder brother to you on the one hand, and as a Son of God on the other. My devotion to my brothers has placed me in charge of the Sonship, which I render complete because I share it. This may appear to contradict the statement "I and my Father are one," but there are two parts to the statement in recognition that the Father is greater.

5. Revelations are indirectly inspired by me because I am close to the Holy Spirit, and alert to the revelation-readiness of my brothers. I can thus bring down to them more than they can draw down to themselves. The Holy Spirit mediates higher to lower communication, keeping the direct channel from God to you open for revelation. Revelation is not reciprocal. It proceeds from God to you, but not from you to God.

III. Atonement and Miracles

1. I am in charge of the process of Atonement, which I undertook to begin. When you offer a miracle to any of my brothers, you do it to *yourself* and me. The reason you come before me is that I do not need miracles for my own Atonement, but I stand at the end in case you fail temporarily. My part in the Atonement is the cancelling out of all errors that you could not otherwise correct. When you have been restored to the recognition of your original state, you naturally become part of the Atonement yourself. As you share my unwillingness to accept error in yourself and others, you must join the great crusade to correct it; listen to my voice, learn to undo error and act to correct it. The power to work miracles belongs to you. I will provide the opportunities to do them, but you must be ready and willing. Doing them will bring conviction in the ability, because conviction comes through accomplishment. The ability is the potential, the achievement is its expression, and the Atonement, which is the natural profession of the children of God, is the purpose.
2. "Heaven and earth shall pass away" means that they will not continue to exist as separate states. My word, which is the resurrection and the life, shall not pass away because life is eternal. You are the work of God, and His work is wholly lovable and wholly loving. This is how a man must think of himself in his heart, because this is what he is.
3. The forgiven are the means of the Atonement. Being filled with spirit, they forgive in return. Those who are released must join in releasing their brothers, for this is the plan of the Atonement. Miracles are the way in which minds that serve the Holy Spirit unite with me for the salvation or release of all of God's creations.
7. Miracles arise from a mind that is ready for them. By being united this mind goes out to everyone, even without the awareness of the miracle worker himself. The impersonal nature of miracles is because the Atonement itself is one, uniting all creations with their Creator. As an expression of what you truly are, the miracle places the mind in a state of grace. The mind then naturally welcomes the Host within and the stranger without. When you bring in the stranger, he becomes your brother.

IV. The Escape from Darkness

1. The escape from darkness involves two stages: First, the recognition that darkness cannot hide. This step usually entails fear. Second, the recognition that there is nothing you want to hide even if you could.

This step brings escape from fear. When you have become willing to hide nothing, you will not only be willing to enter into communion but will also understand peace and joy.

2. Holiness can never be really hidden in darkness, but you can deceive yourself about it. This deception makes you fearful because you realize in your heart it *is* a deception, and you exert enormous efforts to establish its reality. The miracle sets reality where it belongs. Reality belongs only to spirit, and the miracle acknowledges only truth. It thus dispels illusions about yourself, and puts you in communion with yourself and God. The miracle joins in the Atonement by placing the mind in the service of the Holy Spirit. This establishes the proper function of the mind and corrects its errors, which are merely lacks of love. Your mind can be possessed by illusions, but spirit is eternally free. If a mind perceives without love, it perceives an empty shell and is unaware of the spirit within. But the Atonement restores spirit to its proper place. The mind that serves spirit *is* invulnerable.

3. Darkness is lack of light as sin is lack of love. It has no unique properties of its own. It is an example of the "scarcity" belief, from which only error can proceed. Truth is always abundant. Those who perceive and acknowledge that they have everything have no needs of any kind. The purpose of the Atonement is to restore everything to you; or rather, to restore it to your awareness. You were given everything when you were created, just as everyone was.

QUESTION 2. How would you compare miracles with revelation?

V. Wholeness and Spirit

3. When the Atonement has been completed, all talents will be shared by all the Sons of God. God is not partial. All His children have His total Love, and all His gifts are freely given to everyone alike. "Except ye become as little children" means that unless you fully recognize your complete dependence on God, you cannot know the real power of the Son in his true relationship with the Father. The specialness of God's Sons does not stem from exclusion but from inclusion. All my brothers are special. If they believe they are deprived of anything, their perception becomes distorted. When this occurs the whole family of God, or the Sonship, is impaired in its relationships.

4. Ultimately, every member of the family of God must return. The miracle calls him to return because it blesses and honors him, even though he may be absent in spirit. "God is not mocked" is not a warning but a reassurance. God *would* be mocked if any of His

creations lacked holiness. The creation is whole, and the mark of wholeness is holiness. Miracles are affirmations of Sonship, which is a state of completion and abundance.

VI. The Illusion of Needs

1. You who want peace can find it only by complete forgiveness. No learning is acquired by anyone unless he wants to learn it and believes in some way that he needs it. While lack does not exist in the creation of God, it is very apparent in what you have made. It is, in fact, the essential difference between them. Lack implies that you would be better off in a state somehow different from the one you are in. Until the "separation," which is the meaning of the "fall," nothing was lacking. There were no needs at all. Needs arise only when you deprive yourself. You act according to the particular order of needs you establish. This, in turn, depends on your perception of what you are.

2. A sense of separation from God is the only lack you really need correct. This sense of separation would never have arisen if you had not distorted your perception of truth, and had thus perceived yourself as lacking. The idea of order of needs arose because, having made this fundamental error, you had already fragmented yourself into levels with different needs. As you integrate you become one, and your needs become one accordingly. Unified needs lead to unified action, because this produces a lack of conflict.

3. The idea of orders of need, which follows from the original error that one can be separated from God, requires correction at its own level before the error of perceiving levels at all can be corrected. You cannot behave effectively while you function on different levels. However, while you do, correction must be introduced vertically from the bottom up. This is because you think you live in space, where concepts such as "up" and "down" are meaningful. Ultimately, space is as meaningless as time. Both are merely beliefs.

4. The real purpose of this world is to use it to correct your unbelief. You can never control the effects of fear yourself, because you made fear, and you believe in what you made. In attitude, then, though not in content, you resemble your Creator, Who has perfect faith in His creations *because* He created them. Belief produces the acceptance of existence. That is why you can believe what no one else thinks is true. It is true for you because it was made by you.

5. All aspects of fear are untrue because they do not exist at the creative level, and therefore do not exist at all. To whatever extent

you are willing to submit your beliefs to this test, to that extent are your perceptions corrected. In sorting out the false from the true, the miracle proceeds along these lines:

> *Perfect love casts out fear.*
> *If fear exists,*
> *Then there is not perfect love.*

> *But:*

> *Only perfect love exists.*
> *If there is fear,*
> *It produces a state that does not exist.*

Believe this and you will be free. Only God can establish this solution, and this faith *is* His gift.

VII. Distortions of Miracle Impulses

1. Your distorted perceptions produce a dense cover over miracle impulses, making it hard for them to reach your own awareness. The confusion of miracle impulses with physical impulses is a major perceptual distortion. Physical impulses are misdirected miracle impulses. All real pleasure comes from doing God's Will. This is because *not* doing it is a denial of Self. Denial of Self results in illusions, while correction of the error brings release from it. Do not deceive yourself into believing that you can relate in peace to God or to your brothers with anything external.

2. Child of God, you were created to create the good, the beautiful and the holy. Do not forget this. The Love of God, for a little while, must still be expressed through one body to another, because vision is still so dim. You can use your body best to help you enlarge your perception so you can achieve real vision, of which the physical eye is incapable. Learning to do this is the body's only true usefulness.

3. Fantasy is a distorted form of vision. Fantasies of any kind are distortions, because they always involve twisting perception into unreality. Actions that stem from distortions are literally the reactions of those who know not what they do. Fantasy is an attempt to control reality according to false needs. Twist reality in any way and you are perceiving destructively. Fantasies are a means of making false associations and attempting to obtain pleasure from them. But although you can perceive false associations, you can never make them real except to yourself. You believe in what you make. If you offer miracles,

you will be equally strong in your belief in them. The strength of your conviction will then sustain the belief of the miracle receiver. Fantasies become totally unnecessary as the wholly satisfying nature of reality becomes apparent to both giver and receiver. Reality is "lost" through usurpation, which produces tyranny. As long as a single "slave" remains to walk the earth, your release is not complete. Complete restoration of the Sonship is the only goal of the miracle-minded.

4. This is a course in mind training. All learning involves attention and study at some level. Some of the later parts of the course rest too heavily on these earlier sections not to require their careful study. You will also need them for preparation. Without this, you may become much too fearful of what is to come to make constructive use of it. However, as you study these earlier sections, you will begin to see some of the implications that will be amplified later on.

5. A solid foundation is necessary because of the confusion between fear and awe to which I have already referred, and which is often made. I have said that awe is inappropriate in connection with the Sons of God, because you should not experience awe in the presence of your equals. However, it was also emphasized that awe is proper in the Presence of your Creator. I have been careful to clarify my role in the Atonement without either over- or understating it. I am also trying to do the same with yours. I have stressed that awe is not an appropriate reaction to me because of our inherent equality. Some of the later steps in this course, however, involve a more direct approach to God Himself. It would be unwise to start on these steps without careful preparation, or awe will be confused with fear, and the experience will be more traumatic than beatific. Healing is of God in the end. The means are being carefully explained to you. Revelation may occasionally reveal the end to you, but to reach it the means are needed.

QUESTION 3. What is "the only lack you really need" to correct?

Chapter 2. THE SEPARATION AND THE ATONEMENT

I. The Origins of Separation

1. To extend is a fundamental aspect of God which He gave to His Son. In the creation, God extended Himself to His creations and imbued them with the same loving Will to create. You have not only been fully created, but have also been created perfect. There is no emptiness in you. Because of your likeness to your Creator you are creative. No child of God can lose this ability because it is inherent in what he is, but he can use it inappropriately by projecting. The inappropriate use of extension, or projection, occurs when you believe that some emptiness or lack exists in you, and that you can fill it with your own ideas instead of truth. This process involves the following steps:

First, you believe that what God created can be changed by your own mind.

Second, you believe that what is perfect can be rendered imperfect or lacking.

Third, you believe that you can distort the creations of God, including yourself.

Fourth, you believe that you can create yourself, and that the direction of your own creation is up to you.

2. These related distortions represent a picture of what actually occurred in the separation, or the "detour into fear." None of this existed before the separation, nor does it actually exist now. Everything God created is like Him. Extension, as undertaken by God, is similar to the inner radiance that the children of the Father inherit from Him. Its real source is internal. This is as true of the Son as of the Father. In this sense the creation includes both the creation of the Son by God, and the Son's creations when his mind is healed. This requires God's endowment of the Son with free will, because all loving creation is freely given in one continuous line, in which all aspects are of the same order.

3. The Garden of Eden, or the pre-separation condition, was a state of mind in which nothing was needed. When Adam listened to the "lies of the serpent," all he heard was untruth. You do not have to continue to believe what is not true unless you choose to do so. All that can literally disappear in the twinkling of an eye because it is merely a misperception. What is seen in dreams seems to be very real. Yet the Bible says that a deep sleep fell upon Adam, and

nowhere is there reference to his waking up. The world has not yet experienced any comprehensive reawakening or rebirth. Such a rebirth is impossible as long as you continue to project or miscreate. It still remains within you, however, to extend as God extended His Spirit to you. In reality this is your only choice, because your free will was given you for your joy in creating the perfect.

4. All fear is ultimately reducible to the basic misperception that you have the ability to usurp the power of God. Of course, you neither can nor have been able to do this. Here is the real basis for your escape from fear. The escape is brought about by your acceptance of the Atonement, which enables you to realize that your errors never really occurred. Only after the deep sleep fell upon Adam could he experience nightmares. If a light is suddenly turned on while someone is dreaming a fearful dream, he may initially interpret the light itself as part of his dream and be afraid of it. However, when he awakens, the light is correctly perceived as the release from the dream, which is then no longer accorded reality. This release does not depend on illusions. The knowledge that illuminates not only sets you free, but also shows you clearly that you *are* free.

5. Whatever lies you may believe are of no concern to the miracle, which can heal any of them with equal ease. It makes no distinctions among misperceptions. Its sole concern is to distinguish between truth on the one hand, and error on the other. Some miracles may seem to be of greater magnitude than others. But remember the first principle in this course; there is no order of difficulty in miracles. In reality you are perfectly unaffected by all expressions of lack of love. These can be from yourself and others, from yourself to others, or from others to you. Peace is an attribute *in* you. You cannot find it outside. Illness is some form of external searching. Health is inner peace. It enables you to remain unshaken by lack of love from without and capable, through your acceptance of miracles, of correcting the conditions proceeding from lack of love in others.

II. The Atonement as Defense

2. True denial is a powerful protective device. You can and should deny any belief that error can hurt you. This kind of denial is not a concealment but a correction. Your right mind depends on it. Denial of error is a strong defense of truth, but denial of truth results in miscreation, the projections of the ego. In the service of the right mind the denial of error frees the mind, and re-establishes the freedom of

the will. When the will is really free it cannot miscreate, because it recognizes only truth.

4. The Atonement is the only defense that cannot be used destructively because it is not a device you made. The Atonement *principle* was in effect long before the Atonement began. The principle was love and the Atonement was an *act* of love. Acts were not necessary before the separation, because belief in space and time did not exist. It was only after the separation that the Atonement and the conditions necessary for its fulfillment were planned. Then a defense so splendid was needed that it could not be misused, although it could be refused. Refusal could not, however, turn it into a weapon of attack, which is the inherent characteristic of other defenses. The Atonement thus becomes the only defense that is not a two-edged sword. It can only heal.

5. The Atonement was built into the space-time belief to set a limit on the need for the belief itself, and ultimately to make learning complete. The Atonement is the final lesson. Learning itself, like the classrooms in which it occurs, is temporary. The ability to learn has no value when change is no longer necessary. The eternally creative have nothing to learn. You can learn to improve your perceptions, and can become a better and better learner. This will bring you into closer and closer accord with the Sonship; but the Sonship itself is a perfect creation and perfection is not a matter of degree. Only while there is a belief in differences is learning meaningful.

III. The Altar of God

2. For perfect effectiveness the Atonement belongs at the center of the inner altar, where it undoes the separation and restores the wholeness of the mind. Before the separation the mind was invulnerable to fear, because fear did not exist. Both the separation and the fear are miscreations that must be undone for the restoration of the temple, and for the opening of the altar to receive the Atonement. This heals the separation by placing within you the one effective defense against all separation thoughts and making you perfectly invulnerable.

3. The acceptance of the Atonement by everyone is only a matter of time. This may appear to contradict free will because of the inevitability of the final decision, but this is not so. You can temporize and you are capable of enormous procrastination, but you cannot depart entirely from your Creator, Who set the limits on your ability to miscreate. An imprisoned will engenders a situation which, in the extreme, becomes altogether intolerable. Tolerance for pain may be high, but it is not without limit. Eventually everyone begins to recognize, however

dimly, that there *must* be a better way. As this recognition becomes more firmly established, it becomes a turning point. This ultimately reawakens spiritual vision, simultaneously weakening the investment in physical sight. The alternating investment in the two levels of perception is usually experienced as conflict, which can become very acute. But the outcome is as certain as God.

4. Spiritual vision literally cannot see error, and merely looks for Atonement. All solutions the physical eye seeks dissolve. Spiritual vision looks within and recognizes immediately that the altar has been defiled and needs to be repaired and protected. Perfectly aware of the right defense it passes over all others, looking past error to truth. Because of the strength of its vision, it brings the mind into its service. This re-establishes the power of the mind and makes it increasingly unable to tolerate delay, realizing that it only adds unnecessary pain. As a result, the mind becomes increasingly sensitive to what it would once have regarded as very minor intrusions of discomfort.

5. The children of God are entitled to the perfect comfort that comes from perfect trust. Until they achieve this, they waste themselves and their true creative powers on useless attempts to make themselves more comfortable by inappropriate means. But the real means are already provided, and do not involve any effort at all on their part. The Atonement is the only gift that is worthy of being offered at the altar of God, because of the value of the altar itself. It was created perfect and is entirely worthy of receiving perfection. God and His creations are completely dependent on Each Other. He depends on them *because* He created them perfect. He gave them His peace so they could not be shaken and could not be deceived. Whenever you are afraid you *are* deceived, and your mind cannot serve the Holy Spirit. This starves you by denying you your daily bread. God is lonely without His Sons, and they are lonely without Him. They must learn to look upon the world as a means of healing the separation. The Atonement is the guarantee that they will ultimately succeed.

IV. Healing as Release from Fear

1. Our emphasis is now on healing. The miracle is the means, the Atonement is the principle, and healing is the result. To speak of "a miracle of healing" is to combine two orders of reality inappropriately. Healing is not a miracle. The Atonement, or the final miracle, is a remedy and any type of healing is a result. The kind of error to which Atonement is applied is irrelevant. All healing is essentially the release

from fear. To undertake this you cannot be fearful yourself. You do not understand healing because of your own fear.

2. A major step in the Atonement plan is to undo error at all levels. Sickness or "not-right-mindedness" is the result of level confusion, because it always entails the belief that what is amiss on one level can adversely affect another. We have referred to miracles as the means of correcting level confusion, for all mistakes must be corrected at the level on which they occur. Only the mind is capable of error. The body can act wrongly only when it is responding to misthought. The body cannot create, and the belief that it can, a fundamental error, produces all physical symptoms. Physical illness represents a belief in magic. The whole distortion that made magic rests on the belief that there is a creative ability in matter which the mind cannot control. This error can take two forms; it can be believed that the mind can miscreate in the body, or that the body can miscreate in the mind. When it is understood that the mind, the only level of creation, cannot create beyond itself, neither type of confusion need occur.

QUESTION 4. What is the Holy Spirit's plan called the "Atonement" and what will be the end result of this plan?

V. The Function of the Miracle Worker

2. Magic is the mindless or the miscreative use of mind. Physical medications are forms of "spells," but if you are afraid to use the mind to heal, you should not attempt to do so. The very fact that you are afraid makes your mind vulnerable to miscreation. You are therefore likely to misunderstand any healing that might occur, and because egocentricity and fear usually occur together, you may be unable to accept the real Source of the healing. Under these conditions, it is safer for you to rely temporarily on physical healing devices, because you cannot misperceive them as your own creations. As long as your sense of vulnerability persists, you should not attempt to perform miracles.

5. *The sole responsibility of the miracle worker is to accept the Atonement for himself.* This means you recognize that mind is the only creative level, and that its errors are healed by the Atonement. Once you accept this, your mind can only heal. By denying your mind any destructive potential and reinstating its purely constructive powers, you place yourself in a position to undo the level confusion of others. The message you then give to them is the truth that their minds are similarly constructive, and their miscreations cannot hurt them. By affirming this you release the mind from overevaluating

its own learning device, and restore the mind to its true position as the learner.

6. It should be emphasized again that the body does not learn any more than it creates. As a learning device it merely follows the learner, but if it is falsely endowed with self-initiative, it becomes a serious obstruction to the very learning it should facilitate. Only the mind is capable of illumination. Spirit is already illuminated and the body in itself is too dense. The mind, however, can bring its illumination to the body by recognizing that it is not the learner, and is therefore unamenable to learning. The body is, however, easily brought into alignment with a mind that has learned to look beyond it toward the light.

9. Healing is an ability that developed after the separation, before which it was unnecessary. Like all aspects of the belief in space and time, it is temporary. However, as long as time persists, healing is needed as a means of protection. This is because healing rests on charity, and charity is a way of perceiving the perfection of another even if you cannot perceive it in yourself. Most of the loftier concepts of which you are capable now are time-dependent. Charity is really a weaker reflection of a much more powerful love-encompassment that is far beyond any form of charity you can conceive of as yet. Charity is essential to right-mindedness in the limited sense in which it can now be attained.

10. Charity is a way of looking at another as if he had already gone far beyond his actual accomplishments in time. Since his own thinking is faulty he cannot see the Atonement for himself, or he would have no need of charity. The charity that is accorded him is both an acknowledgment that he needs help, and a recognition that he will accept it. Both of these perceptions clearly imply their dependence on time, making it apparent that charity still lies within the limitations of this world. I said before that only revelation transcends time. The miracle, as an expression of charity, can only shorten it. It must be understood, however, that whenever you offer a miracle to another, you are shortening the suffering of both of you. This corrects retroactively as well as progressively.

A. Special Principles of Miracle Workers

16. Miracle-minded forgiveness is *only* correction. It has no element of judgment at all. The statement "Father forgive them for they know not what they do" in no way evaluates *what* they do. It is an appeal to God to heal their minds. There is no reference to the outcome of the error. That does not matter.

18. You can do much on behalf of your own healing and that of others if, in a situation calling for help, you think of it this way:

> *I am here only to be truly helpful.*
> *I am here to represent Him Who sent me.*
> *I do not have to worry about what to say or what*
> *   to do, because He Who sent me will direct me.*
> *I am content to be wherever He wishes, knowing*
> *   He goes there with me.*
> *I will be healed as I let Him teach me to heal.*

VI. Fear and Conflict

4. The correction of fear *is* your responsibility. When you ask for release from fear, you are implying that it is not. You should ask, instead, for help in the conditions that have brought the fear about. These conditions always entail a willingness to be separate. At that level you *can* help it. You are much too tolerant of mind wandering, and are passively condoning your mind's miscreations. The particular result does not matter, but the fundamental error does. The correction is always the same. Before you choose to do anything, ask me if your choice is in accord with mine. If you are sure that it is, there will be no fear.

5. Fear is always a sign of strain, arising whenever what you want conflicts with what you do. This situation arises in two ways: First, you can choose to do conflicting things, either simultaneously or successively. This produces conflicted behavior, which is intolerable to you because the part of the mind that wants to do something else is outraged. Second, you can behave as you think you should, but without entirely wanting to do so. This produces consistent behavior, but entails great strain. In both cases, the mind and the behavior are out of accord, resulting in a situation in which you are doing what you do not wholly want to do. This arouses a sense of coercion that usually produces rage, and projection is likely to follow. Whenever there is fear, it is because you have not made up your mind. Your mind is therefore split, and your behavior inevitably becomes erratic. Correcting at the behavioral level can shift the error from the first to the second type, but will not obliterate the fear.

6. It is possible to reach a state in which you bring your mind under my guidance without conscious effort, but this implies a willingness that you have not developed as yet. The Holy Spirit cannot ask more than you are willing to do. The strength to do comes from your

undivided decision. There is no strain in doing God's Will as soon as you recognize that it is also your own. The lesson here is quite simple, but particularly apt to be overlooked. I will therefore repeat it, urging you to listen. Only your mind can produce fear. It does so whenever it is conflicted in what it wants, producing inevitable strain because wanting and doing are discordant. This can be corrected only by accepting a unified goal.

7. The first corrective step in undoing the error is to know first that the conflict is an expression of fear. Say to yourself that you must somehow have chosen not to love, or the fear could not have arisen. Then the whole process of correction becomes nothing more than a series of pragmatic steps in the larger process of accepting the Atonement as the remedy. These steps may be summarized in this way:

> Know first that this is fear.
> Fear arises from lack of love.
> The only remedy for lack of love is perfect love.
> Perfect love is the Atonement.

8. I have emphasized that the miracle, or the expression of Atonement, is always a sign of respect *from* the worthy *to* the worthy. The recognition of this worth is re-established by the Atonement. It is obvious, then, that when you are afraid, you have placed yourself in a position where you need Atonement. You have done something loveless, having chosen without love. This is precisely the situation for which the Atonement was offered. The need for the remedy inspired its establishment. As long as you recognize only the need for the remedy, you will remain fearful. However, as soon as you accept the remedy, you have abolished the fear. This is how true healing occurs.

9. Everyone experiences fear. Yet it would take very little right thinking to realize why fear occurs. Few appreciate the real power of the mind, and no one remains fully aware of it all the time. However, if you hope to spare yourself from fear there are some things you must realize, and realize fully. The mind is very powerful, and never loses its creative force. It never sleeps. Every instant it is creating. It is hard to recognize that thought and belief combine into a power surge that can literally move mountains. It appears at first glance that to believe such power about yourself is arrogant, but that is not the real reason you do not believe it. You prefer to believe that your thoughts cannot exert real influence because you are actually afraid of them. This may allay awareness of the guilt, but at the cost of perceiving the mind as

impotent. If you believe that what you think is ineffectual you may cease to be afraid of it, but you are hardly likely to respect it. There *are* no idle thoughts. All thinking produces form at some level.

VII. Cause and Effect

3. Both miracles and fear come from thoughts. If you are not free to choose one, you would also not be free to choose the other. By choosing the miracle you *have* rejected fear, if only temporarily. You have been fearful of everyone and everything. You are afraid of God, of me and of yourself. You have misperceived or miscreated Us, and believe in what you have made. You would not have done this if you were not afraid of your own thoughts. The fearful *must* miscreate, because they misperceive creation. When you miscreate you are in pain. The cause and effect principle now becomes a real expediter, though only temporarily. Actually, "Cause" is a term properly belonging to God, and His "Effect" is His Son. This entails a set of Cause and Effect relationships totally different from those you introduce into miscreation. The fundamental conflict in this world, then, is between creation and miscreation. All fear is implicit in the second, and all love in the first. The conflict is therefore one between love and fear.

4. It has already been said that you believe you cannot control fear because you yourself made it, and your belief in it seems to render it out of your control. Yet any attempt to resolve the error through attempting the mastery of fear is useless. In fact, it asserts the power of fear by the very assumption that it need be mastered. The true resolution rests entirely on mastery through love. In the interim, however, the sense of conflict is inevitable, since you have placed yourself in a position where you believe in the power of what does not exist.

VIII. The Meaning of the Last Judgment

3. The Last Judgment is generally thought of as a procedure undertaken by God. Actually it will be undertaken by my brothers with my help. It is a final healing rather than a meting out of punishment, however much you may think that punishment is deserved. Punishment is a concept totally opposed to right-mindedness, and the aim of the Last Judgment is to restore right-mindedness to you. The Last Judgment might be called a process of right evaluation. It simply means that everyone will finally come to understand what is worthy and what

is not. After this, the ability to choose can be directed rationally. Until this distinction is made, however, the vacillations between free and imprisoned will cannot but continue.

4. The first step toward freedom involves a sorting out of the false from the true. This is a process of separation in the constructive sense, and reflects the true meaning of the Apocalypse. Everyone will ultimately look upon his own creations and choose to preserve only what is good, just as God Himself looked upon what He had created and knew that it was good. At this point, the mind can begin to look with love on its own creations because of their worthiness. At the same time the mind will inevitably disown its miscreations which, without belief, will no longer exist.

5. The term "Last Judgment" is frightening not only because it has been projected onto God, but also because of the association of "last" with death. This is an outstanding example of upside-down perception. If the meaning of the Last Judgment is objectively examined, it is quite apparent that it is really the doorway to life. No one who lives in fear is really alive. Your own last judgment cannot be directed toward yourself, because you are not your own creation. You can, however, apply it meaningfully and at any time to everything you have made, and retain in your memory only what is creative and good. This is what your right-mindedness cannot but dictate. The purpose of time is solely to "give you time" to achieve this judgment. It is your own perfect judgment of your own perfect creations. When everything you retain is lovable, there is no reason for fear to remain with you. This is your part in the Atonement.

QUESTION 5. What is your only responsibility in order to be a miracle worker, and what is your responsibility in relation to fear?

Chapter 3. THE INNOCENT PERCEPTION

I. Atonement without Sacrifice

1. A further point must be perfectly clear before any residual fear still associated with miracles can disappear. The crucifixion did not establish the Atonement; the resurrection did. Many sincere Christians have misunderstood this. No one who is free of the belief in scarcity could possibly make this mistake. If the crucifixion is seen from an upside-down point of view, it does appear as if God permitted and even encouraged one of His Sons to suffer because he was good. This particularly unfortunate interpretation, which arose out of projection, has led many people to be bitterly afraid of God. Such anti-religious concepts enter into many religions. Yet the real Christian should pause and ask, "How could this be?" Is it likely that God Himself would be capable of the kind of thinking which His Own words have clearly stated is unworthy of His Son?

7. The Atonement itself radiates nothing but truth. It therefore epitomizes harmlessness and sheds only blessing. It could not do this if it arose from anything but perfect innocence. Innocence is wisdom because it is unaware of evil, and evil does not exist. It is, however, perfectly aware of everything that is true. The resurrection demonstrated that nothing can destroy truth. Good can withstand any form of evil, as light abolishes forms of darkness. The Atonement is therefore the perfect lesson. It is the final demonstration that all the other lessons I taught are true. If you can accept this one generalization now, there will be no need to learn from many smaller lessons. You are released from all errors if you believe this.

8. The innocence of God is the true state of the mind of His Son. In this state your mind knows God, for God is not symbolic; He is Fact. Knowing His Son as he is, you realize that the Atonement, not sacrifice, is the only appropriate gift for God's altar, where nothing except perfection belongs. The understanding of the innocent is truth. That is why their altars are truly radiant.

II. Miracles as True Perception

3. When you lack confidence in what someone will do, you are attesting to your belief that he is not in his right mind. This is hardly a miracle-based frame of reference. It also has the disastrous effect of denying the power of the miracle. The miracle perceives everything

as it is. If nothing but the truth exists, right-minded seeing cannot see anything but perfection. I have said that only what God creates or what you create with the same Will has any real existence. This, then, is all the innocent can see. They do not suffer from distorted perception.

4.   You are afraid of God's Will because you have used your own mind, which He created in the likeness of His Own, to miscreate. The mind can miscreate only when it believes it is not free. An "imprisoned" mind is not free because it is possessed, or held back, by itself. It is therefore limited, and the will is not free to assert itself. To be one is to be of one mind or will. When the Will of the Sonship and the Father are One, their perfect accord is Heaven.

5.   Nothing can prevail against a Son of God who commends his spirit into the Hands of his Father. By doing this the mind awakens from its sleep and remembers its Creator. All sense of separation disappears. The Son of God is part of the Holy Trinity, but the Trinity Itself is One. There is no confusion within Its Levels, because They are of one Mind and one Will. This single purpose creates perfect integration and establishes the peace of God. Yet this vision can be perceived only by the truly innocent. Because their hearts are pure, the innocent defend true perception instead of defending themselves against it. Understanding the lesson of the Atonement they are without the wish to attack, and therefore they see truly. This is what the Bible means when it says, "When he shall appear (or be perceived) we shall be like him, for we shall see him as he is."

6.   The way to correct distortions is to withdraw your faith in them and invest it only in what is true. You cannot make untruth true. If you are willing to accept what is true in everything you perceive, you let it be true for you. Truth overcomes all error, and those who live in error and emptiness can never find lasting solace. If you perceive truly you are cancelling out misperceptions in yourself and in others simultaneously. Because you see them as they are, you offer them your acceptance of their truth so they can accept it for themselves. This is the healing that the miracle induces.

III. Perception versus Knowledge

1.   We have been emphasizing perception, and have said very little about knowledge as yet. This is because perception must be straightened out before you can know anything. To know is to be certain. Uncertainty means that you do not know. Knowledge is power because it is certain, and certainty is strength. Perception

is temporary. As an attribute of the belief in space and time, it is subject to either fear or love. Misperceptions produce fear and true perceptions foster love, but neither brings certainty because all perception varies. That is why it is not knowledge. True perception is the basis for knowledge, but knowing is the affirmation of truth and beyond all perceptions.

2. All your difficulties stem from the fact that you do not recognize yourself, your brother or God. To recognize means to "know again," implying that you knew before. You can see in many ways because perception involves interpretation, and this means that it is not whole or consistent. The miracle, being a way of perceiving, is not knowledge. It is the right answer to a question, but you do not question when you know. Questioning illusions is the first step in undoing them. The miracle, or the right answer, corrects them. Since perceptions change, their dependence on time is obvious. How you perceive at any given time determines what you do, and actions must occur in time. Knowledge is timeless, because certainty is not questionable. You know when you have ceased to ask questions.

3. The questioning mind perceives itself in time, and therefore looks for future answers. The closed mind believes the future and the present will be the same. This establishes a seemingly stable state that is usually an attempt to counteract an underlying fear that the future will be worse than the present. This fear inhibits the tendency to question at all.

4. True vision is the natural perception of spiritual sight, but it is still a correction rather than a fact. Spiritual sight is symbolic, and therefore not a device for knowing. It is, however, a means of right perception, which brings it into the proper domain of the miracle. A "vision of God" would be a miracle rather than a revelation. The fact that perception is involved at all removes the experience from the realm of knowledge. That is why visions, however holy, do not last.

5. The Bible tells you to know yourself, or to be certain. Certainty is always of God. When you love someone you have perceived him as he is, and this makes it possible for you to know him. Until you first perceive him as he is you cannot know him. While you ask questions about him you are clearly implying that you do not know God. Certainty does not require action. When you say you are acting on the basis of knowledge, you are really confusing knowledge with perception. Knowledge provides the strength for creative thinking, but not for right doing. Perception, miracles and doing are closely related. Knowledge is the result of revelation and induces only thought. Even

in its most spiritualized form perception involves the body. Knowledge comes from the altar within and is timeless because it is certain. To perceive the truth is not the same as to know it.

7. If you attack error in another, you will hurt yourself. You cannot know your brother when you attack him. Attack is always made upon a stranger. You are making him a stranger by misperceiving him, and so you cannot know him. It is because you have made him a stranger that you are afraid of him. Perceive him correctly so that you can know him. There are no strangers in God's creation. To create as He created you can create only what you know, and therefore accept as yours. God knows His children with perfect certainty. He created them by knowing them. He recognizes them perfectly. When they do not recognize each other, they do not recognize Him.

IV. Error and the Ego

1. The abilities you now possess are only shadows of your real strength. All of your present functions are divided and open to question and doubt. This is because you are not certain how you will use them, and are therefore incapable of knowledge. You are also incapable of knowledge because you can still perceive lovelessly. Perception did not exist until the separation introduced degrees, aspects and intervals. Spirit has no levels, and all conflict arises from the concept of levels. Only the Levels of the Trinity are capable of unity. The levels created by the separation cannot but conflict. This is because they are meaningless to each other.

2. Consciousness, the level of perception, was the first split introduced into the mind after the separation, making the mind a perceiver rather than a creator. Consciousness is correctly identified as the domain of the ego. The ego is a wrong-minded attempt to perceive yourself as you wish to be, rather than as you are. Yet you can know yourself only as you are, because that is all you can be sure of. Everything else *is* open to question.

3. The ego is the questioning aspect of the post-separation self, which was made rather than created. It is capable of asking questions but not of perceiving meaningful answers, because these would involve knowledge and cannot be perceived. The mind is therefore confused, because only One-mindedness can be without confusion. A separated or divided mind *must* be confused. It is necessarily uncertain about what it is. It has to be in conflict because it is out of accord with itself. This makes its aspects strangers to each other, and this is the essence of the fear-prone condition, in which attack is always possible. You

have every reason to feel afraid as you perceive yourself. This is why you cannot escape from fear until you realize that you did not and could not create yourself. You can never make your misperceptions true, and your creation is beyond your own error. That is why you must eventually choose to heal the separation.

4. Right-mindedness is not to be confused with the knowing mind, because it is applicable only to right perception. You can be right-minded or wrong-minded, and even this is subject to degrees, clearly demonstrating that knowledge is not involved. The term "rightminded-ness" is properly used as the correction for "wrong-mindedness," and applies to the state of mind that induces accurate perception. It is miracle-minded because it heals misperception, and this is indeed a miracle in view of how you perceive yourself.

5. Perception always involves some misuse of mind, because it brings the mind into areas of uncertainty. The mind is very active. When it chooses to be separated it chooses to perceive. Until then it wills only to know. Afterwards it can only choose ambiguously, and the only way out of ambiguity is clear perception. The mind returns to its proper function only when it wills to know. This places it in the service of spirit, where perception is changed. The mind chooses to divide itself when it chooses to make its own levels. But it could not entirely separate itself from spirit, because it is from spirit that it derives its whole power to make or create. Even in miscreation the mind is affirming its Source, or it would merely cease to be. This is impossible, because the mind belongs to spirit which God created and which is therefore eternal.

6. The ability to perceive made the body possible, because you must perceive *something* and *with* something. That is why perception involves an exchange or translation, which knowledge does not need. The interpretative function of perception, a distorted form of creation, then permits you to interpret the body as yourself in an attempt to escape from the conflict you have induced. Spirit, which knows, could not be reconciled with this loss of power, because it is incapable of darkness. This makes spirit almost inaccessible to the mind and entirely inaccessible to the body. Thereafter, spirit is perceived as a threat, because light abolishes darkness merely by showing you it is not there. Truth will always overcome error in this way. This cannot be an active process of correction because, as I have already emphasized, knowledge does not do anything. It can be perceived as an attacker, but it cannot attack. What you perceive as its attack is your own vague recognition that knowledge can always be remembered, never having been destroyed.

7.   God and His creations remain in surety, and therefore know that no miscreation exists. Truth cannot deal with errors that you want. I was a man who remembered spirit and its knowledge. As a man I did not attempt to counteract error with knowledge, but to correct error from the bottom up. I demonstrated both the powerlessness of the body and the power of the mind. By uniting my will with that of my Creator, I naturally remembered spirit and its real purpose. I cannot unite your will with God's for you, but I can erase all misperceptions from your mind if you will bring it under my guidance. Only your misperceptions stand in your way. Without them your choice is certain. Sane perception induces sane choosing. I cannot choose for you, but I can help you make your own right choice. "Many are called but few are chosen" should be, "All are called but few choose to listen." Therefore, they do not choose right. The "chosen ones" are merely those who choose right sooner. Right minds can do this now, and they will find rest unto their souls. God knows you only in peace, and this *is* your reality.

QUESTION 6. How is perception different than knowledge?

V. Beyond Perception

1.   I have said that the abilities you possess are only shadows of your real strength, and that perception, which is inherently judgmental, was introduced only after the separation. No one has been sure of anything since. I have also made it clear that the resurrection was the means for the return to knowledge, which was accomplished by the union of my will with the Father's. We can now establish a distinction that will clarify some of our subsequent statements.

2.   Since the separation, the words "create" and "make" have become confused. When you make something, you do so out of a specific sense of lack or need. Anything made for a specific purpose has no true generalizability. When you make something to fill a perceived lack, you are tacitly implying that you believe in separation. The ego has invented many ingenious thought systems for this purpose. None of them is creative. Inventiveness is wasted effort even in its most ingenious form. The highly specific nature of invention is not worthy of the abstract creativity of God's creations.

4.   The fundamental question you continually ask yourself cannot properly be directed to yourself at all. You keep asking what it is you are. This implies that the answer is not only one you know, but is also one that is up to you to supply. Yet you cannot perceive yourself

correctly. You have no image to be perceived. The word "image" is always perception-related, and not a part of knowledge. Images are symbolic and stand for something else. The idea of "changing your image" recognizes the power of perception, but also implies that there is nothing stable to know.

6.   Prayer is a way of asking for something. It is the medium of miracles. But the only meaningful prayer is for forgiveness, because those who have been forgiven have everything. Once forgiveness has been accepted, prayer in the usual sense becomes utterly meaningless. The prayer for forgiveness is nothing more than a request that you may be able to recognize what you already have. In electing perception instead of knowledge, you placed yourself in a position where you could resemble your Father only by perceiving miraculously. You have lost the knowledge that you yourself are a miracle of God. Creation is your Source and your only real function.

8.   What happens to perceptions if there are no judgments and nothing but perfect equality? Perception becomes impossible. Truth can only be known. All of it is equally true, and knowing any part of it is to know all of it. Only perception involves partial awareness. Knowledge transcends the laws governing perception, because partial knowledge is impossible. It is all one and has no separate parts. You who are really one with it need but know yourself and your knowledge is complete. To know God's miracle is to know Him.

9.   Forgiveness is the healing of the perception of separation. Correct perception of your brother is necessary, because minds have chosen to see themselves as separate. Spirit knows God completely. That is its miraculous power. The fact that each one has this power completely is a condition entirely alien to the world's thinking. The world believes that if anyone has everything, there is nothing left. But God's miracles are as total as His Thoughts because they *are* His Thoughts.

10.   As long as perception lasts prayer has a place. Since perception rests on lack, those who perceive have not totally accepted the Atonement and given themselves over to truth. Perception is based on a separated state, so that anyone who perceives at all needs healing. Communion, not prayer, is the natural state of those who know. God and His miracle are inseparable. How beautiful indeed are the Thoughts of God who live in His light! Your worth is beyond perception because it is beyond doubt. Do not perceive yourself in different lights. Know yourself in the One Light where the miracle that is you is perfectly clear.

VI. Judgment and the Authority Problem

2. The choice to judge rather than to know is the cause of the loss of peace. Judgment is the process on which perception but not knowledge rests. I have discussed this before in terms of the selectivity of perception, pointing out that evaluation is its obvious prerequisite. Judgment always involves rejection. It never emphasizes only the positive aspects of what is judged, whether in you or in others. What has been perceived and rejected, or judged and found wanting, remains in your mind because it has been perceived. One of the illusions from which you suffer is the belief that what you judged against has no effect. This cannot be true unless you also believe that what you judged against does not exist. You evidently do not believe this, or you would not have judged against it. In the end it does not matter whether your judgment is right or wrong. Either way you are placing your belief in the unreal. This cannot be avoided in any type of judgment, because it implies the belief that reality is yours to select *from*.

3. You have no idea of the tremendous release and deep peace that comes from meeting yourself and your brothers totally without judgment. When you recognize what you are and what your brothers are, you will realize that judging them in any way is without meaning. In fact, their meaning is lost to you precisely *because* you are judging them. All uncertainty comes from the belief that you are under the coercion of judgment. You do not need judgment to organize your life, and you certainly do not need it to organize yourself. In the presence of knowledge all judgment is automatically suspended, and this is the process that enables recognition to replace perception.

4. You are very fearful of everything you have perceived but have refused to accept. You believe that, because you have refused to accept it, you have lost control over it. This is why you see it in nightmares, or in pleasant disguises in what seem to be your happier dreams. Nothing that you have refused to accept can be brought into awareness. It is not dangerous in itself, but you have made it seem dangerous to you.

5. When you feel tired, it is because you have judged yourself as capable of being tired. When you laugh at someone, it is because you have judged him as unworthy. When you laugh at yourself you must laugh at others, if only because you cannot tolerate the idea of being more unworthy than they are. All this makes you feel tired because it is essentially disheartening. You are not really capable of being tired, but you are very capable of wearying yourself. The strain of constant judgment is virtually intolerable. It is curious that an ability

so debilitating would be so deeply cherished. Yet if you wish to be the author of reality, you will insist on holding on to judgment. You will also regard judgment with fear, believing that it will someday be used against you. This belief can exist only to the extent that you believe in the efficacy of judgment as a weapon of defense for your own authority.

6. God offers only mercy. Your words should reflect only mercy, because that is what you have received and that is what you should give. Justice is a temporary expedient, or an attempt to teach you the meaning of mercy. It is judgmental only because you are capable of injustice.

7. I have spoken of different symptoms, and at that level there is almost endless variation. There is, however, only one cause for all of them: the authority problem. This *is* "the root of all evil." Every symptom the ego makes involves a contradiction in terms, because the mind is split between the ego and the Holy Spirit, so that whatever the ego makes is incomplete and contradictory. This untenable position is the result of the authority problem which, because it accepts the one inconceivable thought as its premise, can produce only ideas that are inconceivable.

8. The issue of authority is really a question of authorship. When you have an authority problem, it is always because you believe you are the author of yourself and project your delusion onto others. You then perceive the situation as one in which others are literally fighting you for your authorship. This is the fundamental error of all those who believe they have usurped the power of God. This belief is very frightening to them, but hardly troubles God. He is, however, eager to undo it, not to punish His children, but only because He knows that it makes them unhappy. God's creations are given their true Authorship, but you prefer to be anonymous when you choose to separate yourself from your Author. Being uncertain of your true Authorship, you believe that your creation was anonymous. This leaves you in a position where it sounds meaningful to believe that you created yourself. The dispute over authorship has left such uncertainty in your mind that it may even doubt whether you really exist at all.

9. Only those who give over all desire to reject can know that their own rejection is impossible. You have not usurped the power of God, but you *have* lost it. Fortunately, to lose something does not mean that it has gone. It merely means that you do not remember where it is. Its existence does not depend on your ability to identify it, or even to place it. It is possible to look on reality without judgment and merely know that it is there.

10. Peace is a natural heritage of spirit. Everyone is free to refuse to accept his inheritance, but he is not free to establish what his inheritance is. The problem everyone must decide is the fundamental question of authorship. All fear comes ultimately, and sometimes by way of very devious routes, from the denial of Authorship. The offense is never to God, but only to those who deny Him. To deny His Authorship is to deny yourself the reason for your peace, so that you see yourself only in segments. This strange perception *is* the authority problem.

11. There is no one who does not feel that he is imprisoned in some way. If this is the result of his own free will he must regard his will as not free, or the circular reasoning in this position would be quite apparent. Free will must lead to freedom. Judgment always imprisons because it separates segments of reality by the unstable scales of desire. Wishes are not facts. To wish is to imply that willing is not sufficient. Yet no one in his right mind believes that what is wished is as real as what is willed. Instead of "Seek ye first the Kingdom of Heaven" say, "*Will* ye first the Kingdom of Heaven," and you have said, "I know what I am and I accept my own inheritance."

QUESTION 7. What is the authority problem?

VII. Creating versus the Self-Image

1. Every system of thought must have a starting point. It begins with either a making or a creating, a difference we have already discussed. Their resemblance lies in their power as foundations. Their difference lies in what rests upon them. Both are cornerstones for systems of belief by which one lives. It is a mistake to believe that a thought system based on lies is weak. Nothing made by a child of God is without power. It is essential to realize this, because otherwise you will be unable to escape from the prison you have made.

4. Eating of the fruit of the tree of knowledge is a symbolic expression for usurping the ability for self-creating. This is the only sense in which God and His creations are not co-creators. The belief that they are is implicit in the "self-concept," or the tendency of the self to make an image of itself. Images are perceived, not known. Knowledge cannot deceive, but perception can. You can perceive yourself as self-creating, but you cannot do more than believe it. You cannot make it true. And, as I said before, when you finally perceive correctly you can only be glad that you cannot. Until then, however, the belief that you can is the foundation stone in your thought system, and all your defenses are used to attack ideas that might bring it to

light. You still believe you are an image of your own making. Your mind is split with the Holy Spirit on this point, and there is no resolution while you believe the one thing that is literally inconceivable. That is why you cannot create and are filled with fear about what you make.

5. The mind can make the belief in separation very real and very fearful, and this belief *is* the "devil." It is powerful, active, destructive and clearly in opposition to God, because it literally denies His Fatherhood. Look at your life and see what the devil has made. But realize that this making will surely dissolve in the light of truth, because its foundation is a lie. Your creation by God is the only Foundation that cannot be shaken, because the light is in it. Your starting point is truth, and you must return to your Beginning. Much has been seen since then, but nothing has really happened. Your Self is still in peace, even though your mind is in conflict. You have not yet gone back far enough, and that is why you become so fearful. As you approach the Beginning, you feel the fear of the destruction of your thought system upon you as if it were the fear of death. There is no death, but there *is* a belief in death.

6. The branch that bears no fruit will be cut off and will wither away. Be glad! The light will shine from the true Foundation of life, and your own thought system will stand corrected. It cannot stand otherwise. You who fear salvation are choosing death. Life and death, light and darkness, knowledge and perception, are irreconcilable. To believe that they can be reconciled is to believe that God and His Son can *not*. Only the oneness of knowledge is free of conflict. Your Kingdom is not of this world because it was given you from beyond this world. Only in this world is the idea of an authority problem meaningful. The world is not left by death but by truth, and truth can be known by all those for whom the Kingdom was created, and for whom it waits.

Chapter 4. THE ILLUSIONS OF THE EGO

I. Right Teaching and Right Learning

1. A good teacher clarifies his own ideas and strengthens them by teaching them. Teacher and pupil are alike in the learning process. They are in the same order of learning, and unless they share their lessons conviction will be lacking. A good teacher must believe in the ideas he teaches, but he must meet another condition; he must believe in the students to whom he offers the ideas.

2. Many stand guard over their ideas because they want to protect their thought systems as they are, and learning means change. Change is always fearful to the separated, because they cannot conceive of it as a move towards healing the separation. They always perceive it as a move toward further separation, because the separation was their first experience of change. You believe that if you allow no change to enter into your ego you will find peace. This profound confusion is possible only if you maintain that the same thought system can stand on two foundations. Nothing can reach spirit from the ego, and nothing can reach the ego from spirit. Spirit can neither strengthen the ego nor reduce the conflict within it. The ego *is* a contradiction. Your self and God's Self *are* in opposition. They are opposed in source, in direction and in outcome. They are fundamentally irreconcilable, because spirit cannot perceive and the ego cannot know. They are therefore not in communication and can never be in communication. Nevertheless, the ego can learn, even though its maker can be misguided. He cannot, however, make the totally lifeless out of the life-given.

3. Spirit need not be taught, but the ego must be. Learning is ultimately perceived as frightening because it leads to the relinquishment, not the destruction, of the ego to the light of spirit. This is the change the ego must fear, because it does not share my charity. My lesson was like yours, and because I learned it I can teach it. I will never attack your ego, but I am trying to teach you how its thought system arose. When I remind you of your true creation, your ego cannot but respond with fear.

4. Teaching and learning are your greatest strengths now, because they enable you to change your mind and help others to change theirs. Refusing to change your mind will not prove that the separation has not occurred. The dreamer who doubts the reality of his dream while he is still dreaming is not really healing his split mind. You dream of a separated ego and believe in a world that rests upon it.

This is very real to you. You cannot undo it by not changing your mind about it. If you are willing to renounce the role of guardian of your thought system and open it to me, I will correct it very gently and lead you back to God.

5. Every good teacher hopes to give his students so much of his own learning that they will one day no longer need him. This is the one true goal of the teacher. It is impossible to convince the ego of this, because it goes against all of its own laws. But remember that laws are set up to protect the continuity of the system in which the lawmaker believes. It is natural for the ego to try to protect itself once you have made it, but it is not natural for you to want to obey its laws unless *you* believe them. The ego cannot make this choice because of the nature of its origin. You can, because of the nature of yours.

6. Egos can clash in any situation, but spirit cannot clash at all. If you perceive a teacher as merely "a larger ego" you will be afraid, because to enlarge an ego would be to increase anxiety about separation. I will teach with you and live with you if you will think with me, but my goal will always be to absolve you finally from the need for a teacher. This is the opposite of the ego-oriented teacher's goal. He is concerned with the effect of his ego on other egos, and therefore interprets their interaction as a means of ego preservation. I would not be able to devote myself to teaching if I believed this, and you will not be a devoted teacher as long as you believe it. I am constantly being perceived as a teacher either to be exalted or rejected, but I do not accept either perception for myself.

7. Your worth is not established by teaching or learning. Your worth is established by God. As long as you dispute this everything you do will be fearful, particularly any situation that lends itself to the belief in superiority and inferiority. Teachers must be patient and repeat their lessons until they are learned. I am willing to do this, because I have no right to set your learning limits for you. Again,—nothing you do or think or wish or make is necessary to establish your worth. This point is not debatable except in delusions. Your ego is never at stake because God did not create it. Your spirit is never at stake because He did. Any confusion on this point is delusional, and no form of devotion is possible as long as this delusion lasts.

8. The ego tries to exploit all situations into forms of praise for itself in order to overcome its doubts. It will remain doubtful as long as you believe in its existence. You who made it cannot trust it, because in your right mind you realize it is not real. The only sane solution is not to try to change reality, which is indeed a fearful attempt, but to accept it as it is. You are part of reality, which stands unchanged beyond the reach of

your ego but within easy reach of spirit. When you are afraid, be still and know that God is real, and you are His beloved Son in whom He is well pleased. Do not let your ego dispute this, because the ego cannot know what is as far beyond its reach as you are.

9. God is not the author of fear. You are. You have chosen to create unlike Him, and have therefore made fear for yourself. You are not at peace because you are not fulfilling your function. God gave you a very lofty function that you are not meeting. Your ego has chosen to be afraid instead of meeting it. When you awaken you will not be able to understand this, because it is literally incredible. *Do not believe the incredible now.* Any attempt to increase its believableness is merely to postpone the inevitable. The word "inevitable" is fearful to the ego, but joyous to the spirit. God is inevitable, and you cannot avoid Him any more than He can avoid you.

10. The ego is afraid of the spirit's joy, because once you have experienced it you will withdraw all protection from the ego, and become totally without investment in fear. Your investment is great now because fear is a witness to the separation, and your ego rejoices when you witness to it. Leave it behind! Do not listen to it and do not preserve it. Listen only to God, Who is as incapable of deception as is the spirit He created. Release yourself and release others. Do not present a false and unworthy picture of yourself to others, and do not accept such a picture of them yourself.

11. The ego has built a shabby and unsheltering home for you, because it cannot build otherwise. Do not try to make this impoverished house stand. Its weakness is your strength. Only God could make a home that is worthy of His creations, who have chosen to leave it empty by their own dispossession. Yet His home will stand forever, and is ready for you when you choose to enter it. Of this you can be wholly certain. God is as incapable of creating the perishable as the ego is of making the eternal.

12. Of your ego you can do nothing to save yourself or others, but of your spirit you can do everything for the salvation of both. Humility is a lesson for the ego, not for the spirit. Spirit is beyond humility, because it recognizes its radiance and gladly sheds its light everywhere. The meek shall inherit the earth because their egos are humble, and this gives them truer perception. The Kingdom of Heaven is the spirit's right, whose beauty and dignity are far beyond doubt, beyond perception, and stand forever as the mark of the Love of God for His creations, who are wholly worthy of Him and only of Him. Nothing else is sufficiently worthy to be a gift for a creation of God Himself.

13. I will substitute for your ego if you wish, but never for your spirit. A father can safely leave a child with an elder brother who has shown himself responsible, but this involves no confusion about the child's origin. The brother can protect the child's body and his ego, but he does not confuse himself with the father because he does this. I can be entrusted with your body and your ego only because this enables you not to be concerned with them, and lets me teach you their unimportance. I could not understand their importance to you if I had not once been tempted to believe in them myself. Let us undertake to learn this lesson together so we can be free of them together. I need devoted teachers who share my aim of healing the mind. Spirit is far beyond the need of your protection or mine. Remember this:

> In this world you need not have tribulation because I have overcome the world. That is why you should be of good cheer.

QUESTION 8. What are "your greatest strengths now"?

II. The Ego and False Autonomy

1. It is reasonable to ask how the mind could ever have made the ego. In fact, it is the best question you could ask. There is, however, no point in giving an answer in terms of the past because the past does not matter, and history would not exist if the same errors were not being repeated in the present. Abstract thought applies to knowledge because knowledge is completely impersonal, and examples are irrelevant to its understanding. Perception, however, is always specific, and therefore quite concrete.

2. Everyone makes an ego or a self for himself, which is subject to enormous variation because of its instability. He also makes an ego for everyone else he perceives, which is equally variable. Their interaction is a process that alters both, because they were not made by or with the Unalterable. It is important to realize that this alteration can and does occur as readily when the interaction takes place in the mind as when it involves physical proximity. Thinking about another ego is as effective in changing relative perception as is physical interaction. There could be no better example that the ego is only an idea and not a fact.

3. Your own state of mind is a good example of how the ego was made. When you threw knowledge away it is as if you never had it. This is so apparent that one need only recognize it to see that it does happen. If this occurs in the present, why is it surprising that it occurred

in the past? Surprise is a reasonable response to the unfamiliar, though hardly to something that occurs with such persistence. But do not forget that the mind need not work that way, even though it does work that way now.

4. Think of the love of animals for their offspring, and the need they feel to protect them. That is because they regard them as part of themselves. No one dismisses something he considers part of himself. You react to your ego much as God does to His creations,—with love, protection and charity. Your reactions to the self you made are not surprising. In fact, they resemble in many ways how you will one day react to your real creations, which are as timeless as you are. The question is not how you respond to the ego, but what you believe you are. Belief is an ego function, and as long as your origin is open to belief you are regarding it from an ego viewpoint. When teaching is no longer necessary you will merely know God. Belief that there is another way of perceiving is the loftiest idea of which ego thinking is capable. That is because it contains a hint of recognition that the ego is not the Self.

5. Undermining the ego's thought system must be perceived as painful, even though this is anything but true. Babies scream in rage if you take away a knife or scissors, although they may well harm themselves if you do not. In this sense you are still a baby. You have no sense of real self-preservation, and are likely to decide that you need precisely what would hurt you most. Yet whether or not you recognize it now, you have agreed to cooperate in the effort to become both harmless and helpful, attributes that must go together. Your attitudes even toward this are necessarily conflicted, because all attitudes are ego-based. This will not last. Be patient a while and remember that the outcome is as certain as God.

6. Only those who have a real and lasting sense of abundance can be truly charitable. This is obvious when you consider what is involved. To the ego, to give anything implies that you will have to do without it. When you associate giving with sacrifice, you give only because you believe that you are somehow getting something better, and can therefore do without the thing you give. "Giving to get" is an inescapable law of the ego, which always evaluates itself in relation to other egos. It is therefore continually preoccupied with the belief in scarcity that gave rise to it. Its whole perception of other egos as real is only an attempt to convince itself that *it* is real. "Self-esteem" in ego terms means nothing more than that the ego has deluded itself into accepting its reality, and is therefore temporarily less predatory. This "self-esteem" is

always vulnerable to stress, a term which refers to any perceived threat to the ego's existence.

7. The ego literally lives by comparisons. Equality is beyond its grasp, and charity becomes impossible. The ego never gives out of abundance, because it was made as a substitute for it. That is why the concept of "getting" arose in the ego's thought system. Appetites are "getting" mechanisms, representing the ego's need to confirm itself. This is as true of body appetites as it is of the so-called "higher ego needs." Body appetites are not physical in origin. The ego regards the body as its home, and tries to satisfy itself through the body. But the idea that this is possible is a decision of the mind, which has become completely confused about what is really possible.

8. The ego believes it is completely on its own, which is merely another way of describing how it thinks it originated. This is such a fearful state that it can only turn to other egos and try to unite with them in a feeble attempt at identification, or attack them in an equally feeble show of strength. It is not free, however, to open the premise to question, because the premise is its foundation. The ego is the mind's belief that it is completely on its own. The ego's ceaseless attempts to gain the spirit's acknowledgment and thus establish its own existence are useless. Spirit in its knowledge is unaware of the ego. It does not attack it; it merely cannot conceive of it at all. While the ego is equally unaware of spirit, it does perceive itself as being rejected by something greater than itself. This is why self-esteem in ego terms must be delusional. The creations of God do not create myths, although creative effort can be turned to mythology. It can do so, however, only under one condition; what it makes is then no longer creative. Myths are entirely perceptual, and so ambiguous in form and characteristically good-and-evil in nature that the most benevolent of them is not without fearful connotations.

10. Salvation is nothing more than "right-mindedness," which is not the One-mindedness of the Holy Spirit, but which must be achieved before One-mindedness is restored. Right-mindedness leads to the next step automatically, because right perception is uniformly without attack, and therefore wrong-mindedness is obliterated. The ego cannot survive without judgment, and is laid aside accordingly. The mind then has only one direction in which it can move. Its direction is always automatic, because it cannot but be dictated by the thought system to which it adheres.

11. It cannot be emphasized too often that correcting perception is merely a temporary expedient. It is necessary only because mis-perception is a block to knowledge, while accurate perception is a steppingstone towards it. The whole value of right perception lies

in the inevitable realization that *all* perception is unnecessary. This removes the block entirely. You may ask how this is possible as long as you appear to be living in this world. That is a reasonable question. You must be careful, however, that you really understand it. Who is the "you" who are living in this world? Spirit is immortal, and immortality is a constant state. It is as true now as it ever was or ever will be, because it implies no change at all. It is not a continuum, nor is it understood by being compared to an opposite. Knowledge never involves comparisons. That is its main difference from everything else the mind can grasp.

III. Love without Conflict

3. It is surely apparent by now why the ego regards spirit as its "enemy." The ego arose from the separation, and its continued existence depends on your continuing belief in the separation. The ego must offer you some sort of reward for maintaining this belief. All it can offer is a sense of temporary existence, which begins with its own beginning and ends with its own ending. It tells you this life is your existence because it is its own. Against this sense of temporary existence spirit offers you the knowledge of permanence and unshakable being. No one who has experienced the revelation of this can ever fully believe in the ego again. How can its meager offering to you prevail against the glorious gift of God?

4. You who identify with your ego cannot believe God loves you. You do not love what you made, and what you made does not love you. Being made out of the denial of the Father, the ego has no allegiance to its maker. You cannot conceive of the real relationship that exists between God and His creations because of your hatred for the self you made. You project onto the ego the decision to separate, and this conflicts with the love you feel for the ego because you made it. No love in this world is without this ambivalence, and since no ego has experienced love without ambivalence the concept is beyond its understanding. Love will enter immediately into any mind that truly wants it, but it must want it truly. This means that it wants it without ambivalence, and this kind of wanting is wholly without the ego's "drive to get."

6. No force except your own will is strong enough or worthy enough to guide you. In this you are as free as God, and must remain so forever. Let us ask the Father in my name to keep you mindful of His Love for you and yours for Him. He has never failed to answer this request, because it asks only for what He has already willed. Those

who call truly are always answered. Thou shalt have no other gods before Him because there *are* none.

7. It has never really entered your mind to give up every idea you ever had that opposes knowledge. You retain thousands of little scraps of fear that prevent the Holy One from entering. Light cannot penetrate through the walls you make to block it, and it is forever unwilling to destroy what you have made. No one can see through a wall, but I can step around it. Watch your mind for the scraps of fear, or you will be unable to ask me to do so. I can help you only as our Father created us. I will love you and honor you and maintain complete respect for what you have made, but I will not uphold it unless it is true. I will never forsake you any more than God will, but I must wait as long as you choose to forsake yourself. Because I wait in love and not in impatience, you will surely ask me truly. I will come in response to a single unequivocal call.

8. Watch carefully and see what it is you are really asking for. Be very honest with yourself in this, for we must hide nothing from each other. If you will really try to do this, you have taken the first step toward preparing your mind for the Holy One to enter. We will prepare for this together, for once He has come, you will be ready to help me make other minds ready for Him. How long will you deny Him His Kingdom?

9. In your own mind, though denied by the ego, is the declaration of your release. *God has given you everything.* This one fact means the ego does not exist, and this makes it profoundly afraid. In the ego's language, "to have" and "to be" are different, but they are identical to the Holy Spirit. The Holy Spirit knows that you both *have* everything and *are* everything. Any distinction in this respect is meaningful only when the idea of "getting," which implies a lack, has already been accepted. That is why we make no distinction between *having* the Kingdom of God and *being* the Kingdom of God.

10. The calm being of God's Kingdom, which in your sane mind is perfectly conscious, is ruthlessly banished from the part of the mind the ego rules. The ego is desperate because it opposes literally invincible odds, whether you are asleep or awake. Consider how much vigilance you have been willing to exert to protect your ego, and how little to protect your right mind. Who but the insane would undertake to believe what is not true, and then protect this belief at the cost of truth?

QUESTION 9. What is the ego?

IV. This Need Not Be

5. When you feel guilty, remember that the ego has indeed violated the laws of God, but *you* have not. Leave the "sins" of the ego to me. That is what Atonement is for. But until you change your mind about those whom your ego has hurt, the Atonement cannot release you. While you feel guilty your ego is in command, because only the ego can experience guilt. *This need not be.*

6. Watch your mind for the temptations of the ego, and do not be deceived by it. It offers you nothing. When you have given up this voluntary dis-spiriting, you will see how your mind can focus and rise above fatigue and heal. Yet you are not sufficiently vigilant against the demands of the ego to disengage yourself. *This need not be.*

7. The habit of engaging with God and His creations is easily made if you actively refuse to let your mind slip away. The problem is not one of concentration; it is the belief that no one, including yourself, is worth consistent effort. Side with me consistently against this deception, and do not permit this shabby belief to pull you back. The disheartened are useless to themselves and to me, but only the ego can *be* disheartened.

8. Have you really considered how many opportunities you have had to gladden yourself, and how many of them you have refused? There is no limit to the power of a Son of God, but he can limit the expression of his power as much as he chooses. Your mind and mine can unite in shining your ego away, releasing the strength of God into everything you think and do. Do not settle for anything less than this, and refuse to accept anything but this as your goal. Watch your mind carefully for any beliefs that hinder its accomplishment, and step away from them. Judge how well you have done this by your own feelings, for this is the one right use of judgment. Judgment, like any other defense, can be used to attack or protect; to hurt or to heal. The ego *should* be brought to judgment and found wanting there. Without your own allegiance, protection and love, the ego cannot exist. Let it be judged truly and you must withdraw allegiance, protection and love from it.

9. You are a mirror of truth, in which God Himself shines in perfect light. To the ego's dark glass you need but say, "I will not look there because I know these images are not true." Then let the Holy One shine on you in peace, knowing that this and only this must be. His Mind shone on you in your creation and brought your mind into being. His Mind still shines on you and must shine through you. Your ego cannot prevent Him from shining on you, but it can prevent you from letting Him shine through you.

10. The First Coming of Christ is merely another name for the creation, for Christ is the Son of God. The Second Coming of Christ means nothing more than the end of the ego's rule and the healing of the mind. I was created like you in the First, and I have called you to join with me in the Second. I am in charge of the Second Coming, and my judgment, which is used only for protection, cannot be wrong because it never attacks. Yours may be so distorted that you believe I was mistaken in choosing you. I assure you this is a mistake of your ego. Do not mistake it for humility. Your ego is trying to convince you that it is real and I am not, because if I am real, I am no more real than you are. That knowledge, and I assure you that it *is* knowledge, means that Christ has come into your mind and healed it.

11. I do not attack your ego. I do work with your higher mind, the home of the Holy Spirit, whether you are asleep or awake, just as your ego does with your lower mind, which is its home. I am your vigilance in this, because you are too confused to recognize your own hope. I am not mistaken. Your mind will elect to join with mine, and together we are invincible. You and your brother will yet come together in my name, and your sanity will be restored. I raised the dead by knowing that life is an eternal attribute of everything that the living God created. Why do you believe it is harder for me to inspire the dis-spirited or to stabilize the unstable? I do not believe that there is an order of difficulty in miracles; you do. I have called and you will answer. I understand that miracles are natural, because they are expressions of love. My calling you is as natural as your answer, and as inevitable.

V. The Ego-Body Illusion

3. Any thought system that confuses God and the body must be insane. Yet this confusion is essential to the ego, which judges only in terms of threat or non-threat to itself. In one sense the ego's fear of God is at least logical, since the idea of Him does dispel the ego. But fear of the body, with which the ego identifies so closely, makes no sense at all.

4. The body is the ego's home by its own election. It is the only identification with which the ego feels safe, since the body's vulnerability is its own best argument that you cannot be of God. This is the belief that the ego sponsors eagerly. Yet the ego hates the body, because it cannot accept it as good enough to be its home. Here is where the mind becomes actually dazed. Being told by the ego that it is really part of the body and that the body is its protector, the

mind is also told that the body cannot protect it. Therefore, the mind asks, "Where can I go for protection?" to which the ego replies, "Turn to me." The mind, and not without cause, reminds the ego that it has itself insisted that it is identified with the body, so there is no point in turning to *it* for protection. The ego has no real answer to this because there is none, but it does have a typical solution. It obliterates the question from the mind's awareness. Once out of awareness the question can and does produce uneasiness, but it cannot be answered because it cannot be asked.

5. This is the question that *must* be asked: "Where can I go for protection?" "Seek and ye shall find" does not mean that you should seek blindly and desperately for something you would not recognize. Meaningful seeking is consciously undertaken, consciously organized and consciously directed. The goal must be formulated clearly and kept in mind. Learning and wanting to learn are inseparable. You learn best when you believe what you are trying to learn is of value to you. However, not everything you may want to learn has lasting value. Indeed, many of the things you want to learn may be chosen *because* their value will not last.

6. The ego thinks it is an advantage not to commit itself to anything that is eternal, because the eternal must come from God. Eternalness is the one function the ego has tried to develop, but has systematically failed to achieve. The ego compromises with the issue of the eternal, just as it does with all issues touching on the real question in any way. By becoming involved with tangential issues, it hopes to hide the real question and keep it out of mind. The ego's characteristic busyness with nonessentials is for precisely that purpose. Preoccupations with problems set up to be incapable of solution are favorite ego devices for impeding learning progress. In all these diversionary tactics, however, the one question that is never asked by those who pursue them is, "What for?" This is the question that *you* must learn to ask in connection with everything. What is the purpose? Whatever it is, it will direct your efforts automatically. When you make a decision of purpose, then, you have made a decision about your future effort; a decision that will remain in effect unless you change your mind.

VI. The Rewards of God

1. The ego does not recognize the real source of "threat," and if you associate yourself with the ego, you do not understand the situation as it is. Only your allegiance to it gives the ego any power over you. I have spoken of the ego as if it were a separate thing, acting on its

own. This was necessary to persuade you that you cannot dismiss it lightly, and must realize how much of your thinking is ego-directed. We cannot safely let it go at that, however, or you will regard yourself as necessarily conflicted as long as you are here, or as long as you believe that you are here. The ego is nothing more than a part of your belief about yourself. Your other life has continued without interruption, and has been and always will be totally unaffected by your attempts to dissociate it.

2. In learning to escape from illusions, your debt to your brother is something you must never forget. It is the same debt that you owe to me. Whenever you act egotistically towards another, you are throwing away the graciousness of your indebtedness and the holy perception it would produce. The term "holy" can be used here because, as you learn how much you are indebted to the whole Sonship, which includes me, you come as close to knowledge as perception can. The gap is then so small that knowledge can easily flow across it and obliterate it forever.

3. You have very little trust in me as yet, but it will increase as you turn more and more often to me instead of to your ego for guidance. The results will convince you increasingly that this choice is the only sane one you can make. No one who learns from experience that one choice brings peace and joy while another brings chaos and disaster needs additional convincing. Learning through rewards is more effective than learning through pain, because pain is an ego illusion, and can never induce more than a temporary effect. The rewards of God, however, are immediately recognized as eternal. Since this recognition is made by you and not the ego, the recognition itself establishes that you and your ego cannot be identical. You may believe that you have already accepted this difference, but you are by no means convinced as yet. The fact that you believe you must escape from the ego shows this; but you cannot escape from the ego by humbling it or controlling it or punishing it.

4. The ego and the spirit do not know each other. The separated mind cannot maintain the separation except by dissociating. Having done this, it denies all truly natural impulses, not because the ego is a separate thing, but because you want to believe that *you* are. The ego is a device for maintaining this belief, but it is still only your decision to use the device that enables it to endure.

5. How can you teach someone the value of something he has deliberately thrown away? He must have thrown it away because he did not value it. You can only show him how miserable he is without it, and slowly bring it nearer so he can learn how his misery lessens as he approaches it. This teaches him to associate his misery with its absence, and the opposite of misery with its presence. It gradually becomes

desirable as he changes his mind about its worth. I am teaching you to associate misery with the ego and joy with the spirit. You have taught yourself the opposite. You are still free to choose, but can you really want the rewards of the ego in the presence of the rewards of God?

6. My trust in you is greater than yours in me at the moment, but it will not always be that way. Your mission is very simple. You are asked to live so as to demonstrate that you are not an ego, and I do not choose God's channels wrongly. The Holy One shares my trust, and accepts my Atonement decisions because my will is never out of accord with His. I have said before that I am in charge of the Atonement. This is only because I completed my part in it as a man, and can now complete it through others. My chosen channels cannot fail, because I will lend them my strength as long as theirs is wanting.

7. I will go with you to the Holy One, and through my perception He can bridge the little gap. Your gratitude to your brother is the only gift I want. I will bring it to God for you, knowing that to know your brother *is* to know God. If you are grateful to your brother, you are grateful to God for what He created. Through your gratitude you come to know your brother, and one moment of real recognition makes everyone your brother because each of them is of your Father. Love does not conquer all things, but it does set all things right. Because you are the Kingdom of God I can lead you back to your own creations. You do not recognize them now, but what has been dissociated is still there.

8. As you come closer to a brother you approach me, and as you withdraw from him I become distant to you. Salvation is a collaborative venture. It cannot be undertaken successfully by those who disengage themselves from the Sonship, because they are disengaging themselves from me. God will come to you only as you will give Him to your brothers. Learn first of them and you will be ready to hear God. That is because the function of love is one.

QUESTION 10. What is "the question that *you* must learn to ask in connection with everything"?

VII. Creation and Communication

1. It is clear that while the content of any particular ego illusion does not matter, its correction is more helpful in a specific context. Ego illusions are quite specific, although the mind is naturally abstract. Part of the mind becomes concrete, however, when it splits. The concrete part believes in the ego, because the ego depends on the concrete.

The ego is the part of the mind that believes your existence is defined by separation.

2. Everything the ego perceives is a separate whole, without the relationships that imply being. The ego is thus against communication, except insofar as it is utilized to establish separateness rather than to abolish it. The communication system of the ego is based on its own thought system, as is everything else it dictates. Its communication is controlled by its need to protect itself, and it will disrupt communication when it experiences threat. This disruption is a reaction to a specific person or persons. The specificity of the ego's thinking, then, results in spurious generalization which is really not abstract at all. It merely responds in certain specific ways to everything it perceives as related.

3. In contrast, spirit reacts in the same way to everything it knows is true, and does not respond at all to anything else. Nor does it make any attempt to establish what is true. It knows that what is true is everything that God created. It is in complete and direct communication with every aspect of creation, because it is in complete and direct communication with its Creator. This communication is the Will of God. Creation and communication are synonymous. God created every mind by communicating His Mind to it, thus establishing it forever as a channel for the reception of His Mind and Will. Since only beings of a like order can truly communicate, His creations naturally communicate with Him and like Him. This communication is perfectly abstract, since its quality is universal in application and not subject to any judgment, any exception or any alteration. God created you by this and for this. The mind can distort its function, but it cannot endow itself with functions it was not given. That is why the mind cannot totally lose the ability to communicate, even though it may refuse to utilize it on behalf of being.

4. Existence as well as being rests on communication. Existence, however, is specific in how, what and with whom communication is judged to be worth undertaking. Being is completely without these distinctions. It is a state in which the mind is in communication with everything that is real. To whatever extent you permit this state to be curtailed you are limiting your sense of your own reality, which becomes total only by recognizing all reality in the glorious context of its real relationship to you. This is your reality. Do not desecrate it or recoil from it. It is your real home, your real temple and your real Self.

5. God, Who encompasses all being, created beings who have everything individually, but who want to share it to increase their joy. Nothing real can be increased except by sharing. That is why God

created you. Divine Abstraction takes joy in sharing. That is what creation means. "How," "what" and "to whom" are irrelevant, because real creation gives everything, since it can create only like itself. Remember that in the Kingdom there is no difference between *having* and *being*, as there is in existence. In the state of being the mind gives everything always.

6. The Bible repeatedly states that you should praise God. This hardly means that you should tell Him how wonderful He is. He has no ego with which to accept such praise, and no perception with which to judge it. But unless you take your part in the creation, His joy is not complete because yours is incomplete. And this He does know. He knows it in His Own Being and its experience of His Son's experience. The constant going out of His Love is blocked when His channels are closed, and He is lonely when the minds He created do not communicate fully with Him.

7. God has kept your Kingdom for you, but He cannot share His joy with you until you know it with your whole mind. Revelation is not enough, because it is only communication *from* God. God does not need revelation returned to Him, which would clearly be impossible, but He does want it brought to others. This cannot be done with the actual revelation; its content cannot be expressed, because it is intensely personal to the mind that receives it. It can, however, be returned by that mind to other minds, through the attitudes the knowledge from the revelation brings.

8. God is praised whenever any mind learns to be wholly helpful. This is impossible without being wholly harmless, because the two beliefs must coexist. The truly helpful are invulnerable, because they are not protecting their egos and so nothing can hurt them. Their helpfulness is their praise of God, and He will return their praise of Him because they are like Him, and they can rejoice together. God goes out to them and through them, and there is great joy throughout the Kingdom. Every mind that is changed adds to this joy with its individual willingness to share in it. The truly helpful are God's miracle workers, whom I direct until we are all united in the joy of the Kingdom. I will direct you to wherever you can be truly helpful, and to whoever can follow my guidance through you.

Chapter 5. HEALING AND WHOLENESS

I. The Invitation to the Holy Spirit

1. Healing is a thought by which two minds perceive their oneness and become glad. This gladness calls to every part of the Sonship to rejoice with them, and lets God go out into them and through them. Only the healed mind can experience revelation with lasting effect, because revelation is an experience of pure joy. If you do not choose to be wholly joyous, your mind cannot have what it does not choose to be. Remember that spirit knows no difference between *having* and *being*. The higher mind thinks according to the laws spirit obeys, and therefore honors only the laws of God. To spirit getting is meaningless and giving is all. Having everything, spirit holds everything by giving it, and thus creates as the Father created. While this kind of thinking is totally alien to having things, even to the lower mind it is quite comprehensible in connection with ideas. If you share a physical possession, you do divide its ownership. If you share an idea, however, you do not lessen it. All of it is still yours although all of it has been given away. Further, if the one to whom you give it accepts it as his, he reinforces it in your mind and thus increases it. If you can accept the concept that the world is one of ideas, the whole belief in the false association the ego makes between giving and losing is gone.

5. The Holy Spirit is the Christ Mind which is aware of the knowledge that lies beyond perception. He came into being with the separation as a protection, inspiring the Atonement principle at the same time. Before that there was no need for healing, for no one was comfortless. The Voice of the Holy Spirit is the Call to Atonement, or the restoration of the integrity of the mind. When the Atonement is complete and the whole Sonship is healed there will be no Call to return. But what God creates is eternal. The Holy Spirit will remain with the Sons of God, to bless their creations and keep them in the light of joy.

6. God honored even the miscreations of His children because they had made them. But He also blessed His children with a way of thinking that could raise their perceptions so high they could reach almost back to Him. The Holy Spirit is the Mind of the Atonement. He represents a state of mind close enough to One-mindedness that transfer to it is at last possible. Perception is not knowledge, but it can be transferred to knowledge, or cross over into it. It might even be more helpful here to use the literal meaning of transferred or "carried over," since the last step is taken by God.

II. The Voice for God

2. The Holy Spirit is the spirit of joy. He is the Call to return with which God blessed the minds of His separated Sons. This is the vocation of the mind. The mind had no calling until the separation, because before that it had only being, and would not have understood the Call to right thinking. The Holy Spirit is God's Answer to the separation; the means by which the Atonement heals until the whole mind returns to creating.
3. The principle of Atonement and the separation began at the same time. When the ego was made, God placed in the mind the Call to joy. This Call is so strong that the ego always dissolves at Its sound. That is why you must choose to hear one of two voices within you. One you made yourself, and that one is not of God. But the other is given you by God, Who asks you only to listen to it. The Holy Spirit is in you in a very literal sense. His is the Voice that calls you back to where you were before and will be again. It is possible even in this world to hear only that Voice and no other. It takes effort and great willingness to learn. It is the final lesson that I learned, and God's Sons are as equal as learners as they are as Sons.
5. God does not guide, because He can share only perfect knowledge. Guidance is evaluative, because it implies there is a right way and also a wrong way, one to be chosen and the other to be avoided. By choosing one you give up the other. The choice for the Holy Spirit is the choice for God. God is not in you in a literal sense; you are part of Him.
9. My mind will always be like yours, because we were created as equals. It was only my decision that gave me all power in Heaven and earth. My only gift to you is to help you make the same decision. This decision is the choice to share it, because the decision itself *is* the decision to share. It is made by giving, and is therefore the one choice that resembles true creation. I am your model for decision. By deciding for God I showed you that this decision can be made, and that you can make it.
10. I have assured you that the Mind that decided for me is also in you, and that you can let it change you just as it changed me. This Mind is unequivocal, because it hears only one Voice and answers in only one way. You are the light of the world with me. Rest does not come from sleeping but from waking. The Holy Spirit is the Call to awaken and be glad. The world is very tired, because it is the idea of weariness. Our task is the joyous one of waking it to the Call for God. Everyone will answer the Call of the Holy Spirit, or the Sonship cannot be as One. What better vocation could there be for any part of the Kingdom than to restore it to the perfect integration

that can make it whole? Hear only this through the Holy Spirit within you, and teach your brothers to listen as I am teaching you.

QUESTION 11. What is the nature and role of the Holy Spirit, and how is the Holy Spirit related to the Atonement?

III. The Guide to Salvation

1. The way to recognize your brother is by recognizing the Holy Spirit in him. I have already said that the Holy Spirit is the Bridge for the transfer of perception to knowledge, so we can use the terms as if they were related, because in His Mind they are. This relationship must be in His Mind because, unless it were, the separation between the two ways of thinking would not be open to healing. He is part of the Holy Trinity, because His Mind is partly yours and also partly God's. This needs clarification, not in statement but in experience.

2. The Holy Spirit is the idea of healing. Being thought, the idea gains as it is shared. Being the Call *for* God, it is also the idea *of* God. Since you are part of God it is also the idea of yourself, as well as of all His creations. The idea of the Holy Spirit shares the property of other ideas because it follows the laws of the universe of which it is a part. It is strengthened by being given away. It increases in you as you give it to your brother. Your brother does not have to be aware of the Holy Spirit in himself or in you for this miracle to occur. He may have dissociated the Call for God, just as you have. This dissociation is healed in both of you as you become aware of the Call for God in him, and thus acknowledge Its being.

3. There are two diametrically opposed ways of seeing your brother. They must both be in your mind, because you are the perceiver. They must also be in his, because you are perceiving him. See him through the Holy Spirit in his mind, and you will recognize Him in yours. What you acknowledge in your brother you are acknowledging in yourself, and what you share you strengthen.

5. Delay is of the ego, because time is its concept. Both time and delay are meaningless in eternity. I have said before that the Holy Spirit is God's Answer to the ego. Everything of which the Holy Spirit reminds you is in direct opposition to the ego's notions, because true and false perceptions are themselves opposed. The Holy Spirit has the task of undoing what the ego has made. He undoes it at the same level on which the ego operates, or the mind would be unable to understand the change.

6. I have repeatedly emphasized that one level of the mind is not understandable to another. So it is with the ego and the Holy Spirit; with time and eternity. Eternity is an idea of God, so the Holy Spirit understands it perfectly. Time is a belief of the ego, so the lower mind, which is the ego's domain, accepts it without question. The only aspect of time that is eternal is *now*.

7. The Holy Spirit is the Mediator between the interpretations of the ego and the knowledge of the spirit. His ability to deal with symbols enables Him to work with the ego's beliefs in its own language. His ability to look beyond symbols into eternity enables Him to understand the laws of God, for which He speaks. He can therefore perform the function of reinterpreting what the ego makes, not by destruction but by understanding. Understanding is light, and light leads to knowledge. The Holy Spirit is in light because He is in you who are light, but you yourself do not know this. It is therefore the task of the Holy Spirit to reinterpret you on behalf of God.

8. You cannot understand yourself alone. This is because you have no meaning apart from your rightful place in the Sonship, and the rightful place of the Sonship is God. This is your life, your eternity and your Self. It is of this that the Holy Spirit reminds you. It is this that the Holy Spirit sees. This vision frightens the ego because it is so calm. Peace is the ego's greatest enemy because, according to its interpretation of reality, war is the guarantee of its survival. The ego becomes strong in strife. If you believe there is strife you will react viciously, because the idea of danger has entered your mind. The idea itself is an appeal to the ego. The Holy Spirit is as vigilant as the ego to the call of danger, opposing it with His strength just as the ego welcomes it. The Holy Spirit counters this welcome by welcoming peace. Eternity and peace are as closely related as are time and war.

9. Perception derives meaning from relationships. Those you accept are the foundations of your beliefs. The separation is merely another term for a split mind. The ego is the symbol of separation, just as the Holy Spirit is the symbol of peace. What you perceive in others you are strengthening in yourself. You may let your mind misperceive, but the Holy Spirit lets your mind reinterpret its own misperceptions.

10. The Holy Spirit is the perfect Teacher. He uses only what your mind already understands to teach you that you do not understand it. The Holy Spirit can deal with a reluctant learner without going counter to his mind, because part of it is still for God. Despite the ego's attempts to conceal this part, it is still much stronger than the ego, although the ego does not recognize it. The Holy Spirit recognizes it perfectly because it is His Own dwelling place; the place in the mind where He is at

home. You are at home there, too, because it is a place of peace, and peace is of God. You who are part of God are not at home except in His peace. If peace is eternal, you are at home only in eternity.

11. The ego made the world as it perceives it, but the Holy Spirit, the reinterpreter of what the ego made, sees the world as a teaching device for bringing you home. The Holy Spirit must perceive time, and reinterpret it into the timeless. He must work through opposites, because He must work with and for a mind that is in opposition. Correct and learn, and be open to learning. You have not made truth, but truth can still set you free. Look as the Holy Spirit looks, and understand as He understands. His understanding looks back to God in remembrance of me. He is in communion with God always, and He is part of you. He is your Guide to salvation, because He holds the remembrance of things past and to come, and brings them to the present. He holds this gladness gently in your mind, asking only that you increase it in His Name by sharing it to increase His joy in you.

IV. Teaching and Healing

2. What the ego makes it keeps to itself, and so it is without strength. Its existence is unshared. It does not die; it was merely never born. Physical birth is not a beginning; it is a continuing. Everything that continues has already been born. It will increase as you are willing to return the unhealed part of your mind to the higher part, returning it undivided to creation. I have come to give you the foundation, so your own thoughts can make you really free. You have carried the burden of unshared ideas that are too weak to increase, but having made them you did not realize how to undo them. You cannot cancel out your past errors alone. They will not disappear from your mind without the Atonement, a remedy not of your making. The Atonement must be understood as a pure act of sharing. That is what I meant when I said it is possible even in this world to listen to one Voice. If you are part of God and the Sonship is One, you cannot be limited to the self the ego sees.

3. Every loving thought held in any part of the Sonship belongs to every part. It is shared *because* it is loving. Sharing is God's way of creating, and also yours. The ego can keep you in exile from the Kingdom, but in the Kingdom itself it has no power. Ideas of the spirit do not leave the mind that thinks them, nor can they conflict with each other. However, ideas of the ego can conflict because they occur at different levels and also include opposite thoughts at the same level. *It is impossible to share opposing thoughts.* You can share

only the thoughts that are of God and that He keeps for you. And of such is the Kingdom of Heaven. The rest remains with you until the Holy Spirit has reinterpreted them in the light of the Kingdom, making them, too, worthy of being shared. When they have been sufficiently purified He lets you give them away. The decision to share them *is* their purification.

6. The Holy Spirit atones in all of us by undoing, and thus lifts the burden you have placed in your mind. By following Him you are led back to God where you belong, and how can you find the way except by taking your brother with you? My part in the Atonement is not complete until you join it and give it away. As you teach so shall you learn. I will never leave you or forsake you, because to forsake you would be to forsake myself and God Who created me. You forsake yourself and God if you forsake any of your brothers. You must learn to see them as they are, and understand they belong to God as you do. How could you treat your brother better than by rendering unto God the things that are God's?

7. The Atonement gives you the power of a healed mind, but the power to create is of God. Therefore, those who have been forgiven must devote themselves first to healing because, having received the idea of healing, they must give it to hold it. The full power of creation cannot be expressed as long as any of God's ideas is withheld from the Kingdom. The joint will of the Sonship is the only creator that can create like the Father, because only the complete can think completely, and the thinking of God lacks nothing. Everything you think that is not through the Holy Spirit *is* lacking.

QUESTION 12. What is the significance of sharing, and what is the opposite of sharing?

V. The Ego's Use of Guilt

2. In Heaven there is no guilt, because the Kingdom is attained through the Atonement, which releases you to create. The word "create" is appropriate here because, once what you have made is undone by the Holy Spirit, the blessed residue is restored and therefore continues in creation. What is truly blessed is incapable of giving rise to guilt, and must give rise to joy. This makes it invulnerable to the ego because its peace is unassailable. It is invulnerable to disruption because it is whole. Guilt is *always* disruptive. Anything that engenders fear is divisive because it obeys the law of division. If the ego is the symbol of the separation, it is also the symbol of guilt. Guilt is more

than merely not of God. It is the symbol of attack on God. This is a totally meaningless concept except to the ego, but do not underestimate the power of the ego's belief in it. This is the belief from which all guilt really stems.

3. The ego is the part of the mind that believes in division. How could part of God detach itself without believing it is attacking Him? We spoke before of the authority problem as based on the concept of usurping God's power. The ego believes that this is what you did because it believes that it *is* you. If you identify with the ego, you must perceive yourself as guilty. Whenever you respond to your ego you will experience guilt, and you will fear punishment. The ego is quite literally a fearful thought. However ridiculous the idea of attacking God may be to the sane mind, never forget that the ego is not sane. It represents a delusional system, and speaks for it. Listening to the ego's voice means that you believe it is possible to attack God, and that a part of Him has been torn away by you. Fear of retaliation from without follows, because the severity of the guilt is so acute that it must be projected.

4. Whatever you accept into your mind has reality for you. It is your acceptance of it that makes it real. If you enthrone the ego in your mind, your allowing it to enter makes it your reality. This is because the mind is capable of creating reality or making illusions. I said before that you must learn to think with God. To think with Him is to think like Him. This engenders joy, not guilt, because it is natural. Guilt is a sure sign that your thinking is unnatural. Unnatural thinking will always be attended with guilt, because it is the belief in sin. The ego does not perceive sin as a lack of love, but as a positive act of assault. This is necessary to the ego's survival because, as soon as you regard sin as a lack, you will automatically attempt to remedy the situation. And you will succeed. The ego regards this as doom, but you must learn to regard it as freedom.

5. The guiltless mind cannot suffer. Being sane, the mind heals the body because *it* has been healed. The sane mind cannot conceive of illness because it cannot conceive of attacking anyone or anything. I said before that illness is a form of magic. It might be better to say that it is a form of magical solution. The ego believes that by punishing itself it will mitigate the punishment of God. Yet even in this it is arrogant. It attributes to God a punishing intent, and then takes this intent as its own prerogative. It tries to usurp all the functions of God as it perceives them, because it recognizes that only total allegiance can be trusted.

6. The ego cannot oppose the laws of God any more than you can, but it can interpret them according to what it wants, just as you can.

That is why the question, "What do you want?" must be answered. You are answering it *every* minute and *every* second, and each moment of decision is a judgment that is anything but ineffectual. Its effects will follow automatically until the decision is changed. Remember, though, that the alternatives themselves are unalterable. The Holy Spirit, like the ego, is a decision. Together they constitute all the alternatives the mind can accept and obey. The Holy Spirit and the ego are the only choices open to you. God created one, and so you cannot eradicate it. You made the other, and so you can. Only what God creates is irreversible and unchangeable. What you made can always be changed because, when you do not think like God, you are not really thinking at all. Delusional ideas are not real thoughts, although you can believe in them. But you are wrong. The function of thought comes from God and is in God. As part of His Thought, you *cannot* think apart from Him.

7. Irrational thought is disordered thought. God Himself orders your thought because your thought was created by Him. Guilt feelings are always a sign that you do not know this. They also show that you believe you can think apart from God, and want to. Every disordered thought is attended by guilt at its inception, and maintained by guilt in its continuance. Guilt is inescapable by those who believe they order their own thoughts, and must therefore obey their dictates. This makes them feel responsible for their errors without recognizing that, by accepting this responsibility, they are reacting irresponsibly. If the sole responsibility of the miracle worker is to accept the Atonement for himself, and I assure you that it is, then the responsibility for *what* is atoned for cannot be yours. The dilemma cannot be resolved except by accepting the solution of undoing. You *would* be responsible for the effects of all your wrong thinking if it could not be undone. The purpose of the Atonement is to save the past in purified form only. If you accept the remedy for disordered thought, a remedy whose efficacy is beyond doubt, how can its symptoms remain?

8. The continuing decision to remain separated is the only possible reason for continuing guilt feelings. We have said this before, but did not emphasize the destructive results of the decision. Any decision of the mind will affect both behavior and experience. What you want you expect. This is not delusional. Your mind *does* make your future, and it will turn it back to full creation at any minute if it accepts the Atonement first. It will also return to full creation the instant it has done so. Having given up its disordered thought, the proper ordering of thought becomes quite apparent.

VI. Time and Eternity

1. God in His knowledge is not waiting, but His Kingdom is bereft while *you* wait. All the Sons of God are waiting for your return, just as you are waiting for theirs. Delay does not matter in eternity, but it is tragic in time. You have elected to be in time rather than eternity, and therefore believe you *are* in time. Yet your election is both free and alterable. You do not belong in time. Your place is only in eternity, where God Himself placed you forever.

2. Guilt feelings are the preservers of time. They induce fears of retaliation or abandonment, and thus ensure that the future will be like the past. This is the ego's continuity. It gives the ego a false sense of security by believing that you cannot escape from it. But you can and must. God offers you the continuity of eternity in exchange. When you choose to make this exchange, you will simultaneously exchange guilt for joy, viciousness for love, and pain for peace. My role is only to unchain your will and set it free. Your ego cannot accept this freedom, and will oppose it at every possible moment and in every possible way. And as its maker, you recognize what it can do because you gave it the power to do it.

9. "The wicked shall perish" becomes a statement of Atonement, if the word "perish" is understood as "be undone." Every loveless thought must be undone, a word the ego cannot even understand. To the ego, to be undone means to be destroyed. The ego will not be destroyed because it is part of your thought, but because it is uncreative and therefore unsharing, it will be reinterpreted to release you from fear. The part of your mind that you have given to the ego will merely return to the Kingdom, where your whole mind belongs. You can delay the completion of the Kingdom, but you cannot introduce the concept of fear into it.

VII. The Decision for God

5. Whenever you are not wholly joyous, it is because you have reacted with a lack of love to one of God's creations. Perceiving this as "sin" you become defensive because you expect attack. The decision to react in this way is yours, and can therefore be undone. It cannot be undone by repentance in the usual sense, because this implies guilt. If you allow yourself to feel guilty, you will reinforce the error rather than allow it to be undone for you.

6. Decision cannot be difficult. This is obvious, if you realize that you must already have decided not to be wholly joyous if that is how you

feel. Therefore, the first step in the undoing is to recognize that you actively decided wrongly, but can as actively decide otherwise. Be very firm with yourself in this, and keep yourself fully aware that the undoing process, which does not come from you, is nevertheless within you because God placed it there. Your part is merely to return your thinking to the point at which the error was made, and give it over to the Atonement in peace. Say this to yourself as sincerely as you can, remembering that the Holy Spirit will respond fully to your slightest invitation:

> *I must have decided wrongly, because I am not at peace.*
> *I made the decision myself, but I can also decide otherwise.*
> *I want to decide otherwise, because I want to be at peace.*
> *I do not feel guilty, because the Holy Spirit will undo all the*
> *consequences of my wrong decision if I will let Him.*
> *I choose to let Him, by allowing Him to decide for God for me.*

QUESTION 13. How are the ego and guilt related and will the ego eventually be destroyed?

Chapter 6. THE LESSONS OF LOVE
Introduction

1. The relationship of anger to attack is obvious, but the relationship of anger to fear is not always so apparent. Anger always involves projection of separation, which must ultimately be accepted as one's own responsibility, rather than being blamed on others. Anger cannot occur unless you believe that you have been attacked, that your attack is justified in return, and that you are in no way responsible for it. Given these three wholly irrational premises, the equally irrational conclusion that a brother is worthy of attack rather than of love must follow. What can be expected from insane premises except an insane conclusion? The way to undo an insane conclusion is to consider the sanity of the premises on which it rests. You cannot *be* attacked, attack *has* no justification, and you *are* responsible for what you believe.

2. You have been asked to take me as your model for learning, since an extreme example is a particularly helpful learning device. Everyone teaches, and teaches all the time. This is a responsibility you inevitably assume the moment you accept any premise at all, and no one can organize his life without some thought system. Once you have developed a thought system of any kind, you live by it and teach it. Your capacity for allegiance to a thought system may be misplaced, but it is still a form of faith and can be redirected.

I. The Message of the Crucifixion

1. For learning purposes, let us consider the crucifixion again. I did not dwell on it before because of the fearful connotations you may associate with it. The only emphasis laid upon it so far has been that it was not a form of punishment. Nothing, however, can be explained in negative terms only. There is a positive interpretation of the crucifixion that is wholly devoid of fear, and therefore wholly benign in what it teaches, if it is properly understood.

2. The crucifixion is nothing more than an extreme example. Its value, like the value of any teaching device, lies solely in the kind of learning it facilitates. It can be, and has been, misunderstood. This is only because the fearful are apt to perceive fearfully. I have already told you that you can always call on me to share my decision, and thus make it stronger. I have also told you that the crucifixion was the last useless journey the Sonship need take, and that it represents release from fear to anyone who understands it. While I emphasized only the resurrection before, the purpose of the crucifixion and how it actually led to the

resurrection was not clarified then. Nevertheless, it has a definite contribution to make to your own life, and if you will consider it without fear, it will help you understand your own role as a teacher.

4. Assault can ultimately be made only on the body. There is little doubt that one body can assault another, and can even destroy it. Yet if destruction itself is impossible, anything that is destructible cannot be real. Its destruction, therefore, does not justify anger. To the extent to which you believe that it does, you are accepting false premises and teaching them to others. The message the crucifixion was intended to teach was that it is not necessary to perceive any form of assault in persecution, because you cannot *be* persecuted. If you respond with anger, you must be equating yourself with the destructible, and are therefore regarding yourself insanely.

6. As I have said before, "As you teach so shall you learn." If you react as if you are persecuted, you are teaching persecution. This is not a lesson a Son of God should want to teach if he is to realize his own salvation. Rather, teach your own perfect immunity, which is the truth in you, and realize that it cannot *be* assailed. Do not try to protect it yourself, or you are believing that it is assailable. You are not asked to be crucified, which was part of my own teaching contribution. You are merely asked to follow my example in the face of much less extreme temptations to misperceive, and not to accept them as false justifications for anger. There can be no justification for the unjustifiable. Do not believe there is, and do not teach that there is. Remember always that what you believe you will teach. Believe with me, and we will become equal as teachers.

7. Your resurrection is your reawakening. I am the model for rebirth, but rebirth itself is merely the dawning on your mind of what is already in it. God placed it there Himself, and so it is true forever. I believed in it, and therefore accepted it as true for me. Help me to teach it to our brothers in the name of the Kingdom of God, but first believe that it is true for you, or you will teach amiss. My brothers slept during the so-called "agony in the garden," but I could not be angry with them because I knew I could not *be* abandoned.

9. I elected, for your sake and mine, to demonstrate that the most outrageous assault, as judged by the ego, does not matter. As the world judges these things, but not as God knows them, I was betrayed, abandoned, beaten, torn, and finally killed. It was clear that this was only because of the projection of others onto me, since I had not harmed anyone and had healed many.

10. We are still equal as learners, although we do not need to have equal experiences. The Holy Spirit is glad when you can learn from

mine, and be reawakened by them. That is their only purpose, and that is the only way in which I can be perceived as the way, the truth and the life. When you hear only one Voice you are never called on to sacrifice. On the contrary, by being able to hear the Holy Spirit in others you can learn from their experiences, and can gain from them without experiencing them directly yourself. That is because the Holy Spirit is One, and anyone who listens is inevitably led to demonstrate His way for all.

11. You are not persecuted, nor was I. You are not asked to repeat my experiences because the Holy Spirit, Whom we share, makes this unnecessary. To use my experiences constructively, however, you must still follow my example in how to perceive them. My brothers and yours are constantly engaged in justifying the unjustifiable. My one lesson, which I must teach as I learned it, is that no perception that is out of accord with the judgment of the Holy Spirit can be justified. I undertook to show this was true in an extreme case, merely because it would serve as a good teaching aid to those whose temptation to give in to anger and assault would not be so extreme. I will with God that none of His Sons should suffer.

12. The crucifixion cannot be shared because it is the symbol of projection, but the resurrection is the symbol of sharing because the reawakening of every Son of God is necessary to enable the Sonship to know its Wholeness. Only this is knowledge.

13. The message of the crucifixion is perfectly clear:

Teach only love, for that is what you are.

14. If you interpret the crucifixion in any other way, you are using it as a weapon for assault rather than as the call for peace for which it was intended. The Apostles often misunderstood it, and for the same reason that anyone misunderstands it. Their own imperfect love made them vulnerable to projection, and out of their own fear they spoke of the "wrath of God" as His retaliatory weapon. Nor could they speak of the crucifixion entirely without anger, because their sense of guilt had made them angry.

16. As you read the teachings of the Apostles, remember that I told them myself that there was much they would understand later, because they were not wholly ready to follow me at the time. I do not want you to allow any fear to enter into the thought system toward which I am guiding you. I do not call for martyrs but for teachers. No one is punished for sins, and the Sons of God are not sinners. Any concept of punishment involves the projection of blame, and reinforces the idea that blame is justified. The result is a lesson in blame, for all behavior teaches the beliefs that motivate it. The crucifixion was the result of

clearly opposed thought systems; the perfect symbol of the "conflict" between the ego and the Son of God. This conflict seems just as real now, and its lessons must be learned now as well as then.

17. I do not need gratitude, but you need to develop your weakened ability to be grateful, or you cannot appreciate God. He does not need your appreciation, but *you* do. You cannot love what you do not appreciate, for fear makes appreciation impossible. When you are afraid of what you are you do not appreciate it, and will therefore reject it. As a result, you will teach rejection.

18. The power of the Sons of God is present all the time, because they were created as creators. Their influence on each other is without limit, and must be used for their joint salvation. Each one must learn to teach that all forms of rejection are meaningless. The separation is the notion of rejection. As long as you teach this you will believe it. This is not as God thinks, and you must think as He thinks if you are to know Him again.

19. Remember that the Holy Spirit is the Communication Link between God the Father and His separated Sons. If you will listen to His Voice you will know that you cannot either hurt or be hurt, and that many need your blessing to help them hear this for themselves. When you perceive only this need in them, and do not respond to any other, you will have learned of me and will be as eager to share your learning as I am.

QUESTION 14. What four false perceptions support the illusion that anger is justified, and what is the message of the crucifixion?

II. The Alternative to Projection

1. Any split in mind must involve a rejection of part of it, and this *is* the belief in separation. The Wholeness of God, which is His peace, cannot be appreciated except by a whole mind that recognizes the Wholeness of God's creation. By this recognition it knows its Creator. Exclusion and separation are synonymous, as are separation and dissociation. We have said before that the separation was and is dissociation, and that once it occurs projection becomes its main defense, or the device that keeps it going. The reason, however, may not be so obvious as you think.

2. What you project you disown, and therefore do not believe is yours. You are excluding yourself by the very judgment that you are different from the one on whom you project. Since you have also judged against what you project, you continue to attack it because you continue to keep it separated. By doing this unconsciously, you try to keep the

fact that you attacked yourself out of awareness, and thus imagine that you have made yourself safe.

3. Yet projection will always hurt you. It reinforces your belief in your own split mind, and its only purpose is to keep the separation going. It is solely a device of the ego to make you feel different from your brothers and separated from them. The ego justifies this on the grounds that it makes you seem "better" than they are, thus obscuring your equality with them still further. Projection and attack are inevitably related, because projection is always a means of justifying attack. Anger without projection is impossible. The ego uses projection only to destroy your perception of both yourself and your brothers. The process begins by excluding something that exists in you but which you do not want, and leads directly to excluding you from your brothers.

4. We have learned, however, that there *is* an alternative to projection. Every ability of the ego has a better use, because its abilities are directed by the mind, which has a better Voice. The Holy Spirit extends and the ego projects. As their goals are opposed, so is the result.

5. The Holy Spirit begins by perceiving you as perfect. Knowing this perfection is shared He recognizes it in others, thus strengthening it in both. Instead of anger this arouses love for both, because it establishes inclusion. Perceiving equality, the Holy Spirit perceives equal needs. This invites Atonement automatically, because Atonement is the one need in this world that is universal. To perceive yourself this way is the only way in which you can find happiness in the world. That is because it is the acknowledgment that you are not in this world, for the world *is* unhappy.

6. How else can you find joy in a joyless place except by realizing that you are not there? You cannot be anywhere God did not put you, and God created you as part of Him. That is both where you are and what you are. It is completely unalterable. It is total inclusion. You cannot change it now or ever. It is forever true. It is not a belief, but a Fact. Anything that God created is as true as He is. Its truth lies only in its perfect inclusion in Him Who alone is perfect. To deny this is to deny yourself and Him, since it is impossible to accept one without the other.

7. The perfect equality of the Holy Spirit's perception is the reflection of the perfect equality of God's knowing. The ego's perception has no counterpart in God, but the Holy Spirit remains the Bridge between perception and knowledge. By enabling you to use perception in a way that reflects knowledge, you will ultimately remember it. The ego would prefer to believe that this memory is impossible, yet it is *your* perception the Holy Spirit guides. Your perception will end where it

began. Everything meets in God, because everything was created by Him and in Him.

8. God created His Sons by extending His Thought, and retaining the extensions of His Thought in His Mind. All His Thoughts are thus perfectly united within themselves and with each other. The Holy Spirit enables you to perceive this wholeness *now*. God created you to create. You cannot extend His Kingdom until you know of its wholeness.

9. Thoughts begin in the mind of the thinker, from which they reach outward. This is as true of God's Thinking as it is of yours. Because your mind is split, you can perceive as well as think. Yet perception cannot escape the basic laws of mind. You perceive from your mind and project your perceptions outward. Although perception of any kind is unreal, you made it and the Holy Spirit can therefore use it well. He can inspire perception and lead it toward God. This convergence seems to be far in the future only because your mind is not in perfect alignment with the idea, and therefore does not want it now.

10. The Holy Spirit uses time, but does not believe in it. Coming from God He uses everything for good, but He does not believe in what is not true. Since the Holy Spirit is in your mind, your mind can also believe only what is true. The Holy Spirit can speak only for this, because He speaks for God. He tells you to return your whole mind to God, because it has never left Him. If it has never left Him, you need only perceive it as it is to be returned. The full awareness of the Atonement, then, is the recognition that *the separation never occurred*. The ego cannot prevail against this because it is an explicit statement that the ego never occurred.

11. The ego can accept the idea that return is necessary because it can so easily make the idea seem difficult. Yet the Holy Spirit tells you that even return is unnecessary, because what never happened cannot be difficult. However, you can *make* the idea of return both necessary and difficult. Yet it is surely clear that the perfect need nothing, and you cannot experience perfection as a difficult accomplishment, because that is what you are. This is the way in which you must perceive God's creations, bringing all of your perceptions into the one line the Holy Spirit sees. This line is the direct line of communication with God, and lets your mind converge with His. There is no conflict anywhere in this perception, because it means that all perception is guided by the Holy Spirit, Whose Mind is fixed on God. Only the Holy Spirit can resolve conflict, because only the Holy Spirit is conflict-free. He perceives only what is true in your mind, and extends outward only to what is true in other minds.

12. The difference between the ego's projection and the Holy Spirit's extension is very simple. The ego projects to exclude, and therefore to deceive. The Holy Spirit extends by recognizing Himself in every mind, and thus perceives them as one. Nothing conflicts in this perception, because what the Holy Spirit perceives is all the same. Wherever He looks He sees Himself, and because He is united He offers the whole Kingdom always. This is the one message God gave to Him and for which He must speak, because that is what He is. The peace of God lies in that message, and so the peace of God lies in you. The great peace of the Kingdom shines in your mind forever, but it must shine outward to make you aware of it.

13. The Holy Spirit was given you with perfect impartiality, and only by recognizing Him impartially can you recognize Him at all. The ego is legion, but the Holy Spirit is One. No darkness abides anywhere in the Kingdom, but your part is only to allow no darkness to abide in your own mind. This alignment with light is unlimited, because it is in alignment with the light of the world. Each of us is the light of the world, and by joining our minds in this light we proclaim the Kingdom of God together and as one.

III. The Relinquishment of Attack

3. The only safety lies in extending the Holy Spirit, because as you see His gentleness in others your own mind perceives itself as totally harmless. Once it can accept this fully, it sees no need to protect itself. The protection of God then dawns upon it, assuring it that it is perfectly safe forever. The perfectly safe are wholly benign. They bless because they know that they are blessed. Without anxiety the mind is wholly kind, and because it extends beneficence it is beneficent. Safety is the complete relinquishment of attack. No compromise is possible in this. Teach attack in any form and you have learned it, and it will hurt you. Yet this learning is not immortal, and you can unlearn it by not teaching it.

4. Since you cannot *not* teach, your salvation lies in teaching the exact opposite of everything the ego believes. This is how you will learn the truth that will set you free, and will keep you free as others learn it of you. The only way to have peace is to teach peace. By teaching peace you must learn it yourself, because you cannot teach what you still dissociate. Only thus can you win back the knowledge that you threw away. An idea that you share you must have. It awakens in your mind through the conviction of teaching it. Everything you teach you are learning. Teach only love, and learn that love is yours and you are love.

IV. The Only Answer

1. Remember that the Holy Spirit is the Answer, not the question. The ego always speaks first. It is capricious and does not mean its maker well. It believes, and correctly, that its maker may withdraw his support from it at any moment. If it meant you well it would be glad, as the Holy Spirit will be glad when He has brought you home and you no longer need His guidance. The ego does not regard itself as part of you. Herein lies its primary error, the foundation of its whole thought system.

2. When God created you He made you part of Him. That is why attack within the Kingdom is impossible. You made the ego without love, and so it does not love you. You could not remain within the Kingdom without love, and since the Kingdom *is* love, you believe that you are without it. This enables the ego to regard itself as separate and outside its maker, thus speaking for the part of your mind that believes *you* are separate and outside the Mind of God. The ego, then, raised the first question that was ever asked, but one it can never answer. That question, "What are you?" was the beginning of doubt. The ego has never answered any questions since, although it has raised a great many. The most inventive activities of the ego have never done more than obscure the question, because you have the answer and *the ego is afraid of you.*

3. You cannot understand the conflict until you fully understand the basic fact that the ego cannot know anything. The Holy Spirit does not speak first, *but He always answers.* Everyone has called upon Him for help at one time or another and in one way or another, and has been answered. Since the Holy Spirit answers truly He answers for all time, which means that *everyone* has the answer *now.*

5. The ego uses the body to conspire against your mind, and because the ego realizes that its "enemy" can end them both merely by recognizing they are not part of you, they join in the attack together. This is perhaps the strangest perception of all, if you consider what it really involves. The ego, which is not real, attempts to persuade the mind, which *is* real, that the mind is the ego's learning device; and further, that the body is more real than the mind is. No one in his right mind could possibly believe this, and no one in his right mind does believe it.

6. Hear, then, the one answer of the Holy Spirit to all the questions the ego raises: You are a child of God, a priceless part of His Kingdom, which He created as part of Him. Nothing else exists and only this is real. You have chosen a sleep in which you have had bad dreams, but

the sleep is not real and God calls you to awake. There will be nothing left of your dream when you hear Him, because you will awaken. Your dreams contain many of the ego's symbols and they have confused you. Yet that was only because you were asleep and did not know. When you wake you will see the truth around you and in you, and you will no longer believe in dreams because they will have no reality for you. Yet the Kingdom and all that you have created there will have great reality for you, because they are beautiful and true.

12. God does not teach. To teach is to imply a lack, which God knows is not there. God is not conflicted. Teaching aims at change, but God created only the changeless. The separation was not a loss of perfection, but a failure in communication. A harsh and strident form of communication arose as the ego's voice. It could not shatter the peace of God, but it could shatter *yours*. God did not blot it out, because to eradicate it would be to attack it. Being questioned, He did not question. He merely gave the Answer. His Answer is your Teacher.

V. The Lessons of the Holy Spirit

1. Like any good teacher, the Holy Spirit knows more than you do now, but He teaches only to make you equal with Him. You had already taught yourself wrongly, having believed what was not true. You did not believe in your own perfection. Would God teach you that you had made a split mind, when He knows your mind only as whole? What God does know is that His communication channels are not open to Him, so that He cannot impart His joy and know that His children are wholly joyous. Giving His joy is an ongoing process, not in time but in eternity. God's extending outward, though not His completeness, is blocked when the Sonship does not communicate with Him as one. So He thought, "My children sleep and must be awakened."

4. The Holy Spirit never itemizes errors because He does not frighten children, and those who lack wisdom *are* children. Yet He always answers their call, and His dependability makes them more certain. Children *do* confuse fantasy and reality, and they are frightened because they do not recognize the difference. The Holy Spirit makes no distinction among dreams. He merely shines them away. His light is always the Call to awaken, whatever you have been dreaming. Nothing lasting lies in dreams, and the Holy Spirit, shining with the light from God Himself, speaks only for what lasts forever.

QUESTION 15. The ego functions using the projection of guilt and separation, but what is the alternative to projection?

Chapter 7. THE GIFTS OF THE KINGDOM

I. The Last Step

7. God does not take steps, because His accomplishments are not gradual. He does not teach, because His creations are changeless. He does nothing last, because He created first and for always. It must be understood that the word "first" as applied to Him is not a time concept. He is first in the sense that He is the First in the Holy Trinity Itself. He is the Prime Creator, because He created His co-creators. Because He did, time applies neither to Him nor to what He created. The "last step" that God will take was therefore true in the beginning, is true now, and will be true forever. What is timeless is always there, because its being is eternally changeless. It does not change by increase, because it was forever created to increase. If you perceive it as not increasing you do not know what it is. You also do not know Who created it. God does not reveal this to you because it was never hidden. His light was never obscured, because it is His Will to share it. How can what is fully shared be withheld and then revealed?

II. The Law of the Kingdom

1. To heal is the only kind of thinking in this world that resembles the Thought of God, and because of the elements they share, can transfer easily to it. When a brother perceives himself as sick, he is perceiving himself as not whole, and therefore in need. If you, too, see him this way, you are seeing him as if he were absent from the Kingdom or separated from it, thus making the Kingdom itself obscure to both of you. Sickness and separation are not of God, but the Kingdom is. If you obscure the Kingdom, you are perceiving what is not of God.
2. To heal, then, is to correct perception in your brother and yourself by sharing the Holy Spirit with him. This places you both within the Kingdom, and restores its wholeness in your mind. This reflects creation, because it unifies by increasing and integrates by extending. What you project or extend is real for you. This is an immutable law of the mind in this world as well as in the Kingdom. However, the content is different in this world, because the thoughts it governs are very different from the Thoughts in the Kingdom. Laws must be adapted to circumstances if they are to maintain order. The outstanding characteristic of the laws of mind as they operate in this world is that by obeying them, and I assure you that you must obey them,

you can arrive at diametrically opposed results. This is because the laws have been adapted to the circumstances of this world, in which diametrically opposed outcomes seem possible because you can respond to two conflicting voices.

III. The Reality of the Kingdom

5. God has lit your mind Himself, and keeps your mind lit by His light because His light is what your mind is. This is totally beyond question, and when you question it you are answered. The Answer merely undoes the question by establishing the fact that to question reality is to question meaninglessly. That is why the Holy Spirit never questions. His sole function is to undo the questionable and thus lead to certainty. The certain are perfectly calm, because they are not in doubt. They do not raise questions, because nothing questionable enters their minds. This holds them in perfect serenity, because this is what they share, knowing what they are.

IV. Healing as the Recognition of Truth

1. Truth can only *be* recognized and *need* only be recognized. Inspiration is of the Holy Spirit, and certainty is of God according to His laws. Both, therefore, come from the same Source, since inspiration comes from the Voice for God and certainty comes from the laws of God. Healing does not come directly from God, Who knows His creations as perfectly whole. Yet healing is still of God, because it proceeds from His Voice and from His laws. It is their result, in a state of mind that does not know Him. The state is unknown to Him and therefore does not exist, but those who sleep are unaware. Because they are unaware, they do not know.

5. The ego's goal is as unified as the Holy Spirit's, and it is because of this that their goals can never be reconciled in any way or to any extent. The ego always seeks to divide and separate. The Holy Spirit always seeks to unify and heal. As you heal you are healed, because the Holy Spirit sees no order of difficulty in healing. Healing is the way to undo the belief in differences, being the only way of perceiving the Sonship as one. This perception is therefore in accord with the laws of God, even in a state of mind that is out of accord with His. The strength of right perception is so great that it brings the mind into accord with His, because it serves His Voice, which is in all of you.

6. To think you can oppose the Will of God is a real delusion. The ego believes that it can, and that it can offer you its own "will" as a gift.

You do not want it. It is not a gift. It is nothing at all. God has given you a gift that you both *have* and *are*. When you do not use it, you forget that you have it. By not remembering it, you do not know what you are. Healing, then, is a way of approaching knowledge by thinking in accordance with the laws of God, and recognizing their universality. Without this recognition, you have made the laws meaningless to you. Yet the laws are not meaningless, since all meaning is contained by them and in them.

7. Seek ye first the Kingdom of Heaven, because that is where the laws of God operate truly, and they can operate only truly because they are the laws of truth. But seek this only, because you can find nothing else. There *is* nothing else. God is All in all in a very literal sense. All being is in Him Who is all Being. You are therefore in Him since your being is His. Healing is a way of forgetting the sense of danger the ego has induced in you, by not recognizing its existence in your brother. This strengthens the Holy Spirit in both of you, because it is a refusal to acknowledge fear. Love needs only this invitation. It comes freely to all the Sonship, being what the Sonship is. By your awakening to it, you are merely forgetting what you are not. This enables you to remember what you are.

V. Healing and the Changelessness of Mind

3. Healing is the one ability everyone can develop and must develop if he is to be healed. Healing is the Holy Spirit's form of communication in this world, and the only one He accepts. He recognizes no other, because He does not accept the ego's confusion of mind and body. Minds can communicate, but they cannot hurt. The body in the service of the ego can hurt other bodies, but this cannot occur unless the body has already been confused with the mind. This situation, too, can be used either for healing or for magic, but you must remember that magic always involves the belief that healing is harmful. This belief is its totally insane premise, and so it proceeds accordingly.

4. Healing only strengthens. Magic always tries to weaken. Healing perceives nothing in the healer that everyone else does not share with him. Magic always sees something "special" in the healer, which he believes he can offer as a gift to someone who does not have it. He may believe that the gift comes from God to him, but it is quite evident that he does not understand God if he thinks he has something that others lack.

7. The unhealed healer wants gratitude from his brothers, but he is not grateful to them. That is because he thinks he is giving something

to them, and is not receiving something equally desirable in return. His teaching is limited because he is learning so little. His healing lesson is limited by his own ingratitude, which is a lesson in sickness. True learning is constant, and so vital in its power for change that a Son of God can recognize his power in one instant and change the world in the next. That is because, by changing his mind, he has changed the most powerful device that was ever given him for change. This in no way contradicts the changelessness of mind as God created it, but you think that you have changed it as long as you learn through the ego. This places you in a position of needing to learn a lesson that seems contradictory;—you must learn to change your mind about your mind. Only by this can you learn that it *is* changeless.

8. When you heal, that is exactly what you *are* learning. You are recognizing the changeless mind in your brother by realizing that he could not have changed his mind. That is how you perceive the Holy Spirit in him. It is only the Holy Spirit in him that never changes His Mind. He himself may think he can, or he would not perceive himself as sick. He therefore does not know what his Self is. If you see only the changeless in him you have not really changed him. By changing your mind about his *for* him, you help him undo the change his ego thinks it has made in him.

9. As you can hear two voices, so you can see in two ways. One way shows you an image, or an idol that you may worship out of fear, but will never love. The other shows you only truth, which you will love because you will understand it. Understanding is appreciation, because what you understand you can identify with, and by making it part of you, you have accepted it with love. That is how God Himself created you; in understanding, in appreciation and in love. The ego is totally unable to understand this, because it does not understand what it makes, does not appreciate it and does not love it. It incorporates to take away. It literally believes that *every* time it deprives someone of something, it has increased. I have spoken often of the increase of the Kingdom by your creations, which can only be created as you were. The whole glory and perfect joy that *is* the Kingdom lies in you to give. Do you not want to give it?

10. You cannot forget the Father because I am with you, and I cannot forget Him. To forget me is to forget yourself and Him Who created you. Our brothers are forgetful. That is why they need your remembrance of me and of Him Who created me. Through this remembrance, you can change their minds about themselves, as I can change yours. Your mind is so powerful a light that you can look into theirs and enlighten them, as I can enlighten yours. I do not want to share my body in communion

because this is to share nothing. Would I try to share an illusion with the most holy children of a most holy Father? Yet I do want to share my mind with you because we are of one Mind, and that Mind is ours. See only this Mind everywhere, because only this is everywhere and in everything. It is everything because it encompasses all things within itself. Blessed are you who perceive only this, because you perceive only what is true.

11. Come therefore unto me, and learn of the truth in you. The mind we share is shared by all our brothers, and as we see them truly they will be healed. Let your mind shine with mine upon their minds, and by our gratitude to them make them aware of the light in them. This light will shine back upon you and on the whole Sonship, because this is your proper gift to God. He will accept it and give it to the Sonship, because it is acceptable to Him and therefore to His Sons. This is true communion with the Holy Spirit, Who sees the altar of God in everyone, and by bringing it to your appreciation, He calls upon you to love God and His creation. You can appreciate the Sonship only as one. This is part of the law of creation, and therefore governs all thought.

QUESTION 16. What is the significance of light in relation to your mind and in relation to your brothers and sisters in the Sonship?

VI. From Vigilance to Peace

1. Although you can love the Sonship only as one, you can perceive it as fragmented. It is impossible, however, to see something in part of it that you will not attribute to all of it. That is why attack is never discrete, and why it must be relinquished entirely. If it is not relinquished entirely it is not relinquished at all. Fear and love make or create, depending on whether the ego or the Holy Spirit begets or inspires them, but they *will* return to the mind of the thinker and they will affect his total perception. That includes his concept of God, of His creations and of his own. He will not appreciate any of Them if he regards Them fearfully. He will appreciate all of Them if he regards Them with love.

2. The mind that accepts attack cannot love. That is because it believes it can destroy love, and therefore does not understand what love is. If it does not understand what love is, it cannot perceive itself as loving. This loses the awareness of being, induces feelings of unreality and results in utter confusion. Your thinking has done this because of its power, but your thinking can also save you from this

because its power is not of your making. Your ability to direct your thinking as you choose is part of its power. If you do not believe you can do this you have denied the power of your thought, and thus rendered it powerless in your belief.

4. The ego cannot afford to know anything. Knowledge is total, and the ego does not believe in totality. This unbelief is its origin, and while the ego does not love you it *is* faithful to its own antecedents, begetting as it was begotten. Mind always reproduces as it was produced. Produced by fear, the ego reproduces fear. This is its allegiance, and this allegiance makes it treacherous to love because you *are* love. Love is your power, which the ego must deny. It must also deny everything this power gives you *because* it gives you everything. No one who has everything wants the ego. Its own maker, then, does not want it. Rejection is therefore the only decision the ego could possibly encounter, if the mind that made it knew itself. And if it recognized any part of the Sonship, it *would* know itself.

5. The ego therefore opposes all appreciation, all recognition, all sane perception and all knowledge. It perceives their threat as total, because it senses that all commitments the mind makes are total. Forced, therefore, to detach itself from you, it is willing to attach itself to anything else. But there *is* nothing else. The mind can, however, make up illusions, and if it does so it will believe in them, because that is how it made them.

6. The Holy Spirit undoes illusions without attacking them, because He cannot perceive them at all. They therefore do not exist for Him. He resolves the apparent conflict they engender by perceiving conflict as meaningless. I have said before that the Holy Spirit perceives the conflict exactly as it is, and it *is* meaningless. The Holy Spirit does not want you to understand conflict; He wants you to realize that, because conflict is meaningless, it is not understandable. As I have already said, understanding brings appreciation and appreciation brings love. Nothing else can be understood, because nothing else is real and therefore nothing else has meaning.

VII. The Totality of the Kingdom

1. Whenever you deny a blessing to a brother *you* will feel deprived, because denial is as total as love. It is as impossible to deny part of the Sonship as it is to love it in part. Nor is it possible to love it totally at times. You cannot be totally committed sometimes. Denial has no power in itself, but you can give it the power of your mind, whose power is without limit. If you use it to deny reality, reality is gone for you.

Reality cannot be partly appreciated. That is why denying any part of it means you have lost the awareness of all of it. Yet denial is a defense, and so it is as capable of being used positively as well as negatively. Used negatively it will be destructive, because it will be used for attack. But in the service of the Holy Spirit, it can help you recognize part of reality, and thus appreciate all of it. Mind is too powerful to be subject to exclusion. You will never be able to exclude yourself from your thoughts.

2.   When a brother acts insanely, he is offering you an opportunity to bless him. His need is yours. You need the blessing you can offer him. There is no way for you to have it except by giving it. This is the law of God, and it has no exceptions. What you deny you lack, not because it is lacking, but because you have denied it in another and are therefore not aware of it in yourself. Every response you make is determined by what you think you are, and what you want to be *is* what you think you are. What you want to be, then, must determine *every* response you make.

3.   You do not need God's blessing because that you have forever, but you do need yours. The ego's picture of you is deprived, unloving and vulnerable. You cannot love this. Yet you can very easily escape from this image by leaving it behind. You are not there and that is not you. Do not see this picture in anyone, or you have accepted it *as* you. All illusions about the Sonship are dispelled together as they were made together. Teach no one that he is what you would not want to be. Your brother is the mirror in which you see the image of yourself as long as perception lasts. And perception will last until the Sonship knows itself as whole. You made perception and it must last as long as you want it.

4.   Illusions are investments. They will last as long as you value them. Values are relative, but they are powerful because they are mental judgments. The only way to dispel illusions is to withdraw all investment from them, and they will have no life for you because you will have put them out of your mind. While you include them in it, you are giving life to them. Except there is nothing there to receive your gift.

5.   The gift of life is yours to give, because it was given you. You are unaware of your gift because you do not give it. You cannot make nothing live, since nothing cannot be enlivened. Therefore, you are not extending the gift you both *have* and *are*, and so you do not know your being. All confusion comes from not extending life, because that is not the Will of your Creator. You can do nothing apart from Him, and you *do* do nothing apart from Him. Keep His way to remember

yourself, and teach His way lest you forget yourself. Give only honor to the Sons of the living God, and count yourself among them gladly.

6. Only honor is a fitting gift for those whom God Himself created worthy of honor, and whom He honors. Give them the appreciation God accords them always, because they are His beloved Sons in whom He is well pleased. You cannot be apart from them because you are not apart from Him. Rest in His Love and protect your rest by loving. But love everything He created, of which you are a part, or you cannot learn of His peace and accept His gift for yourself and as yourself. You cannot know your own perfection until you have honored all those who were created like you.

VIII. The Unbelievable Belief

4. You cannot perpetuate an illusion about another without perpetuating it about yourself. There is no way out of this, because it is impossible to fragment the mind. To fragment is to break into pieces, and mind cannot attack or be attacked. The belief that it can, an error the ego always makes, underlies its whole use of projection. It does not understand what mind is, and therefore does not understand what *you* are. Yet its existence is dependent on your mind, because the ego is your belief. The ego is a confusion in identification. Never having had a consistent model, it never developed consistently. It is the product of the misapplication of the laws of God by distorted minds that are misusing their power.

5. *Do not be afraid of the ego*. It depends on your mind, and as you made it by believing in it, so you can dispel it by withdrawing belief from it. Do not project the responsibility for your belief in it onto anyone else, or you will preserve the belief. When you are willing to accept sole responsibility for the ego's existence you will have laid aside all anger and all attack, because they come from an attempt to project responsibility for your own errors. But having accepted the errors as yours, do not keep them. Give them over quickly to the Holy Spirit to be undone completely, so that all their effects will vanish from your mind and from the Sonship as a whole.

6. The Holy Spirit will teach you to perceive beyond your belief, because truth is beyond belief and His perception is true. The ego can be completely forgotten at any time, because it is a totally incredible belief, and no one can keep a belief he has judged to be unbelievable. The more you learn about the ego, the more you realize that it cannot be believed. The incredible cannot be understood because

it is unbelievable. The meaninglessness of perception based on the unbelievable is apparent, but it may not be recognized as being beyond belief, because it is made *by* belief.

7. The whole purpose of this course is to teach you that the ego is unbelievable and will forever be unbelievable. You who made the ego by believing the unbelievable cannot make this judgment alone. By accepting the Atonement for yourself, you are deciding against the belief that you can be alone, thus dispelling the idea of separation and affirming your true identification with the whole Kingdom as literally part of you. This identification is as beyond doubt as it is beyond belief. Your wholeness has no limits because being is infinity.

IX. The Extension of the Kingdom

3. The extension of God's Being is spirit's only function. Its fullness cannot be contained, any more than can the fullness of its Creator. Fullness is extension. The ego's whole thought system blocks extension, and thus blocks your only function. It therefore blocks your joy, so that you perceive yourself as unfulfilled. Unless you create you *are* unfulfilled, but God does not know unfulfillment and therefore you must create. You may not know your own creations, but this can no more interfere with their reality than your unawareness of your spirit can interfere with its being.

4. The Kingdom is forever extending because it is in the Mind of God. You do not know your joy because you do not know your own Self-fullness. Exclude any part of the Kingdom from yourself and you are not whole. A split mind cannot perceive its fullness, and needs the miracle of its wholeness to dawn upon it and heal it. This reawakens the wholeness in it, and restores it to the Kingdom because of its acceptance of wholeness. The full appreciation of the mind's Self-fullness makes selfishness impossible and extension inevitable. That is why there is perfect peace in the Kingdom. Spirit is fulfilling its function, and only complete fulfillment is peace.

7. Be confident that you have never lost your Identity and the extensions which maintain It in wholeness and peace. Miracles are an expression of this confidence. They are reflections of both your proper identification with your brothers, and of your awareness that your identification is maintained by extension. The miracle is a lesson in total perception. By including any part of totality in the lesson, you have included the whole.

X. The Confusion of Pain and Joy

3. The Holy Spirit will direct you only so as to avoid pain. Surely no one would object to this goal if he recognized it. The problem is not whether what the Holy Spirit says is true, but whether you want to listen to what He says. You no more recognize what is painful than you know what is joyful, and are, in fact, very apt to confuse the two. The Holy Spirit's main function is to teach you to tell them apart. What is joyful to you is painful to the ego, and as long as you are in doubt about what you are, you will be confused about joy and pain. This confusion is the cause of the whole idea of sacrifice. Obey the Holy Spirit, and you will be giving up the ego. But you will be sacrificing nothing. On the contrary, you will be gaining everything. If you believed this, there would be no conflict.

4. That is why you need to demonstrate the obvious to yourself. It is not obvious to you. You believe that doing the opposite of God's Will can be better for you. You also believe that it is possible to *do* the opposite of God's Will. Therefore, you believe that an impossible choice is open to you, and one which is both fearful and desirable. Yet God wills. He does not wish. Your will is as powerful as His because it *is* His. The ego's wishes do not mean anything, because the ego wishes for the impossible. You can wish for the impossible, but you can will only with God. This is the ego's weakness and your strength.

QUESTION 17. You made the ego, but what does the Course say about letting go of your identification with the ego?

Chapter 8. THE JOURNEY BACK

I. The Direction of the Curriculum

1. Knowledge is not the motivation for learning this course. Peace is. This is the prerequisite for knowledge only because those who are in conflict are not peaceful, and peace is the condition of knowledge because it is the condition of the Kingdom. Knowledge can be restored only when you meet its conditions. This is not a bargain made by God, Who makes no bargains. It is merely the result of your misuse of His laws on behalf of an imaginary will that is not His. Knowledge *is* His Will. If you are opposing His Will, how can you have knowledge? I have told you what knowledge offers you, but perhaps you do not yet regard this as wholly desirable. If you did you would not be so ready to throw it away when the ego asks for your allegiance.

2. The distractions of the ego may seem to interfere with your learning, but the ego has no power to distract you unless you give it the power to do so. The ego's voice is an hallucination. You cannot expect it to say "I am not real." Yet you are not asked to dispel your hallucinations alone. You are merely asked to evaluate them in terms of their results will be removed from your mind for you.

II. The Difference between Imprisonment and Freedom

3. The ego cannot teach you anything as long as your will is free, because you will not listen to it. It is not your will to be imprisoned because your will is free. That is why the ego is the denial of free will. It is never God Who coerces you, because He shares His Will with you. His Voice teaches only in accordance with His Will, but that is not the Holy Spirit's lesson because that is what you *are*. The lesson is that your will and God's cannot be out of accord because they are one. This is the undoing of everything the ego tries to teach. It is not, then, only the direction of the curriculum that must be unconflicted, but also the content.

4. The ego tries to teach that you want to oppose God's Will. This unnatural lesson cannot be learned, and the attempt to learn it is a violation of your own freedom, making you afraid of your will *because* it is free. The Holy Spirit opposes any imprisoning of the will of a Son of God, knowing that the Will of the Son is the Father's. The Holy Spirit leads you steadily along the path of freedom, teaching you how to disregard or look beyond everything that would hold you back.

6. The Holy Spirit's teaching takes only *one* direction and has only *one* goal. His direction is freedom and His goal is God. Yet He cannot conceive of God without you, because it is not God's Will to *be* without you. When you have learned that your will is God's, you could no more will to be without Him than He could will to be without you. This is freedom and this is joy. Deny yourself this and you are denying God His Kingdom, because He created you for this.

7. When I said, "All power and glory are yours because the Kingdom is His," this is what I meant: The Will of God is without limit, and all power and glory lie within it. It is boundless in strength and in love and in peace. It has no boundaries because its extension is unlimited, and it encompasses all things because it created all things. By creating all things, it made them part of itself. You are the Will of God because that is how you were created. Because your Creator creates only like Himself, you are like Him. You are part of Him Who is all power and glory, and are therefore as unlimited as He is.

III. The Holy Encounter

1. Glory to God in the highest, and to you because He has so willed it. Ask and it shall be given you, because it has already *been* given. Ask for light and learn that you *are* light. If you want understanding and enlightenment you will learn it, because your decision to learn it is the decision to listen to the Teacher Who knows of light, and can therefore teach it to you. There is no limit on your learning because there is no limit on your mind. There is no limit on His teaching because He was created to teach. Understanding His function perfectly He fulfills it perfectly, because that is His joy and yours.

4. When you meet anyone, remember it is a holy encounter. As you see him you will see yourself. As you treat him you will treat yourself. As you think of him you will think of yourself. Never forget this, for in him you will find yourself or lose yourself. Whenever two Sons of God meet, they are given another chance at salvation. Do not leave anyone without giving salvation to him and receiving it yourself. For I am always there with you, in remembrance of *you*.

5. The goal of the curriculum, regardless of the teacher you choose, is "Know thyself." There is nothing else to seek. Everyone is looking for himself and for the power and glory he thinks he has lost. Whenever you are with anyone, you have another opportunity to find them. Your power and glory are in him because they are yours. The ego tries to find them in yourself alone, because it does not know where to look. The Holy Spirit teaches you that if you look only at yourself you

cannot find yourself, because that is not what you are. Whenever you are with a brother, you are learning what you are because you are teaching what you are. He will respond either with pain or with joy, depending on which teacher you are following. He will be imprisoned or released according to your decision, and so will you. Never forget your responsibility to him, because it is your responsibility to yourself. Give him his place in the Kingdom and you will have yours.

6. The Kingdom cannot be found alone, and you who are the Kingdom cannot find yourself alone. To achieve the goal of the curriculum, then, you cannot listen to the ego, whose purpose is to defeat its own goal. The ego does not know this, because it does not know anything. But you can know it, and you will know it if you are willing to look at what the ego would make of you. This is your responsibility, because once you have really looked at it you *will* accept the Atonement for yourself. What other choice could you make? Having made this choice you will understand why you once believed that, when you met someone else, you thought he *was* someone else. And every holy encounter in which you enter fully will teach you this is not so.

7. You can encounter only part of yourself because you are part of God, Who is everything. His power and glory are everywhere, and you cannot be excluded from them. The ego teaches that your strength is in you alone. The Holy Spirit teaches that all strength is in God and *therefore* in you. God wills no one suffer. He does not will anyone to suffer for a wrong decision, including you. That is why He has given you the means for undoing it. Through His power and glory all your wrong decisions are undone completely, releasing you and your brother from every imprisoning thought any part of the Sonship holds. Wrong decisions have no power, because they are not true. The imprisonment they seem to produce is no more true than they are.

IV. The Gift of Freedom

2. I am come as a light into a world that does deny itself everything. It does this simply by dissociating itself from everything. It is therefore an illusion of isolation, maintained by fear of the same loneliness that *is* its illusion. I said that I am with you always, even unto the end of the world. That is why I am the light of the world. If I am with you in the loneliness of the world, the loneliness is gone. You cannot maintain the illusion of loneliness if you are not alone. My purpose, then, is still to overcome the world. I do not attack it, but my light must dispel it because of what it is. Light does not attack darkness, but it does shine it away. If my light goes with you everywhere, you shine it away with me. The light becomes

ours, and you cannot abide in darkness any more than darkness can abide wherever you go. The remembrance of me is the remembrance of yourself, and of Him Who sent me to you.

3. You were in darkness until God's Will was done completely by any part of the Sonship. When this was done, it was perfectly accomplished by all. How else could it be perfectly accomplished? My mission was simply to unite the will of the Sonship with the Will of the Father by being aware of the Father's Will myself. This is the awareness I came to give you, and your problem in accepting it is the problem of this world. Dispelling it is salvation, and in this sense I *am* the salvation of the world. The world must therefore despise and reject me, because the world *is* the belief that love is impossible. If you will accept the fact that I am with you, you are denying the world and accepting God. My will is His, and your decision to hear me is the decision to hear His Voice and abide in His Will. As God sent me to you so will I send you to others. And I will go to them with you, so we can teach them peace and union.

4. Do you not think the world needs peace as much as you do? Do you not want to give it to the world as much as you want to receive it? For unless you do, you will not receive it. If you want to have it of me, you must give it. Healing does not come from anyone else. You must accept guidance from within. The guidance must be what you want, or it will be meaningless to you. That is why healing is a collaborative venture. I can tell you what to do, but you must collaborate by believing that I know what you should do. Only then will your mind choose to follow me. Without this choice you could not be healed because you would have decided against healing, and this rejection of my decision for you makes healing impossible.

5. Healing reflects our joint will. This is obvious when you consider what healing is for. Healing is the way in which the separation is overcome. Separation is overcome by union. It cannot be overcome by separating. The decision to unite must be unequivocal, or the mind itself is divided and not whole. Your mind is the means by which you determine your own condition, because mind is the mechanism of decision. It is the power by which you separate or join, and experience pain or joy accordingly. My decision cannot overcome yours, because yours is as powerful as mine. If it were not so the Sons of God would be unequal. All things are possible through our joint decision, but mine alone cannot help you. Your will is as free as mine, and God Himself would not go against it. I cannot will what God does not will. I can offer my strength to make yours invincible, but I cannot oppose your decision without competing with it and thereby violating God's Will for you.

6. Nothing God created can oppose your decision, as nothing God created can oppose His Will. God gave your will its power, which I can only acknowledge in honor of His. If you want to be like me I will help you, knowing that we are alike. If you want to be different, I will wait until you change your mind. I can teach you, but only you can choose to listen to my teaching. How else can it be, if God's Kingdom is freedom? Freedom cannot be learned by tyranny of any kind, and the perfect equality of all God's Sons cannot be recognized through the dominion of one mind over another. God's Sons are equal in will, all being the Will of their Father. This is the only lesson I came to teach.
8. Freedom is the only gift you can offer to God's Sons, being an acknowledgment of what they are and what He is. Freedom is creation, because it is love. Whom you seek to imprison you do not love. Therefore, when you seek to imprison anyone, including yourself, you do not love him and you cannot identify with him. When you imprison yourself you are losing sight of your true identification with me and with the Father. Your identification is with the Father *and* with the Son. It cannot be with One and not the Other. If you are part of One you must be part of the Other, because They are One. The Holy Trinity is holy *because* It is One. If you exclude yourself from this union, you are perceiving the Holy Trinity as separated. You must be included in It, because It is everything. Unless you take your place in It and fulfill your function as part of It, the Holy Trinity is as bereft as you are. No part of It can be imprisoned if Its truth is to be known.

V. The Undivided Will of the Sonship

2. The undivided will of the Sonship is the perfect creator, being wholly in the likeness of God, Whose Will it is. You cannot be exempt from it if you are to understand what it is and what you are. By the belief that your will is separate from mine, you are exempting yourself from the Will of God which *is* yourself. Yet to heal is still to make whole. Therefore, to heal is to unite with those who are like you, because perceiving this likeness is to recognize the Father. If your perfection is in Him and only in Him, how can you know it without recognizing Him? The recognition of God is the recognition of yourself. There is no separation of God and His creation. You will realize this when you understand that there is no separation between your will and mine. Let the Love of God shine upon you by your acceptance of me. My reality is yours and His. By joining your mind with mine you are signifying your awareness that the Will of God is One.

4. When you unite with me you are uniting without the ego, because I have renounced the ego in myself and therefore cannot unite with yours. Our union is therefore the way to renounce the ego in you. The truth in both of us is beyond the ego. Our success in transcending the ego is guaranteed by God, and I share this confidence for both of us and all of us. I bring God's peace back to all His children because I received it of Him for us all. Nothing can prevail against our united wills because nothing can prevail against God's.

5. Would you know the Will of God for you? Ask it of me who know it for you and you will find it. I will deny you nothing, as God denies me nothing. Ours is simply the journey back to God Who is our home. Whenever fear intrudes anywhere along the road to peace, it is because the ego has attempted to join the journey with us and cannot do so. Sensing defeat and angered by it, the ego regards itself as rejected and becomes retaliative. You are invulnerable to its retaliation because I am with you. On this journey you have chosen me as your companion *instead* of the ego. Do not attempt to hold on to both, or you will try to go in different directions and will lose the way.

6. The ego's way is not mine, but it is also not yours. The Holy Spirit has one direction for all minds, and the one He taught me is yours. Let us not lose sight of His direction through illusions, for only illusions of another direction can obscure the one for which God's Voice speaks in all of us. Never accord the ego the power to interfere with the journey. It has none, because the journey is the way to what is true. Leave all illusions behind, and reach beyond all attempts of the ego to hold you back. I go before you because I am beyond the ego. Reach, therefore, for my hand because you want to transcend the ego. My strength will never be wanting, and if you choose to share it you will do so. I give it willingly and gladly, because I need you as much as you need me.

QUESTION 18. Can you find the divine only by looking within yourself, and what must you do to find your place in God's Kingdom?

VI. The Treasure of God

4. Listen to the story of the prodigal son, and learn what God's treasure is and yours: This son of a loving father left his home and thought he had squandered everything for nothing of any value, although he had not understood its worthlessness at the time. He was ashamed to return to his father, because he thought he had hurt him. Yet when he came home the father welcomed him with joy, because the son himself *was* his father's treasure. He wanted nothing else.

5. God wants only His Son because His Son is His only treasure. You want your creations as He wants His. Your creations are your gift to the Holy Trinity, created in gratitude for your creation. They do not leave you any more than you left your Creator, but they extend your creation as God extended Himself to you. Can the creations of God Himself take joy in what is not real? And what is real except the creations of God and those that are created like His? Your creations love you as you love your Father for the gift of creation. There is no other gift that is eternal, and therefore there is no other gift that is true. How, then, can you accept anything else or give anything else, and expect joy in return? And what else but joy would you want? You made neither yourself nor your function. You made only the decision to be unworthy of both. Yet you cannot make yourself unworthy because you are the treasure of God, and what He values is valuable. There can be no question of its worth, because its value lies in God's sharing Himself with it and establishing its value forever.

8. There is no question but one you should ever ask of yourself;—"Do I want to know my Father's Will for me?" He will not hide it. He has revealed it to me because I asked it of Him, and learned of what He had already given. Our function is to work together, because apart from each other we cannot function at all. The whole power of God's Son lies in all of us, but not in any of us alone. God would not have us be alone because *He* does not will to be alone. That is why He created His Son, and gave him the power to create with Him. Our creations are as holy as we are, and we are the Sons of God Himself, as holy as He is. Through our creations we extend our love, and thus increase the joy of the Holy Trinity. You do not understand this, because you who are God's Own treasure do not regard yourself as valuable. Given this belief, you cannot understand anything.

9. I share with God the knowledge of the value He puts upon you. My devotion to you is of Him, being born of my knowledge of myself and Him. We cannot be separated. Whom God has joined cannot be separated, and God has joined all His Sons with Himself. Can you be separated from your life and your being? The journey to God is merely the reawakening of the knowledge of where you are always, and what you are forever. It is a journey without distance to a goal that has never changed. Truth can only be experienced. It cannot be described and it cannot be explained. I can make you aware of the conditions of truth, but the experience is of God. Together we can meet its conditions, but truth will dawn upon you of itself.

VII. The Body as a Means of Communication

2.   Remember that the Holy Spirit interprets the body only as a means of communication. Being the Communication Link between God and His separated Sons, the Holy Spirit interprets everything you have made in the light of what He is. The ego separates through the body. The Holy Spirit reaches through it to others. You do not perceive your brothers as the Holy Spirit does, because you do not regard bodies solely as a means of joining minds and uniting them with yours and mine. This interpretation of the body will change your mind entirely about its value. Of itself it has none.

3.   If you use the body for attack, it is harmful to you. If you use it only to reach the minds of those who believe they are bodies, and teach them *through* the body that this is not so, you will understand the power of the mind that is in you. If you use the body for this and only for this, you cannot use it for attack. In the service of uniting it becomes a beautiful lesson in communion, which has value until communion *is*. This is God's way of making unlimited what you have limited. The Holy Spirit does not see the body as you do, because He knows the only reality of anything is the service it renders God on behalf of the function He gives it.

5.   Yet all loss comes only from your own misunderstanding. Loss of any kind is impossible. But when you look upon a brother as a physical entity, his power and glory are "lost" to you and so are yours. You have attacked him, but you must have attacked yourself first. Do not see him this way for your own salvation, which must bring him his. Do not allow him to belittle himself in your mind, but give him freedom from his belief in littleness, and thus escape from yours. As part of you, he is holy. As part of me, you are. To communicate with part of God Himself is to reach beyond the Kingdom to its Creator, through His Voice which He has established as part of you.

10.   Healing is the result of using the body solely for communication. Since this is natural it heals by making whole, which is also natural. All mind is whole, and the belief that part of it is physical, or not mind, is a fragmented or sick interpretation. Mind cannot be made physical, but it can be made manifest *through* the physical if it uses the body to go beyond itself. By reaching out, the mind extends itself. It does not stop at the body, for if it does it is blocked in its purpose. A mind that has been blocked has allowed itself to be vulnerable to attack, because it has turned against itself.

11. The removal of blocks, then, is the only way to guarantee help and healing. Help and healing are the normal expressions of a mind that is working through the body, but not *in* it. If the mind believes the body is its goal it will distort its perception of the body, and by blocking its own extension beyond it, will induce illness by fostering separation. Perceiving the body as a separate entity cannot but foster illness, because it is not true. A medium of communication loses its usefulness if it is used for anything else. To use a medium of communication as a medium of attack is an obvious confusion in purpose.

15. Joy is unified purpose, and unified purpose is only God's. When yours is unified it is His. Believe you can interfere with His purpose, and you need salvation. You have condemned yourself, but condemnation is not of God. Therefore it is not true. No more are any of its seeming results. When you see a brother as a body, you are condemning him because you have condemned yourself. Yet if all condemnation is unreal, and it must be unreal since it is a form of attack, then it can *have* no results.

16. Do not allow yourself to suffer from imagined results of what is not true. Free your mind from the belief that this is possible. In its complete impossibility lies your only hope for release. But what other hope would you want? Freedom from illusions lies only in not believing them. There is no attack, but there *is* unlimited communication and therefore unlimited power and wholeness. The power of wholeness is extension. Do not arrest your thought in this world, and you will open your mind to creation in God.

VIII. The Body as Means or End

9. The Holy Spirit teaches you to use your body only to reach your brothers, so He can teach His message through you. This will heal them and therefore heal you. Everything used in accordance with its function as the Holy Spirit sees it cannot be sick. Everything used otherwise is. Do not allow the body to be a mirror of a split mind. Do not let it be an image of your own perception of littleness. Do not let it reflect your decision to attack. Health is seen as the natural state of everything when interpretation is left to the Holy Spirit, Who perceives no attack on anything. Health is the result of relinquishing all attempts to use the body lovelessly. Health is the beginning of the proper perspective on life under the guidance of the one Teacher Who knows what life is, being the Voice for Life Itself.

IX. Healing as Corrected Perception

1. I said before that the Holy Spirit is the Answer. He is the Answer to everything, because He knows what the answer to everything is. The ego does not know what a real question is, although it asks an endless number. Yet you can learn this as you learn to question the value of the ego, and thus establish your ability to evaluate its questions. When the ego tempts you to sickness do not ask the Holy Spirit to heal the body, for this would merely be to accept the ego's belief that the body is the proper aim of healing. Ask, rather, that the Holy Spirit teach you the right *perception* of the body, for perception alone can be distorted. Only perception can be sick, because only perception can be wrong.

2. Wrong perception is the wish that things be as they are not. The reality of everything is totally harmless, because total harmlessness is the condition of its reality. It is also the condition of your awareness of its reality. You do not have to seek reality. It will seek you and find you when you meet its conditions. Its conditions are part of what it is. And this part only is up to you. The rest is of itself. You need do so little because your little part is so powerful that it will bring the whole to you. Accept, then, your little part, and let the whole be yours.

3. Wholeness heals because it is of the mind. All forms of sickness, even unto death, are physical expressions of the fear of awakening. They are attempts to reinforce sleeping out of fear of waking. This is a pathetic way of trying not to see by rendering the faculties for seeing ineffectual. "Rest in peace" is a blessing for the living, not the dead, because rest comes from waking, not from sleeping. Sleep is withdrawing; waking is joining. Dreams are illusions of joining, because they reflect the ego's distorted notions about what joining is. Yet the Holy Spirit, too, has use for sleep, and can use dreams on behalf of waking if you will let Him.

4. How you wake is the sign of how you have used sleep. To whom did you give it? Under which teacher did you place it? Whenever you wake dispiritedly, it was not given to the Holy Spirit. Only when you awaken joyously have you utilized sleep according to His purpose. You can indeed be "drugged" by sleep, if you have misused it on behalf of sickness. Sleep is no more a form of death than death is a form of unconsciousness. Complete unconsciousness is impossible. You can rest in peace only because you are awake.

5. Healing is release from the fear of waking and the substitution of the decision to wake. The decision to wake is the reflection of the

will to love, since all healing involves replacing fear with love. The Holy Spirit cannot distinguish among degrees of error, for if He taught that one form of sickness is more serious than another, He would be teaching that one error can be more real than another. His function is to distinguish only between the false and the true, replacing the false with the true.

7. The Bible enjoins you to be perfect, to heal all errors, to take no thought of the body as separate and to accomplish all things in my name. This is not my name alone, for ours is a shared identification. The Name of God's Son is One, and you are enjoined to do the works of love because we share this Oneness. Our minds are whole because they are one. If you are sick you are withdrawing from me. Yet you cannot withdraw from me alone. You can only withdraw from yourself *and* me.

8. You have surely begun to realize that this is a very practical course, and one that means exactly what it says. I would not ask you to do things you cannot do, and it is impossible that I could do things you cannot do. Given this, and given this quite literally, nothing can prevent you from doing exactly what I ask, and everything argues *for* your doing it. I give you no limits because God lays none upon you. When you limit yourself we are not of one mind, and that is sickness. Yet sickness is not of the body, but of the mind. All forms of sickness are signs that the mind is split, and does not accept a unified purpose.

9. The unification of purpose, then, is the Holy Spirit's only way of healing. This is because it is the only level at which healing means anything. The re-establishing of meaning in a chaotic thought system *is* the way to heal it. Your task is only to meet the conditions for meaning, since meaning itself is of God. Yet your return to meaning is essential to His, because your meaning is part of His. Your healing, then, is part of His health, since it is part of His Wholeness. He cannot lose this, but you *can* not know it. Yet it is still His Will for you, and His Will must stand forever and in all things.

QUESTION 19. What is the best way to utilize the body?

Chapter 9. THE ACCEPTANCE
OF THE ATONEMENT

I. The Acceptance of Reality

1. Fear of the Will of God is one of the strangest beliefs the human mind has ever made. It could not possibly have occurred unless the mind were already profoundly split, making it possible for it to be afraid of what it really is. Reality cannot "threaten" anything except illusions, since reality can only uphold truth. The very fact that the Will of God, which is what you are, is perceived as fearful, demonstrates that you *are* afraid of what you are. It is not, then, the Will of God of which you are afraid, but yours.

2. Your will is not the ego's, and that is why the ego is against you. What seems to be the fear of God is really the fear of your own reality. It is impossible to learn anything consistently in a state of panic. If the purpose of this course is to help you remember what you are, and if you believe that what you are is fearful, then it must follow that you will not learn this course. Yet the reason for the course is that you do not what you are.

3. If you do not know what your reality is, why would you be so sure that it is fearful? The association of truth and fear, which would be highly artificial at most, is particularly inappropriate in the minds of those who do not know what truth is. All this could mean is that you are arbitrarily associating something beyond your awareness with something you do not want. It is evident, then, that you are judging something of which you are totally unaware. You have set up this strange situation so that it is impossible to escape from it without a Guide Who *does* know what your reality is. The purpose of this Guide is merely to remind you of what you want. He is not attempting to force an alien will upon you. He is merely making *every* possible effort, within the limits you impose on Him, to re-establish your own will in your awareness.

7. You may insist that the Holy Spirit does not answer you, but it might be wiser to consider the kind of questioner you are. You do not ask only for what you want. This is because you are afraid you might receive it, and you would. That is why you persist in asking the teacher who could not possibly give you what you want. Of him you can never learn what it is, and this gives you the illusion of safety. Yet you cannot be safe *from* truth, but only *in* truth. Reality is the only safety. Your will is your salvation because it is the same as God's. The separation is nothing more than the belief that it is different.

9. Ultimately everyone must remember the Will of God, because ultimately everyone must recognize himself. This recognition is the recognition that his will and God's are one. In the presence of truth, there are no unbelievers and no sacrifices. In the security of reality, fear is totally meaningless. To deny what is can only *seem* to be fearful. Fear cannot be real without a cause, and God is the only Cause. God is Love and you do want Him. This *is* your will. Ask for this and you will be answered, because you will be asking only for what belongs to you.

10. When you ask the Holy Spirit for what would hurt you He cannot answer because nothing can hurt you, and so you are asking for nothing. Any wish that stems from the ego is a wish for nothing, and to ask for it is not a request. It is merely a denial in the form of a request. The Holy Spirit is not concerned with form, being aware only of meaning. The ego cannot ask the Holy Spirit for anything, because there is complete communication failure between them. Yet *you* can ask for everything of the Holy Spirit, because your requests to Him are real, being of your right mind. Would the Holy Spirit deny the Will of God? And could He fail to recognize it in His Son?

11. You do not recognize the enormous waste of energy you expend in denying truth. What would you say of someone who persists in attempting the impossible, believing that to achieve it is to succeed? The belief that you must have the impossible in order to be happy is totally at variance with the principle of creation. God could not will that happiness depended on what you could never have. The fact that God is Love does not require belief, but it does require acceptance. It is indeed possible for you to deny facts, although it is impossible for you to change them. If you hold your hands over your eyes, you will not see because you are interfering with the laws of seeing. If you deny love, you will not know it because your cooperation is the law of its being. You cannot change laws you did not make, and the laws of happiness were created for you, not by you.

13. God in His devotion to you created you devoted to everything, and gave you what you are devoted *to*. Otherwise you would not have been created perfect. Reality is everything, and you have everything because you are real. You cannot make the unreal because the absence of reality is fearful, and fear cannot be created. As long as you believe that fear is possible, you will not create. Opposing orders of reality make reality meaningless, and reality *is* meaning.

14. Remember, then, that God's Will is already possible, and nothing else will ever be. This is the simple acceptance of reality, because only that is real. You cannot distort reality and know what it is. And if you

do distort reality you will experience anxiety, depression and ultimately panic, because you are trying to make yourself unreal. When you feel these things, do not try to look beyond yourself for truth, for truth can only be within you. Say, therefore:

Christ is in me, and where He is God must be,
for Christ is part of Him.

II. The Answer to Prayer

4. If you would know your prayers are answered, never doubt a Son of God. Do not question him and do not confound him, for your faith in him is your faith in yourself. If you would know God and His Answer, believe in me whose faith in you cannot be shaken. Can you ask of the Holy Spirit truly, and doubt your brother? Believe his words are true because of the truth that is in him. You will unite with the truth in him, and his words will *be* true. As you hear him you will hear me. Listening to truth is the only way you can hear it now, and finally know it.

5. The message your brother gives you is up to you. What does he say to you? What would you have him say? Your decision about him determines the message you receive. Remember that the Holy Spirit is in him, and His Voice speaks to you through him. What can so holy a brother tell you except truth? But are you listening to it? Your brother may not know who he is, but there is a light in his mind that does know. This light can shine into yours, giving truth to his words and making you able to hear them. His words are the Holy Spirit's answer to you. Is your faith in him strong enough to let you hear?

6. You can no more pray for yourself alone than you can find joy for yourself alone. Prayer is the restatement of inclusion, directed by the Holy Spirit under the laws of God. Salvation is of your brother. The Holy Spirit extends from your mind to his, and answers *you*. You cannot hear the Voice for God in yourself alone, because you are not alone. And His answer is only for what you are. You will not know the trust I have in you unless you extend it. You will not trust the guidance of the Holy Spirit, or believe that it is for you unless you hear it in others. It must be for your brother *because* it is for you. Would God have created a Voice for you alone? Could you hear His answer except as He answers all of God's Sons? Hear of your brother what you would have me hear of you, for you would not want me to be deceived.

7. I love you for the truth in you, as God does. Your deceptions may deceive you, but they cannot deceive me. Knowing what you are, I cannot doubt you. I hear only the Holy Spirit in you, Who speaks to me through you. If you would hear me, hear my brothers in whom

God's Voice speaks. The answer to all prayers lies in them. You will be answered as you hear the answer in everyone. Do not listen to anything else or you will not hear truly.

III. The Correction of Error

1. The alertness of the ego to the errors of other egos is not the kind of vigilance the Holy Spirit would have you maintain. Egos are critical in terms of the kind of "sense" they stand for. They understand this kind of sense, because it is sensible to them. To the Holy Spirit it makes no sense at all.

2. To the ego it is kind and right and good to point out errors and "correct" them. This makes perfect sense to the ego, which is unaware of what errors are and what correction is. Errors are of the ego, and correction of errors lies in the relinquishment of the ego. When you correct a brother, you are telling him that he is wrong. He may be making no sense at the time, and it is certain that, if he is speaking from the ego, he will not be making sense. But your task is still to tell him he is right. You do not tell him this verbally, if he is speaking foolishly. He needs correction at another level, because his error is at another level. He is still right, because he is a Son of God. His ego is always wrong, no matter what it says or does.

3. If you point out the errors of your brother's ego you must be seeing through yours, because the Holy Spirit does not perceive his errors. This *must* be true, since there is no communication between the ego and the Holy Spirit. The ego makes no sense, and the Holy Spirit does not attempt to understand anything that arises from it. Since He does not understand it, He does not judge it, knowing that nothing the ego makes means anything.

4. When you react at all to errors, you are not listening to the Holy Spirit. He has merely disregarded them, and if you attend to them you are not hearing Him. If you do not hear Him, you are listening to your ego and making as little sense as the brother whose errors you perceive. This cannot be correction. Yet it is more than merely a lack of correction for him. It is the giving up of correction in yourself.

5. When a brother behaves insanely, you can heal him only by perceiving the sanity in him. If you perceive his errors and accept them, you are accepting yours. If you want to give yours over to the Holy Spirit, you must do this with his. Unless this becomes the one way in which you handle all errors, you cannot understand how all errors are undone. How is this different from telling you that what you teach

you learn? Your brother is as right as you are, and if you think he is wrong you are condemning yourself.

6. *You* cannot correct yourself. Is it possible, then, for you to correct another? Yet you can see him truly, because it is possible for you to *see* yourself truly. It is not up to you to change your brother, but merely to accept him as he is. His errors do not come from the truth that is in him, and only this truth is yours. His errors cannot change this, and can have no effect at all on the truth in you. To perceive errors in anyone, and to react to them as if they were real, is to make them real to you. You will not escape paying the price for this, not because you are being punished for it, but because you are following the wrong guide and will therefore lose your way.

7. Your brother's errors are not of him, any more than yours are of you. Accept his errors as real, and you have attacked yourself. If you would find your way and keep it, see only truth beside you for you walk together. The Holy Spirit in you forgives all things in you and in your brother. His errors are forgiven with yours. Atonement is no more separate than love. Atonement cannot be separate because it comes from love. Any attempt you make to correct a brother means that you believe correction by you is possible, and this can only be the arrogance of the ego. Correction is of God, Who does not know of arrogance.

8. The Holy Spirit forgives everything because God created everything. Do not undertake His function, or you will forget yours. Accept only the function of healing in time, because that is what time is for. God gave you the function to create in eternity. You do not need to learn that, but you do need to learn to want it. For that all learning was made. This is the Holy Spirit's use of an ability that you do not need, but that you made. Give it to Him! You do not understand how to use it. He will teach you how to see yourself without condemnation, by learning how to look on everything without it. Condemnation will then not be real to you, and all your errors will be forgiven.

QUESTION 20. What are errors, and what is the best attitude to have about errors of others and about correcting your own errors?

IV. The Holy Spirit's Plan of Forgiveness

1. Atonement is for all, because it is the way to undo the belief that anything is for you alone. To forgive is to overlook. Look, then, beyond error and do not let your perception rest upon it, for you will believe what your perception holds. Accept as true only what your brother is, if you would know yourself. Perceive what he is not and you cannot know

what you are, because you see him falsely. Remember always that your Identity is shared, and that Its sharing is Its reality.

2. You have a part to play in the Atonement, but the plan of the Atonement is beyond you. You do not understand how to overlook errors, or you would not make them. It would merely be further error to believe either that you do not make them, or that you can correct them without a Guide to correction. And if you do not follow this Guide, your errors will not be corrected. The plan is not yours because of your limited ideas about what you are. This sense of limitation is where all errors arise. The way to undo them, therefore, is not *of* you but *for* you.

3. The Atonement is a lesson in sharing, which is given you because *you have forgotten how to do it.* The Holy Spirit merely reminds you of the natural use of your abilities. By reinterpreting the ability to attack into the ability to share, He translates what you have made into what God created. If you would accomplish this through Him you cannot look on your abilities through the eyes of the ego, or you will judge them as *it* does. All their harmfulness lies in the ego's judgment. All their helpfulness lies in the judgment of the Holy Spirit.

4. The ego, too, has a plan of forgiveness because you are asking for one, though not of the right teacher. The ego's plan, of course, makes no sense and will not work. By following its plan you will merely place yourself in an impossible situation, to which the ego always leads you. The ego's plan is to have you see error clearly first, and then overlook it. Yet how can you overlook what you have made real? By seeing it clearly, you have made it real and *cannot* overlook it. This is where the ego is forced to appeal to "mysteries," insisting that you must accept the meaningless to save yourself. Many have tried to do this in my name, forgetting that my words make perfect sense because they come from God. They are as sensible now as they ever were, because they speak of ideas that are eternal.

5. Forgiveness that is learned of me does not use fear to undo fear. Nor does it make real the unreal and then destroy it. Forgiveness through the Holy Spirit lies simply in looking beyond error from the beginning, and thus keeping it unreal for you. Do not let any belief in its realness enter your mind, or you will also believe that you must undo what you have made in order to be forgiven. What has no effect does not exist, and to the Holy Spirit the effects of error are nonexistent. By steadily and consistently cancelling out all its effects, everywhere and in all respects, He teaches that the ego does not exist and proves it.

6. Follow the Holy Spirit's teaching in forgiveness, then, because forgiveness is His function and He knows how to fulfill it perfectly. That

is what I meant when I said that miracles are natural, and when they do not occur something has gone wrong. Miracles are merely the sign of your willingness to follow the Holy Spirit's plan of salvation, recognizing that you do not understand what it is. His work is not your function, and unless you accept this you cannot learn what your function is.

V. The Unhealed Healer

3. There is an advantage to bringing nightmares into awareness, but only to teach that they are not real, and that anything they contain is meaningless. The unhealed healer cannot do this because he does not believe it. All unhealed healers follow the ego's plan for forgiveness in one form or another. If they are theologians they are likely to condemn themselves, teach condemnation and advocate a fearful solution. Projecting condemnation onto God, they make Him appear retaliative, and fear His retribution. What they have done is merely to identify with the ego, and by perceiving what *it* does, condemn themselves because of this confusion. It is understandable that there have been revolts against this concept, but to revolt against it is still to believe in it.

6. What, then, should happen? When God said, "Let there be light," there *was* light. Can you find light by analyzing darkness, as the psychotherapist does, or like the theologian, by acknowledging darkness in yourself and looking for a distant light to remove it, while emphasizing the distance? Healing is not mysterious. Nothing will change unless it is understood, since light *is* understanding. A "miserable sinner" cannot be healed without magic, nor can an "unimportant mind" esteem itself without magic.

7. Both forms of the ego's approach, then, must arrive at an impasse; the characteristic "impossible situation" to which the ego always leads. It may help someone to point out where he is heading, but the point is lost unless he is also helped to change his direction. The unhealed healer cannot do this for him, since he cannot do it for himself. The only meaningful contribution the healer can make is to present an example of one whose direction has been changed *for* him, and who no longer believes in nightmares of any kind. The light in his mind will therefore answer the questioner, who must decide with God that there is light *because* he sees it. And by his acknowledgment the healer knows it is there. That is how perception ultimately is translated into knowledge. The miracle worker begins by perceiving light, and translates his perception into sureness by continually extending it and accepting its acknowledgment. Its effects assure him it is there.

8. A therapist does not heal; *he lets healing be*. He can point to darkness but he cannot bring light of himself, for light is not of him. Yet, being *for* him, it must also be for his patient. The Holy Spirit is the only Therapist. He makes healing clear in any situation in which He is the Guide. You can only let Him fulfill His function. He needs no help for this. He will tell you exactly what to do to help anyone He sends to you for help, and will speak to him through you if you do not interfere. Remember that you choose the guide for helping, and the wrong choice will not help. But remember also that the right one will. Trust Him, for help is His function, and He is of God. As you awaken other minds to the Holy Spirit through Him, and not yourself, you will understand that you are not obeying the laws of this world. But the laws you are obeying work. "The good is what works" is a sound though insufficient statement. Only the good *can* work. Nothing else works at all.

VI. The Acceptance of Your Brother

3. If your brothers are part of you, will you accept them? Only they can teach you what you are, for your learning is the result of what you taught them. What you call upon in them you call upon in yourself. And as you call upon it in them it becomes real to you. God has but one Son, knowing them all as One. Only God Himself is more than they but they are not less than He is. Would you know what this means? If what you do to my brother you do to me, and if you do everything for yourself because we are part of you, everything we do belongs to you as well. Everyone God created is part of you and shares His glory with you. His glory belongs to Him, but it is equally yours. You cannot, then, be less glorious than He is.
4. God is more than you only because He created you, but not even this would He keep from you. Therefore you can create as He did, and your dissociation will not alter this. Neither God's light nor yours is dimmed because you do not see. Because the Sonship must create as one, you remember creation whenever you recognize part of creation. Each part you remember adds to your wholeness because each part *is* whole. Wholeness is indivisible, but you cannot learn of your wholeness until you see it everywhere. You can know yourself only as God knows His Son, for knowledge is shared with God. When you awake in Him you will know your magnitude by accepting His limitlessness as yours. But meanwhile you will judge it as you judge your brother's, and will accept it as you accept his.
5. You are not yet awake, but you can learn how to awaken. Very simply, the Holy Spirit teaches you to awaken others. As you see them

waken you will learn what waking means, and because you have chosen to wake them, their gratitude and their appreciation of what you have given them will teach you its value. They will become the witnesses to your reality, as you were created witness to God's. Yet when the Sonship comes together and accepts its Oneness it will be known by its creations, who witness to its reality as the Son does to the Father.

6. Miracles have no place in eternity, because they are reparative. Yet while you still need healing, your miracles are the only witnesses to your reality that you can recognize. You cannot perform a miracle for yourself, because miracles are a way of giving acceptance and receiving it. In time the giving comes first, though they are simultaneous in eternity, where they cannot be separated. When you have learned they are the same, the need for time is over.

VII. The Two Evaluations

3. It is perfectly obvious that if the Holy Spirit looks with love on all He perceives, He looks with love on you. His evaluation of you is based on His knowledge of what you are, and so He evaluates you truly. And this evaluation must be in your mind, because He is. The ego is also in your mind, because you have accepted it there. Its evaluation of you, however, is the exact opposite of the Holy Spirit's, because the ego does not love you. It is unaware of what you are, and wholly mistrustful of everything it perceives because its perceptions are so shifting. The ego is therefore capable of suspiciousness at best and viciousness at worst. That is its range. It cannot exceed it because of its uncertainty. And it can never go beyond it because it can never *be* certain.

4. You, then, have two conflicting evaluations of yourself in your mind, and they cannot both be true. You do not yet realize how completely different these evaluations are, because you do not understand how lofty the Holy Spirit's perception of you really is. He is not deceived by anything you do, because He never forgets what you are. The ego is deceived by everything you do, especially when you respond to the Holy Spirit, because at such times its confusion increases. The ego is, therefore, particularly likely to attack you when you react lovingly, because it has evaluated you as unloving and you are going against its judgment. The ego will attack your motives as soon as they become clearly out of accord with its perception of you. This is when it will shift abruptly from suspiciousness to viciousness, since its uncertainty is increased. Yet it is surely pointless to attack in return. What can this

mean except that you are agreeing with the ego's evaluation of what you are?

5. If you choose to see yourself as unloving you will not be happy. You are condemning yourself and must therefore regard yourself as inadequate. Would you look to the ego to help you escape from a sense of inadequacy it has produced, and must maintain for its existence? Can you escape from its evaluation of you by using its methods for keeping this picture intact?

6. You cannot evaluate an insane belief system from within it. Its range precludes this. You can only go beyond it, look back from a point where sanity exists and *see the contrast*. Only by this contrast can insanity be judged as insane. With the grandeur of God in you, you have chosen to be little and to lament your littleness. Within the system that dictated this choice the lament is inevitable. Your littleness is taken for granted there and you do not ask, "Who granted it?" The question is meaningless within the ego's thought system, because it would open the whole thought system to question.

QUESTION 21. How would you compare the Holy Spirit's forgiveness through overlooking errors with the ego's plan of forgiveness?

Chapter 10. THE IDOLS OF SICKNESS

Introduction

1. Nothing beyond yourself can make you fearful or loving, because nothing is beyond you. Time and eternity are both in your mind, and will conflict until you perceive time solely as a means to regain eternity. You cannot do this as long as you believe that anything happening to you is caused by factors outside yourself. You must learn that time is solely at your disposal, and that nothing in the world can take this responsibility from you. You can violate God's laws in your imagination, but you cannot escape from them. They were established for your protection and are as inviolate as your safety.

2. God created nothing beside you and nothing beside you exists, for you are part of Him. What except Him can exist? Nothing beyond Him can happen, because nothing except Him is real. Your creations add to Him as you do, but nothing is added that is different because everything has always been. What can upset you except the ephemeral, and how can the ephemeral be real if you are God's only creation and He created you eternal? Your holy mind establishes everything that happens to you. Every response you make to everything you perceive is up to you, because your mind determines your perception of it.

3. God does not change His Mind about you, for He is not uncertain of Himself. And what He knows can be known, because He does not know it only for Himself. He created you for Himself, but He gave you the power to create for yourself so you would be like Him. That is why your mind is holy. Can anything exceed the Love of God? Can anything, then, exceed your will? Nothing can reach you from beyond it because, being in God, you encompass everything. Believe this, and you will realize how much is up to you. When anything threatens your peace of mind, ask yourself, "Has God changed His Mind about me?" Then accept His decision, for it is indeed changeless, and refuse to change your mind about yourself. God will never decide against you, or He would be deciding against Himself.

I. At Home in God

2. You are at home in God, dreaming of exile but perfectly capable of awakening to reality. Is it your decision to do so? You recognize from your own experience that what you see in dreams you think is real while you are asleep. Yet the instant you waken you realize that everything

that seemed to happen in the dream did not happen at all. You do not think this strange, even though all the laws of what you awaken to were violated while you slept. Is it not possible that you merely shifted from one dream to another, without really waking?

3. Would you bother to reconcile what happened in conflicting dreams, or would you dismiss both together if you discovered that reality is in accord with neither? You do not remember being awake. When you hear the Holy Spirit you may feel better because loving then seems possible to you, but you do not remember yet that it once was so. And it is in this remembering that you will know it can be so again. What is possible has not yet been accomplished. Yet what has once been is so now, if it is eternal. When you remember, you will know that what you remember is eternal, and therefore is now.

4. You will remember everything the instant you desire it wholly, for if to desire wholly is to create, you will have willed away the separation, returning your mind simultaneously to your Creator and your creations. Knowing Them you will have no wish to sleep, but only the desire to waken and be glad. Dreams will be impossible because you will want only truth, and being at last your will, it will be yours.

II. The Decision to Forget

1. Unless you first know something you cannot dissociate it. Knowledge must precede dissociation, so that dissociation is nothing more than a decision to forget. What has been forgotten then appears to be fearful, but only because the dissociation is an attack on truth. You are fearful *because* you have forgotten. And you have replaced your knowledge by an awareness of dreams because you are afraid of your dissociation, not of what you have dissociated. When what you have dissociated is accepted, it ceases to be fearful.

2. Yet to give up the dissociation of reality brings more than merely lack of fear. In this decision lie joy and peace and the glory of creation. Offer the Holy Spirit only your willingness to remember, for He retains the knowledge of God and of yourself for you, waiting for your acceptance. Give up gladly everything that would stand in the way of your remembering, for God is in your memory. His Voice will tell you that you are part of Him when you are willing to remember Him and know your own reality again. Let nothing in this world delay your remembering of Him, for in this remembering is the knowledge of yourself.

3. To remember is merely to restore to your mind *what is already there.* You do not make what you remember; you merely accept again what is

already there, but was rejected. The ability to accept truth in this world is the perceptual counterpart of creating in the Kingdom. God will do His part if you will do yours, and His return in exchange for yours is the exchange of knowledge for perception. Nothing is beyond His Will for you. But signify your will to remember Him, and behold! He will give you everything but for the asking.

4. When you attack, you are denying yourself. You are specifically teaching yourself that you are not what you are. Your denial of reality precludes the acceptance of God's gift, because you have accepted something else in its place. If you understand that this is always an attack on truth, and truth is God, you will realize why it is always fearful. If you further recognize that you are part of God, you will understand why it is that you always attack yourself first.

5. All attack is Self attack. It cannot be anything else. Arising from your own decision not to be what you are, it is an attack on your identification. Attack is thus the way in which your identification is lost, because when you attack, you must have forgotten what you are. And if your reality is God's, when you attack you are not remembering Him. This is not because He is gone, but because you are actively choosing not to remember Him.

6. If you realized the complete havoc this makes of your peace of mind you could not make such an insane decision. You make it only because you still believe it can get you something you want. It follows, then, that you want something other than peace of mind, but you have not considered what it must be. Yet the logical outcome of your decision is perfectly clear, if you will only look at it. By deciding against your reality, you have made yourself vigilant *against* God and His Kingdom. And it is this vigilance that makes you afraid to remember Him.

III. The God of Sickness

1. You have not attacked God and you do love Him. Can you change your reality? No one can will to destroy himself. When you think you are attacking yourself, it is a sure sign that you hate what you *think* you are. And this, and only this, can be attacked by you. What you think you are can be very hateful, and what this strange image makes you do can be very destructive. Yet the destruction is no more real than the image, although those who make idols do worship them. The idols are nothing, but their worshippers are the Sons of God in sickness. God would have them released from their sickness and returned to His Mind. He will not limit your power to help them, because He has given it to you. Do not be afraid of it, because it is your salvation.

2. What Comforter can there be for the sick children of God except His power through you? Remember that it does not matter where in the Sonship He is accepted. He is always accepted for all, and when your mind receives Him the remembrance of Him awakens throughout the Sonship. Heal your brothers simply by accepting God for them. Your minds are not separate, and God has only one channel for healing because He has but one Son. God's remaining Communication Link with all His children joins them together, and them to Him. To be aware of this is to heal them because it is the awareness that no one is separate, and so no one is sick.

3. To believe that a Son of God can be sick is to believe that part of God can suffer. Love cannot suffer, because it cannot attack. The remembrance of love therefore brings invulnerability with it. Do not side with sickness in the presence of a Son of God even if he believes in it, for your acceptance of God in him acknowledges the Love of God he has forgotten. Your recognition of him as part of God reminds him of the truth about himself, which he is denying. Would you strengthen his denial of God and thus lose sight of yourself? Or would you remind him of his wholeness and remember your Creator with him?

7. When a brother is sick it is because he is not asking for peace, and therefore does not know he has it. The acceptance of peace is the denial of illusion, and sickness *is* an illusion. Yet every Son of God has the power to deny illusions anywhere in the Kingdom, merely by denying them completely in himself. I can heal you because I know you. I know your value for you, and it is this value that makes you whole. A whole mind is not idolatrous, and does not know of conflicting laws. I will heal you merely because I have only one message, and it is true. Your faith in it will make you whole when you have faith in me.

IV. The End of Sickness

7. The miracle is the act of a Son of God who has laid aside all false gods, and calls on his brothers to do likewise. It is an act of faith, because it is the recognition that his brother can do it. It is a call to the Holy Spirit in his mind, a call that is strengthened by joining. Because the miracle worker has heard God's Voice, he strengthens It in a sick brother by weakening his belief in sickness, which he does not share. The power of one mind can shine into another, because all the lamps of God were lit by the same spark. It is everywhere and it is eternal.

8. In many only the spark remains, for the Great Rays are obscured. Yet God has kept the spark alive so that the Rays can never be completely forgotten. If you but see the little spark you will learn of the

greater light, for the Rays are there unseen. Perceiving the spark will heal, but knowing the light will create. Yet in the returning the little light must be acknowledged first, for the separation was a descent from magnitude to littleness. But the spark is still as pure as the Great Light, because it is the remaining call of creation. Put all your faith in it, and God Himself will answer you.

V. The Denial of God

3. Allegiance to the denial of God is the ego's religion. The god of sickness obviously demands the denial of health, because health is in direct opposition to its own survival. But consider what this means to you. Unless you are sick you cannot keep the gods you made, for only in sickness could you possibly want them. Blasphemy, then, is *self-destructive*, not God-destructive. It means that you are willing not to know yourself in order to be sick. This is the offering your god demands because, having made him out of your insanity, he is an insane idea. He has many forms, but although he may seem to be many different things he is but one idea;—the denial of God.

6. Son of God, you have not sinned, but you have been much mistaken. Yet this can be corrected and God will help you, knowing that you could not sin against Him. You denied Him because you loved Him, knowing that if you recognized your love for Him, you could not deny Him. Your denial of Him therefore means that you love Him, and that you know He loves you. Remember that what you deny you must have once known. And if you accept denial, you can accept its undoing.

10. You do not realize how much you have denied yourself, and how much God, in His Love, would not have it so. Yet He would not interfere with you, because He would not know His Son if he were not free. To interfere with you would be to attack Himself, and God is not insane. When you deny Him *you* are insane. Would you have Him share your insanity? God will never cease to love His Son, and His Son will never cease to love Him. That was the condition of His Son's creation, fixed forever in the Mind of God. To know that is sanity. To deny it is insanity. God gave Himself to you in your creation, and His gifts are eternal. Would you deny yourself to Him?

QUESTION 22. What do bedtime dreams have in common with the dream of this world in apparent banishment from God, and is it helpful for you to sympathize with your brother by agreeing with his belief in his sickness?

Chapter 11. GOD OR THE EGO

Introduction

3. You make by projection, but God creates by extension. The cornerstone of God's creation is you, for His thought system is light. Remember the Rays that are there unseen. The more you approach the center of His thought system, the clearer the light becomes. The closer you come to the foundation of the ego's thought system, the darker and more obscure becomes the way. Yet even the little spark in your mind is enough to lighten it. Bring this light fearlessly with you, and bravely hold it up to the foundation of the ego's thought system. Be willing to judge it with perfect honesty. Open the dark cornerstone of terror on which it rests, and bring it out into the light. There you will see that it rested on meaninglessness, and that everything of which you have been afraid was based on nothing.

4. My brother, you are part of God and part of me. When you have at last looked at the ego's foundation without shrinking you will also have looked upon ours. I come to you from our Father to offer you everything again. Do not refuse it in order to keep a dark cornerstone hidden, for its protection will not save you. I give you the lamp and I will go with you. You will not take this journey alone. I will lead you to your true Father, Who hath need of you, as I have. Will you not answer the call of love with joy?

I. The Gifts of Fatherhood

2. To be alone is to be separated from infinity, but how can this be if infinity has no end? No one can be beyond the limitless, because what has no limits must be everywhere. There are no beginnings and no endings in God, Whose universe is Himself. Can you exclude yourself from the universe, or from God Who *is* the universe? I and my Father are one with you, for you are part of Us. Do you really believe that part of God can be missing or lost to Him?

3. If you were not part of God, His Will would not be unified. Is this conceivable? Can part of His Mind contain nothing? If your place in His Mind cannot be filled by anyone except you, and your filling it was your creation, without you there would be an empty place in God's Mind. Extension cannot be blocked, and it has no voids. It continues forever, however much it is denied. Your denial of its reality may arrest it in

time, but not in eternity. That is why your creations have not ceased to be extended, and why so much is waiting for your return.

6.   God has given you a place in His Mind that is yours forever. Yet you can keep it only by giving it, as it was given you. Could you be alone there, when it was given you because God did not will to be alone? God's Mind cannot be lessened. It can only be increased, for everything He creates has the function of creating. Love does not limit, and what it creates is not limited. To give without limit is God's Will for you, because only this can bring you the joy that is His and that He wills to share with you. Your love is as boundless as His because it *is* His.

7.   Could any part of God be without His Love, and could any part of His Love be contained? God is your heritage, because His one gift is Himself. How can you give except like Him if you would know His gift to you? Give, then, without limit and without end, to learn how much He has given you. Your ability to accept Him depends on your willingness to give as He gives. Your fatherhood and your Father are One. God wills to create, and your will is His. It follows, then, that you will to create, since your will follows from His. And being an extension of His Will, yours must be the same.

8.   Yet what you will you do not know. This is not strange when you realize that to deny is to "not know." God's Will is that you are His Son. By denying this you deny your own will, and therefore do not know what it is. You must ask what God's Will is in everything, because it is yours. You do not know what it is, but the Holy Spirit remembers it for you. Ask Him, therefore, what God's Will is for you, and He will tell you yours. It cannot be too often repeated that you do not know it. Whenever what the Holy Spirit tells you appears to be coercive, it is only because you have not recognized your will.

9.   The projection of the ego makes it appear as if God's Will is outside yourself, and therefore not yours. In this interpretation it *seems* possible for God's Will and yours to conflict. God, then, may seem to demand of you what you do not want to give, and thus deprive you of what you want. Would God, Who wants only your will, be capable of this? Your will is His life, which He has given to you. Even in time you cannot live apart from Him. Sleep is not death. What He created can sleep, but cannot die. Immortality is His Will for His Son, and His Son's will for himself. God's Son cannot will death for himself because his Father is life, and His Son is like Him. Creation is your will *because* it is His.

10.   You cannot be happy unless you do what you will truly, and you cannot change this because it is immutable. It is immutable by God's Will and yours, for otherwise His Will would not be extended. You are

afraid to know God's Will, because you believe it is not yours. This belief is your whole sickness and your whole fear. Every symptom of sickness and fear arises here, because this is the belief that makes you *want* not to know. Believing this you hide in darkness, denying that the light is in you.

11. You are asked to trust the Holy Spirit only because He speaks for you. He is the Voice for God, but never forget that God did not will to be alone. He shares His Will with you; He does not thrust it upon you. Always remember that what He gives He keeps, so that nothing He gives can contradict Him. You who share His life must share it to know it, for sharing *is* knowing. Blessed are you who learn that to hear the Will of your Father is to know your own. For it is your will to be like Him, Whose will it is that it be so. God's Will is that His Son be one, and united with Him in His Oneness. That is why healing is the beginning of the recognition that your will is His.

II. The Invitation to Healing

1. If sickness is separation, the decision to heal and to be healed is the first step toward recognizing what you truly want. Every attack is a step away from this, and every healing thought brings it closer. The Son of God *has* both Father and Son, because he *is* both Father and Son. To unite *having* and *being* is to unite your will with His, for He wills you Himself. And you will yourself to Him because, in your perfect understanding of Him, you know there is but one Will. Yet when you attack any part of God and His Kingdom your understanding is not perfect, and what you really want is therefore lost to you.

2. Healing thus becomes a lesson in understanding, and the more you practice it the better teacher and learner you become. If you have denied truth, what better witnesses to its reality could you have than those who have been healed by it? But be sure to count yourself among them, for in your willingness to join them is your healing accomplished. Every miracle that you accomplish speaks to you of the Fatherhood of God. Every healing thought that you accept, either from your brother or in your own mind, teaches you that you are God's Son. In every hurtful thought you hold, wherever you perceive it, lies the denial of God's Fatherhood and of your Sonship.

III. from Darkness to Light

1. When you are weary, remember you have hurt yourself. Your Comforter will rest you, but you cannot. You do not know how, for if

you did you could never have grown weary. Unless you hurt yourself you could never suffer in any way, for that is not God's Will for His Son. Pain is not of Him, for He knows no attack and His peace surrounds you silently. God is very quiet, for there is no conflict in Him. Conflict is the root of all evil, for being blind it does not see whom it attacks. Yet it always attacks the Son of God, and the Son of God is you.

2. God's Son is indeed in need of comfort, for he knows not what he does, believing his will is not his own. The Kingdom is his, and yet he wanders homeless. At home in God he is lonely, and amid all his brothers he is friendless. Would God let this be real, when He did not will to be alone Himself? And if your will is His it cannot be true of you, because it is not true of Him.

3. O my child, if you knew what God wills for you, your joy would be complete! And what He wills has happened, for it was always true. When the light comes and you have said, "God's Will is mine," you will see such beauty that you will know it is not of you. Out of your joy you will create beauty in His Name, for your joy could no more be contained than His. The bleak little world will vanish into nothingness, and your heart will be so filled with joy that it will leap into Heaven, and into the Presence of God. I cannot tell you what this will be like, for your heart is not ready. Yet I can tell you, and remind you often, that what God wills for Himself He wills for you, and what He wills for you is yours.

4. The way is not hard, but it *is* very different. Yours is the way of pain, of which God knows nothing. That way is hard indeed, and very lonely. Fear and grief are your guests, and they go with you and abide with you on the way. But the dark journey is not the way of God's Son. Walk in light and do not see the dark companions, for they are not fit companions for the Son of God, who was created *of* light and *in* light. The Great Light always surrounds you and shines out from you. How can you see the dark companions in a light such as this? If you see them, it is only because you are denying the light. But deny them instead, for the light is here and the way is clear.

5. God hides nothing from His Son, even though His Son would hide himself. Yet the Son of God cannot hide his glory, for God wills him to be glorious, and gave him the light that shines in him. You will never lose your way, for God leads you. When you wander, you but undertake a journey that is not real. The dark companions, the dark way, are all illusions. Turn toward the light, for the little spark in you is part of a light so great that it can sweep you out of all darkness forever. For your Father *is* your Creator, and you *are* like Him.

7. Only God's Comforter can comfort you. In the quiet of His temple, He waits to give you the peace that is yours. Give His peace, that you may enter the temple and find it waiting for you. But be holy in the Presence of God, or you will not know that you are there. For what is unlike God cannot enter His Mind, because it was not His Thought and therefore does not belong to Him. And your mind must be as pure as His, if you would know what belongs to you. Guard carefully His temple, for He Himself dwells there and abides in peace. You cannot enter God's Presence with the dark companions beside you, but you also cannot enter alone. All your brothers must enter with you, for until you have accepted them *you* cannot enter. For you cannot understand wholeness unless you are whole, and no part of the Son can be excluded if he would know the Wholeness of his Father.

8. In your mind you can accept the whole Sonship and bless it with the light your Father gave it. Then you will be worthy to dwell in the temple with Him, because it is your will not to be alone. God blessed His Son forever. If you will bless him in time, you will be in eternity. Time cannot separate you from God if you use it on behalf of the eternal.

IV. The Inheritance of God's Son

4. *Only you can deprive yourself of anything.* Do not oppose this realization, for it is truly the beginning of the dawn of light. Remember also that the denial of this simple fact takes many forms, and these you must learn to recognize and to oppose steadfastly, without exception. This is a crucial step in the reawakening. The beginning phases of this reversal are often quite painful, for as blame is withdrawn from without, there is a strong tendency to harbor it within. It is difficult at first to realize that this is exactly the same thing, for there is no distinction between within and without.

5. If your brothers are part of you and you blame them for your deprivation, you are blaming yourself. And you cannot blame yourself without blaming them. That is why blame must be undone, not seen elsewhere. Lay it to yourself and you cannot know yourself, for only the ego blames at all. Self-blame is therefore ego identification, and as much an ego defense as blaming others. *You cannot enter God's Presence if you attack His Son.* When His Son lifts his voice in praise of his Creator, he will hear the Voice for his Father. Yet the Creator cannot be praised without His Son, for Their glory is shared and They are glorified together.

6. Christ is at God's altar, waiting to welcome His Son. But come wholly without condemnation, for otherwise you will believe that the

door is barred and you cannot enter. The door is not barred, and it is impossible that you cannot enter the place where God would have you be. But love yourself with the Love of Christ, for so does your Father love you. You can refuse to enter, but you cannot bar the door that Christ holds open. Come unto me who hold it open for you, for while I live it cannot be shut, and I live forever. God is my life and yours, and nothing is denied by God to His Son.

7. At God's altar Christ waits for the restoration of Himself in you. God knows His Son as wholly blameless as Himself, and He is approached through the appreciation of His Son. Christ waits for your acceptance of Him as yourself, and of His Wholeness as yours. For Christ is the Son of God, Who lives in His Creator and shines with His glory. Christ is the extension of the Love and the loveliness of God, as perfect as His Creator and at peace with Him.

8. Blessed is the Son of God whose radiance is of his Father, and whose glory he wills to share as his Father shares it with him. There is no condemnation in the Son, for there is no condemnation in the Father. Sharing the perfect Love of the Father the Son must share what belongs to Him, for otherwise he will not know the Father or the Son. Peace be unto you who rest in God, and in whom the whole Sonship rests.

QUESTION 23. What does light mean to God and to you, and what is the relationship between God's Will and your will?

V. The "Dynamics" of the Ego

13. The ego analyzes; the Holy Spirit accepts. The appreciation of wholeness comes only through acceptance, for to analyze means to break down or to separate out. The attempt to understand totality by breaking it down is clearly the characteristically contradictory approach of the ego to everything. The ego believes that power, understanding and truth lie in separation, and to establish this belief it must attack. Unaware that the belief cannot be established, and obsessed with the conviction that separation is salvation, the ego attacks everything it perceives by breaking it into small, disconnected parts, without meaningful relationships and therefore without meaning. The ego will always substitute chaos for meaning, for if separation is salvation, harmony is threat.

14. The ego's interpretations of the laws of perception are, and would have to be, the exact opposite of the Holy Spirit's. The ego focuses on error and overlooks truth. It makes real every mistake it perceives, and

with characteristically circular reasoning concludes that because of the mistake consistent truth must be meaningless. The next step, then, is obvious. If consistent truth is meaningless, inconsistency must be true. Holding error clearly in mind, and protecting what it has made real, the ego proceeds to the next step in its thought system: Error is real and truth is error.

16. Do not underestimate the appeal of the ego's demonstrations to those who would listen. Selective perception chooses its witnesses carefully, and its witnesses are consistent. The case for insanity is strong to the insane. For reasoning ends at its beginning, and no thought system transcends its source. Yet reasoning without meaning cannot demonstrate anything, and those who are convinced by it must be deluded. Can the ego teach truly when it overlooks truth? Can it perceive what it has denied? Its witnesses do attest to its denial, but hardly to what it has denied. The ego looks straight at the Father and does not see Him, for it has denied His Son.

17. Would *you* remember the Father? Accept His Son and you will remember Him. Nothing can demonstrate that His Son is unworthy, for nothing can prove that a lie is true. What you see of His Son through the eyes of the ego is a demonstration that His Son does not exist, yet where the Son is the Father must be. Accept what God does not deny, and it will demonstrate its truth. The witnesses for God stand in His light and behold what He created. Their silence is the sign that they have beheld God's Son, and in the Presence of Christ they need demonstrate nothing, for Christ speaks to them of Himself and of His Father. They are silent because Christ speaks to them, and it is His words they speak.

18. Every brother you meet becomes a witness for Christ or for the ego, depending on what you perceive in him. Everyone convinces you of what you want to perceive, and of the reality of the kingdom you have chosen for your vigilance. Everything you perceive is a witness to the thought system you want to be true. Every brother has the power to release you, if you choose to be free. You cannot accept false witness of him unless you have evoked false witnesses against him. If he speaks not of Christ to you, you spoke not of Christ to him. You hear but your own voice, and if Christ speaks through you, you will hear Him.

VI. Waking to Redemption

1. It is impossible not to believe what you see, but it is equally impossible to see what you do not believe. Perceptions are built up on the basis of experience, and experience leads to beliefs. It is not until

beliefs are fixed that perceptions stabilize. In effect, then, what you believe you *do* see. That is what I meant when I said, "Blessed are ye who have not seen and still believe," for those who believe in the resurrection will see it. The resurrection is the complete triumph of Christ over the ego, not by attack but by transcendence. For Christ does rise above the ego and all its works, and ascends to the Father and His Kingdom.

2. Would you join in the resurrection or the crucifixion? Would you condemn your brothers or free them? Would you transcend your prison and ascend to the Father? These questions are all the same, and are answered together. There has been much confusion about what perception means, because the word is used both for awareness and for the interpretation of awareness. Yet you cannot be aware without interpretation, for what you perceive *is* your interpretation.

3. This course is perfectly clear. If you do not see it clearly, it is because you are interpreting against it, and therefore do not believe it. And since belief determines perception, you do not perceive what it means and therefore do not accept it. Yet different experiences lead to different beliefs, and with them different perceptions. For perceptions are learned *with* beliefs, and experience does teach. I am leading you to a new kind of experience that you will become less and less willing to deny. Learning of Christ is easy, for to perceive with Him involves no strain at all. His perceptions are your natural awareness, and it is only the distortions you introduce that tire you. Let the Christ in you interpret for you, and do not try to limit what you see by narrow little beliefs that are unworthy of God's Son. For until Christ comes into His Own, the Son of God will see himself as Fatherless.

4. I am *your* resurrection and *your* life. You live in me because you live in God. And everyone lives in you, as you live in everyone. Can you, then, perceive unworthiness in a brother and not perceive it in yourself? And can you perceive it in yourself and not perceive it in God? Believe in the resurrection because it has been accomplished, and it has been accomplished in you. This is as true now as it will ever be, for the resurrection is the Will of God, which knows no time and no exceptions. But make no exceptions yourself, or you will not perceive what has been accomplished for you. For we ascend unto the Father together, as it was in the beginning, is now and ever shall be, for such is the nature of God's Son as his Father created him.

5. Do not underestimate the power of the devotion of God's Son, nor the power the god he worships has over him. For he places himself at the altar of his god, whether it be the god he made or the God Who created him. That is why his slavery is as complete as his freedom,

for he will obey only the god he accepts. The god of crucifixion demands that he crucify, and his worshippers obey. In his name they crucify themselves, believing that the power of the Son of God is born of sacrifice and pain. The God of resurrection demands nothing, for He does not will to take away. He does not require obedience, for obedience implies submission. He would only have you learn your will and follow it, not in the spirit of sacrifice and submission, but in the gladness of freedom.

6. Resurrection must compel your allegiance gladly, because it is the symbol of joy. Its whole compelling power lies in the fact that it represents what you want to be. The freedom to leave behind everything that hurts you and humbles you and frightens you cannot be thrust upon you, but it can be offered you through the grace of God. And you can accept it by His grace, for God is gracious to His Son, accepting him without question as His Own. Who, then, is *your* own? The Father has given you all that is His, and He Himself is yours with them. Guard them in their resurrection, for otherwise you will not awake in God, safely surrounded by what is yours forever.

9. You will awaken to your own call, for the Call to awake is within you. If I live in you, you are awake. Yet you must see the works I do through you, or you will not perceive that I have done them unto you. Do not set limits on what you believe I can do through you, or you will not accept what I can do *for* you. Yet it is done already, and unless you give all that you have received you will not know that your redeemer liveth, and that you have awakened with him. Redemption is recognized only by sharing it.

10. God's Son *is* saved. Bring only this awareness to the Sonship, and you will have a part in the redemption as valuable as mine. For your part must be like mine if you learn it of me. If you believe that yours is limited, you are limiting mine. There is no order of difficulty in miracles because all of God's Sons are of equal value, and their equality is their oneness. The whole power of God is in every part of Him, and nothing contradictory to His Will is either great or small. What does not exist has no size and no measure. To God all things are possible. And to Christ it is given to be like the Father.

VII. The Condition of Reality

1. The world as you perceive it cannot have been created by the Father, for the world is not as you see it. God created only the eternal, and everything you see is perishable. Therefore, there must be another world that you do not see. The Bible speaks of a new Heaven and

a new earth, yet this cannot be literally true, for the eternal are not re-created. To perceive anew is merely to perceive again, implying that before, or in the interval between, you were not perceiving at all. What, then, is the world that awaits your perception when you see it?

2. Every loving thought that the Son of God ever had is eternal. The loving thoughts his mind perceives in this world are the world's only reality. They are still perceptions, because he still believes that he is separate. Yet they are eternal because they are loving. And being loving they are like the Father, and therefore cannot die. The real world can actually be perceived. All that is necessary is a willingness to perceive nothing else. For if you perceive both good and evil, you are accepting both the false and the true and making no distinction between them.

3. The ego may see some good, but never only good. That is why its perceptions are so variable. It does not reject goodness entirely, for that you could not accept. But it always adds something that is not real to the real, thus confusing illusion and reality. For perceptions cannot be partly true. If you believe in truth and illusion, you cannot tell which is true. To establish your personal autonomy you tried to create unlike your Father, believing that what you made is capable of being unlike Him. Yet everything true *is* like Him. Perceiving only the real world will lead you to the real Heaven, because it will make you capable of understanding it.

4. The perception of goodness is not knowledge, but the denial of the opposite of goodness enables you to recognize a condition in which opposites do not exist. And this *is* the condition of knowledge. Without this awareness you have not met its conditions, and until you do you will not know it is yours already. You have made many ideas that you have placed between yourself and your Creator, and these beliefs are the world as you perceive it. Truth is not absent here, but it is obscure. You do not know the difference between what you have made and what God created, and so you do not know the difference between what you have made and what *you* have created. To believe that you can perceive the real world is to believe that you can know yourself. You can know God because it is His Will to be known. The real world is all that the Holy Spirit has saved for you out of what you have made, and to perceive only this is salvation, because it is the recognition that reality is only what is true.

VIII. The Problem and the Answer

1. This is a very simple course. Perhaps you do not feel you need a course which, in the end, teaches that only reality is true. But do you

believe it? When you perceive the real world, you will recognize that you did not believe it. Yet the swiftness with which your new and only real perception will be translated into knowledge will leave you but an instant to realize that this alone is true. And then everything you made will be forgotten; the good and the bad, the false and the true. For as Heaven and earth become one, even the real world will vanish from your sight. The end of the world is not its destruction, but its translation into Heaven. The reinterpretation of the world is the transfer of all perception to knowledge.

3. You do not know the meaning of anything you perceive. Not one thought you hold is wholly true. The recognition of this is your firm beginning. You are not misguided; you have accepted no guide at all. Instruction in perception is your great need, for you understand nothing. Recognize this but do not accept it, for understanding is your inheritance. Perceptions are learned, and you are not without a Teacher. Yet your willingness to learn of Him depends on your willingness to question everything you learned of yourself, for you who learned amiss should not be your own teacher.

4. No one can withhold truth except from himself. Yet God will not refuse you the Answer He gave. Ask, then, for what is yours, but which you did not make, and do not defend yourself against truth. You made the problem God has answered. Ask yourself, therefore, but one simple question:

Do I want the problem or do I want the answer?

Decide for the answer and you will have it, for you will see it as it is, and it is yours already.

5. You may complain that this course is not sufficiently specific for you to understand and use. Yet perhaps you have not done what it specifically advocates. This is not a course in the play of ideas, but in their practical application. Nothing could be more specific than to be told that if you ask you will receive. The Holy Spirit will answer every specific problem as long as you believe that problems are specific. His answer is both many and one, as long as you believe that the one is many. You may be afraid of His specificity, for fear of what you think it will demand of you. Yet only by asking will you learn that nothing of God demands anything of you. God gives; He does not take. When you refuse to ask, it is because you believe that asking is taking rather than sharing.

9. Ask anything of God's Son and his Father will answer you, for Christ is not deceived in His Father and His Father is not deceived in

Him. Do not, then, be deceived in your brother, and see only his loving thoughts as his reality, for by denying that his mind is split you will heal yours. Accept him as his Father accepts him and heal him unto Christ, for Christ is his healing and yours. Christ is the Son of God Who is in no way separate from His Father, Whose every thought is as loving as the Thought of His Father by which He was created. Be not deceived in God's Son, for thereby you must be deceived in yourself. And being deceived in yourself you are deceived in your Father, in Whom no deceit is possible.

QUESTION 24. What are the characteristics of your perceptions of the real world, and why do these perceptions lead to awakening in Heaven?

Chapter 12. THE HOLY SPIRIT'S CURRICULUM

I. The Judgment of the Holy Spirit

1. You have been told not to make error real, and the way to do this is very simple. If you want to believe in error, you would have to make it real because it is not true. But truth is real in its own right, and to believe in truth *you do not have to do anything.* Understand that you do not respond to anything directly, but to your interpretation of it. Your interpretation thus becomes the justification for the response. That is why analyzing the motives of others is hazardous to you. If you decide that someone is really trying to attack you or desert you or enslave you, you will respond as if he had actually done so, having made his error real to you. To interpret error is to give it power, and having done this you will overlook truth.

2. The analysis of ego motivation is very complicated, very obscuring, and never without your own ego involvement. The whole process represents a clear-cut attempt to demonstrate your own ability to understand what you perceive. This is shown by the fact that you react to your interpretations as if they were correct. You may then control your reactions behaviorally, but not emotionally. This would obviously be a split or an attack on the integrity of your mind, pitting one level within it against another.

3. There is but one interpretation of motivation that makes any sense. And because it is the Holy Spirit's judgment it requires no effort at all on your part. Every loving thought is true. Everything else is an appeal for healing and help, regardless of the form it takes. Can anyone be justified in responding with anger to a brother's plea for help? No response can be appropriate except the willingness to give it to him, for this and only this is what he is asking for. Offer him anything else, and you are assuming the right to attack his reality by interpreting it as you see fit. Perhaps the danger of this to your own mind is not yet fully apparent. If you believe that an appeal for help is something else you will react to something else. Your response will therefore be inappropriate to reality as it is, but not to your perception of it.

6. Only appreciation is an appropriate response to your brother. Gratitude is due him for both his loving thoughts and his appeals for help, for both are capable of bringing love into your awareness if you perceive them truly. And all your sense of strain comes from your attempts not to do just this. How simple, then, is God's plan for

salvation. There is but one response to reality, for reality evokes no conflict at all. There is but one Teacher of reality, Who understands what it is. He does not change His Mind about reality because reality does not change. Although your interpretations of reality are meaningless in your divided state, His remain consistently true. He gives them to you because they are *for* you. Do not attempt to "help" a brother in your way, for you cannot help yourself. But hear his call for the Help of God, and you will recognize your own need for the Father.

7. Your interpretations of your brother's needs are your interpretation of yours. By giving help you are asking for it, and if you perceive but one need in yourself you will be healed. For you will recognize God's Answer as you want It to be, and if you want It in truth, It will be truly yours. Every appeal you answer in the Name of Christ brings the remembrance of your Father closer to your awareness. For the sake of your need, then, hear every call for help as what it is, so God can answer *you*.

8. By applying the Holy Spirit's interpretation of the reactions of others more and more consistently, you will gain an increasing awareness that His criteria are equally applicable to you. For to recognize fear is not enough to escape from it, although the recognition is necessary to demonstrate the need for escape. The Holy Spirit must still translate the fear into truth. If you were left with the fear, once you had recognized it, you would have taken a step away from reality, not towards it. Yet we have repeatedly emphasized the need to recognize fear and face it without disguise as a crucial step in the undoing of the ego. Consider how well the Holy Spirit's interpretation of the motives of others will serve you then. Having taught you to accept only loving thoughts in others and to regard everything else as an appeal for help, He has taught you that fear itself is an appeal for help. This is what recognizing fear really means. If you do not protect it, He will reinterpret it. That is the ultimate value in learning to perceive attack as a call for love. We have already learned that fear and attack are inevitably associated. If only attack produces fear, and if you see attack as the call for help that it is, the unreality of fear must dawn on you. For fear *is* a call for love, in unconscious recognition of what has been denied.

9. Fear is a symptom of your own deep sense of loss. If when you perceive it in others you learn to supply the loss, the basic cause of fear is removed. Thereby you teach yourself that fear does not exist in you. The means for removing it is in yourself, and you have demonstrated this by giving it. Fear and love are the only emotions of which you are capable. One is false, for it was made out of denial; and denial depends

on the belief in what is denied for its own existence. By interpreting fear correctly as a positive affirmation of the underlying belief it masks, you are undermining its perceived usefulness by rendering it useless. Defenses that do not work at all are automatically discarded. If you raise what fear conceals to clear-cut unequivocal predominance, fear becomes meaningless. You have denied its power to conceal love, which was its only purpose. The veil that you have drawn across the face of love has disappeared.

10. If you would look upon love, which *is* the world's reality, how could you do better than to recognize, in *every* defense against it, the underlying appeal *for* it? And how could you better learn of its reality than by answering the appeal for it by giving it? The Holy Spirit's interpretation of fear does dispel it, for the awareness of truth cannot be denied. Thus does the Holy Spirit replace fear with love and translate error into truth. And thus will you learn of Him how to replace your dream of separation with the fact of unity. For the separation is only the denial of union, and correctly interpreted, attests to your eternal knowledge that union is true.

II. The Way to Remember God

1. Miracles are merely the translation of denial into truth. If to love oneself is to heal oneself, those who are sick do not love themselves. Therefore, they are asking for the love that would heal them, but which they are denying to themselves. If they knew the truth about themselves they could not be sick. The task of the miracle worker thus becomes *to deny the denial of truth*. The sick must heal themselves, for the truth is in them. Yet having obscured it, the light in another mind must shine into theirs because that light *is* theirs.

2. The light in them shines as brightly regardless of the density of the fog that obscures it. If you give no power to the fog to obscure the light, it has none. For it has power only if the Son of God gives power to it. He must himself withdraw that power, remembering that all power is of God. You can remember this for all the Sonship. Do not allow your brother not to remember, for his forgetfulness is yours. But your remembering is his, for God cannot be remembered alone. *This is what you have forgotten.* To perceive the healing of your brother as the healing of yourself is thus the way to remember God. For you forgot your brothers with Him, and God's Answer to your forgetting is but the way to remember.

3. Perceive in sickness but another call for love, and offer your brother what he believes he cannot offer himself. Whatever the sickness, there

is but one remedy. You will be made whole as you make whole, for to perceive in sickness the appeal for health is to recognize in hatred the call for love. And to give a brother what he really wants is to offer it unto yourself, for your Father wills you to know your brother as yourself. Answer his call for love, and yours is answered. Healing is the Love of Christ for His Father and for Himself.

7. A little while and you will see me, for I am not hidden because *you* are hiding. I will awaken you as surely as I awakened myself, for I awoke for you. In my resurrection is your release. Our mission is to escape from crucifixion, not from redemption. Trust in my help, for I did not walk alone, and I will walk with you as our Father walked with me. Do you not know that I walked with Him in peace? And does not that mean that peace goes with *us* on the journey?

8. There is no fear in perfect love. We will but be making perfect to you what is already perfect in you. You do not fear the unknown but the known. You will not fail in your mission because I did not fail in mine. Give me but a little trust in the name of the complete trust I have in you, and we will easily accomplish the goal of perfection together. For perfection *is*, and cannot be denied. To deny the denial of perfection is not so difficult as to deny truth, and what we can accomplish together will be believed when you see it as accomplished.

9. You who have tried to banish love have not succeeded, but you who choose to banish fear must succeed. The Lord is with you, but you know it not. Yet your Redeemer liveth, and abideth in you in the peace out of which He was created. Would you not exchange this awareness for the awareness of fear? When we have overcome fear—not by hiding it, not by minimizing it, and not by denying its full import in any way—this is what you will really see. You cannot lay aside the obstacles to real vision without looking upon them, for to lay aside means to judge against. If you will look, the Holy Spirit will judge, and He will judge truly. Yet He cannot shine away what you keep hidden, for you have not offered it to Him and He cannot take it from you.

10. We are therefore embarking on an organized, well-structured and carefully planned program aimed at learning how to offer to the Holy Spirit everything you do not want. He knows what to do with it. You do not understand how to use what He knows. Whatever is given Him that is not of God is gone. Yet you must look at it yourself in perfect willingness, for otherwise His knowledge remains useless to you. Surely He will not fail to help you, since help is His only purpose. Do you not have greater reason for fearing the world as you perceive it, than for looking at the cause of fear and letting it go forever?

III. The Investment in Reality

1. I once asked you to sell all you have and give to the poor and follow me. This is what I meant: If you have no investment in anything in this world, you can teach the poor where their treasure is. The poor are merely those who have invested wrongly, and they are poor indeed! Because they are in need it is given you to help them, since you are among them. Consider how perfectly your lesson would be learned if you were unwilling to share their poverty. For poverty is lack, and there is but one lack since there is but one need.

2. Suppose a brother insists on having you do something you think you do not want to do. His very insistence should tell you that he believes salvation lies in it. If you insist on refusing and experience a quick response of opposition, you are believing that your salvation lies in *not* doing it. You, then, are making the same mistake he is, and are making his error real to both of you. Insistence means investment, and what you invest in is always related to your notion of salvation. The question is always twofold; first, *what* is to be saved? And second, *how* can it be saved?

3. Whenever you become angry with a brother, for whatever reason, you are believing that the ego is to be saved, and to be saved by attack. If he attacks, you are agreeing with this belief; and if you attack, you are reinforcing it. *Remember that those who attack are poor.* Their poverty asks for gifts, not for further impoverishment. You who could help them are surely acting destructively if you accept their poverty as yours. If you had not invested as they had, it would never occur to you to overlook their need.

4. *Recognize what does not matter*, and if your brothers ask you for something "outrageous," do it *because* it does not matter. Refuse, and your opposition establishes that it does matter to you. It is only you, therefore, who have made the request outrageous, and every request of a brother is for you. Why would you insist in denying him? For to do so is to deny yourself and impoverish both. He is asking for salvation, as you are. Poverty is of the ego, and never of God. No "outrageous" requests can be made of one who recognizes what is valuable and wants to accept nothing else.

6. To identify with the ego is to attack yourself and make yourself poor. That is why everyone who identifies with the ego feels deprived. What he experiences then is depression or anger, because what he did was to exchange Self-love for self-hate, making him afraid of himself. He does not realize this. Even if he is fully aware of anxiety he does not perceive its source as his own ego identification, and he always tries to

handle it by making some sort of insane "arrangement" with the world. He always perceives this world as outside himself, for this is crucial to his adjustment. He does not realize that he makes this world, for there is no world outside of him.

7. If only the loving thoughts of God's Son are the world's reality, the real world must be in his mind. His insane thoughts, too, must be in his mind, but an internal conflict of this magnitude he cannot tolerate. A split mind is endangered, and the recognition that it encompasses completely opposed thoughts within itself is intolerable. Therefore the mind projects the split, not the reality. Everything you perceive as the outside world is merely your attempt to maintain your ego identification, for everyone believes that identification is salvation. Yet consider what has happened, for thoughts do have consequences to the thinker. You have become at odds with the world as you perceive it, because you think it is antagonistic to you. This is a necessary consequence of what you have done. You have projected outward what is antagonistic to what is inward, and therefore you would have to perceive it this way. That is why you must realize that your hatred is in your mind and not outside it before you can get rid of it; and why you must get rid of it before you can perceive the world as it really is.

9. The world you perceive is a world of separation. Perhaps you are willing to accept even death to deny your Father. Yet He would not have it so, and so it is not so. You still cannot will against Him, and that is why you have no control over the world you made. It is not a world of will because it is governed by the desire to be unlike God, and this desire is not will. The world you made is therefore totally chaotic, governed by arbitrary and senseless "laws," and without meaning of any kind. For it is made out of what you do not want, projected from your mind because you are afraid of it. Yet this world is only in the mind of its maker, along with his real salvation. Do not believe it is outside of yourself, for only by recognizing where it is will you gain control over it. For you do have control over your mind, since the mind is the mechanism of decision.

QUESTION 25. Is the world outside your mind or inside your mind?

IV. Seeking and Finding

1. The ego is certain that love is dangerous, and this is always its central teaching. It never puts it this way; on the contrary, everyone who believes that the ego is salvation seems to be intensely engaged in the search for love. Yet the ego, though encouraging the search for love

very actively, makes one proviso; do not find it. Its dictates, then, can be summed up simply as: "Seek and do *not* find." This is the one promise the ego holds out to you, and the one promise it will keep. For the ego pursues its goal with fanatic insistence, and its judgment, though severely impaired, is completely consistent.

4. Do you realize that the ego must set you on a journey which cannot but lead to a sense of futility and depression? To seek and not to find is hardly joyous. Is this the promise you would keep? The Holy Spirit offers you another promise, and one that will lead to joy. For His promise is always, "Seek and you *will* find," and under His guidance you cannot be defeated. His is the journey to accomplishment, and the goal He sets before you He will give you. For He will never deceive God's Son whom He loves with the Love of the Father.

V. The Sane Curriculum

1. Only love is strong because it is undivided. The strong do not attack because they see no need to do so. Before the idea of attack can enter your mind, you must have perceived yourself as weak. Because you attacked yourself and believed that the attack was effective, you behold yourself as weakened. No longer perceiving yourself and your brothers as equal, and regarding yourself as weaker, you attempt to "equalize" the situation you made. You use attack to do so because you believe that attack was successful in weakening you.

2. That is why the recognition of your own invulnerability is so important to the restoration of your sanity. For if you accept your invulnerability, you are recognizing that attack has no effect. Although you have attacked yourself, you will be demonstrating that nothing really happened. Therefore, by attacking you have not done anything. Once you realize this you will no longer see any sense in attack, for it manifestly does not work and cannot protect you. Yet the recognition of your invulnerability has more than negative value. If your attacks on yourself have failed to weaken you, you are still strong. You therefore have no need to "equalize" the situation to establish your strength.

3. You will never realize the utter uselessness of attack except by recognizing that your attack on yourself has no effects. For others do react to attack if they perceive it, and if you are trying to attack them you will be unable to avoid interpreting this as reinforcement. The only place you can cancel out all reinforcement is in yourself. For you are always the first point of your attack, and if this has never been, it has no consequences.

4. The Holy Spirit's Love is your strength, for yours is divided and therefore not real. You cannot trust your own love when you attack it. You cannot learn of perfect love with a split mind, because a split mind has made itself a poor learner. You tried to make the separation eternal, because you wanted to retain the characteristics of creation, but with your own content. Yet creation is not of you, and poor learners do need special teaching.

9. Your learning potential, properly understood, is limitless because it will lead you to God. You can teach the way to Him and learn it, if you follow the Teacher Who knows the way to Him and understands His curriculum for learning it. The curriculum is totally unambiguous, because the goal is not divided and the means and the end are in complete accord. You need offer only undivided attention. Everything else will be given you. For you really want to learn aright, and nothing can oppose the decision of God's Son. His learning is as unlimited as he is.

VI. The Vision of Christ

1. The ego is trying to teach you how to gain the whole world and lose your own soul. The Holy Spirit teaches that you cannot lose your soul and there is no gain in the world, for of itself it profits nothing. To invest without profit is surely to impoverish yourself, and the overhead is high. Not only is there no profit in the investment, but the cost to you is enormous. For this investment costs you the world's reality by denying yours, and gives you nothing in return. You cannot sell your soul, but you can sell your awareness of it. You cannot perceive your soul, but you will not know it while you perceive something else as more valuable.

2. The Holy Spirit is your strength because He knows nothing but the spirit as you. He is perfectly aware that you do not know yourself, and perfectly aware of how to teach you to remember what you are. Because He loves you, He will gladly teach you what He loves, for He wills to share it. Remembering you always, He cannot let you forget your worth. For the Father never ceases to remind Him of His Son, and He never ceases to remind His Son of the Father. God is in your memory because of Him. You chose to forget your Father but you do not really want to do so, and therefore you can decide otherwise. As it was my decision, so is it yours.

3. You do not want the world. The only thing of value in it is whatever part of it you look upon with love. This gives it the only reality it will ever have. Its value is not in itself, but yours is in you. As self-value

comes from self-extension, so does the perception of self-value come from the extension of loving thoughts outward. Make the world real unto yourself, for the real world is the gift of the Holy Spirit, and so it belongs to you.

4. Correction is for all who cannot see. To open the eyes of the blind is the Holy Spirit's mission, for He knows that they have not lost their vision, but merely sleep. He would awaken them from the sleep of forgetting to the remembering of God. Christ's eyes are open, and He will look upon whatever you see with love if you accept His vision as yours. The Holy Spirit keeps the vision of Christ for every Son of God who sleeps. In His sight the Son of God is perfect, and He longs to share His vision with you. He will show you the real world because God gave you Heaven. Through Him your Father calls His Son to remember. The awakening of His Son begins with his investment in the real world, and by this he will learn to re-invest in himself. For reality is one with the Father and the Son, and the Holy Spirit blesses the real world in Their Name.

5. When you have seen this real world, as you will surely do, you will remember Us. Yet you must learn the cost of sleeping, and refuse to pay it. Only then will you decide to awaken. And then the real world will spring to your sight, for Christ has never slept. He is waiting to be seen, for He has never lost sight of you. He looks quietly on the real world, which He would share with you because He knows of the Father's Love for Him. And knowing this, He would give you what is yours. In perfect peace He waits for you at His Father's altar, holding out the Father's Love to you in the quiet light of the Holy Spirit's blessing. For the Holy Spirit will lead everyone home to his Father, where Christ waits as his Self.

6. Every child of God is one in Christ, for his being is in Christ as Christ's is in God. Christ's Love for you is His Love for His Father, which He knows because He knows His Father's Love for Him. When the Holy Spirit has at last led you to Christ at the altar to His Father, perception fuses into knowledge because perception has become so holy that its transfer to holiness is merely its natural extension. Love transfers to love without any interference, for the two are one. As you perceive more and more common elements in all situations, the transfer of training under the Holy Spirit's guidance increases and becomes generalized. Gradually you learn to apply it to everyone and everything, for its applicability is universal. When this has been accomplished, perception and knowledge have become so similar that they share the unification of the laws of God.

7. What is one cannot be perceived as separate, and the denial of the separation is the reinstatement of knowledge. At the altar of God, the holy perception of God's Son becomes so enlightened that light streams into it, and the spirit of God's Son shines in the Mind of the Father and becomes one with it. Very gently does God shine upon Himself, loving the extension of Himself that is His Son. The world has no purpose as it blends into the purpose of God. For the real world has slipped quietly into Heaven, where everything eternal in it has always been. There the Redeemer and the redeemed join in perfect love of God and of each other. Heaven is your home, and being in God it must also be in you.

VII. Looking Within

9. The power of decision is your one remaining freedom as a prisoner of this world. You can decide to see it right. What you made of it is not its reality, for its reality is only what you give it. You cannot really give anything but love to anyone or anything, nor can you really receive anything but love from them. If you think you have received anything else, it is because you have looked within and thought you saw the power to give something else within yourself. It was only this decision that determined what you found, for it was the decision for what you sought.

10. You are afraid of me because you looked within and are afraid of what you saw. Yet you could not have seen reality, for the reality of your mind is the loveliest of God's creations. Coming only from God, its power and grandeur could only bring you peace *if you really looked upon it*. If you are afraid, it is because you saw something that is not there. Yet in that same place you could have looked upon me and all your brothers, in the perfect safety of the Mind which created us. For we are there in the peace of the Father, Who wills to extend His peace through you.

11. When you have accepted your mission to extend peace you will find peace, for by making it manifest you will see it. Its holy witnesses will surround you because you called upon them, and they will come to you. I have heard your call and I have answered it, but you will not look upon me nor hear the answer that you sought. That is because you do not yet want *only* that. Yet as I become more real to you, you will learn that you do want only that. And you will see me as you look within, and we will look upon the real world together. Through the eyes of Christ, only the real world exists and only the real world can be

seen. As you decide so will you see. And all that you see but witnesses to your decision.

12. When you look within and see me, it will be because you have decided to manifest truth. And as you manifest it you will see it both without and within. You will see it without *because* you saw it first within. Everything you behold without is a judgment of what you beheld within. If it is your judgment it will be wrong, for judgment is not your function. If it is the judgment of the Holy Spirit it will be right, for judgment *is* His function. You share His function only by judging as He does, reserving no judgment at all for yourself. You will judge against yourself, but He will judge *for* you.

QUESTION 26. What enables you to see the real world of loving thoughts, and what are the various results of having the vision of the real world?

VIII. The Attraction of Love for Love

4. Because of your Father's Love you can never forget Him, for no one can forget what God Himself placed in his memory. You can deny it, but you cannot lose it. A Voice will answer every question you ask, and a vision will correct the perception of everything you see. For what you have made invisible is the only truth, and what you have not heard is the only Answer. God would reunite you with yourself, and did not abandon you in your distress. You are waiting only for Him, and do not know it. Yet His memory shines in your mind and cannot be obliterated. It is no more past than future, being forever always.

5. You have but to ask for this memory, and you will remember. Yet the memory of God cannot shine in a mind that has obliterated it and wants to keep it so. For the memory of God can dawn only in a mind that chooses to remember, and that has relinquished the insane desire to control reality. You who cannot even control yourself should hardly aspire to control the universe. But look upon what you have made of it, and rejoice that it is not so.

6. Son of God, be not content with nothing! What is not real cannot be seen and has no value. God could not offer His Son what has no value, nor could His Son receive it. You were redeemed the instant you thought you had deserted Him. Everything you made has never been, and is invisible because the Holy Spirit does not see it. Yet what He does see is yours to behold, and through His vision your perception is healed. You have made invisible the only truth that this world holds. Valuing nothing, you have sought nothing. By making nothing real to you, you

have seen it. *But it is not there.* And Christ is invisible to you because of what you have made visible to yourself.

7.   Yet it does not matter how much distance you have tried to interpose between your awareness and truth. God's Son can be seen because his vision is shared. The Holy Spirit looks upon him, and sees nothing else in you. What is invisible to you is perfect in His sight, and encompasses all of it. He has remembered you because He forgot not the Father. You looked upon the unreal and found despair. Yet by seeking the unreal, what else could you find? The unreal world *is* a thing of despair, for it can never be. And you who share God's Being with Him could never be content without reality. What God did not give you has no power over you, and the attraction of love for love remains irresistible. For it is the function of love to unite all things unto itself, and to hold all things together by extending its wholeness.

8.   The real world was given you by God in loving exchange for the world you made and the world you see. Only take it from the hand of Christ and look upon it. Its reality will make everything else invisible, for beholding it is total perception. And as you look upon it you will remember that it was always so. Nothingness will become invisible, for you will at last have seen truly. Redeemed perception is easily translated into knowledge, for only perception is capable of error and perception has never been. Being corrected it gives place to knowledge, which is forever the only reality. The Atonement is but the way back to what was never lost. Your Father could not cease to love His Son.

Chapter 13. THE GUILTLESS WORLD

II. The Guiltless Son of God

1. The ultimate purpose of projection is always to get rid of guilt. Yet, characteristically, the ego attempts to get rid of guilt from its viewpoint only, for much as the ego wants to retain guilt *you* find it intolerable, since guilt stands in the way of your remembering God, Whose pull is so strong that you cannot resist it. On this issue, then, the deepest split of all occurs, for if you are to retain guilt, as the ego insists, *you cannot be you.* Only by persuading you that it is you could the ego possibly induce you to project guilt, and thereby keep it in your mind.

6. I have said that the crucifixion is the symbol of the ego. When it was confronted with the real guiltlessness of God's Son it did attempt to kill him, and the reason it gave was that guiltlessness is blasphemous to God. To the ego, the *ego* is God, and guiltlessness must be interpreted as the final guilt that fully justifies murder. You do not yet understand that any fear you may experience in connection with this course stems ultimately from this interpretation, but if you will consider your reactions to it you will become increasingly convinced that this is so.

7. This course has explicitly stated that its goal for you is happiness and peace. Yet you are afraid of it. You have been told again and again that it will set you free, yet you sometimes react as if it is trying to imprison you. You often dismiss it more readily than you dismiss the ego's thought system. To some extent, then, you must believe that by not learning the course you are protecting yourself. And you do not realize that it is only your guiltlessness that *can* protect you.

8. The Atonement has always been interpreted as the release from guilt, and this is correct if it is understood. Yet even when I interpret it for you, you may reject it and do not accept it for yourself. You have perhaps recognized the futility of the ego and its offerings, but though you do not want them, you may not yet look upon the alternative with gladness. In the extreme, you are afraid of redemption and you believe it will kill you. Make no mistake about the depth of this fear. For you believe that, in the presence of truth, you might turn on yourself and destroy yourself.

9. Little child, this is not so. Your "guilty secret" is nothing, and if you will but bring it to the light, the light will dispel it. And then no dark cloud will remain between you and the remembrance of your Father, for you will remember His guiltless Son, who did not die because he is immortal. And you will see that you were redeemed with him, and

have never been separated from him. In this understanding lies your remembering, for it is the recognition of love without fear. There will be great joy in Heaven on your homecoming, and the joy will be yours. For the redeemed son of man is the guiltless Son of God, and to recognize him *is* your redemption.

III. The Fear of Redemption

1. You may wonder why it is so crucial that you look upon your hatred and realize its full extent. You may also think that it would be easy enough for the Holy Spirit to show it to you, and to dispel it without the need for you to raise it to awareness yourself. Yet there is one more obstacle you have interposed between yourself and the Atonement. We have said that no one will countenance fear if he recognizes it. Yet in your disordered state of mind you are not afraid of fear. You do not like it, but it is not your desire to attack that really frightens you. You are not seriously disturbed by your hostility. You keep it hidden because you are more afraid of what it covers. You could look even upon the ego's darkest cornerstone without fear if you did not believe that, without the ego, you would find within yourself something you fear even more. You are not really afraid of crucifixion. Your real terror is of redemption.
2. Under the ego's dark foundation is the memory of God, and it is of this that you are really afraid. For this memory would instantly restore you to your proper place, and it is this place that you have sought to leave. Your fear of attack is nothing compared to your fear of love. You would be willing to look even upon your savage wish to kill God's Son, if you did not believe that it saves you from love. For this wish caused the separation, and you have protected it because you do not want the separation healed. You realize that, by removing the dark cloud that obscures it, your love for your Father would impel you to answer His Call and leap into Heaven. You believe that attack is salvation because it would prevent you from this. For still deeper than the ego's foundation, and much stronger than it will ever be, is your intense and burning love of God, and His for you. This is what you really want to hide.
3. In honesty, is it not harder for you to say "I love" than "I hate"? You associate love with weakness and hatred with strength, and your own real power seems to you as your real weakness. For you could not control your joyous response to the call of love if you heard it, and the whole world you thought you made would vanish. The Holy Spirit, then, seems to be attacking your fortress, for you would shut out God, and He does not will to be excluded.

4. You have built your whole insane belief system because you think you would be helpless in God's Presence, and you would save yourself from His Love because you think it would crush you into nothingness. You are afraid it would sweep you away from yourself and make you little, because you believe that magnitude lies in defiance, and that attack is grandeur. You think you have made a world God would destroy; and by loving Him, which you do, you would throw this world away, which you *would*. Therefore, you have used the world to cover your love, and the deeper you go into the blackness of the ego's foundation, the closer you come to the Love that is hidden there. *And it is this that frightens you.*

5. You can accept insanity because you made it, but you cannot accept love because you did not. You would rather be a slave of the crucifixion than a Son of God in redemption. Your individual death seems more valuable than your living oneness, for what is given you is not so dear as what you made. You are more afraid of God than of the ego, and love cannot enter where it is not welcome. But hatred can, for it enters of its own volition and cares not for yours.

6. You must look upon your illusions and not keep them hidden, because they do not rest on their own foundation. In concealment they appear to do so, and thus they seem to be self-sustained. This is the fundamental illusion on which the others rest. For beneath them, and concealed as long as they are hidden, is the loving mind that thought it made them in anger. And the pain in this mind is so apparent, when it is uncovered, that its need of healing cannot be denied. Not all the tricks and games you offer it can heal it, for here is the real crucifixion of God's Son.

7. And yet he is not crucified. Here is both his pain and his healing, for the Holy Spirit's vision is merciful and His remedy is quick. Do not hide suffering from His sight, but bring it gladly to Him. Lay before His eternal sanity all your hurt, and let Him heal you. Do not leave any spot of pain hidden from His light, and search your mind carefully for any thoughts you may fear to uncover. For He will heal every little thought you have kept to hurt you and cleanse it of its littleness, restoring it to the magnitude of God.

8. Beneath all the grandiosity you hold so dear is your real call for help. For you call for love to your Father as your Father calls you to Himself. In that place which you have hidden, you will only to unite with the Father, in loving remembrance of Him. You will find this place of truth as you see it in your brothers, for though they may deceive themselves, like you they long for the grandeur that is in them. And perceiving it you will welcome it, and it will be yours. For grandeur is

the right of God's Son, and no illusions can satisfy him or save him from what he is. Only his love is real, and he will be content only with his reality.

9. Save him from his illusions that you may accept the magnitude of your Father in peace and joy. But exempt no one from your love, or you will be hiding a dark place in your mind where the Holy Spirit is not welcome. And thus you will exempt yourself from His healing power, for by not offering total love you will not be healed completely. Healing must be as complete as fear, for love cannot enter where there is one spot of fear to mar its welcome.

10. You who prefer separation to sanity cannot obtain it in your right mind. You were at peace until you asked for special favor. And God did not give it for the request was alien to Him, and you could not ask this of a Father Who truly loved His Son. Therefore you made of Him an unloving father, demanding of Him what only such a father could give. And the peace of God's Son was shattered, for he no longer understood his Father. He feared what he had made, but still more did he fear his real Father, having attacked his own glorious equality with Him.

11. In peace he needed nothing and asked for nothing. In war he demanded everything and found nothing. For how could the gentleness of love respond to his demands, except by departing in peace and returning to the Father? If the Son did not wish to remain in peace, he could not remain at all. For a darkened mind cannot live in the light, and it must seek a place of darkness where it can believe it is where it is not. God did not allow this to happen. Yet you demanded that it happen, and therefore believed that it was so.

QUESTION 27. Why are you attracted to love and yet afraid of both love and redemption, and what happened the first time you requested "special favor" (special love) from God?

V. The Two Emotions

1. I have said you have but two emotions, love and fear. One is changeless but continually exchanged, being offered by the eternal to the eternal. In this exchange it is extended, for it increases as it is given. The other has many forms, for the content of individual illusions differs greatly. Yet they have one thing in common; they are all insane. They are made of sights that are not seen, and sounds that are not heard. They make up a private world that cannot be shared. For they are

meaningful only to their maker, and so they have no meaning at all. In this world their maker moves alone, for only he perceives them.

8. Vision depends on light. You cannot see in darkness. Yet in darkness, in the private world of sleep, you see in dreams although your eyes are closed. And it is here that what you see you made. But let the darkness go and all you made you will no longer see, for sight of it depends upon denying vision. Yet from denying vision it does not follow you cannot see. But this is what denial does, for by it you accept insanity, believing you can make a private world and rule your own perception. Yet for this, light must be excluded. Dreams disappear when light has come and you can see.

9. Do not seek vision through your eyes, for you made your way of seeing that you might see in darkness, and in this you are deceived. Beyond this darkness, and yet still within you, is the vision of Christ, Who looks on all in light. Your "vision" comes from fear, as His from love. And He sees for you, as your witness to the real world. He is the Holy Spirit's manifestation, looking always on the real world, and calling forth its witnesses and drawing them to you. He loves what He sees within you, and He would extend it. And He will not return unto the Father until He has extended your perception even unto Him. And there perception is no more, for He has returned you to the Father with Him.

10. You have but two emotions, and one you made and one was given you. Each is a way of seeing, and different worlds arise from their different sights. See through the vision that is given you, for through Christ's vision He beholds Himself. And seeing what He is, He knows His Father. Beyond your darkest dreams He sees God's guiltless Son within you, shining in perfect radiance that is undimmed by your dreams. And this *you* will see as you look with Him, for His vision is His gift of love to you, given Him of the Father for you.

11. The Holy Spirit is the light in which Christ stands revealed. And all who would behold Him can see Him, for they have asked for light. Nor will they see Him alone, for He is no more alone than they are. Because they saw the Son, they have risen in Him to the Father. And all this will they understand, because they looked within and saw beyond the darkness the Christ in them, and recognized Him. In the sanity of His vision they looked upon themselves with love, seeing themselves as the Holy Spirit sees them. And with this vision of the truth in them came all the beauty of the world to shine upon them.

VI. Finding the Present

1. To perceive truly is to be aware of all reality through the awareness of your own. But for this no illusions can rise to meet your sight, for reality leaves no room for any error. This means that you perceive a brother only as you see him *now*. His past has no reality in the present, so you cannot see it. Your past reactions to him are also not there, and if it is to them that you react, you see but an image of him that you made and cherish instead of him. In your questioning of illusions, ask yourself if it is really sane to perceive what was as now. If you remember the past as you look upon your brother, you will be unable to perceive the reality that is now.

2. You consider it "natural" to use your past experience as the reference point from which to judge the present. Yet this is *unnatural* because it is delusional. When you have learned to look on everyone with no reference at all to the past, either his or yours as you perceived it, you will be able to learn from what you see *now*. For the past can cast no shadow to darken the present, *unless you are afraid of light*. And only if you are would you choose to bring darkness with you, and by holding it in your mind, see it as a dark cloud that shrouds your brothers and conceals their reality from your sight.

6. Judgment and condemnation are behind you, and unless you bring them with you, you will see that you are free of them. Look lovingly upon the present, for it holds the only things that are forever true. All healing lies within it because its continuity is real. It extends to all aspects of the Sonship at the same time, and thus enables them to reach each other. The present is before time was, and will be when time is no more. In it are all things that are eternal, and they are one. Their continuity is timeless and their communication is unbroken, for they are not separated by the past. Only the past can separate, and it is nowhere.

8. Now is the time of salvation, for now is the release from time. Reach out to all your brothers, and touch them with the touch of Christ. In timeless union with them is your continuity, unbroken because it is wholly shared. God's guiltless Son is only light. There is no darkness in him anywhere, for he is whole. Call all your brothers to witness to his wholeness, as I am calling you to join with me. Each voice has a part in the song of redemption, the hymn of gladness and thanksgiving for the light to the Creator of light. The holy light that shines forth from God's Son is the witness that his light is of his Father.

10. Child of Light, you know not that the light is in you. Yet you will find it through its witnesses, for having given light to them they will return it. Each one you see in light brings your light closer to your awareness. Love always leads to love. The sick, who ask for love, are grateful for it, and in their joy they shine with holy thanks. And this they offer you who gave them joy. They are your guides to joy, for having received it of you they would keep it. You have established them as guides to peace, for you have made it manifest in them. And seeing it, its beauty calls you home.

11. There is a light that this world cannot give. Yet you can give it, as it was given you. And as you give it, it shines forth to call you from the world and follow it. For this light will attract you as nothing in this world can do. And you will lay aside the world and find another. This other world is bright with love which you have given it. And here will everything remind you of your Father and His holy Son. Light is unlimited, and spreads across this world in quiet joy. All those you brought with you will shine on you, and you will shine on them in gratitude because they brought you here. Your light will join with theirs in power so compelling, that it will draw the others out of darkness as you look on them.

VII. Attainment of the Real World

1. Sit quietly and look upon the world you see, and tell yourself: "The real world is not like this. It has no buildings and there are no streets where people walk alone and separate. There are no stores where people buy an endless list of things they do not need. It is not lit with artificial light, and night comes not upon it. There is no day that brightens and grows dim. There is no loss. Nothing is there but shines, and shines forever."

2. The world you see must be denied, for sight of it is costing you a different kind of vision. *You cannot see both worlds*, for each of them involves a different kind of seeing, and depends on what you cherish. The sight of one is possible because you have denied the other. Both are not true, yet either one will seem as real to you as the amount to which you hold it dear. And yet their power is not the same, because their real attraction to you is unequal.

5. You have been wrong about the world because you have misjudged yourself. From such a twisted reference point, what could you see? All seeing starts with the perceiver, who judges what is true and what is false. And what he judges false he does not see. You who would judge reality cannot see it, for whenever judgment enters reality has slipped away. The out of mind *is* out of sight, because what is denied is there

but is not recognized. Christ is still there, although you know Him not. His Being does not depend upon your recognition. He lives within you in the quiet present, and waits for you to leave the past behind and enter into the world He holds out to you in love.

6.   No one in this distracted world but has seen some glimpses of the other world about him. Yet while he still lays value on his own, he will deny the vision of the other, maintaining that he loves what he loves not, and following not the road that love points out. Love leads so gladly! As you follow Him, you will rejoice that you have found His company, and learned of Him the joyful journey home. You wait but for yourself. To give this sad world over and exchange your errors for the peace of God is but *your* will. And Christ will always offer you the Will of God, in recognition that you share it with Him.

8.   The peace of God passeth your understanding only in the past. Yet here it *is*, and you can understand it *now*. God loves His Son forever, and His Son returns his Father's Love forever. The real world is the way that leads you to remembrance of the one thing that is wholly true and wholly yours. For all else you have lent yourself in time, and it will fade. But this one thing is always yours, being the gift of God unto His Son. Your one reality was given you, and by it God created you as one with Him.

9.   You will first dream of peace, and then awaken to it. Your first exchange of what you made for what you want is the exchange of nightmares for the happy dreams of love. In these lie your true perceptions, for the Holy Spirit corrects the world of dreams, where all perception is. Knowledge needs no correction. Yet the dreams of love lead unto knowledge. In them you see nothing fearful, and because of this they are the welcome that you offer knowledge. Love waits on welcome, not on time, and the real world is but your welcome of what always was. Therefore the call of joy is in it, and your glad response is your awakening to what you have not lost.

QUESTION 28. How are light, vision, and Christ related?

VIII. From Perception to Knowledge

1.   All healing is release from the past. That is why the Holy Spirit is the only Healer. He teaches that the past does not exist, a fact which belongs to the sphere of knowledge, and which therefore no one in the world can know. It would indeed be impossible to be in the world with this knowledge. For the mind that knows this unequivocally knows also it dwells in eternity, and utilizes no perception at all. It therefore does not consider where it is, because the concept "where" does not mean

anything to it. It knows that it is *everywhere*, just as it has *everything*, and forever.

2. The very real difference between perception and knowledge becomes quite apparent if you consider this: There is nothing partial about knowledge. Every aspect is whole, and therefore no aspect is separate. You are an aspect of knowledge, being in the Mind of God, Who knows you. All knowledge must be yours, for in you is all knowledge. Perception, at its loftiest, is never complete. Even the perception of the Holy Spirit, as perfect as perception can be, is without meaning in Heaven. Perception can reach everywhere under His guidance, for the vision of Christ beholds everything in light. Yet no perception, however holy, will last forever.

3. Perfect perception, then, has many elements in common with knowledge, making transfer to it possible. Yet the last step must be taken by God, because the last step in your redemption, which seems to be in the future, was accomplished by God in your creation. The separation has not interrupted it. Creation cannot be interrupted. The separation is merely a faulty formulation of reality, with no effect at all. The miracle, without a function in Heaven, is needful here. Aspects of reality can still be seen, and they will replace aspects of unreality. Aspects of reality can be seen in everything and everywhere. Yet only God can gather them together, by crowning them as one with the final gift of eternity.

4. Apart from the Father and the Son, the Holy Spirit has no function. He is not separate from Either, being in the Mind of Both, and knowing that Mind is One. He is a Thought of God, and God has given Him to you because He has no Thoughts He does not share. His message speaks of timelessness in time, and that is why Christ's vision looks on everything with love. Yet even Christ's vision is not His reality. The golden aspects of reality that spring to light under His loving gaze are partial glimpses of the Heaven that lies beyond them.

5. This is the miracle of creation; *that it is one forever*. Every miracle you offer to the Son of God is but the true perception of one aspect of the whole. Though every aspect *is* the whole, you cannot know this until you see that every aspect is the same, perceived in the same light and therefore one. Everyone seen without the past thus brings you nearer to the end of time by bringing healed and healing sight into the darkness, and enabling the world to see. For light must come into the darkened world to make Christ's vision possible even here. Help Him to give His gift of light to all who think they wander in the darkness, and let Him gather them into His quiet sight that makes them one.

6. They are all the same; all beautiful and equal in their holiness. And He will offer them unto His Father as they were offered unto Him.

There is one miracle, as there is one reality. And every miracle you do contains them all, as every aspect of reality you see blends quietly into the one reality of God. The only miracle that ever was is God's most holy Son, created in the one reality that is his Father. Christ's vision is His gift to you. His Being is His Father's gift to Him.

7. Be you content with healing, for Christ's gift you can bestow, and your Father's gift you cannot lose. Offer Christ's gift to everyone and everywhere, for miracles, offered the Son of God through the Holy Spirit, attune you to reality. The Holy Spirit knows your part in the redemption, and who are seeking you and where to find them. Knowledge is far beyond your individual concern. You who are part of it and all of it need only realize that it is of the Father, not of you. Your role in the redemption leads you to it by re-establishing its oneness in your mind.

8. When you have seen your brothers as yourself you will be released to knowledge, having learned to free yourself through Him Who knows of freedom. Unite with me under the holy banner of His teaching, and as we grow in strength the power of God's Son will move in us, and we will leave no one untouched and no one left alone. And suddenly time will be over, and we will all unite in the eternity of God the Father. The holy light you saw outside yourself, in every miracle you offered to your brothers, will be returned to you. And knowing that the light is in you, your creations will be there with you, as you are in your Father.

IX. The Cloud of Guilt

2. Release from guilt is the ego's whole undoing. *Make no one fearful*, for his guilt is yours, and by obeying the ego's harsh commandments you bring its condemnation on yourself, and you will not escape the punishment it offers those who obey it. The ego rewards fidelity to it with pain, for faith in it *is* pain. And faith can be rewarded only in terms of the belief in which the faith was placed. Faith makes the power of belief, and where it is invested determines its reward. For faith is always given what is treasured, and what is treasured is returned to you.

4. Atonement brings a re-evaluation of everything you cherish, for it is the means by which the Holy Spirit can separate the false and the true, which you have accepted into your mind without distinction. Therefore you cannot value one without the other, and guilt has become as true for you as innocence. You do not believe the Son of God is guiltless because you see the past, and see him not. When you condemn a brother you are saying, "I who was guilty choose to remain so." You have denied his freedom, and by so doing you have denied the

witness unto yours. You could as easily have freed him from the past, and lifted from his mind the cloud of guilt that binds him to it. And in his freedom would have been your own.

6. See no one, then, as guilty, and you will affirm the truth of guiltlessness unto yourself. In every condemnation that you offer the Son of God lies the conviction of your own guilt. If you would have the Holy Spirit make you free of it, accept His offer of Atonement for all your brothers. For so you learn that it is true for you. Remember always that it is impossible to condemn the Son of God in part. Those whom you see as guilty become the witnesses to guilt in you, and you will see it there, for it *is* there until it is undone. Guilt is always in your mind, which has condemned itself. Project it not, for while you do, it cannot be undone. With everyone whom you release from guilt great is the joy in Heaven, where the witnesses to your fatherhood rejoice.

7. Guilt makes you blind, for while you see one spot of guilt within you, you will not see the light. And by projecting it the world seems dark, and shrouded in your guilt. You throw a dark veil over it, and cannot see it because you cannot look within. You are afraid of what you would see there, but it is not there. *The thing you fear is gone.* If you would look within you would see only the Atonement, shining in quiet and in peace upon the altar to your Father.

8. Do not be afraid to look within. The ego tells you all is black with guilt within you, and bids you not to look. Instead, it bids you look upon your brothers, and see the guilt in them. Yet this you cannot do without remaining blind. For those who see their brothers in the dark, and guilty in the dark in which they shroud them, are too afraid to look upon the light within. Within you is not what you believe is there, and what you put your faith in. Within you is the holy sign of perfect faith your Father has in you. He does not value you as you do. He knows Himself, and knows the truth in you. He knows there is no difference, for He knows not of differences. Can you see guilt where God knows there is perfect innocence? You can deny His knowledge, but you cannot change it. Look, then, upon the light He placed within you, and learn that what you feared was there has been replaced with love.

X. Release from Guilt

6. As long as you believe that guilt is justified in any way, in anyone, whatever he may do, you will not look within, where you would always find Atonement. The end of guilt will never come as long as you believe there is a reason for it. For you must learn that guilt is always totally

insane, and has no reason. The Holy Spirit seeks not to dispel reality. If guilt were real, Atonement would not be. The purpose of Atonement is to dispel illusions, not to establish them as real and then forgive them.

7. The Holy Spirit does not keep illusions in your mind to frighten you, and show them to you fearfully to demonstrate what He has saved you from. What He has saved you from is gone. Give no reality to guilt, and see no reason for it. The Holy Spirit does what God would have Him do, and has always done so. He has seen separation, but knows of union. He teaches healing, but He also knows of creation. He would have you see and teach as He does, and through Him. Yet what He knows you do not know, though it is yours.

8. *Now* it is given you to heal and teach, to make what will be *now*. As yet it is not now. The Son of God believes that he is lost in guilt, alone in a dark world where pain is pressing everywhere upon him from without. When he has looked within and seen the radiance there, he will remember how much his Father loves him. And it will seem incredible that he ever thought his Father loved him not, and looked upon him as condemned. The moment that you realize guilt is insane, wholly unjustified and wholly without reason, you will not fear to look upon the Atonement and accept it wholly.

9. You who have been unmerciful to yourself do not remember your Father's Love. And looking without mercy upon your brothers, you do not remember how much you love Him. Yet it is forever true. In shining peace within you is the perfect purity in which you were created. Fear not to look upon the lovely truth in you. Look through the cloud of guilt that dims your vision, and look past darkness to the holy place where you will see the light. The altar to your Father is as pure as He Who raised it to Himself. Nothing can keep from you what Christ would have you see. His Will is like His Father's, and He offers mercy to every child of God, as He would have you do.

10. Release from guilt as you would be released. There is no other way to look within and see the light of love, shining as steadily and as surely as God Himself has always loved His Son. *And as His Son loves Him.* There is no fear in love, for love is guiltless. You who have always loved your Father can have no fear, for any reason, to look within and see your holiness. You cannot be as you believed you were. Your guilt is without reason because it is not in the Mind of God, where you are. And this *is* reason, which the Holy Spirit would restore to you. He would remove only illusions. All else He would have you see. And in Christ's vision He would show you the perfect purity that is forever within God's Son.

11.   You cannot enter into real relationships with any of God's Sons unless you love them all and equally. Love is not special. If you single out part of the Sonship for your love, you are imposing guilt on all your relationships and making them unreal. You can love only as God loves. Seek not to love unlike Him, for there is no love apart from His. Until you recognize that this is true, you will have no idea what love is like. No one who condemns a brother can see himself as guiltless and in the peace of God. If he is guiltless and in peace and sees it not, he is delusional, and has not looked upon himself. To him I say:

> *Behold the Son of God, and look upon his purity and be still. In quiet look upon his holiness, and offer thanks unto his Father that no guilt has ever touched him.*

12.   No illusion that you have ever held against him has touched his innocence in any way. His shining purity, wholly untouched by guilt and wholly loving, is bright within you. Let us look upon him together and love him. For in love of him is your guiltlessness. But look upon yourself, and gladness and appreciation for what you see will banish guilt forever. I thank You, Father, for the purity of Your most holy Son, whom You have created guiltless forever.

13.   Like you, my faith and my belief are centered on what I treasure. The difference is that I love *only* what God loves with me, and because of this I treasure you beyond the value that you set on yourself, even unto the worth that God has placed upon you. I love all that He created, and all my faith and my belief I offer unto it. My faith in you is as strong as all the love I give my Father. My trust in you is without limit, and without the fear that you will hear me not. I thank the Father for your loveliness, and for the many gifts that you will let me offer to the Kingdom in honor of its wholeness that is of God.

14.   Praise be to you who make the Father One with His Own Son. Alone we are all lowly, but together we shine with brightness so intense that none of us alone can even think of it. Before the glorious radiance of the Kingdom guilt melts away, and transformed into kindness will never more be what it was. Every reaction you experience will be so purified that it is fitting as a hymn of praise unto your Father. See only praise of Him in what He has created, for He will never cease His praise of you. United in this praise we stand before the gates of Heaven where we will surely enter in our sinlessness. God loves you. Could I, then, lack faith in you and love Him perfectly?

XI. The Peace of Heaven

3. When we are all united in Heaven, you will value nothing that you value here. For nothing that you value here do you value wholly, and so you do not value it at all. Value is where God placed it, and the value of what God esteems cannot be judged, for it has been established. It is wholly of value. It can merely be appreciated or not. To value it partially is not to know its value. In Heaven is everything God values, and nothing else. Heaven is perfectly unambiguous. Everything is clear and bright, and calls forth one response. There is no darkness and there is no contrast. There is no variation. There is no interruption. There is a sense of peace so deep that no dream in this world has ever brought even a dim imagining of what it is.

QUESTION 29. How would you compare partial awareness with the awareness of wholeness, and if you love everyone except one person whom you see as guilty, what will the result be?

Chapter 14. TEACHING FOR TRUTH

II. The Happy Learner

6. If you would be a happy learner, you must give everything you have learned to the Holy Spirit, to be unlearned for you. And then begin to learn the joyous lessons that come quickly on the firm foundation that truth is true. For what is builded there *is* true, and built on truth. The universe of learning will open up before you in all its gracious simplicity. With truth before you, you will not look back.

7. The happy learner meets the conditions of learning here, as he meets the conditions of knowledge in the Kingdom. All this lies in the Holy Spirit's plan to free you from the past, and open up the way to freedom for you. For truth *is* true. What else could ever be, or ever was? This simple lesson holds the key to the dark door that you believe is locked forever. You made this door of nothing, and behind it *is* nothing. The key is only the light that shines away the shapes and forms and fears of nothing. Accept this key to freedom from the hands of Christ Who gives it to you, that you may join Him in the holy task of bringing light. For, like your brothers, you do not realize the light has come and freed you from the sleep of darkness.

8. Behold your brothers in their freedom, and learn of them how to be free of darkness. The light in you will waken them, and they will not leave you asleep. The vision of Christ is given the very instant that it is perceived. Where everything is clear, it is all holy. The quietness of its simplicity is so compelling that you will realize it is impossible to deny the simple truth. For there is nothing else. God is everywhere, and His Son is in Him with everything. Can he sing the dirge of sorrow when this is true?

III. The Decision for Guiltlessness

4. Each day, each hour and minute, even each second, you are deciding between the crucifixion and the resurrection; between the ego and the Holy Spirit. The ego is the choice for guilt; the Holy Spirit the choice for guiltlessness. The power of decision is all that is yours. What you can decide between is fixed, because there are no alternatives except truth and illusion. And there is no overlap between them, because they are opposites which cannot be reconciled and cannot both be true. You are guilty or guiltless, bound or free, unhappy or happy.

6. No penalty is ever asked of God's Son except by himself and of himself. Every chance given him to heal is another opportunity to

replace darkness with light and fear with love. If he refuses it he binds himself to darkness, because he did not choose to free his brother and enter light with him. By giving power to nothing, he throws away the joyous opportunity to learn that nothing has no power. And by not dispelling darkness, he became afraid of darkness and of light. The joy of learning that darkness has no power over the Son of God is the happy lesson the Holy Spirit teaches, and would have you teach with Him. It is His joy to teach it, as it will be yours.

7. The way to teach this simple lesson is merely this: Guiltlessness is invulnerability. Therefore, make your invulnerability manifest to everyone. Teach him that, whatever he may try to do to you, your perfect freedom from the belief that you can be harmed shows him that he is guiltless. He can do nothing that can hurt you, and by refusing to allow him to think he can, you teach him that the Atonement, which you have accepted for yourself, is also his. There is nothing to forgive. No one can hurt the Son of God. His guilt is wholly without cause, and being without cause, cannot exist.

8. God is the only Cause, and guilt is not of Him. Teach no one he has hurt you, for if you do, you teach yourself that what is not of God has power over you. *The causeless cannot be.* Do not attest to it, and do not foster belief in it in any mind. Remember always that mind is one, and cause is one. You will learn communication with this oneness only when you learn to deny the causeless, and accept the Cause of God as yours. The power that God has given to His Son *is* his, and nothing else can His Son see or choose to look upon without imposing on himself the penalty of guilt, in place of all the happy teaching the Holy Spirit would gladly offer him.

9. Whenever you choose to make decisions for yourself you are thinking destructively, and the decision will be wrong. It will hurt you because of the concept of decision that led to it. It is not true that you can make decisions by yourself or for yourself alone. No thought of God's Son can be separate or isolated in its effects. Every decision is made for the whole Sonship, directed in and out, and influencing a constellation larger than anything you ever dreamed of.

11. It will never happen that you must make decisions for yourself. You are not bereft of help, and Help that knows the answer. Would you be content with little, which is all that you alone can offer yourself, when He Who gives you everything will simply offer it to you? He will never ask what you have done to make you worthy of the gift of God. Ask it not therefore of yourself. Instead, accept His answer, for He knows that you are worthy of everything God wills for you. Do not try to escape the gift of God He so freely and so gladly offers you.

He offers you but what God gave Him for you. You need not decide whether or not you are deserving of it. God knows you are.

12. Would you deny the truth of God's decision, and place your pitiful appraisal of yourself in place of His calm and unswerving value of His Son? Nothing can shake God's conviction of the perfect purity of everything that He created, for it *is* wholly pure. Do not decide against it, for being of Him it must be true. Peace abides in every mind that quietly accepts the plan God set for its Atonement, relinquishing its own. You know not of salvation, for you do not understand it. Make no decisions about what it is or where it lies, but ask the Holy Spirit everything, and leave all decisions to His gentle counsel.

13. The One Who knows the plan of God that God would have you follow can teach you what it is. Only His wisdom is capable of guiding you to follow it. Every decision you undertake alone but signifies that you would define what salvation *is*, and what you would be saved *from*. The Holy Spirit knows that all salvation is escape from guilt. You have no other "enemy," and against this strange distortion of the purity of the Son of God the Holy Spirit is your only Friend. He is the strong protector of the innocence that sets you free. And it is His decision to undo everything that would obscure your innocence from your unclouded mind.

14. Let Him, therefore, be the only Guide that you would follow to salvation. He knows the way, and leads you gladly on it. With Him you will not fail to learn that what God wills for you *is* your will. Without His guidance you will think you know alone, and will decide against your peace as surely as you decided that salvation lay in you alone. Salvation is of Him to Whom God gave it for you. He has not forgotten it. Forget Him not and He will make *every* decision for you, for your salvation and the peace of God in you.

16. Say to the Holy Spirit only, "Decide for me," and it is done. For His decisions are reflections of what God knows about you, and in this light, error of any kind becomes impossible. Why would you struggle so frantically to anticipate all you cannot know, when all knowledge lies behind every decision the Holy Spirit makes for you? Learn of His wisdom and His Love, and teach His answer to everyone who struggles in the dark. For you decide for them and for yourself.

IV. Your Function in the Atonement

3. When you have let all that obscured the truth in your most holy mind be undone for you, and therefore stand in grace before your Father, He will give Himself to you as He has always done. Giving Himself is all He knows, and so it is all knowledge. For what He knows

not cannot be, and therefore cannot be given. Ask not to be forgiven, for this has already been accomplished. Ask, rather, to learn how to forgive, and to restore what always was to your unforgiving mind. Atonement becomes real and visible to those who use it. On earth this is your only function, and you must learn that it is all you want to learn. You will feel guilty till you learn this. For in the end, whatever form it takes, your guilt arises from your failure to fulfill your function in God's Mind with all of yours. Can you escape this guilt by failing to fulfill your function here?

4. You need not understand creation to do what must be done before that knowledge would be meaningful to you. God breaks no barriers; neither did He make them. When you release them they are gone. God will not fail, nor ever has in anything. Decide that God is right and you are wrong about yourself. He created you out of Himself, but still within Him. He knows what you are. Remember that there is no second to Him. There cannot, therefore, be anyone without His Holiness, nor anyone unworthy of His perfect Love. Fail not in your function of loving in a loveless place made out of darkness and deceit, for thus are darkness and deceit undone. Fail not yourself, but instead offer to God and you His blameless Son. For this small gift of appreciation for His Love, God will Himself exchange your gift for His.

6. When you have learned how to decide with God, all decisions become as easy and as right as breathing. There is no effort, and you will be led as gently as if you were being carried down a quiet path in summer. Only your own volition seems to make deciding hard. The Holy Spirit will not delay in answering your every question what to do. He knows. And He will tell you, and then do it for you. You who are tired will find this is more restful than sleep. For you can bring your guilt into sleeping, but not into this.

8. Your task is not to make reality. It is here without your making, but not without you. You who have tried to throw yourself away and valued God so little, hear me speak for Him and for yourself. You cannot understand how much your Father loves you, for there is no parallel in your experience of the world to help you understand it. There is nothing on earth with which it can compare, and nothing you have ever felt apart from Him resembles it ever so faintly. You cannot even give a blessing in perfect gentleness. Would you know of One Who gives forever, and Who knows of nothing except giving?

9. The children of Heaven live in the light of the blessing of their Father, because they know that they are sinless. The Atonement was established as the means of restoring guiltlessness to minds that

have denied it, and thus denied Heaven to themselves. Atonement teaches you the true condition of the Son of God. It does not teach you what you are, or what your Father is. The Holy Spirit, Who remembers this for you, merely teaches you how to remove the blocks that stand between you and what you know. His memory is yours. If you remember what you have made, you are remembering nothing. Remembrance of reality is in Him, and therefore in you.

10. The guiltless and the guilty are totally incapable of understanding one another. Each perceives the other as like himself, making both unable to communicate, because each sees the other unlike the way he sees himself. God can communicate only to the Holy Spirit in your mind, because only He shares the knowledge of what you are with God. And only the Holy Spirit can answer God for you, for only He knows what God is. Everything else that you have placed within your mind cannot exist, for what is not in communication with the Mind of God has never been. Communication with God is life. Nothing without it is at all.

QUESTION 30. What is the importance of your power of decision?

V. The Circle of Atonement

2. Everyone has a special part to play in the Atonement, but the message given to each one is always the same; *God's Son is guiltless.* Each one teaches the message differently, and learns it differently. Yet until he teaches it and learns it, he will suffer the pain of dim awareness that his true function remains unfulfilled in him. The burden of guilt is heavy, but God would not have you bound by it. His plan for your awaking is as perfect as yours is fallible. You know not what you do, but He Who knows is with you. His gentleness is yours, and all the love you share with God He holds in trust for you. He would teach you nothing except how to be happy.

3. Blessed Son of a wholly blessing Father, joy was created for you. Who can condemn whom God has blessed? There is nothing in the Mind of God that does not share His shining innocence. Creation is the natural extension of perfect purity. Your only calling here is to devote yourself, with active willingness, to the denial of guilt in all its forms. To accuse is *not to understand.* The happy learners of the Atonement become the teachers of the innocence that is the right of all that God created. Deny them not what is their due, for you will not withhold it from them alone.

4. The inheritance of the Kingdom is the right of God's Son, given him in his creation. Do not try to steal it from him, or you will ask for guilt and will experience it. Protect his purity from every thought that would steal it away and keep it from his sight. Bring innocence to light, in answer to the call of the Atonement. Never allow purity to remain hidden, but shine away the heavy veils of guilt within which the Son of God has hidden himself from his own sight.

6. Teachers of innocence, each in his own way, have joined together, taking their part in the unified curriculum of the Atonement. There is no unity of learning goals apart from this. There is no conflict in this curriculum, which has one aim however it is taught. Each effort made on its behalf is offered for the single purpose of release from guilt, to the eternal glory of God and His creation. And every teaching that points to this points straight to Heaven, and the peace of God. There is no pain, no trial, no fear that teaching this can fail to overcome. The power of God Himself supports this teaching, and guarantees its limitless results.

7. Join your own efforts to the power that cannot fail and must result in peace. No one can be untouched by teaching such as this. You will not see yourself beyond the power of God if you teach only this. You will not be exempt from the effects of this most holy lesson, which seeks but to restore what is the right of God's creation. From everyone whom you accord release from guilt you will inevitably learn your innocence. The circle of Atonement has no end. And you will find ever-increasing confidence in your safe inclusion in the circle with everyone you bring within its safety and its perfect peace.

8. Peace, then, be unto everyone who becomes a teacher of peace. For peace is the acknowledgment of perfect purity, from which no one is excluded. Within its holy circle is everyone whom God created as His Son. Joy is its unifying attribute, with no one left outside to suffer guilt alone. The power of God draws everyone to its safe embrace of love and union. Stand quietly within this circle, and attract all tortured minds to join with you in the safety of its peace and holiness. Abide with me within it, as a teacher of Atonement, not of guilt.

11. Each one you see you place within the holy circle of Atonement or leave outside, judging him fit for crucifixion or for redemption. If you bring him into the circle of purity, you will rest there with him. If you leave him without, you join him there. Judge not except in quietness which is not of you. Refuse to accept anyone as without the blessing of Atonement, and bring him into it by blessing him. Holiness must be shared, for therein lies everything that makes it holy. Come gladly to the holy circle, and look out in peace on all who think they are outside.

Cast no one out, for here is what he seeks along with you. Come, let us join him in the holy place of peace which is for all of us, united as one within the Cause of peace.

VI. The Light of Communication

2. The quiet light in which the Holy Spirit dwells within you is merely perfect openness, in which nothing is hidden and therefore nothing is fearful. Attack will always yield to love if it is brought to love, not hidden from it. There is no darkness that the light of love will not dispel, unless it is concealed from love's beneficence. What is kept apart from love cannot share its healing power, because it has been separated off and kept in darkness. The sentinels of darkness watch over it carefully, and you who made these guardians of illusion out of nothing are now afraid of them.

5. You have regarded the separation as a means for breaking your communication with your Father. The Holy Spirit reinterprets it as a means of re-establishing what was not broken, but *has* been made obscure. All things you made have use to Him, for His most holy purpose. He knows you are not separate from God, but He perceives much in your mind that lets you think you are. All this and nothing else would He separate from you. The power of decision, which you made in place of the power of creation, He would teach you how to use on your behalf. You who made it to crucify yourself must learn of Him how to apply it to the holy cause of restoration.

VII. Sharing Perception with the Holy Spirit

2. The search for truth is but the honest searching out of everything that interferes with truth. Truth *is*. It can neither be lost nor sought nor found. It is there, wherever you are, being within you. Yet it can be recognized or unrecognized, real or false to you. If you hide it, it becomes unreal to you *because* you hid it and surrounded it with fear. Under each cornerstone of fear on which you have erected your insane system of belief, the truth lies hidden. Yet you cannot know this, for by hiding truth in fear, you see no reason to believe that the more you look at fear the less you see it, and the clearer what it conceals becomes.

4. Our emphasis has been on bringing what is undesirable to the desirable; what you do not want to what you do. You will realize that salvation must come to you this way, if you consider what dissociation is. Dissociation is a distorted process of thinking whereby two systems

of belief which cannot coexist are both maintained. If they are brought together, their joint acceptance becomes impossible. But if one is kept in darkness from the other, their separation seems to keep them both alive and equal in their reality. Their joining thus becomes the source of fear, for if they meet, acceptance must be withdrawn from one of them. You cannot have them both, for each denies the other. Apart, this fact is lost from sight, for each in a separate place can be endowed with firm belief. Bring them together, and the fact of their complete incompatibility is instantly apparent. One will go, because the other is seen in the same place.

6. The Holy Spirit asks of you but this; bring to Him every secret you have locked away from Him. Open every door to Him, and bid Him enter the darkness and lighten it away. At your request He enters gladly. He brings the light to darkness if you make the darkness open to Him. But what you hide He cannot look upon. He sees for you, and unless you look with Him He cannot see. The vision of Christ is not for Him alone, but for Him with you. Bring, therefore, all your dark and secret thoughts to Him, and look upon them with Him. He holds the light, and you the darkness. They cannot coexist when both of You together look on them. His judgment must prevail, and He will give it to you as you join your perception to His.

7. Joining with Him in seeing is the way in which you learn to share with Him the interpretation of perception that leads to knowledge. You cannot see alone. Sharing perception with Him Whom God has given you teaches you how to recognize what you see. It is the recognition that nothing you see means anything alone. Seeing with Him will show you that all meaning, including yours, comes not from double vision, but from the gentle fusing of everything into *one* meaning, *one* emotion and *one* purpose. God has one purpose which He shares with you. The single vision which the Holy Spirit offers you will bring this oneness to your mind with clarity and brightness so intense you could not wish, for all the world, not to accept what God would have you have. Behold your will, accepting it as His, with all His Love as yours. All honor to you through Him, and through Him unto God.

VIII. The Holy Meeting Place

4. There is no substitute for truth. And truth will make this plain to you as you are brought into the place where you must meet with truth. And there you must be led, through gentle understanding which can lead you nowhere else. Where God is, there are you. Such is the truth. Nothing can change the knowledge, given you by God, into

unknowingness. Everything God created knows its Creator. For this is how creation is accomplished by the Creator and by His creations. In the holy meeting place are joined the Father and His creations, and the creations of His Son with Them together. There is one link that joins Them all together, holding Them in the oneness out of which creation happens.

5. The link with which the Father joins Himself to those He gives the power to create can never be dissolved. Heaven itself is union with all of creation, and with its one Creator. And Heaven remains the Will of God for you. Lay no gifts other than this upon your altars, for nothing can coexist with it. Here your little offerings are brought together with the gift of God, and only what is worthy of the Father will be accepted by the Son, for whom it is intended. To whom God gives Himself, He *is* given. Your little gifts will vanish on the altar, where He has placed His Own.

QUESTION 31. Who is called to enter the circle of Atonement, and what does the Holy Spirit ask of you?

IX. The Reflection of Holiness

2. Bringing the ego to God is but to bring error to truth, where it stands corrected because it is the opposite of what it meets. It is undone because the contradiction can no longer stand. How long can contradiction stand when its impossible nature is clearly revealed? What disappears in light is not attacked. It merely vanishes because it is not true. Different realities are meaningless, for reality must be one. It cannot change with time or mood or chance. Its changelessness is what makes it real. This cannot be undone. Undoing is for unreality. And this reality will do for you.

3. Merely by being what it is, does truth release you from everything that it is not. The Atonement is so gentle you need but whisper to it, and all its power will rush to your assistance and support. You are not frail with God beside you. Yet without Him you are nothing. The Atonement offers you God. The gift that you refused is held by Him in you. The Holy Spirit holds it there for you. God has not left His altar, though His worshippers placed other gods upon it. The temple still is holy, for the Presence that dwells within it *is* Holiness.

4. In the temple, Holiness waits quietly for the return of them that love it. The Presence knows they will return to purity and to grace. The graciousness of God will take them gently in, and cover all their sense of pain and loss with the immortal assurance of their Father's Love. There, fear of death will be replaced with joy of life. For God is life,

and they abide in life. Life is as holy as the Holiness by which it was created. The Presence of Holiness lives in everything that lives, for Holiness created life, and leaves not what It created holy as Itself.

5. In this world you can become a spotless mirror, in which the Holiness of your Creator shines forth from you to all around you. You can reflect Heaven here. Yet no reflections of the images of other gods must dim the mirror that would hold God's reflection in it. Earth can reflect Heaven or hell; God or the ego. You need but leave the mirror clean and clear of all the images of hidden darkness you have drawn upon it. God will shine upon it of Himself. Only the clear reflection of Himself can be perceived upon it.

6. Reflections are seen in light. In darkness they are obscure, and their meaning seems to lie only in shifting interpretations, rather than in themselves. The reflection of God needs no interpretation. It is clear. Clean but the mirror, and the message that shines forth from what the mirror holds out for everyone to see, no one can fail to understand. It is the message that the Holy Spirit is holding to the mirror that is in him. He recognizes it because he has been taught his need for it, but knows not where to look to find it. Let him, then, see it in you and share it with you.

7. Could you but realize for a single instant the power of healing that the reflection of God, shining in you, can bring to all the world, you could not wait to make the mirror of your mind clean to receive the image of the holiness that heals the world. The image of holiness that shines in your mind is not obscure, and will not change. Its meaning to those who look upon it is not obscure, for everyone perceives it as the same. All bring their different problems to its healing light, and all their problems find but healing there.

8. The response of holiness to any form of error is always the same. There is no contradiction in what holiness calls forth. Its one response is healing, without regard for what is brought to it. Those who have learned to offer only healing, because of the reflection of holiness in them, are ready at last for Heaven. There, holiness is not a reflection, but rather the actual condition of what was but reflected to them here. God is no image, and His creations, as part of Him, hold Him in them in truth. They do not merely reflect truth, for they *are* truth.

X. The Equality of Miracles

7. The only judgment involved is the Holy Spirit's one division into two categories; one of love, and the other the call for love. You cannot safely make this division, for you are much too confused either

to recognize love, or to believe that everything else is nothing but a call for love. You are too bound to form, and not to content. What you consider content is not content at all. It is merely form, and nothing else. For you do not respond to what a brother really offers you, but only to the particular perception of his offering by which the ego judges it.

8. The ego is incapable of understanding content, and is totally unconcerned with it. To the ego, if the form is acceptable the content must be. Otherwise it will attack the form. If you believe you understand something of the "dynamics" of the ego, let me assure you that you understand nothing of it. For of yourself you could not understand it. The study of the ego is not the study of the mind. In fact, the ego enjoys studying itself, and thoroughly approves the undertakings of students who would "analyze" it, thus approving its importance. Yet they but study form with meaningless content. For their teacher is senseless, though careful to conceal this fact behind impressive sounding words, but which lack any consistent sense when they are put together.

9. This is characteristic of the ego's judgments. Separately, they seem to hold, but put them together and the system of thought that arises from joining them is incoherent and utterly chaotic. For form is not enough for meaning, and the underlying lack of content makes a cohesive system impossible. Separation therefore remains the ego's chosen condition. For no one alone can judge the ego truly. Yet when two or more join together in searching for truth, the ego can no longer defend its lack of content. The fact of union tells them it is not true.

10. It is impossible to remember God in secret and alone. For remembering Him means you are not alone, and are willing to remember it. Take no thought for yourself, for no thought you hold *is* for yourself. If you would remember your Father, let the Holy Spirit order your thoughts and give only the answer with which He answers you. Everyone seeks for love as you do, but knows it not unless he joins with you in seeking it. If you undertake the search together, you bring with you a light so powerful that what you see is given meaning. The lonely journey fails because it has excluded what it would find.

11. As God communicates to the Holy Spirit in you, so does the Holy Spirit translate His communications through you, so you can understand them. God has no secret communications, for everything of Him is perfectly open and freely accessible to all, being for all. Nothing lives in secret, and what you would hide from the Holy Spirit is nothing. Every interpretation you would lay upon a brother is senseless. Let the Holy Spirit show him to you, and teach you both

his love and his call for love. Neither his mind nor yours holds more than these two orders of thought.

12. The miracle is the recognition that this is true. Where there is love, your brother must give it to you because of what it is. But where there is a call for love, you must give it because of what you are. Earlier I said this course will teach you how to remember what you are, restoring to you your Identity. We have already learned that this Identity is shared. The miracle becomes the means of sharing It. By supplying your Identity wherever It is not recognized, you will recognize It. And God Himself, Who wills to be with His Son forever, will bless each recognition of His Son with all the Love He holds for him. Nor will the power of all His Love be absent from any miracle you offer to His Son. How, then, can there be any order of difficulty among them?

XI. The Test of Truth

3. Atonement teaches you how to escape forever from everything that you have taught yourself in the past, by showing you only what you are *now*. Learning has been accomplished before its effects are manifest. Learning is therefore in the past, but its influence determines the present by giving it whatever meaning it holds for you. *Your* learning gives the present no meaning at all. Nothing you have ever learned can help you understand the present, or teach you how to undo the past. Your past is what you have taught yourself. *Let* it all go. Do not attempt to understand any event or anything or anyone in its "light," for the darkness in which you try to see can only obscure. Put no confidence at all in darkness to illuminate your understanding, for if you do you contradict the light, and thereby think you see the darkness. Yet darkness cannot be seen, for it is nothing more than a condition in which seeing becomes impossible.

5. You have one test, as sure as God, by which to recognize if what you learned is true. If you are wholly free of fear of any kind, and if all those who meet or even think of you share in your perfect peace, then you can be sure that you have learned God's lesson, and not your own. Unless all this is true, there are dark lessons in your mind that hurt and hinder you, and everyone around you. The absence of perfect peace means but one thing: You think you do not will for God's Son what his Father wills for him. Every dark lesson teaches this, in one form or another. And each bright lesson with which the Holy Spirit will replace the dark ones you do not accept, teaches you that you will with the Father and His Son.

6. Do not be concerned about how you can learn a lesson so completely different from everything that you have taught yourself. How would you know? Your part is very simple. You need only recognize that everything you learned you do not want. Ask to be taught, and do not use your experiences to confirm what you have learned. When your peace is threatened or disturbed in any way, say to yourself:

> I do not know what anything, including this, means. And
> so I do not know how to respond to it. And I will not use
> my own past learning as the light to guide me now.

By this refusal to attempt to teach yourself what you do not know, the Guide Whom God has given you will speak to you. He will take His rightful place in your awareness the instant you abandon it, and offer it to Him.

7. You cannot be your guide to miracles, for it is you who made them necessary. And because you did, the means on which you can depend for miracles has been provided for you. God's Son can make no needs his Father will not meet, if he but turn to Him ever so little. Yet He cannot compel His Son to turn to Him and remain Himself. It is impossible that God lose His Identity, for if He did, you would lose yours. And being yours He cannot change Himself, for your Identity is changeless. The miracle acknowledges His changelessness by seeing His Son as he always was, and not as he would make himself. The miracle brings the effects that only guiltlessness can bring, and thus establishes the fact that guiltlessness must be.

12. Those who remember always that they know nothing, and who have become willing to learn everything, will learn it. But whenever they trust themselves, they will not learn. They have destroyed their motivation for learning by thinking they already know. Think not you understand anything until you pass the test of perfect peace, for peace and understanding go together and never can be found alone. Each brings the other with it, for it is the law of God they be not separate. They are cause and effect, each to the other, so where one is absent the other cannot be.

QUESTION 32. Holiness is yours, but what can you do with your mind to help others with your holiness, and what are the two categories of thought you need to adopt as your way of perceiving your brother and yourself?

Chapter 15. THE HOLY INSTANT

I. The Two Uses of Time

6. How bleak and despairing is the ego's use of time! And how terrifying! For underneath its fanatical insistence that the past and future be the same is hidden a far more insidious threat to peace. The ego does not advertise its final threat, for it would have its worshippers still believe that it can offer them escape. But the belief in guilt must lead to the belief in hell, and always does. The only way in which the ego allows the fear of hell to be experienced is to bring hell here, but always as a foretaste of the future. For no one who considers himself as deserving of hell can believe that punishment will end in peace.

7. The Holy Spirit teaches thus: There is no hell. Hell is only what the ego has made of the present. The belief in hell is what prevents you from understanding the present, because you are afraid of it. The Holy Spirit leads as steadily to Heaven as the ego drives to hell. For the Holy Spirit, Who knows only the present, uses it to undo the fear by which the ego would make the present useless. There is no escape from fear in the ego's use of time. For time, according to its teaching, is nothing but a teaching device for compounding guilt until it becomes all-encompassing, demanding vengeance forever.

8. The Holy Spirit would undo all of this *now*. Fear is not of the present, but only of the past and future, which do not exist. There is no fear in the present when each instant stands clear and separated from the past, without its shadow reaching out into the future. Each instant is a clean, untarnished birth, in which the Son of God emerges from the past into the present. And the present extends forever. It is so beautiful and so clean and free of guilt that nothing but happiness is there. No darkness is remembered, and immortality and joy are now.

13. How long is an instant? It is as short for your brother as it is for you. Practice giving this blessed instant of freedom to all who are enslaved by time, and thus make time their friend for them. The Holy Spirit gives their blessed instant to you through your giving it. As you give it, He offers it to you. Be not unwilling to give what you would receive of Him, for you join with Him in giving. In the crystal cleanness of the release you give is your instantaneous escape from guilt. You must be holy if you offer holiness.

IV. Practicing the Holy Instant

1. This course is not beyond immediate learning, unless you believe that what God wills takes time. And this means only that you would rather delay the recognition that His Will is so. The holy instant is this instant and every instant. The one you want it to be it is. The one you would not have it be is lost to you. You must decide when it is. Delay it not. For beyond the past and future, where you will not find it, it stands in shimmering readiness for your acceptance. Yet you cannot bring it into glad awareness while you do not want it, for it holds the whole release from littleness.

2. Your practice must therefore rest upon your willingness to let all littleness go. The instant in which magnitude dawns upon you is but as far away as your desire for it. As long as you desire it not and cherish littleness instead, by so much is it far from you. By so much as you want it will you bring it nearer. Think not that you can find salvation in your own way and have it. Give over every plan you have made for your salvation in exchange for God's. His will content you, and nothing else can bring you peace. For peace is of God, and no one beside Him.

5. I stand within the holy instant, as clear as you would have me. And the extent to which you learn to accept me is the measure of the time in which the holy instant will be yours. I call to you to make the holy instant yours at once, for the release from littleness in the mind of the host of God depends on willingness, and not on time.

6. The reason this course is simple is that truth is simple. Complexity is of the ego, and is nothing more than the ego's attempt to obscure the obvious. You could live forever in the holy instant, beginning now and reaching to eternity, but for a very simple reason. Do not obscure the simplicity of this reason, for if you do, it will be only because you prefer not to recognize it and not to let it go. The simple reason, simply stated, is this: The holy instant is a time in which you receive and give perfect communication. This means, however, that it is a time in which your mind is open, both to receive and give. It is the recognition that all minds are in communication. It therefore seeks to change nothing, but merely to accept everything.

8. Every thought you would keep hidden shuts communication off, because you would have it so. It is impossible to recognize perfect communication while breaking communication holds value to you. Ask yourself honestly, "Would I want to have perfect communication, and am I wholly willing to let everything that interferes with it go forever?" If the answer is no, then the Holy Spirit's readiness to give it to you is not enough to make it yours, for you are not ready to share it with Him. And it cannot come into a mind that has decided to oppose it.

For the holy instant is given and received with equal willingness, being the acceptance of the single Will that governs all thought.
9. The necessary condition for the holy instant does not require that you have no thoughts that are not pure. But it does require that you have none that you would keep. Innocence is not of your making. It is given you the instant you would have it. Atonement would not be if there were no need for it. You will not be able to accept perfect communication as long as you would hide it from yourself. For what you would hide *is* hidden from you. In your practice, then, try only to be vigilant against deception, and seek not to protect the thoughts you would keep to yourself. Let the Holy Spirit's purity shine them away, and bring all your awareness to the readiness for purity He offers you. Thus will He make you ready to acknowledge that you are host to God, and hostage to no one and to nothing.

V. The Holy Instant and Special Relationships

1. The holy instant is the Holy Spirit's most useful learning device for teaching you love's meaning. For its purpose is to suspend judgment entirely. Judgment always rests on the past, for past experience is the basis on which you judge. Judgment becomes impossible without the past, for without it you do not understand anything. You would make no attempt to judge, because it would be quite apparent to you that you do not understand what anything means. You are afraid of this because you believe that without the ego, all would be chaos. Yet I assure you that without the ego, all would be love.
2. The past is the ego's chief learning device, for it is in the past that you learned to define your own needs and acquired methods for meeting them on your own terms. We have said that to limit love to part of the Sonship is to bring guilt into your relationships, and thus make them unreal. If you seek to separate out certain aspects of the totality and look to them to meet your imagined needs, you are attempting to use separation to save you. How, then, could guilt not enter? For separation is the source of guilt, and to appeal to it for salvation is to believe you are alone. To be alone *is* to be guilty. For to experience yourself as alone is to deny the Oneness of the Father and His Son, and thus to attack reality.
3. You cannot love parts of reality and understand what love means. If you would love unlike to God, Who knows no special love, how can you understand it? To believe that *special* relationships, with *special* love, can offer you salvation is the belief that separation is salvation. For it is the complete equality of the Atonement in which salvation lies. How can you decide that special aspects of the Sonship can give you

more than others? The past has taught you this. Yet the holy instant teaches you it is not so.

4. Because of guilt, all special relationships have elements of fear in them. This is why they shift and change so frequently. They are not based on changeless love alone. And love, where fear has entered, cannot be depended on because it is not perfect. In His function as Interpreter of what you made, the Holy Spirit uses special relationships, which you have chosen to support the ego, as learning experiences that point to truth. Under His teaching, *every* relationship becomes a lesson in love.

5. The Holy Spirit knows no one is special. Yet He also perceives that you have made special relationships, which He would purify and not let you destroy. However unholy the reason you made them may be, He can translate them into holiness by removing as much fear as you will let Him. You can place any relationship under His care and be sure that it will not result in pain, if you offer Him your willingness to have it serve no need but His. All the guilt in it arises from your use of it. All the love from His. Do not, then, be afraid to let go your imagined needs, which would destroy the relationship. Your only need is His.

9. God knows you *now*. He remembers nothing, having always known you exactly as He knows you now. The holy instant reflects His knowing by bringing all perception out of the past, thus removing the frame of reference you have built by which to judge your brothers. Once this is gone, the Holy Spirit substitutes His frame of reference for it. His frame of reference is simply God. The Holy Spirit's time-lessness lies only here. For in the holy instant, free of the past, you see that love is in you, and you have no need to look without and snatch love guiltily from where you thought it was.

10. All your relationships are blessed in the holy instant, because the blessing is not limited. In the holy instant the Sonship gains as one, and united in your blessing it becomes one to you. The meaning of love is the meaning God gave to it. Give to it any meaning apart from His, and it is impossible to understand it. God loves every brother as He loves you; neither less nor more. He needs them all equally, and so do you. In time, you have been told to offer miracles as I direct, and let the Holy Spirit bring to you those who are seeking you. Yet in the holy instant you unite directly with God, and all your brothers join in Christ. Those who are joined in Christ are in no way separate. For Christ is the Self the Sonship shares, as God shares His Self with Christ.

11. Think you that you can judge the Self of God? God has created It beyond judgment, out of His need to extend His Love. With love in

you, you have no need except to extend it. In the holy instant there is no conflict of needs, for there is only one. For the holy instant reaches to eternity, and to the Mind of God. And it is only there love has meaning, and only there can it be understood.

VI. The Holy Instant and the Laws of God

4. You do not find it difficult to believe that when another calls on God for love, your call remains as strong. Nor do you think that when God answers him, your hope of answer is diminished. On the contrary, you are more inclined to regard his success as witness to the possibility of yours. That is because you recognize, however dimly, that God is an idea, and so your faith in Him is strengthened by sharing. What you find difficult to accept is the fact that, like your Father, *you* are an idea. And like Him, you can give yourself completely, wholly without loss and only with gain. Herein lies peace, for here there *is* no conflict.
5. In the world of scarcity, love has no meaning and peace is impossible. For gain and loss are both accepted, and so no one is aware that perfect love is in him. In the holy instant you recognize the idea of love in you, and unite this idea with the Mind that thought it, and could not relinquish it. By holding it within itself, there *is* no loss. The holy instant thus becomes a lesson in how to hold all of your brothers in your mind, experiencing not loss but completion. From this it follows you can only give. And this *is* love, for this alone is natural under the laws of God. In the holy instant the laws of God prevail, and only they have meaning. The laws of this world cease to hold any meaning at all. When the Son of God accepts the laws of God as what he gladly wills, it is impossible that he be bound, or limited in any way. In that instant he is as free as God would have him be. For the instant he refuses to be bound, he is not bound.

QUESTION 33. What are the features of the holy instant?

VII. The Needless Sacrifice

1. Beyond the poor attraction of the special love relationship, and always obscured by it, is the powerful attraction of the Father for His Son. There is no other love that can satisfy you, because there *is* no other love. This is the only love that is fully given and fully returned. Being complete, it asks nothing. Being wholly pure, everyone joined in it has everything. This is not the basis for any relationship in which the ego enters. For every relationship on which the ego embarks *is* special.

2. The ego establishes relationships only to get something. And it would keep the giver bound to itself through guilt. It is impossible for the ego to enter into any relationship without anger, for the ego believes that anger makes friends. This is not its statement, but it *is* its purpose. For the ego really believes that it can get and keep *by making guilty*. This is its one attraction; an attraction so weak that it would have no hold at all, except that no one recognizes it. For the ego always seems to attract through love, and has no attraction at all to anyone who perceives that it attracts through guilt.

4. We said before that the ego attempts to maintain and increase guilt, but in such a way that you do not recognize what it would do to you. For it is the ego's fundamental doctrine that what you do to others you have escaped. The ego wishes no one well. Yet its survival depends on your belief that you are exempt from its evil intentions. It counsels, therefore, that if you are host to it, it will enable you to direct its anger outward, thus protecting you. And thus it embarks on an endless, unrewarding chain of special relationships, forged out of anger and dedicated to but one insane belief; that the more anger you invest outside yourself, the safer you become.

10. Whenever you are angry, you can be sure that you have formed a special relationship which the ego has "blessed," for anger is its blessing. Anger takes many forms, but it cannot long deceive those who will learn that love brings no guilt at all, and what brings guilt cannot be love and *must* be anger. All anger is nothing more than an attempt to make someone feel guilty, and this attempt is the only basis the ego accepts for special relationships. Guilt is the only need the ego has, and as long as you identify with it, guilt will remain attractive to you. Yet remember this; to be with a body is not communication. And if you think it is, you will feel guilty about communication and will be afraid to hear the Holy Spirit, recognizing in His Voice your own need to communicate.

11. The Holy Spirit cannot teach through fear. And how can He communicate with you, while you believe that to communicate is to make yourself alone? It is clearly insane to believe that by communicating you will be abandoned. And yet many do believe it. For they think their minds must be kept private or they will lose them, but if their bodies are together their minds remain their own. The union of bodies thus becomes the way in which they would keep minds apart. For bodies cannot forgive. They can only do as the mind directs.

13. Forgiveness lies in communication as surely as damnation lies in guilt. It is the Holy Spirit's teaching function to instruct those who believe communication to be damnation that communication is

salvation. And He will do so, for the power of God in Him and you is joined in a real relationship so holy and so strong, that it can overcome even this without fear.

14. It is through the holy instant that what seems impossible is accomplished, making it evident that it is not impossible. In the holy instant guilt holds no attraction, since communication has been restored. And guilt, whose only purpose is to disrupt communication, has no function here. Here there is no concealment, and no private thoughts. The willingness to communicate attracts communication to it, and overcomes loneliness completely. There is complete forgiveness here, for there is no desire to exclude anyone from your completion, in sudden recognition of the value of his part in it. In the protection of your wholeness, all are invited and made welcome. And you understand that your completion is God's, Whose only need is to have you be complete. For your completion makes you His in your awareness. And here it is that you experience yourself as you were created, and as you are.

VIII. The Only Real Relationship

4. Think but an instant on this: God gave the Sonship to you, to ensure your perfect creation. This was His gift, for as He withheld Himself not from you, He withheld not His creation. Nothing that ever was created but is yours. Your relationships are with the universe. And this universe, being of God, is far beyond the petty sum of all the separate bodies you perceive. For all its parts are joined in God through Christ, where they become like to their Father. Christ knows of no separation from His Father, Who is His one relationship, in which He gives as His Father gives to Him.

IX. The Holy Instant and the Attraction of God

1. As the ego would limit your perception of your brothers to the body, so would the Holy Spirit release your vision and let you see the Great Rays shining from them, so unlimited that they reach to God. It is this shift to vision that is accomplished in the holy instant. Yet it is needful for you to learn just what this shift entails, so you will become willing to make it permanent. Given this willingness it will not leave you, for it *is* permanent. Once you have accepted it as the only perception you want, it is translated into knowledge by the part that God Himself plays in the Atonement, for it is the only step in it He understands. Therefore, in this there will be no delay when you are ready for it. God is ready now, but you are not.

2. Our task is but to continue, as fast as possible, the necessary process of looking straight at all the interference and seeing it exactly as it is.

For it is impossible to recognize as wholly without gratification what you think you want. The body is the symbol of the ego, as the ego is the symbol of the separation. And both are nothing more than attempts to limit communication, and thereby to make it impossible. For communication must be unlimited in order to have meaning, and deprived of meaning, it will not satisfy you completely. Yet it remains the only means by which you can establish real relationships, which have no limits, having been established by God.

3. In the holy instant, where the Great Rays replace the body in awareness, the recognition of relationships without limits is given you. But in order to see this, it is necessary to give up every use the ego has for the body, and to accept the fact that the ego has no purpose you would share with it. For the ego would limit everyone to a body for its own purposes, and while you think it has a purpose, you will choose to utilize the means by which it tries to turn its purpose into accomplishment. This will never be accomplished. Yet you have surely recognized that the ego, whose goals are altogether unattainable, will strive for them with all its might, and will do so with the strength that you have given it.

6. You have no conception of the limits you have placed on your perception, and no idea of all the loveliness that you could see. But this you must remember; the attraction of guilt opposes the attraction of God. His attraction for you remains unlimited, but because your power, being His, is as great as His, you can turn away from love. What you invest in guilt you withdraw from God. And your sight grows weak and dim and limited, for you have attempted to separate the Father from the Son, and limit Their communication. Seek not Atonement in further separation. And limit not your vision of God's Son to what interferes with his release, and what the Holy Spirit must undo to set him free. For his belief in limits *has* imprisoned him.

7. When the body ceases to attract you, and when you place no value on it as a means of getting anything, then there will be no interference in communication and your thoughts will be as free as God's. As you let the Holy Spirit teach you how to use the body only for purposes of communication, and renounce its use for separation and attack which the ego sees in it, you will learn you have no need of a body at all. In the holy instant there are no bodies, and you experience only the attraction of God. Accepting it as undivided you join Him wholly, in an instant, for you would place no limits on your union with Him. The reality of this relationship becomes the only truth that you could ever want. All truth *is* here.

Chapter 16. THE FORGIVENESS OF ILLUSIONS

II. The Power of Holiness

2. There is a tendency to fragment, and then to be concerned about the truth of just a little part of the whole. And this is but a way of avoiding, or looking away from the whole, to what you think you might be better able to understand. For this is but another way in which you would still try to keep understanding to yourself. A better and far more helpful way to think of miracles is this: You do not understand them, either in part or in whole. Yet they have been done through you. Therefore your understanding cannot be necessary. Yet it is still impossible to accomplish what you do not understand. And so there must be Something in you that *does* understand.

4. You have done miracles, but it is quite apparent that you have not done them alone. You have succeeded whenever you have reached another mind and joined with it. When two minds join as one and share one idea equally, the first link in the awareness of the Sonship as One has been made. When you have made this joining as the Holy Spirit bids you, and have offered it to Him to use as He sees fit, His natural perception of your gift enables Him to understand it, and you to use His understanding on your behalf. It is impossible to convince you of the reality of what has clearly been accomplished through your willingness while you believe that you must understand it or else it is not real.

8. Do not interpret against God's Love, for you have many witnesses that speak of it so clearly that only the blind and deaf could fail to see and hear them. This year determine not to deny what has been given you by God. Awake and share it, for that is the only reason He has called to you. His Voice has spoken clearly, and yet you have so little faith in what you heard, because you have preferred to place still greater faith in the disaster you have made. Today, let us resolve together to accept the joyful tidings that disaster is not real and that reality is not disaster. Reality is safe and sure, and wholly kind to everyone and everything. There is no greater love than to accept this and be glad. For love asks only that you be happy, and will give you everything that makes for happiness.

QUESTION 34. What is the link between the special relationship and guilt, and do you need to understand miracles in order to perform them?

IV. The Illusion and the Reality of Love

6. Your task is not to seek for love, but merely to seek and find all of the barriers within yourself that you have built against it. It is not necessary to seek for what is true, but it *is* necessary to seek for what is false. Every illusion is one of fear, whatever form it takes. And the attempt to escape from one illusion into another must fail. If you seek love outside yourself you can be certain that you perceive hatred within, and are afraid of it. Yet peace will never come from the illusion of love, but only from its reality.

12. Your Father can no more forget the truth in you than you can fail to remember it. The Holy Spirit is the Bridge to Him, made from your willingness to unite with Him and created by His joy in union with you. The journey that seemed endless is almost complete, for what *is* endless is very near. You have almost recognized it. Turn with me firmly away from all illusions now, and let nothing stand in the way of truth. We will take the last useless journey away from truth together, and then together we go straight to God, in joyous answer to His Call for His completion.

13. If special relationships of any kind would hinder God's completion, can they have any value to you? What would interfere with God must interfere with you. Only in time does interference in God's completion seem to be possible. The bridge that He would carry you across lifts you from time into eternity. Waken from time, and answer fearlessly the Call of Him Who gave eternity to you in your creation. On this side of the bridge to timelessness you understand nothing. But as you step lightly across it, upheld *by* timelessness, you are directed straight to the Heart of God. At its center, and only there, you are safe forever, because you are complete forever. There is no veil the Love of God in us together cannot lift. The way to truth is open. Follow it with me.

V. The Choice for Completion

3. The special love relationship is the ego's most boasted gift, and one which has the most appeal to those unwilling to relinquish guilt. The "dynamics" of the ego are clearest here, for counting on the attraction of this offering, the fantasies that center around it are often quite overt. Here they are usually judged to be acceptable and even natural. No one considers it bizarre to love and hate together, and even those who believe that hate is sin merely feel guilty, but do not correct it. This is the "natural" condition of the separation, and those who learn that it is not natural at all seem to be the unnatural ones. For this world *is* the opposite of Heaven, being made to be its opposite, and everything

here takes a direction exactly opposite of what is true. In Heaven, where the meaning of love is known, love is the same as union. Here, where the illusion of love is accepted in love's place, love is perceived as separation and exclusion.

4. It is in the special relationship, born of the hidden wish for special love from God, that the ego's hatred triumphs. For the special relationship is the renunciation of the Love of God, and the attempt to secure for the self the specialness that He denied. It is essential to the preservation of the ego that you believe this specialness is not hell, but Heaven. For the ego would never have you see that separation could only be loss, being the one condition in which Heaven could not be.

7. Most curious of all is the concept of the self which the ego fosters in the special relationship. This "self" seeks the relationship to make itself complete. Yet when it finds the special relationship in which it thinks it can accomplish this it gives itself away, and tries to "trade" itself for the self of another. This is not union, for there is no increase and no extension. Each partner tries to sacrifice the self he does not want for one he thinks he would prefer. And he feels guilty for the "sin" of taking, and of giving nothing of value in return. How much value can he place upon a self that he would give away to get a "better" one?

8. The "better" self the ego seeks is always one that is more special. And whoever seems to possess a special self is "loved" for what can be taken from him. Where both partners see this special self in each other, the ego sees "a union made in Heaven." For neither one will recognize that he has asked for hell, and so he will not interfere with the ego's illusion of Heaven, which it offered him to interfere with Heaven. Yet if all illusions are of fear, and they can be of nothing else, the illusion of Heaven is nothing more than an "attractive" form of fear, in which the guilt is buried deep and rises in the form of "love."

13. See in the special relationship nothing more than a meaningless attempt to raise other gods before Him, and by worshipping them to obscure their tininess and His greatness. In the name of your completion you do not want this. For every idol that you raise to place before Him stands before *you*, in place of what you are.

14. Salvation lies in the simple fact that illusions are not fearful because they are not true. They but seem to be fearful to the extent to which you fail to recognize them for what they are; and you will fail to do this to the extent to which you *want* them to be true. And to the same extent you are denying truth, and so are failing to make the simple choice between truth and illusion; God and fantasy. Remember this, and you will have no difficulty in perceiving the decision as just what it is, and nothing more.

15. The core of the separation illusion lies simply in the fantasy of destruction of love's meaning. And unless love's meaning is restored to you, you cannot know yourself who share its meaning. Separation is only the decision *not* to know yourself. This whole thought system is a carefully contrived learning experience, designed to lead away from truth and into fantasy. Yet for every learning that would hurt you, God offers you correction and complete escape from all its consequences.

16. The decision whether or not to listen to this course and follow it is but the choice between truth and illusion. For here is truth, separated from illusion and not confused with it at all. How simple does this choice become when it is perceived as only what it is. For only fantasies make confusion in choosing possible, and they are totally unreal.

17. This year is thus the time to make the easiest decision that ever confronted you, and also the only one. You will cross the bridge into reality simply because you will recognize that God is on the other side, and nothing at all is here. It is impossible not to make the natural decision as this is realized.

VI. The Bridge to the Real World

1. The search for the special relationship is the sign that you equate yourself with the ego and not with God. For the special relationship has value only to the ego. To the ego, unless a relationship has special value it has no meaning, for it perceives all love as special. Yet this cannot be natural, for it is unlike the relationship of God and His Son, and all relationships that are unlike this one *must* be unnatural. For God created love as He would have it be, and gave it as it is. Love has no meaning except as its Creator defined it by His Will. It is impossible to define it otherwise and understand it.

4. The special relationship is totally meaningless without a body. If you value it, you must also value the body. And what you value you will keep. The special relationship is a device for limiting your self to a body, and for limiting your perception of others to theirs. The Great Rays would establish the total lack of value of the special relationship, if they were seen. For in seeing them the body would disappear, because its value would be lost. And so your whole investment in seeing it would be withdrawn from it.

5. You see the world you value. On this side of the bridge you see the world of separate bodies, seeking to join each other in separate unions and to become one by losing. When two individuals seek to become one, they are trying to decrease their magnitude. Each would deny his power, for the separate union excludes the universe. Far more is left

outside than would be taken in, for God is left without and *nothing* taken in. If one such union were made in perfect faith, the universe would enter into it. Yet the special relationship the ego seeks does not include even one whole individual. The ego wants but part of him, and sees only this part and nothing else.

6.   Across the bridge it is so different! For a time the body is still seen, but not exclusively, as it is seen here. The little spark that holds the Great Rays within it is also visible, and this spark cannot be limited long to littleness. Once you have crossed the bridge, the value of the body is so diminished in your sight that you will see no need at all to magnify it. For you will realize that the only value the body has is to enable you to bring your brothers to the bridge with you, and to be released together there.

7.   The bridge itself is nothing more than a transition in the perspective of reality. On this side, everything you see is grossly distorted and completely out of perspective. What is little and insignificant is magnified, and what is strong and powerful cut down to littleness. In the transition there is a period of confusion, in which a sense of actual disorientation may occur. But fear it not, for it means only that you have been willing to let go your hold on the distorted frame of reference that seemed to hold your world together. This frame of reference is built around the special relationship. Without this illusion there could be no meaning you would still seek here.

11.   The new perspective you will gain from crossing over will be the understanding of where Heaven *is*. From this side, it seems to be outside and across the bridge. Yet as you cross to join it, it will join with you and become one with you. And you will think, in glad astonishment, that for all this you gave up *nothing*! The joy of Heaven, which has no limit, is increased with each light that returns to take its rightful place within it. Wait no longer, for the Love of God and *you*. And may the holy instant speed you on the way, as it will surely do if you but let it come to you.

12.   The Holy Spirit asks only this little help of you: Whenever your thoughts wander to a special relationship which still attracts you, enter with Him into a holy instant, and there let Him release you. He needs only your willingness to share His perspective to give it to you completely. And your willingness need not be complete because His is perfect. It is His task to atone for your unwillingness by His perfect faith, and it is His faith you share with Him there. Out of your recognition of your unwillingness for your release, His perfect willingness is given you. Call upon Him, for Heaven is at His Call. And let Him call on Heaven for you.

VII. The End of Illusions

11. Seek and *find* His message in the holy instant, where all illusions are forgiven. From there the miracle extends to bless everyone and to resolve all problems, be they perceived as great or small, possible or impossible. There is nothing that will not give place to Him and to His Majesty. To join in close relationship with Him is to accept relationships as real, and through their reality to give over all illusions for the reality of your relationship with God. Praise be to your relationship with Him and to no other. The truth lies there and nowhere else. You choose this or nothing.

12. *Forgive us our illusions, Father, and help us to accept our true relationship with You, in which there are no illusions, and where none can ever enter. Our holiness is Yours. What can there be in us that needs forgiveness when Yours is perfect? The sleep of forgetfulness is only the unwillingness to remember Your forgiveness and Your Love. Let us not wander into temptation, for the temptation of the Son of God is not Your Will. And let us receive only what You have given, and accept but this into the minds which You created and which You love. Amen.*

QUESTION 35. What is the nature of love in the special love relationship, and what is traded in the bargain of a special love relationship?

Chapter 17. FORGIVENESS AND
THE HOLY RELATIONSHIP

II. The Forgiven World

1. Can you imagine how beautiful those you forgive will look to you? In no fantasy have you ever seen anything so lovely. Nothing you see here, sleeping or waking, comes near to such loveliness. And nothing will you value like unto this, nor hold so dear. Nothing that you remember that made your heart sing with joy has ever brought you even a little part of the happiness this sight will bring you. For you will see the Son of God. You will behold the beauty the Holy Spirit loves to look upon, and which He thanks the Father for. He was created to see this for you, until you learned to see it for yourself. And all His teaching leads to seeing it and giving thanks with Him.

2. This loveliness is not a fantasy. It is the real world, bright and clean and new, with everything sparkling under the open sun. Nothing is hidden here, for everything has been forgiven and there are no fantasies to hide the truth. The bridge between that world and this is so little and so easy to cross, that you could not believe it is the meeting place of worlds so different. Yet this little bridge is the strongest thing that touches on this world at all. This little step, so small it has escaped your notice, is a stride through time into eternity, beyond all ugliness into beauty that will enchant you, and will never cease to cause you wonderment at its perfection.

3. This step, the smallest ever taken, is still the greatest accomplishment of all in God's plan of Atonement. All else is learned, but this is given, complete and wholly perfect. No one but Him Who planned salvation could complete it thus. The real world, in its loveliness, you learn to reach. Fantasies are all undone, and no one and nothing remain still bound by them, and by your own forgiveness you are free to see. Yet what you see is only what you made, with the blessing of your forgiveness on it. And with this final blessing of God's Son upon himself, the real perception, born of the new perspective he has learned, has served its purpose.

4. The stars will disappear in light, and the sun that opened up the world to beauty will vanish. Perception will be meaningless when it has been perfected, for everything that has been used for learning will have no function. Nothing will ever change; no shifts nor shadings, no differences, no variations that made perception possible will still

occur. The perception of the real world will be so short that you will barely have time to thank God for it. For God will take the last step swiftly, when you have reached the real world and have been made ready for Him.

5. The real world is attained simply by the complete forgiveness of the old, the world you see without forgiveness. The great Transformer of perception will undertake with you the careful searching of the mind that made this world, and uncover to you the seeming reasons for your making it. In the light of the real reason that He brings, as you follow Him, He will show you that there is no reason here at all. Each spot His reason touches grows alive with beauty, and what seemed ugly in the darkness of your lack of reason is suddenly released to loveliness. Not even what the Son of God made in insanity could be without a hidden spark of beauty that gentleness could release.

6. All this beauty will rise to bless your sight as you look upon the world with forgiving eyes. For forgiveness literally transforms vision, and lets you see the real world reaching quietly and gently across chaos, removing all illusions that had twisted your perception and fixed it on the past. The smallest leaf becomes a thing of wonder, and a blade of grass a sign of God's perfection.

7. From the forgiven world the Son of God is lifted easily into his home. And there he knows that he has always rested there in peace. Even salvation will become a dream, and vanish from his mind. For salvation is the end of dreams, and with the closing of the dream will have no meaning. Who, awake in Heaven, could dream that there could ever be need of salvation?

8. How much do you want salvation? It will give you the real world, trembling with readiness to be given you. The eagerness of the Holy Spirit to give you this is so intense He would not wait, although He waits in patience. Meet His patience with your impatience at delay in meeting Him. Go out in gladness to meet with your Redeemer, and walk with Him in trust out of this world, and into the real world of beauty and forgiveness.

III. Shadows of the Past

1. To forgive is merely to remember only the loving thoughts you gave in the past, and those that were given you. All the rest must be forgotten. Forgiveness is a selective remembering, based not on your selection. For the shadow figures you would make immortal are "enemies" of reality. Be willing to forgive the Son of God for what he did not do. The shadow figures are the witnesses you bring with you

to demonstrate he did what he did not. Because you bring them, you will hear them. And you who keep them by your own selection do not understand how they came into your mind, and what their purpose is. They represent the evil that you think was done to you. You bring them with you only that you may return evil for evil, hoping that their witness will enable you to think guiltily of another and not harm yourself. They speak so clearly for the separation that no one not obsessed with keeping separation could hear them. They offer you the "reasons" why you should enter into unholy alliances to support the ego's goals, and make your relationships the witness to its power.

4. Time is indeed unkind to the unholy relationship. For time *is* cruel in the ego's hands, as it is kind when used for gentleness. The attraction of the unholy relationship begins to fade and to be questioned almost at once. Once it is formed, doubt must enter in, because its purpose is impossible. The "ideal" of the unholy relationship thus becomes one in which the reality of the other does not enter at all to "spoil" the dream. And the less the other really brings to the relationship, the "better" it becomes. Thus, the attempt at union becomes a way of excluding even the one with whom the union was sought. For it was formed to get him out of it, and join with fantasies in uninterrupted "bliss."

8. The past becomes the justification for entering into a continuing, unholy alliance with the ego against the present. For the present *is* forgiveness. Therefore, the relationships the unholy alliance dictates are not perceived nor felt as *now*. Yet the frame of reference to which the present is referred for meaning is an *illusion* of the past, in which those elements that fit the purpose of the unholy alliance are retained, and all the rest let go. And what is thus let go is all the truth the past could ever offer to the present as witnesses for its reality. What is kept but witnesses to the reality of dreams.

9. It is still up to you to choose to join with truth or with illusion. But remember that to choose one is to let the other go. Which one you choose you will endow with beauty and reality, because the choice depends on which you value more. The spark of beauty or the veil of ugliness, the real world or the world of guilt and fear, truth or illusion, freedom or slavery—it is all the same. For you can never choose except between God and the ego. Thought systems are but true or false, and all their attributes come simply from what they are. Only the Thoughts of God are true. And all that follows from them comes from what they are, and is as true as is the holy Source from which they came.

10. My holy brother, I would enter into all your relationships, and step between you and your fantasies. Let my relationship to you be real to you, and let me bring reality to your perception of your brothers. They were not created to enable you to hurt yourself through them. They were created to create with you. This is the truth that I would interpose between you and your goal of madness. Be not separate from me, and let not the holy purpose of Atonement be lost to you in dreams of vengeance. Relationships in which such dreams are cherished have excluded me. Let me enter in the Name of God and bring you peace, that you may offer peace to me.

V. The Healed Relationship

1. The holy relationship is the expression of the holy instant in living in this world. Like everything about salvation, the holy instant is a practical device, witnessed to by its results. The holy instant never fails. The experience of it is always felt. Yet without expression it is not remembered. The holy relationship is a constant reminder of the experience in which the relationship became what it is. And as the unholy relationship is a continuing hymn of hate in praise of its maker, so is the holy relationship a happy song of praise to the Redeemer of relationships.

2. The holy relationship, a major step toward the perception of the real world, is learned. It is the old, unholy relationship, transformed and seen anew. The holy relationship is a phenomenal teaching accomplishment. In all its aspects, as it begins, develops and becomes accomplished, it represents the reversal of the unholy relationship. Be comforted in this; the only difficult phase is the beginning. For here, the goal of the relationship is abruptly shifted to the exact opposite of what it was. This is the first result of offering the relationship to the Holy Spirit, to use for His purposes.

3. This invitation is accepted immediately, and the Holy Spirit wastes no time in introducing the practical results of asking Him to enter. At once His goal replaces yours. This is accomplished very rapidly, but it makes the relationship seem disturbed, disjunctive and even quite distressing. The reason is quite clear. For the relationship as it *is* is out of line with its own goal, and clearly unsuited to the purpose that has been accepted for it. In its unholy condition, *your* goal was all that seemed to give it meaning. Now it seems to make no sense. Many relationships have been broken off at this point, and the pursuit of the old goal re-established in another relationship. For once the

unholy relationship has accepted the goal of holiness, it can never again be what it was.

4. The temptation of the ego becomes extremely intense with this shift in goals. For the relationship has not as yet been changed sufficiently to make its former goal completely without attraction, and its structure is "threatened" by the recognition of its inappropriateness for meeting its new purpose. The conflict between the goal and the structure of the relationship is so apparent that they cannot coexist. Yet now the goal will not be changed. Set firmly in the unholy relationship, there is no course except to change the relationship to fit the goal. Until this happy solution is seen and accepted as the only way out of the conflict, the relationship may seem to be severely strained.

5. It would not be kinder to shift the goal more slowly, for the contrast would be obscured, and the ego given time to reinterpret each slow step according to its liking. Only a radical shift in purpose could induce a complete change of mind about what the whole relationship is for. As this change develops and is finally accomplished, it grows increasingly beneficent and joyous. But at the beginning, the situation is experienced as very precarious. A relationship, undertaken by two individuals for their unholy purposes, suddenly has holiness for its goal. As these two contemplate their relationship from the point of view of this new purpose, they are inevitably appalled. Their perception of the relationship may even become quite disorganized. And yet, the former organization of their perception no longer serves the purpose they have agreed to meet.

6. This is the time for *faith*. You let this goal be set for you. That was an act of faith. Do not abandon faith, now that the rewards of faith are being introduced. If you believed the Holy Spirit was there to accept the relationship, why would you now not still believe that He is there to purify what He has taken under His guidance? Have faith in your brother in what but seems to be a trying time. The goal *is* set. And your relationship has sanity as its purpose. For now you find yourself in an insane relationship, recognized as such in the light of its goal.

11. You undertook, together, to invite the Holy Spirit into your relationship. He could not have entered otherwise. Although you may have made many mistakes since then, you have also made enormous efforts to help Him do His work. And He has not been lacking in appreciation for all you have done for Him. Nor does He see the mistakes at all. Have you been similarly grateful to your brother? Have you consistently appreciated the good efforts, and overlooked mistakes? Or has your appreciation flickered and grown dim in what seemed to be the light of the mistakes? Perhaps you are now entering

upon a campaign to blame him for the discomfort of the situation in which you find yourself. And by this lack of thanks and gratitude you make yourself unable to express the holy instant, and thus lose sight of it.

14. You and your brother stand together in the holy presence of truth itself. Here is the goal, together with you. Think you not the goal itself will gladly arrange the means for its accomplishment? It is just this same discrepancy between the purpose that has been accepted and the means as they stand now which seems to make you suffer, but which makes Heaven glad. If Heaven were outside you, you could not share in its gladness. Yet because it is within, the gladness, too, is yours. You *are* joined in purpose, but remain still separate and divided on the means. Yet the goal is fixed, firm and unalterable, and the means will surely fall in place because the goal is sure. And you will share the gladness of the Sonship that it is so.

QUESTION 36. What will forgiveness show you in the real world, and what happens when two people join in a holy relationship?

VI. Setting the Goal

1. The practical application of the Holy Spirit's purpose is extremely simple, but it is unequivocal. In fact, in order to be simple it *must* be unequivocal. The simple is merely what is easily understood, and for this it is apparent that it must be clear. The setting of the Holy Spirit's goal is general. Now He will work with you to make it specific, for application *is* specific. There are certain very specific guidelines He provides for any situation, but remember that you do not yet realize their universal application. Therefore, it is essential at this point to use them in each situation separately, until you can more safely look beyond each situation, in an understanding far broader than you now possess.

2. In any situation in which you are uncertain, the first thing to consider, very simply, is "What do I want to come of this? What is it *for?*" The clarification of the goal belongs at the beginning, for it is this which will determine the outcome. In the ego's procedure this is reversed. The situation becomes the determiner of the outcome, which can be anything. The reason for this disorganized approach is evident. The ego does not know what it wants to come of the situation. It is aware of what it does not want, but only that. It has no positive goal at all.

3. Without a clear-cut, positive goal, set at the outset, the situation just seems to happen, and makes no sense until it has already happened.

Then you look back at it, and try to piece together what it must have meant. And you will be wrong. Not only is your judgment in the past, but you have no idea what should happen. No goal was set with which to bring the means in line. And now the only judgment left to make is whether or not the ego likes it; is it acceptable, or does it call for vengeance? The absence of a criterion for outcome, set in advance, makes understanding doubtful and evaluation impossible.

4. The value of deciding in advance what you want to happen is simply that you will perceive the situation as a means to *make* it happen. You will therefore make *every* effort to overlook what interferes with the accomplishment of your objective, and concentrate on everything that helps you meet it. It is quite noticeable that this approach has brought you closer to the Holy Spirit's sorting out of truth and falsity. The true becomes what can be used to meet the goal. The false becomes the useless from this point of view. The situation now has meaning, but only because the goal has made it meaningful.

5. The goal of truth has further practical advantages. If the situation is used for truth and sanity, its outcome must be peace. And this is quite apart from what the outcome *is*. If peace is the condition of truth and sanity, and cannot be without them, where peace is they must be. Truth comes of itself. If you experience peace, it is because the truth has come to you and you will see the outcome truly, for deception cannot prevail against you. You will recognize the outcome *because* you are at peace. Here again you see the opposite of the ego's way of looking, for the ego believes the situation brings the experience. The Holy Spirit knows that the situation is as the goal determines it, and is experienced according to the goal.

6. The goal of truth requires faith. Faith is implicit in the acceptance of the Holy Spirit's purpose, and this faith is all-inclusive. Where the goal of truth is set, there faith must be. The Holy Spirit sees the situation as a whole. The goal establishes the fact that everyone involved in it will play his part in its accomplishment. This is inevitable. No one will fail in anything. This seems to ask for faith beyond you, and beyond what you can give. Yet this is so only from the viewpoint of the ego, for the ego believes in "solving" conflict through fragmentation, and does not perceive the situation as a whole. Therefore, it seeks to split off segments of the situation and deal with them separately, for it has faith in separation and not in wholeness.

7. Confronted with any aspect of the situation that seems to be difficult, the ego will attempt to take this aspect elsewhere, and resolve it there. And it will seem to be successful, except that this attempt conflicts with unity, and must obscure the goal of truth. And

peace will not be experienced except in fantasy. Truth has not come because faith has been denied, being withheld from where it rightfully belonged. Thus do you lose the understanding of the situation the goal of truth would bring. For fantasy solutions bring but the illusion of experience, and the illusion of peace is not the condition in which truth can enter.

VII. The Call for Faith

5. Every situation in which you find yourself is but a means to meet the purpose set for your relationship. See it as something else and you are faithless. Use not your faithlessness. Let it enter and look upon it calmly, but do not use it. Faithlessness is the servant of illusion, and wholly faithful to its master. Use it, and it will carry you straight to illusions. Be tempted not by what it offers you. It interferes, not with the goal, but with the value of the goal to you. Accept not the illusion of peace it offers, but look upon its offering and recognize it *is* illusion.

9. Enter each situation with the faith you give your brother, or you are faithless to your own relationship. Your faith will call the others to share your purpose, as the same purpose called forth the faith in you. And you will see the means you once employed to lead you to illusions transformed to means for truth. Truth calls for faith, and faith makes room for truth. When the Holy Spirit changed the purpose of your relationship by exchanging yours for His, the goal He placed there was extended to every situation in which you enter, or will ever enter. And every situation was thus made free of the past, which would have made it purposeless.

10. You call for faith because of Him Who walks with you in every situation. You are no longer wholly insane, and no longer alone. For loneliness in God must be a dream. You whose relationship shares the Holy Spirit's goal are set apart from loneliness because the truth has come. Its call for faith is strong. Use not your faithlessness against it, for it calls you to salvation and to peace.

VIII. The Conditions of Peace

1. The holy instant is nothing more than a special case, or an extreme example, of what every situation is meant to be. The meaning that the Holy Spirit's purpose has given it is also given to every situation. It calls forth just the same suspension of faithlessness, withheld and left unused, that faith might answer to the call of truth. The holy instant is the shining example, the clear and unequivocal demonstration of the

meaning of every relationship and every situation, seen as a whole. Faith has accepted every aspect of the situation, and faithlessness has not forced any exclusion on it. It is a situation of perfect peace, simply because you have let it be what it is.

2. This simple courtesy is all the Holy Spirit asks of you. Let truth be what it is. Do not intrude upon it, do not attack it, do not interrupt its coming. Let it encompass every situation and bring you peace. Not even faith is asked of you, for truth asks nothing. Let it enter, and it will call forth and secure for you the faith you need for peace. But rise you not against it, for against your opposition it cannot come.

3. Would you not want to make a holy instant of every situation? For such is the gift of faith, freely given wherever faithlessness is laid aside, unused. And then the power of the Holy Spirit's purpose is free to use instead. This power instantly transforms all situations into one sure and continuous means for establishing His purpose, and demonstrating its reality. What has been demonstrated has called for faith, and has been given it. Now it becomes a fact, from which faith can no longer be withheld. The strain of refusing faith to truth is enormous, and far greater than you realize. But to answer truth with faith entails no strain at all.

4. To you who have acknowledged the Call of your Redeemer, the strain of not responding to His Call seems to be greater than before. This is not so. Before, the strain was there, but you attributed it to something else, believing that the "something else" produced it. This was never true. For what the "something else" produced was sorrow and depression, sickness and pain, darkness and dim imaginings of terror, cold fantasies of fear and fiery dreams of hell. And it was nothing but the intolerable strain of refusing to give faith to truth, and see its evident reality.

6. When you accepted truth as the goal for your relationship, you became a giver of peace as surely as your Father gave peace to you. For the goal of peace cannot be accepted apart from its conditions, and you had faith in it for no one accepts what he does not believe is real. Your purpose has not changed, and will not change, for you accepted what can never change. And nothing that it needs to be forever changeless can you now withhold from it. Your release is certain. Give as you have received. And demonstrate that you have risen far beyond any situation that could hold you back, and keep you separate from Him Whose Call you answered.

QUESTION 37. When you are uncertain about a situation, what do you need to consider and clarify in order be led by the Holy Spirit?

Chapter 18. THE PASSING OF THE DREAM

II. The Basis of the Dream

5. Dreams show you that you have the power to make a world as you would have it be, and that because you want it you see it. And while you see it you do not doubt that it is real. Yet here is a world, clearly within your mind, that seems to be outside. You do not respond to it as though you made it, nor do you realize that the emotions the dream produces must come from you. It is the figures in the dream and what they do that seem to make the dream. You do not realize that you are making them act out for you, for if you did the guilt would not be theirs, and the illusion of satisfaction would be gone. In dreams these features are not obscure. You seem to waken, and the dream is gone. Yet what you fail to recognize is that what caused the dream has not gone with it. Your wish to make another world that is not real remains with you. And what you seem to waken to is but another form of this same world you see in dreams. All your time is spent in dreaming. Your sleeping and your waking dreams have different forms, and that is all. Their content is the same. They are your protest against reality, and your fixed and insane idea that you can change it. In your waking dreams, the special relationship has a special place. It is the means by which you try to make your sleeping dreams come true. From this, you do not waken. The special relationship is your determination to keep your hold on unreality, and to prevent yourself from waking. And while you see more value in sleeping than in waking, you will not let go of it.

6. The Holy Spirit, ever practical in His wisdom, accepts your dreams and uses them as means for waking. You would have used them to remain asleep. I said before that the first change, before dreams disappear, is that your dreams of fear are changed to happy dreams. That is what the Holy Spirit does in the special relationship. He does not destroy it, nor snatch it away from you. But He does use it differently, as a help to make His purpose real to you. The special relationship will remain, not as a source of pain and guilt, but as a source of joy and freedom. It will not be for you alone, for therein lay its misery. As its unholiness kept it a thing apart, its holiness will become an offering to everyone.

7. Your special relationship will be a means for undoing guilt in everyone blessed through your holy relationship. It will be a happy dream, and one which you will share with all who come within your sight. Through it, the blessing the Holy Spirit has laid upon it will be

extended. Think not that He has forgotten anyone in the purpose He has given you. And think not that He has forgotten you to whom He gave the gift. He uses everyone who calls on Him as means for the salvation of everyone. And He will waken everyone through you who offered your relationship to Him. If you but recognized His gratitude! Or mine through His! For we are joined as in one purpose, being of one mind with Him.

III. Light in the Dream

4.   You who hold your brother's hand also hold mine, for when you joined each other you were not alone. Do you believe that I would leave you in the darkness that you agreed to leave with me? In your relationship is this world's light. And fear must disappear before you now. Be tempted not to snatch away the gift of faith you offered to your brother. You will succeed only in frightening yourself. The gift is given forever, for God Himself received it. You cannot take it back. You have accepted God. The holiness of your relationship is established in Heaven. You do not understand what you accepted, but remember that your understanding is not necessary. All that was necessary was merely the *wish* to understand. That wish was the desire to be holy. The Will of God is granted you. For you desire the only thing you ever had, or *ever were*.

5.   Each instant that we spend together will teach you that this goal is possible, and will strengthen your desire to reach it. And in your desire lies its accomplishment. Your desire is now in complete accord with all the power of the Holy Spirit's Will. No little, faltering footsteps that you may take can separate your desire from His Will and from His strength. I hold your hand as surely as you agreed to take your brother's. You will not separate, for I stand with you and walk with you in your advance to truth. And where we go we carry God with us.

6.   In your relationship you have joined with me in bringing Heaven to the Son of God, who hid in darkness. You have been willing to bring the darkness to light, and this willingness has given strength to everyone who would remain in darkness. Those who would see *will* see. And they will join with me in carrying their light into the darkness, when the darkness in them is offered to the light, and is removed forever. My need for you, joined with me in the holy light of your relationship, is your need for salvation. Would I not give you what you gave to me? For when you joined your brother, you answered me.

8.   Not one light in Heaven but goes with you. Not one Ray that shines forever in the Mind of God but shines on you. Heaven is joined with

you in your advance to Heaven. When such great lights have joined with you to give the little spark of your desire the power of God Himself, can you remain in darkness? You and your brother are coming home together, after a long and meaningless journey that you undertook apart, and that led nowhere. You have found your brother, and you will light each other's way. And from this light will the Great Rays extend back into darkness and forward unto God, to shine away the past and so make room for His eternal Presence, in which everything is radiant in the light.

IV. The Little Willingness

2. Trust not your good intentions. They are not enough. But trust implicitly your willingness, whatever else may enter. Concentrate only on this, and be not disturbed that shadows surround it. That is why you came. If you could come without them you would not need the holy instant. Come to it not in arrogance, assuming that you must achieve the state its coming brings with it. The miracle of the holy instant lies in your willingness to let it be what it is. And in your willingness for this lies also your acceptance of yourself as you were meant to be.
3. Humility will never ask that you remain content with littleness. But it does require that you be not content with less than greatness that comes not of you. Your difficulty with the holy instant arises from your fixed conviction that you are not worthy of it. And what is this but the determination to be as you would make yourself? God did not create His dwelling place unworthy of Him. And if you believe He cannot enter where He wills to be, you must be interfering with His Will. You do not need the strength of willingness to come from you, but only from His Will.
4. The holy instant does not come from your little willingness alone. It is always the result of your small willingness combined with the unlimited power of God's Will. You have been wrong in thinking that it is needful to prepare yourself for Him. It is impossible to make arrogant preparations for holiness, and not believe that it is up to you to establish the conditions for peace. God has established them. They do not wait upon your willingness for what they are. Your willingness is needed only to make it possible to teach you what they are. If you maintain you are unworthy of learning this, you are interfering with the lesson by believing that you must make the learner different. You did not make the learner, nor can you make him different. Would you first make a miracle yourself, and then expect one to be made *for* you?

5. You merely ask the question. The answer is given. Seek not to answer, but merely to receive the answer as it is given. In preparing for the holy instant, do not attempt to make yourself holy to be ready to receive it. That is but to confuse your role with God's. Atonement cannot come to those who think that they must first atone, but only to those who offer it nothing more than simple willingness to make way for it. Purification is of God alone, and therefore for you. Rather than seek to prepare yourself for Him, try to think thus:

> *I who am host to God am worthy of Him.*
> *He Who established His dwelling place in me created it as*
> *   He would have it be.*
> *It is not needful that I make it ready for Him, but only that*
> *   I do not interfere with His plan to restore to me my own*
> *   awareness of my readiness, which is eternal.*
> *I need add nothing to His plan.*
> *But to receive it, I must be willing not to substitute my own*
> *   in place of it.*

6. And that is all. Add more, and you will merely take away the little that is asked. Remember you made guilt, and that your plan for the escape from guilt has been to bring Atonement to it, and make salvation fearful. And it is only fear that you will add, if you prepare yourself for love. The preparation for the holy instant belongs to Him Who gives it. Release yourself to Him Whose function is release. Do not assume His function for Him. Give Him but what He asks, that you may learn how little is your part, and how great is His.

V. The Happy Dream

2. Never approach the holy instant after you have tried to remove all fear and hatred from your mind. That is *its* function. Never attempt to overlook your guilt before you ask the Holy Spirit's help. That is *His* function. Your part is only to offer Him a little willingness to let Him remove all fear and hatred, and to be forgiven. On your little faith, joined with His understanding, He will build your part in the Atonement and make sure that you fulfill it easily. And with Him, you will build a ladder planted in the solid rock of faith, and rising even to Heaven. Nor will you use it to ascend to Heaven alone.

3. Through your holy relationship, reborn and blessed in every holy instant you do not arrange, thousands will rise to Heaven with you. Can you plan for this? Or could you prepare yourself for such a function? Yet it is possible, because God wills it. Nor will He change

His Mind about it. The means and purpose both belong to Him. You have accepted one; the other will be provided. A purpose such as this, without the means, is inconceivable. He will provide the means to anyone who shares His purpose.

4. Happy dreams come true, not because they are dreams, but only because they are happy. And so they must be loving. Their message is, "Thy Will be done," and not, "I want it otherwise." The alignment of means and purpose is an undertaking impossible for you to understand. You do not even realize you have accepted the Holy Spirit's purpose as your own, and you would merely bring unholy means to its accomplishment. The little faith it needed to change the purpose is all that is required to receive the means and use them.

5. It is no dream to love your brother as yourself. Nor is your holy relationship a dream. All that remains of dreams within it is that it is still a special relationship. Yet it is very useful to the Holy Spirit, Who *has* a special function here. It will become the happy dream through which He can spread joy to thousands on thousands who believe that love is fear, not happiness. Let Him fulfill the function that He gave to your relationship by accepting it for you, and nothing will be wanting that would make of it what He would have it be.

6. When you feel the holiness of your relationship is threatened by anything, stop instantly and offer the Holy Spirit your willingness, in spite of fear, to let Him exchange this instant for the holy one that you would rather have. He will never fail in this. But forget not that your relationship is one, and so it must be that whatever threatens the peace of one is an equal threat to the other. The power of joining its blessing lies in the fact that it is now impossible for you or your brother to experience fear alone, or to attempt to deal with it alone. Never believe that this is necessary, or even possible. Yet just as this is impossible, so is it equally impossible that the holy instant come to either of you without the other. And it will come to both at the request of either.

7. Whoever is saner at the time the threat is perceived should remember how deep is his indebtedness to the other and how much gratitude is due him, and be glad that he can pay his debt by bringing happiness to both. Let him remember this, and say:

> *I desire this holy instant for myself, that I may share it with my brother, whom I love.*
> *It is not possible that I can have it without him, or he without me.*
> *Yet it is wholly possible for us to share it now.*
> *And so I choose this instant as the one to offer to the Holy Spirit, that His blessing may descend on us, and keep us both in peace.*

QUESTION 38. What is required of you to manifest the miracle of the holy instant?

VI. Beyond the Body

1. There is nothing outside you. That is what you must ultimately learn, for it is the realization that the Kingdom of Heaven is restored to you. For God created only this, and He did not depart from it nor leave it separate from Himself. The Kingdom of Heaven is the dwelling place of the Son of God, who left not his Father and dwells not apart from Him. Heaven is not a place nor a condition. It is merely an awareness of perfect Oneness, and the knowledge that there is nothing else; nothing outside this Oneness, and nothing else within.

2. What could God give but knowledge of Himself? What else is there to give? The belief that you could give and get something else, something outside yourself, has cost you the awareness of Heaven and of your Identity. And you have done a stranger thing than you yet realize. You have displaced your guilt to your body from your mind. Yet a body cannot be guilty, for it can do nothing of itself. You who think you hate your body deceive yourself. You hate your mind, for guilt has entered into it, and it would remain separate from your brother's, which it cannot do.

3. Minds are joined; bodies are not. Only by assigning to the mind the properties of the body does separation seem to be possible. And it is mind that seems to be fragmented and private and alone. Its guilt, which keeps it separate, is projected to the body, which suffers and dies because it is attacked to hold the separation in the mind, and let it not know its Identity. Mind cannot attack, but it can make fantasies and direct the body to act them out. Yet it is never what the body does that seems to satisfy. Unless the mind believes the body is actually acting out its fantasies, it will attack the body by increasing the projection of its guilt upon it.

4. In this, the mind is clearly delusional. It cannot attack, but it maintains it can, and uses what it does to hurt the body to prove it can. The mind cannot attack, but it can deceive itself. And this is all it does when it believes it has attacked the body. It can project its guilt, but it will not lose it through projection. And though it clearly can misperceive the function of the body, it cannot change its function from what the Holy Spirit establishes it to be. The body was not made by love. Yet love does not condemn it and can use it lovingly, respecting what the Son of God has made and using it to save him from illusions.

9. The body is outside you, and but seems to surround you, shutting you off from others and keeping you apart from them, and them from you. It is not there. There is no barrier between God and His Son, nor can His Son be separated from Himself except in illusions. This is not his reality, though he believes it is. Yet this could only be if God were wrong. God would have had to create differently, and to have separated Himself from His Son to make this possible. He would have had to create different things, and to establish different orders of reality, only some of which were love. Yet love must be forever like itself, changeless forever, and forever without alternative. And so it is. You cannot put a barrier around yourself, because God placed none between Himself and you.

10. You can stretch out your hand and reach to Heaven. You whose hand is joined with your brother's have begun to reach beyond the body, but not outside yourself, to reach your shared Identity together. Could this be outside you? Where God is not? Is *He* a body, and did He create you as He is not, and where He cannot be? You are surrounded only by Him. What limits can there be on you whom He encompasses?

11. Everyone has experienced what he would call a sense of being transported beyond himself. This feeling of liberation far exceeds the dream of freedom sometimes hoped for in special relationships. It is a sense of actual escape from limitations. If you will consider what this "transportation" really entails, you will realize that it is a sudden unawareness of the body, and a joining of yourself and something else in which your mind enlarges to encompass it. It becomes part of you, as you unite with it. And both become whole, as neither is perceived as separate. What really happens is that you have given up the illusion of a limited awareness, and lost your fear of union. The love that instantly replaces it extends to what has freed you, and unites with it. And while this lasts you are not uncertain of your Identity, and would not limit It. You have escaped from fear to peace, asking no questions of reality, but merely accepting it. You have accepted this instead of the body, and have let yourself be one with something beyond it, simply by not letting your mind be limited by it.

12. This can occur regardless of the physical distance that seems to be between you and what you join; of your respective positions in space; and of your differences in size and seeming quality. Time is not relevant; it can occur with something past, present or anticipated. The "something" can be anything and anywhere; a sound, a sight, a thought, a memory, and even a general idea without specific reference. Yet in every case, you join it without reservation because you love it,

and would be with it. And so you rush to meet it, letting your limits melt away, suspending all the "laws" your body obeys and gently setting them aside.

13. There is no violence at all in this escape. The body is not attacked, but simply properly perceived. It does not limit you, merely because you would not have it so. You are not really "lifted out" of it; it cannot contain you. You go where you would be, gaining, not losing, a sense of Self. In these instants of release from physical restrictions, you experience much of what happens in the holy instant; the lifting of the barriers of time and space, the sudden experience of peace and joy, and, above all, the lack of awareness of the body, and of the questioning whether or not all this is possible.

14. It is possible because you want it. The sudden expansion of awareness that takes place with your desire for it is the irresistible appeal the holy instant holds. It calls to you to be yourself, within its safe embrace. There are the laws of limit lifted for you, to welcome you to openness of mind and freedom. Come to this place of refuge, where you can be yourself in peace. Not through destruction, not through a breaking out, but merely by a quiet melting in. For peace will join you there, simply because you have been willing to let go the limits you have placed upon love, and joined it where it is and where it led you, in answer to its gentle call to be at peace.

VII. I Need Do Nothing

1. You still have too much faith in the body as a source of strength. What plans do you make that do not involve its comfort or protection or enjoyment in some way? This makes the body an end and not a means in your interpretation, and this always means you still find sin attractive. No one accepts Atonement for himself who still accepts sin as his goal. You have thus not met your *one* responsibility. Atonement is not welcomed by those who prefer pain and destruction.

2. There is one thing that you have never done; you have not utterly forgotten the body. It has perhaps faded at times from your sight, but it has not yet completely disappeared. You are not asked to let this happen for more than an instant, yet it is in this instant that the miracle of Atonement happens. Afterwards you will see the body again, but never quite the same. And every instant that you spend without awareness of it gives you a different view of it when you return.

3. At no single instant does the body exist at all. It is always remembered or anticipated, but never experienced just *now*. Only its past and future make it seem real. Time controls it entirely, for sin is

never wholly in the present. In any single instant the attraction of guilt would be experienced as pain and nothing else, and would be avoided. It has no attraction *now*. Its whole attraction is imaginary, and therefore must be thought of in the past or in the future.

4. It is impossible to accept the holy instant without reservation unless, just for an instant, you are willing to see no past or future. You cannot prepare for it without placing it in the future. Release is given you the instant you desire it. Many have spent a lifetime in preparation, and have indeed achieved their instants of success. This course does not attempt to teach more than they learned in time, but it does aim at saving time. You may be attempting to follow a very long road to the goal you have accepted. It is extremely difficult to reach Atonement by fighting against sin. Enormous effort is expended in the attempt to make holy what is hated and despised. Nor is a lifetime of contemplation and long periods of meditation aimed at detachment from the body necessary. All such attempts will ultimately succeed because of their purpose. Yet the means are tedious and very time consuming, for all of them look to the future for release from a state of present unworthiness and inadequacy.

5. Your way will be different, not in purpose but in means. A holy relationship is a means of saving time. One instant spent together with your brother restores the universe to both of you. You *are* prepared. Now you need but to remember you need do nothing. It would be far more profitable now merely to concentrate on this than to consider what you should do. When peace comes at last to those who wrestle with temptation and fight against the giving in to sin; when the light comes at last into the mind given to contemplation; or when the goal is finally achieved by anyone, it always comes with just one happy realization; "*I need do nothing.*"

6. Here is the ultimate release which everyone will one day find in his own way, at his own time. You do not need this time. Time has been saved for you because you and your brother are together. This is the special means this course is using to save you time. You are not making use of the course if you insist on using means which have served others well, neglecting what was made for *you*. Save time for me by only this one preparation, and practice doing nothing else. "I need do nothing" is a statement of allegiance, a truly undivided loyalty. Believe it for just one instant, and you will accomplish more than is given to a century of contemplation, or of struggle against temptation.

7. To do anything involves the body. And if you recognize you need do nothing, you have withdrawn the body's value from your mind. Here is the quick and open door through which you slip past centuries of effort, and escape from time. This is the way in which sin loses all

attraction *right now*. For here is time denied, and past and future gone. Who needs do nothing has no need for time. To do nothing is to rest, and make a place within you where the activity of the body ceases to demand attention. Into this place the Holy Spirit comes, and there abides. He will remain when you forget, and the body's activities return to occupy your conscious mind.

8. Yet there will always be this place of rest to which you can return. And you will be more aware of this quiet center of the storm than all its raging activity. This quiet center, in which you do nothing, will remain with you, giving you rest in the midst of every busy doing on which you are sent. For from this center will you be directed how to use the body sinlessly. It is this center, from which the body is absent, that will keep it so in your awareness of it.

QUESTION 39. What is it like to go beyond the limitations imposed by the body, and what is the Course really recommending when it says "you need do nothing"?

VIII. The Little Garden

1. It is only the awareness of the body that makes love seem limited. For the body *is* a limit on love. The belief in limited love was its origin, and it was made to limit the unlimited. Think not that this is merely allegorical, for it was made to limit *you*. Can you who see yourself within a body know yourself as an idea? Everything you recognize you identify with externals, something outside itself. You cannot even think of God without a body, or in some form you think you recognize.

2. The body cannot know. And while you limit your awareness to its tiny senses, you will not see the grandeur that surrounds you. God cannot come into a body, nor can you join Him there. Limits on love will always seem to shut Him out, and keep you apart from Him. The body is a tiny fence around a little part of a glorious and complete idea. It draws a circle, infinitely small, around a very little segment of Heaven, splintered from the whole, proclaiming that within it is your kingdom, where God can enter not.

3. Within this kingdom the ego rules, and cruelly. And to defend this little speck of dust it bids you fight against the universe. This fragment of your mind is such a tiny part of it that, could you but appreciate the whole, you would see instantly that it is like the smallest sunbeam to the sun, or like the faintest ripple on the surface of the ocean. In its amazing arrogance, this tiny sunbeam has decided it is the sun; this almost imperceptible ripple hails itself as the ocean. Think how alone and frightened is this little thought, this infinitesimal illusion, holding

itself apart against the universe. The sun becomes the sunbeam's "enemy" that would devour it, and the ocean terrifies the little ripple and wants to swallow it.

4. Yet neither sun nor ocean is even aware of all this strange and meaningless activity. They merely continue, unaware that they are feared and hated by a tiny segment of themselves. Even that segment is not lost to them, for it could not survive apart from them. And what it thinks it is in no way changes its total dependence on them for its being. Its whole existence still remains in them. Without the sun the sunbeam would be gone; the ripple without the ocean is inconceivable.

5. Such is the strange position in which those in a world inhabited by bodies seem to be. Each body seems to house a separate mind, a disconnected thought, living alone and in no way joined to the Thought by which it was created. Each tiny fragment seems to be self-contained, needing another for some things, but by no means totally dependent on its one Creator for everything; needing the whole to give it any meaning, for by itself it does mean nothing. Nor has it any life apart and by itself.

6. Like to the sun and ocean your Self continues, unmindful that this tiny part regards itself as you. It is not missing; it could not exist if it were separate, nor would the Whole be whole without it. It is not a separate kingdom, ruled by an idea of separation from the rest. Nor does a fence surround it, preventing it from joining with the rest, and keeping it apart from its Creator. This little aspect is no different from the whole, being continuous with it and at one with it. It leads no separate life, because its life *is* the oneness in which its being was created.

7. Do not accept this little, fenced-off aspect as yourself. The sun and ocean are as nothing beside what you are. The sunbeam sparkles only in the sunlight, and the ripple dances as it rests upon the ocean. Yet in neither sun nor ocean is the power that rests in you. Would you remain within your tiny kingdom, a sorry king, a bitter ruler of all that he surveys, who looks on nothing yet who would still die to defend it? This little self is not your kingdom. Arched high above it and surrounding it with love is the glorious whole, which offers all its happiness and deep content to every part. The little aspect that you think you set apart is no exception.

8. Love knows no bodies, and reaches to everything created like itself. Its total lack of limit *is* its meaning. It is completely impartial in its giving, encompassing only to preserve and keep complete what it would give. In your tiny kingdom you have so little! Should it not, then, be there that you would call on love to enter? Look at the desert—dry and unproductive, scorched and joyless—that makes up

your little kingdom. And realize the life and joy that love would bring to it from where it comes, and where it would return with you.

9. The Thought of God surrounds your little kingdom, waiting at the barrier you built to come inside and shine upon the barren ground. See how life springs up everywhere! The desert becomes a garden, green and deep and quiet, offering rest to those who lost their way and wander in the dust. Give them a place of refuge, prepared by love for them where once a desert was. And everyone you welcome will bring love with him from Heaven for you. They enter one by one into this holy place, but they will not depart as they had come, alone. The love they brought with them will stay with them, as it will stay with you. And under its beneficence your little garden will expand, and reach out to everyone who thirsts for living water, but has grown too weary to go on alone.

10. Go out and find them, for they bring your Self with them. And lead them gently to your quiet garden, and receive their blessing there. So will it grow and stretch across the desert, leaving no lonely little kingdoms locked away from love, and leaving you inside. And you will recognize yourself, and see your little garden gently transformed into the Kingdom of Heaven, with all the Love of its Creator shining upon it.

11. The holy instant is your invitation to love to enter into your bleak and joyless kingdom, and to transform it into a garden of peace and welcome. Love's answer is inevitable. It will come because you came without the body, and interposed no barriers to interfere with its glad coming. In the holy instant, you ask of love only what it offers everyone, neither less nor more. Asking for everything, you will receive it. And your shining Self will lift the tiny aspect that you tried to hide from Heaven straight to Heaven. No part of love calls on the whole in vain. No Son of God remains outside His Fatherhood.

12. Be sure of this; love has entered your special relationship, and entered fully at your weak request. You do not recognize that love has come, because you have not yet let go of all the barriers you hold against your brother. And you and he will not be able to give love welcome separately. You could no more know God alone than He knows you without your brother. But together you could no more be unaware of love than love could know you not, or fail to recognize itself in you.

13. You have reached the end of an ancient journey, not realizing yet that it is over. You are still worn and tired, and the desert's dust still seems to cloud your eyes and keep you sightless. Yet He Whom you welcomed has come to you, and would welcome you. He has

waited long to give you this. Receive it now of Him, for He would have you know Him. Only a little wall of dust still stands between you and your brother. Blow on it lightly and with happy laughter, and it will fall away. And walk into the garden love has prepared for both of you.

IX. The Two Worlds

5. The body will remain guilt's messenger, and will act as it directs as long as you believe that guilt is real. For the reality of guilt is the illusion that seems to make it heavy and opaque, impenetrable, and a real foundation for the ego's thought system. Its thinness and transparency are not apparent until you see the light behind it. And then you see it as a fragile veil before the light.

6. This heavy-seeming barrier, this artificial floor that looks like rock, is like a bank of low dark clouds that seem to be a solid wall before the sun. Its impenetrable appearance is wholly an illusion. It gives way softly to the mountain tops that rise above it, and has no power at all to hold back anyone willing to climb above it and see the sun. It is not strong enough to stop a button's fall, nor hold a feather. Nothing can rest upon it, for it is but an illusion of a foundation. Try but to touch it and it disappears; attempt to grasp it and your hands hold nothing.

8. So should it be with the dark clouds of guilt, no more impenetrable and no more substantial. You will not bruise yourself against them in traveling through. Let your Guide teach you their unsubstantial nature as He leads you past them, for beneath them is a world of light whereon they cast no shadows. Their shadows lie upon the world beyond them, still further from the light. Yet from them to the light their shadows cannot fall.

9. This world of light, this circle of brightness is the real world, where guilt meets with forgiveness. Here the world outside is seen anew, without the shadow of guilt upon it. Here are you forgiven, for here you have forgiven everyone. Here is the new perception, where everything is bright and shining with innocence, washed in the waters of forgiveness, and cleansed of every evil thought you laid upon it. Here there is no attack upon the Son of God, and you are welcome. Here is your innocence, waiting to clothe you and protect you, and make you ready for the final step in the journey inward. Here are the dark and heavy garments of guilt laid by, and gently replaced by purity and love.

10. Yet even forgiveness is not the end. Forgiveness does make lovely, but it does not create. It is the source of healing, but it is the messenger of love and not its Source. Here you are led, that God Himself can take

the final step unhindered, for here does nothing interfere with love, letting it be itself. A step beyond this holy place of forgiveness, a step still further inward but the one *you* cannot take, transports you to something completely different. Here is the Source of light; nothing perceived, forgiven nor transformed. But merely known.

11.   This course will lead to knowledge, but knowledge itself is still beyond the scope of our curriculum. Nor is there any need for us to try to speak of what must forever lie beyond words. We need remember only that whoever attains the real world, beyond which learning cannot go, will go beyond it, but in a different way. Where learning ends there God begins, for learning ends before Him Who is complete where He begins, and where there *is* no end. It is not for us to dwell on what cannot be attained. There is too much to learn. The readiness for knowledge still must be attained.

12.   Love is not learned. Its meaning lies within itself. And learning ends when you have recognized all it is *not*. That is the interference; that is what needs to be undone. Love is not learned, because there never was a time in which you knew it not. Learning is useless in the Presence of your Creator, Whose acknowledgment of you and yours of Him so far transcend all learning that everything you learned is meaningless, replaced forever by the knowledge of love and its one meaning.

13.   Your relationship with your brother has been uprooted from the world of shadows, and its unholy purpose has been safely brought through the barriers of guilt, washed with forgiveness, and set shining and firmly rooted in the world of light. From there it calls to you to follow the course it took, lifted high above the darkness and gently placed before the gates of Heaven. The holy instant in which you and your brother were united is but the messenger of love, sent from beyond forgiveness to remind you of all that lies beyond it. Yet it is through forgiveness that it will be remembered.

14.   And when the memory of God has come to you in the holy place of forgiveness you will remember nothing else, and memory will be as useless as learning, for your only purpose will be creating. Yet this you cannot know until *every* perception has been cleansed and purified, and finally removed forever. Forgiveness removes only the untrue, lifting the shadows from the world and carrying it, safe and sure within its gentleness, to the bright world of new and clean perception. There is your purpose *now*. And it is there that peace awaits you.

QUESTION 40. What is the body's relationship to the ego, to love, to your Self, and to God?

Chapter 19. THE ATTAINMENT OF PEACE

I. Healing and Faith

2. Every situation, properly perceived, becomes an opportunity to heal the Son of God. And he is healed *because* you offered faith to him, giving him to the Holy Spirit and releasing him from every demand your ego would make of him. Thus do you see him free, and in this vision does the Holy Spirit share. And since He shares it He has given it, and so He heals through you. It is this joining Him in a united purpose that makes this purpose real, because you make it whole. And this *is* healing. The body is healed because you came without it, and joined the Mind in which all healing rests.

9. To have faith is to heal. It is the sign that you have accepted the Atonement for yourself, and would therefore share it. By faith, you offer the gift of freedom from the past, which you received. You do not use anything your brother has done before to condemn him now. You freely choose to overlook his errors, looking past all barriers between yourself and him, and seeing them as one. And in that one you see your faith is fully justified. There is no justification for faithlessness, but faith is always justified.

10. Faith is the opposite of fear, as much a part of love as fear is of attack. Faith is the acknowledgment of union. It is the gracious acknowledgment of everyone as a Son of your most loving Father, loved by Him like you, and therefore loved by you as yourself. It is His Love that joins you and your brother, and for His Love you would keep no one separate from yours. Each one appears just as he is perceived in the holy instant, united in your purpose to be released from guilt. You see the Christ in him, and he is healed because you look on what makes faith forever justified in everyone.

11. Faith is the gift of God, through Him Whom God has given you. Faithlessness looks upon the Son of God, and judges him unworthy of forgiveness. But through the eyes of faith, the Son of God is seen already forgiven, free of all the guilt he laid upon himself. Faith sees him only *now* because it looks not to the past to judge him, but would see in him only what it would see in you. It sees not through the body's eyes, nor looks to bodies for its justification. It is the messenger of the new perception, sent forth to gather witnesses unto its coming, and to return their messages to you.

12. Faith is as easily exchanged for knowledge as is the real world. For faith arises from the Holy Spirit's perception, and is the sign you share

it with Him. Faith is a gift you offer to the Son of God through Him, and wholly acceptable to his Father as to Him. And therefore offered you. Your holy relationship, with its new purpose, offers you faith to give unto your brother. Your faithlessness has driven you and him apart, and so you do not recognize salvation in him. Yet faith unites you in the holiness you see, not through the body's eyes, but in the sight of Him Who joined you, and in Whom you are united.

13. Grace is not given to a body, but to a mind. And the mind that receives it looks instantly beyond the body, and sees the holy place where it was healed. There is the altar where the grace was given, in which it stands. Do you, then, offer grace and blessing to your brother, for you stand at the same altar where grace was laid for both of you. And be you healed by grace together, that you may heal through faith.

14. In the holy instant, you and your brother stand before the altar God has raised unto Himself and both of you. Lay faithlessness aside, and come to it together. There will you see the miracle of your relationship as it was made again through faith. And there it is that you will realize that there is nothing faith cannot forgive. No error interferes with its calm sight, which brings the miracle of healing with equal ease to all of them. For what the messengers of love are sent to do they do, returning the glad tidings that it was done to you and your brother who stand together before the altar from which they were sent forth.

II. Sin versus Error

1. It is essential that error be not confused with sin, and it is this distinction that makes salvation possible. For error can be corrected, and the wrong made right. But sin, were it possible, would be irreversible. The belief in sin is necessarily based on the firm conviction that minds, not bodies, can attack. And thus the mind is guilty, and will forever so remain unless a mind not part of it can give it absolution. Sin calls for punishment as error for correction, and the belief that punishment *is* correction is clearly insane.

2. Sin is not an error, for sin entails an arrogance which the idea of error lacks. To sin would be to violate reality, and to succeed. Sin is the proclamation that attack is real and guilt is justified. It assumes the Son of God is guilty, and has thus succeeded in losing his innocence and making himself what God created not. Thus is creation seen as not eternal, and the Will of God open to opposition and defeat. Sin is

the grand illusion underlying all the ego's grandiosity. For by it God Himself is changed, and rendered incomplete.

3. The Son of God can be mistaken; he can deceive himself; he can even turn the power of his mind against himself. But he *cannot* sin. There is nothing he can do that would really change his reality in any way, nor make him really guilty. That is what sin would do, for such is its purpose. Yet for all the wild insanity inherent in the whole idea of sin, it is impossible. For the wages of sin *is* death, and how can the immortal die?

5. Any attempt to reinterpret sin as error is always indefensible to the ego. The idea of sin is wholly sacrosanct to its thought system, and quite unapproachable except with reverence and awe. It is the most "holy" concept in the ego's system; lovely and powerful, wholly true, and necessarily protected with every defense at its disposal. For here lies its "best" defense, which all the others serve. Here is its armor, its protection, and the fundamental purpose of the special relationship in its interpretation.

6. It can indeed be said the ego made its world on sin. Only in such a world could everything be upside down. This is the strange illusion that makes the clouds of guilt seem heavy and impenetrable. The solidness that this world's foundation seems to have is found in this. For sin has changed creation from an idea of God to an ideal the ego wants; a world it rules, made up of bodies, mindless and capable of complete corruption and decay. If this is a mistake, it can be undone easily by truth. Any mistake can be corrected, if truth be left to judge it. But if the mistake is given the status of truth, to what can it be brought? The "holiness" of sin is kept in place by just this strange device. As truth it is inviolate, and everything is brought to *it* for judgment. As a mistake, *it* must be brought to truth. It is impossible to have faith in sin, for sin is faithlessness. Yet it is possible to have faith that a mistake can be corrected.

IV. The Obstacles to Peace

A. The First Obstacle: The Desire to Get Rid of It

1. The first obstacle that peace must flow across is your desire to get rid of it. For it cannot extend unless you keep it. You are the center from which it radiates outward, to call the others in. You are its home; its tranquil dwelling place from which it gently reaches out, but never leaving you. If you would make it homeless, how can it abide within the Son of God? If it would spread across the whole creation, it must

begin with you, and from you reach to everyone who calls, and bring him rest by joining you.

5.   To overcome the world is no more difficult than to surmount your little wall. For in the miracle of your holy relationship, without this barrier, is every miracle contained. There is no order of difficulty in miracles, for they are all the same. Each is a gentle winning over from the appeal of guilt to the appeal of love. How can this fail to be accomplished, wherever it is undertaken? Guilt can raise no real barriers against it. And all that seems to stand between you and your brother must fall away because of the appeal you answered. From you who answered, He Who answered you would call. His home is in your holy relationship. Do not attempt to stand between Him and His holy purpose, for it is yours. But let Him quietly extend the miracle of your relationship to everyone contained in it as it was given.

i. The Attraction of Guilt

10.   The attraction of guilt produces fear of love, for love would never look on guilt at all. It is the nature of love to look upon only the truth, for there it sees itself, with which it would unite in holy union and completion. As love must look past fear, so must fear see love not. For love contains the end of guilt, as surely as fear depends on it. Love is attracted only to love. Overlooking guilt completely, it sees no fear. Being wholly without attack, it could not be afraid. Fear is attracted to what love sees not, and each believes that what the other looks upon does not exist. Fear looks on guilt with just the same devotion that love looks on itself. And each has messengers which it sends forth, and which return to it with messages written in the language in which their going forth was asked.

15.   If you send forth only the messengers the Holy Spirit gives you, wanting no messages but theirs, you will see fear no more. The world will be transformed before your sight, cleansed of all guilt and softly brushed with beauty. The world contains no fear that you laid not upon it. And none you cannot ask love's messengers to remove from it, and see it still. The Holy Spirit has given you His messengers to send to your brother and return to you with what love sees. They have been given to replace the hungry dogs of fear you sent instead. And they go forth to signify the end of fear.

16.   Love, too, would set a feast before you, on a table covered with a spotless cloth, set in a quiet garden where no sound but singing and a softly joyous whispering is ever heard. This is a feast that honors your holy relationship, and at which everyone is welcomed as an honored

guest. And in a holy instant grace is said by everyone together, as they join in gentleness before the table of communion. And I will join you there, as long ago I promised and promise still. For in your new relationship am I made welcome. And where I am made welcome, there I am.

B. The Second Obstacle:
The Belief the Body is Valuable for What It Offers

1. We said that peace must first surmount the obstacle of your desire to get rid of it. Where the attraction of guilt holds sway, peace is not wanted. The second obstacle that peace must flow across, and closely related to the first, is the belief that the body is valuable for what it offers. For here is the attraction of guilt made manifest in the body, and seen in it.
2. This is the value that you think peace would rob you of. This is what you believe that it would dispossess, and leave you homeless. And it is this for which you would deny a home to peace. This "sacrifice" you feel to be too great to make, too much to ask of you. Is it a sacrifice, or a release? What has the body really given you that justifies your strange belief that in it lies salvation? Do you not see that this is the belief in death? Here is the focus of the perception of Atonement as murder. Here is the source of the idea that love is fear.
6. Let me be to you the symbol of the end of guilt, and look upon your brother as you would look on me. Forgive me all the sins you think the Son of God committed. And in the light of your forgiveness he will remember who he is, and forget what never was. I ask for your forgiveness, for if you are guilty, so must I be. But if I surmounted guilt and overcame the world, you were with me. Would you see in me the symbol of guilt or of the end of guilt, remembering that what I signify to you you see within yourself?

i. The Attraction of Pain

12. It is impossible to seek for pleasure through the body and not find pain. It is essential that this relationship be understood, for it is one the ego sees as proof of sin. It is not really punitive at all. It is but the inevitable result of equating yourself with the body, which is the invitation to pain. For it invites fear to enter and become your purpose. The attraction of guilt *must* enter with it, and whatever fear directs the

body to do is therefore painful. It will share the pain of all illusions, and the illusion of pleasure will be the same as pain.

14. Why should the body be anything to you? Certainly what it is made of is not precious. And just as certainly it has no feeling. It transmits to you the feelings that you want. Like any communication medium the body receives and sends the messages that it is given. It has no feeling for them. All of the feeling with which they are invested is given by the sender and the receiver. The ego and the Holy Spirit both recognize this, and both also recognize that here the sender and receiver are the same. The Holy Spirit tells you this with joy. The ego hides it, for it would keep you unaware of it. Who would send messages of hatred and attack if he but understood he sends them to himself? Who would accuse, make guilty and condemn himself?

17. It is not given to the ego's disciples to realize that they have dedicated themselves to death. Freedom is offered them but they have not accepted it, and what is offered must also be received, to be truly given. For the Holy Spirit, too, is a communication medium, receiving from the Father and offering His messages unto the Son. Like the ego, the Holy Spirit is both the sender and the receiver. For what is sent through Him returns to Him, seeking itself along the way, and finding what it seeks. So does the ego find the death *it* seeks, returning it to you.

QUESTION 41. What is the truth about sin and its effects?

C. The Third Obstacle: The Attraction of Death

1. To you and your brother, in whose special relationship the Holy Spirit entered, it is given to release and be released from the dedication to death. For it was offered you, and you accepted. Yet you must learn still more about this strange devotion, for it contains the third obstacle that peace must flow across. No one can die unless he chooses death. What seems to be the fear of death is really its attraction. Guilt, too, is feared and fearful. Yet it could have no hold at all except on those who are attracted to it and seek it out. And so it is with death. Made by the ego, its dark shadow falls across all living things, because the ego is the "enemy" of life.

2. And yet a shadow cannot kill. What is a shadow to the living? They but walk past and it is gone. But what of those whose dedication is not to live; the black-draped "sinners," the ego's mournful chorus, plodding so heavily away from life, dragging their chains and marching in the slow procession that honors their grim master, lord of death?

Touch any one of them with the gentle hands of forgiveness, and watch the chains fall away, along with yours. See him throw aside the black robe he was wearing to his funeral, and hear him laugh at death. The sentence sin would lay upon him he can escape through your forgiveness. This is no arrogance. It is the Will of God. What is impossible to you who chose His Will as yours? What is death to you? Your dedication is not to death, nor to its master. When you accepted the Holy Spirit's purpose in place of the ego's you renounced death, exchanging it for life. We know that an idea leaves not its source. And death is the result of the thought we call the ego, as surely as life is the result of the Thought of God.

D. The Fourth Obstacle: The Fear of God

1. What would you see without the fear of death? What would you feel and think if death held no attraction for you? Very simply, you would remember your Father. The Creator of life, the Source of everything that lives, the Father of the universe and of the universe of universes, and of everything that lies even beyond them would you remember. And as this memory rises in your mind, peace must still surmount a final obstacle, after which is salvation completed, and the Son of God entirely restored to sanity. For here your world *does* end.

2. The fourth obstacle to be surmounted hangs like a heavy veil before the face of Christ. Yet as His face rises beyond it, shining with joy because He is in His Father's Love, peace will lightly brush the veil aside and run to meet Him, and to join with Him at last. For this dark veil, which seems to make the face of Christ Himself like to a leper's, and the bright Rays of His Father's Love that light His face with glory appear as streams of blood, fades in the blazing light beyond it when the fear of death is gone.

3. This is the darkest veil, upheld by the belief in death and protected by its attraction. The dedication to death and to its sovereignty is but the solemn vow, the promise made in secret to the ego never to lift this veil, not to approach it, nor even to suspect that it is there. This is the secret bargain made with the ego to keep what lies beyond the veil forever blotted out and unremembered. Here is your promise never to allow union to call you out of separation; the great amnesia in which the memory of God seems quite forgotten; the cleavage of your Self from you;—*the fear of God*, the final step in your dissociation.

4. See how the belief in death would seem to "save" you. For if this were gone, what could you fear but life? It is the attraction of death that makes life seem to be ugly, cruel and tyrannical. You are no more

afraid of death than of the ego. These are your chosen friends. For in your secret alliance with them you have agreed never to let the fear of God be lifted, so you could look upon the face of Christ and join Him in His Father.

5. Every obstacle that peace must flow across is surmounted in just the same way; the fear that raised it yields to the love beyond, and so the fear is gone. And so it is with this. The desire to get rid of peace and drive the Holy Spirit from you fades in the presence of the quiet recognition that you love Him. The exaltation of the body is given up in favor of the spirit, which you love as you could never love the body. And the appeal of death is lost forever as love's attraction stirs and calls to you. From beyond each of the obstacles to love, Love Itself has called. And each has been surmounted by the power of the attraction of what lies beyond. Your wanting fear seemed to be holding them in place. Yet when you heard the Voice of Love beyond them, you answered and they disappeared.

6. And now you stand in terror before what you swore never to look upon. Your eyes look down, remembering your promise to your "friends." The "loveliness" of sin, the delicate appeal of guilt, the "holy" waxen image of death, and the fear of vengeance of the ego you swore in blood not to desert, all rise and bid you not to raise your eyes. For you realize that if you look on this and let the veil be lifted, *they* will be gone forever. All of your "friends," your "protectors" and your "home" will vanish. Nothing that you remember now will you remember.

7. It seems to you the world will utterly abandon you if you but raise your eyes. Yet all that will occur is you will leave the world forever. This is the re-establishment of *your* will. Look upon it, open-eyed, and you will nevermore believe that you are at the mercy of things beyond you, forces you cannot control, and thoughts that come to you against your will. It *is* your will to look on this. No mad desire, no trivial impulse to forget again, no stab of fear nor the cold sweat of seeming death can stand against your will. For what attracts you from beyond the veil is also deep within you, unseparated from it and completely one.

i. The Lifting of the Veil

8. Forget not that you came this far together, you and your brother. And it was surely not the ego that led you here. No obstacle to peace can be surmounted through its help. It does not open up its secrets, and bid you look on them and go beyond them. It would not have

you see its weakness, and learn it has no power to keep you from the truth. The Guide Who brought you here remains with you, and when you raise your eyes you will be ready to look on terror with no fear at all. But first, lift up your eyes and look on your brother in innocence born of complete forgiveness of his illusions, and through the eyes of faith that sees them not.

9. No one can look upon the fear of God unterrified, unless he has accepted the Atonement and learned illusions are not real. No one can stand before this obstacle alone, for he could not have reached this far unless his brother walked beside him. And no one would dare to look on it without complete forgiveness of his brother in his heart. Stand you here a while and tremble not. You will be ready. Let us join together in a holy instant, here in this place where the purpose, given in a holy instant, has led you. And let us join in faith that He Who brought us here together will offer you the innocence you need, and that you will accept it for my love and His.

10. Nor is it possible to look on this too soon. This is the place to which everyone must come when he is ready. Once he has found his brother he *is* ready. Yet merely to reach the place is not enough. A journey without a purpose is still meaningless, and even when it is over it seems to make no sense. How can you know that it is over unless you realize its purpose is accomplished? Here, with the journey's end before you, you *see* its purpose. And it is here you choose whether to look upon it or wander on, only to return and make the choice again.

11. To look upon the fear of God does need some preparation. Only the sane can look on stark insanity and raving madness with pity and compassion, but not with fear. For only if they share in it does it seem fearful, and you do share in it until you look upon your brother with perfect faith and love and tenderness. Before complete forgiveness you still stand unforgiving. You are afraid of God *because* you fear your brother. Those you do not forgive you fear. And no one reaches love with fear beside him.

12. This brother who stands beside you still seems to be a stranger. You do not know him, and your interpretation of him is very fearful. And you attack him still, to keep what seems to be yourself unharmed. Yet in his hands is your salvation. You see his madness, which you hate because you share it. And all the pity and forgiveness that would heal it gives way to fear. Brother, you need forgiveness of your brother, for you will share in madness or in Heaven together. And you and he will raise your eyes in faith together, or not at all.

13. Beside you is one who offers you the chalice of Atonement, for the Holy Spirit is in him. Would you hold his sins against him, or accept his gift to you? Is this giver of salvation your friend or enemy? Choose which he is, remembering that you will receive of him according to your choice. He has in him the power to forgive your sin, as you for him. Neither can give it to himself alone. And yet your savior stands beside each one. Let him be what he is, and seek not to make of love an enemy.

14. Behold your Friend, the Christ Who stands beside you. How holy and how beautiful He is! You thought He sinned because you cast the veil of sin upon Him to hide His loveliness. Yet still He holds forgiveness out to you, to share His Holiness. This "enemy," this "stranger" still offers you salvation as His Friend. The "enemies" of Christ, the worshippers of sin, know not Whom they attack.

15. This is your brother, crucified by sin and waiting for release from pain. Would you not offer him forgiveness, when only he can offer it to you? For his redemption he will give you yours, as surely as God created every living thing and loves it. And he will give it truly, for it will be both offered and received. There is no grace of Heaven that you cannot offer to your brother, and receive from your most holy Friend. Let him withhold it not, for by receiving it you offer it to him. And he will receive of you what you received of him. Redemption has been given you to give your brother, and thus receive it. Whom you forgive is free, and what you give you share. Forgive the sins your brother thinks he has committed, and all the guilt you think you see in him.

16. Here is the holy place of resurrection, to which we come again; to which we will return until redemption is accomplished and received. Think who your brother is, before you would condemn him. And offer thanks to God that he is holy, and has been given the gift of holiness for you. Join him in gladness, and remove all trace of guilt from his disturbed and tortured mind. Help him to lift the heavy burden of sin you laid upon him and he accepted as his own, and toss it lightly and with happy laughter away from him. Press it not like thorns against his brow, nor nail him to it, unredeemed and hopeless.

17. Give faith to your brother, for faith and hope and mercy are yours to give. Into the hands that give, the gift is given. Look on your brother, and see in him the gift of God you would receive. It is almost Easter, the time of resurrection. Let us give redemption to each other and share in it, that we may rise as one in resurrection, not separate in death. Behold the gift of freedom that I gave the Holy Spirit for you. And be you and your brother free together, as you offer to the

Holy Spirit this same gift. And giving it, receive it of Him in return for what you gave. He leadeth you and me together, that we might meet here in this holy place, and make the same decision.

18. Free your brother here, as I freed you. Give him the selfsame gift, nor look upon him with condemnation of any kind. See him as guiltless as I look on you, and overlook the sins he thinks he sees within himself. Offer your brother freedom and complete release from sin, here in the garden of seeming agony and death. So will we prepare together the way unto the resurrection of God's Son, and let him rise again to glad remembrance of his Father, Who knows no sin, no death, but only life eternal.

19. Together we will disappear into the Presence beyond the veil, not to be lost but found; not to be seen but known. And knowing, nothing in the plan God has established for salvation will be left undone. This is the journey's purpose, without which is the journey meaningless. Here is the peace of God, given to you eternally by Him. Here is the rest and quiet that you seek, the reason for the journey from its beginning. Heaven is the gift you owe your brother, the debt of gratitude you offer to the Son of God in thanks for what he is, and what his Father created him to be.

20. Think carefully how you would look upon the giver of this gift, for as you look on him so will the gift itself appear to be. As he is seen as either the giver of guilt or of salvation, so will his offering be seen and so received. The crucified give pain because they are in pain. But the redeemed give joy because they have been healed of pain. Everyone gives as he receives, but he must choose what it will *be* that he receives. And he will recognize his choice by what he gives, and what is given him. Nor is it given anything in hell or Heaven to interfere with his decision.

21. You came this far because the journey was your choice. And no one undertakes to do what he believes is meaningless. What you had faith in still is faithful, and watches over you in faith so gentle yet so strong that it would lift you far beyond the veil, and place the Son of God safely within the sure protection of his Father. Here is the only purpose that gives this world, and the long journey through this world, whatever meaning lies in them. Beyond this, they are meaningless. You and your brother stand together, still without conviction they have a purpose. Yet it is given you to see this purpose in your holy Friend, and recognize it as your own.

QUESTION 42. What role does love play and what role does your brother play in lifting the veil that separates you from your Home in Heaven?

Chapter 20. THE VISION OF HOLINESS

IV. Entering the Ark

6. The plan is not of you, nor need you be concerned with anything except the part that has been given you to learn. For He Who knows the rest will see to it without your help. But think not that He does not need your part to help Him with the rest. For in your part lies all of it, without which is no part complete, nor is the whole completed without your part. The ark of peace is entered two by two, yet the beginning of another world goes with them. Each holy relationship must enter here, to learn its special function in the Holy Spirit's plan, now that it shares His purpose. And as this purpose is fulfilled, a new world rises in which sin can enter not, and where the Son of God can enter without fear and where he rests a while, to forget imprisonment and to remember freedom. How can he enter, to rest and to remember, without you? Except you be there, he is not complete. And it is his completion that he remembers there.

8. You may wonder how you can be at peace when, while you are in time, there is so much that must be done before the way to peace is open. Perhaps this seems impossible to you. But ask yourself if it is possible that God would have a plan for your salvation that does not work. Once you accept His plan as the one function that you would fulfill, there will be nothing else the Holy Spirit will not arrange for you without your effort. He will go before you making straight your path, and leaving in your way no stones to trip on, and no obstacles to bar your way. Nothing you need will be denied you. Not one seeming difficulty but will melt away before you reach it. You need take thought for nothing, careless of everything except the only purpose that you would fulfill. As that was given you, so will its fulfillment be. God's guarantee will hold against all obstacles, for it rests on certainty and not contingency. It rests on *you*. And what can be more certain than a Son of God?

VIII. The Vision of Sinlessness

1. Vision will come to you at first in glimpses, but they will be enough to show you what is given you who see your brother sinless. Truth is restored to you through your desire, as it was lost to you through your desire for something else. Open the holy place that you closed off by valuing the "something else," and what was never lost will quietly

return. It has been saved for you. Vision would not be necessary had judgment not been made. Desire now its whole undoing, and it is done for you.

3. Your brother's sinlessness is given you in shining light, to look on with the Holy Spirit's vision and to rejoice in along with Him. For peace will come to all who ask for it with real desire and sincerity of purpose, shared with the Holy Spirit and at one with Him on what salvation is. Be willing, then, to see your brother sinless, that Christ may rise before your vision and give you joy. And place no value on your brother's body, which holds him to illusions of what he is. It is his desire to see his sinlessness, as it is yours. And bless the Son of God in your relationship, nor see in him what you have made of him.

5. The body is the sign of weakness, vulnerability and loss of power. Can such a savior help you? Would you turn in your distress and need for help unto the helpless? Is the pitifully little the perfect choice to call upon for strength? Judgment will seem to make your savior weak. Yet it is *you* who need his strength. There is no problem, no event or situation, no perplexity that vision will not solve. All is redeemed when looked upon with vision. For this is not *your* sight, and brings with it the laws beloved of Him Whose sight it is.

6. Everything looked upon with vision falls gently into place, according to the laws brought to it by His calm and certain sight. The end for everything He looks upon is always sure. For it will meet His purpose, seen in unadjusted form and suited perfectly to meet it. Destructiveness becomes benign, and sin is turned to blessing under His gentle gaze. What can the body's eyes perceive, with power to correct? Its eyes adjust to sin, unable to overlook it in any form and seeing it everywhere, in everything. Look through its eyes, and everything will stand condemned before you. All that could save you, you will never see. Your holy relationship, the source of your salvation, will be deprived of meaning, and its most holy purpose bereft of means for its accomplishment.

7. Judgment is but a toy, a whim, the senseless means to play the idle game of death in your imagination. But vision sets all things right, bringing them gently within the kindly sway of Heaven's laws. What if you recognized this world is an hallucination? What if you really understood you made it up? What if you realized that those who seem to walk about in it, to sin and die, attack and murder and destroy themselves, are wholly unreal? Could you have faith in what you see, if you accepted this? And would you see it?

8.   Hallucinations disappear when they are recognized for what they are. This is the healing and the remedy. Believe them not and they are gone. And all you need to do is recognize that *you* did this. Once you accept this simple fact and take unto yourself the power you gave them, you are released from them. One thing is sure; hallucinations serve a purpose, and when that purpose is no longer held they disappear. Therefore, the question never is whether you want them, but always, do you want the purpose that they serve? This world seems to hold out many purposes, each different and with different values. Yet they are all the same. Again there is no order; only a seeming hierarchy of values.

9.   Only two purposes are possible. And one is sin, the other holiness. Nothing is in between, and which you choose determines what you see. For what you see is merely how you elect to meet your goal. Hallucinations serve to meet the goal of madness. They are the means by which the outside world, projected from within, adjusts to sin and seems to witness to its reality. It still is true that nothing is without. Yet upon nothing are all projections made. For it is the projection that gives the "nothing" all the meaning that it holds.

10.   What has no meaning cannot be perceived. And meaning always looks within to find itself, and *then* looks out. All meaning that you give the world outside must thus reflect the sight you saw within; or better, if you saw at all or merely judged against. Vision is the means by which the Holy Spirit translates your nightmares into happy dreams; your wild hallucinations that show you all the fearful outcomes of imagined sin into the calm and reassuring sights with which He would replace them. These gentle sights and sounds are looked on happily, and heard with joy. They are His substitutes for all the terrifying sights and screaming sounds the ego's purpose brought to your horrified awareness. They step away from sin, reminding you that it is not reality which frightens you, and that the errors which you made can be corrected.

11.   When you have looked on what seemed terrifying, and seen it change to sights of loveliness and peace; when you have looked on scenes of violence and death, and watched them change to quiet views of gardens under open skies, with clear, life-giving water running happily beside them in dancing brooks that never waste away; who need persuade you to accept the gift of vision? And after vision, who is there who could refuse what must come after? Think but an instant just on this; you can behold the holiness God gave His Son. And never need you think that there is something else for you to see.

Chapter 21. REASON AND PERCEPTION

Introduction

1. Projection makes perception. The world you see is what you gave it, nothing more than that. But though it is no more than that, it is not less. Therefore, to you it is important. It is the witness to your state of mind, the outside picture of an inward condition. As a man thinketh, so does he perceive. Therefore, seek not to change the world, but choose to change your mind about the world. Perception is a result and not a cause. And that is why order of difficulty in miracles is meaningless. Everything looked upon with vision is healed and holy. Nothing perceived without it means anything. And where there is no meaning, there is chaos.
2. Damnation is your judgment on yourself, and this you will project upon the world. See it as damned, and all you see is what you did to hurt the Son of God. If you behold disaster and catastrophe, you tried to crucify him. If you see holiness and hope, you joined the Will of God to set him free. There is no choice that lies between these two decisions. And you will see the witness to the choice you made, and learn from this to recognize which one you chose. The world you see but shows you how much joy you have allowed yourself to see in you, and to accept as yours. And, if this *is* its meaning, then the power to give it joy must lie within you.

I. The Forgotten Song

6. Listen,—perhaps you catch a hint of an ancient state not quite forgotten; dim, perhaps, and yet not altogether unfamiliar, like a song whose name is long forgotten, and the circumstances in which you heard completely unremembered. Not the whole song has stayed with you, but just a little wisp of melody, attached not to a person or a place or anything particular. But you remember, from just this little part, how lovely was the song, how wonderful the setting where you heard it, and how you loved those who were there and listened with you.
7. The notes are nothing. Yet you have kept them with you, not for themselves, but as a soft reminder of what would make you weep if you remembered how dear it was to you. You could remember, yet you are afraid, believing you would lose the world you learned since then. And yet you know that nothing in the world you learned is half so dear as this. Listen, and see if you remember an ancient song you knew so long ago and held more dear than any melody you taught yourself to cherish since.

8. Beyond the body, beyond the sun and stars, past everything you see and yet somehow familiar, is an arc of golden light that stretches as you look into a great and shining circle. And all the circle fills with light before your eyes. The edges of the circle disappear, and what is in it is no longer contained at all. The light expands and covers everything, extending to infinity forever shining and with no break or limit anywhere. Within it everything is joined in perfect continuity. Nor is it possible to imagine that anything could be outside, for there is nowhere that this light is not.

9. This is the vision of the Son of God, whom you know well. Here is the sight of him who knows his Father. Here is the memory of what you are; a part of this, with all of it within, and joined to all as surely as all is joined in you. Accept the vision that can show you this, and not the body. You know the ancient song, and know it well. Nothing will ever be as dear to you as is this ancient hymn of love the Son of God sings to his Father still.

10. And now the blind can see, for that same song they sing in honor of their Creator gives praise to them as well. The blindness that they made will not withstand the memory of this song. And they will look upon the vision of the Son of God, remembering who he is they sing of. What is a miracle but this remembering? And who is there in whom this memory lies not? The light in one awakens it in all. And when you see it in your brother, you *are* remembering for everyone.

QUESTION 43. What will the Holy Spirit do for you when you accept His plan as your one function, and what is the vision that carries "the memory of what you are"?

II. The Responsibility for Sight

1. We have repeated how little is asked of you to learn this course. It is the same small willingness you need to have your whole relationship transformed to joy; the little gift you offer to the Holy Spirit for which He gives you everything; the very little on which salvation rests; the tiny change of mind by which the crucifixion is changed to resurrection. And being true, it is so simple that it cannot fail to be completely understood. Rejected yes, but not ambiguous. And if you choose against it now it will not be because it is obscure, but rather that this little cost seemed, in your judgment, to be too much to pay for peace.

2. This is the only thing that you need do for vision, happiness, release from pain and the complete escape from sin, all to be given you. Say only this, but mean it with no reservations, for here the power of salvation lies:

*I **am** responsible for what I see.*
I choose the feelings I experience, and I decide upon
    the goal I would achieve.
And everything that seems to happen to me I ask for,
    and receive as I have asked.

Deceive yourself no longer that you are helpless in the face of what is done to you. Acknowledge but that you have been mistaken, and all effects of your mistakes will disappear.

3. It is impossible the Son of God be merely driven by events outside of him. It is impossible that happenings that come to him were not his choice. His power of decision is the determiner of every situation in which he seems to find himself by chance or accident. No accident nor chance is possible within the universe as God created it, outside of which is nothing. Suffer, and you decided sin was your goal. Be happy, and you gave the power of decision to Him Who must decide for God for you. This is the little gift you offer to the Holy Spirit, and even this He gives to you to give yourself. For by this gift is given you the power to release your savior, that he may give salvation unto you.

11. It is as needful that you recognize you made the world you see, as that you recognize that you did not create yourself. *They are the same mistake.* Nothing created not by your Creator has any influence over you. And if you think what you have made can tell you what you see and feel, and place your faith in its ability to do so, you are denying your Creator and believing that you made yourself. For if you think the world you made has power to make you what it wills, you are confusing Son and Father; effect and Source.

III. Faith, Belief and Vision

4. Faith and belief and vision are the means by which the goal of holiness is reached. Through them the Holy Spirit leads you to the real world, and away from all illusions where your faith was laid. This is His direction; the only one He ever sees. And when you wander, He reminds you there is but one. His faith and His belief and vision are all for you. And when you have accepted them completely instead of yours, you will have need of them no longer. For faith and vision and belief are meaningful only before the state of certainty is reached. In Heaven they are unknown. Yet Heaven is reached through them.

7. Faith and belief become attached to vision, as all the means that once served sin are redirected now toward holiness. For what you think is sin is limitation, and whom you try to limit to the body you hate

because you fear. In your refusal to forgive him, you would condemn him to the body because the means for sin are dear to you. And so the body has your faith and your belief. But holiness would set your brother free, removing hatred by removing fear, not as a symptom, but at its source.

IV. The Fear to Look Within

1. The Holy Spirit will never teach you that you are sinful. Errors He will correct, but this makes no one fearful. You are indeed afraid to look within and see the sin you think is there. This you would not be fearful to admit. Fear in association with sin the ego deems quite appropriate, and smiles approvingly. It has no fear to let you feel ashamed. It doubts not your belief and faith in sin. Its temples do not shake because of this. Your faith that sin is there but witnesses to your desire that it *be* there to see. This merely seems to be the source of fear.
2. Remember that the ego is not alone. Its rule is tempered, and its unknown "enemy," Whom it cannot even see, it fears. Loudly the ego tells you not to look inward, for if you do your eyes will light on sin, and God will strike you blind. This you believe, and so you do not look. Yet this is not the ego's hidden fear, nor yours who serve it. Loudly indeed the ego claims it is; too loudly and too often. For underneath this constant shout and frantic proclamation, the ego is not certain it is so. Beneath your fear to look within because of sin is yet another fear, and one which makes the ego tremble.
3. What if you looked within and saw no sin? This "fearful" question is one the ego never asks. And you who ask it now are threatening the ego's whole defensive system too seriously for it to bother to pretend it is your friend. Those who have joined their brothers have detached themselves from their belief that their identity lies in the ego. A holy relationship is one in which you join with what is part of you in truth. And your belief in sin has been already shaken, nor are you now entirely unwilling to look within and see it not.
4. Your liberation still is only partial; still limited and incomplete, yet born within you. Not wholly mad, you have been willing to look on much of your insanity and recognize its madness. Your faith is moving inward, past insanity and on to reason. And what your reason tells you now the ego would not hear. The Holy Spirit's purpose was accepted by the part of your mind the ego knows not of. No more did you. And yet this part, with which you now identify, is not afraid to look upon itself. It knows no sin. How, otherwise, could it have been willing to see the Holy Spirit's purpose as its own?

Chapter 22. SALVATION AND THE HOLY RELATIONSHIP

I. The Message of the Holy Relationship

11. Christ comes to what is like Himself; the same, not different. For He is always drawn unto Himself. What is as like Him as a holy relationship? And what draws you and your brother together draws Him to you. Here are His sweetness and His gentle innocence protected from attack. And here can He return in confidence, for faith in another is always faith in Him. You are indeed correct in looking on your brother as His chosen home, for here you will with Him and with His Father. This is your Father's Will for you, and yours with His. And who is drawn to Christ is drawn to God as surely as Both are drawn to every holy relationship, the home prepared for Them as earth is turned to Heaven.

II. Your Brother's Sinlessness

12. Beyond the body that you interposed between you and your brother, and shining in the golden light that reaches it from the bright, endless circle that extends forever, is your holy relationship, beloved of God Himself. How still it rests, in time and yet beyond, immortal yet on earth. How great the power that lies in it. Time waits upon its will, and earth will be as it would have it be. Here is no separate will, nor the desire that anything be separate. Its will has no exceptions, and what it wills is true. Every illusion brought to its forgiveness is gently overlooked and disappears. For at its center Christ has been reborn, to light His home with vision that overlooks the world. Would you not have this holy home be yours as well? No misery is here, but only joy.

13. All you need do to dwell in quiet here with Christ is share His vision. Quickly and gladly is His vision given anyone who is but willing to see his brother sinless. And no one can remain beyond this willingness, if you would be released entirely from all effects of sin. Would you have partial forgiveness for yourself? Can you reach Heaven while a single sin still tempts you to remain in misery? Heaven is the home of perfect purity, and God created it for you. Look on your holy brother, sinless as yourself, and let him lead you there.

V. Weakness and Defensiveness

6. Forget not, when you feel the need arise to be defensive about anything, you have identified yourself with an illusion. And therefore

feel that you are weak because you are alone. This is the cost of all illusions. Not one but rests on the belief that you are separate. Not one that does not seem to stand, heavy and solid and immovable, between you and your brother. And not one that truth cannot pass over lightly, and so easily that you must be convinced, in spite of what you thought it was, that it is nothing. If you forgive your brother, this *must* happen. For it is your unwillingness to overlook what *seems* to stand between you and your brother that makes it look impenetrable, and defends the illusion of its immovability.

VI. The Light of the Holy Relationship

4. This holy relationship, lovely in its innocence, mighty in strength, and blazing with a light far brighter than the sun that lights the sky you *see*, is chosen of your Father as a means for His Own plan. Be thankful that it serves yours not at all. Nothing entrusted to it can be misused, and nothing given it but will be used. This holy relationship has the power to heal all pain, regardless of its form. Neither you nor your brother alone can serve at all. Only in your joint will does healing lie. For here your healing is, and here will you accept Atonement. And in your healing is the Sonship healed *because* your will and your brother's are joined.

5. Before a holy relationship there is no sin. The form of error is no longer seen, and reason, joined with love, looks quietly on all confusion, observing merely, "This was a mistake." And then the same Atonement you accepted in your relationship corrects the error, and lays a part of Heaven in its place. How blessed are you who let this gift be given! Each part of Heaven that you bring is given you. And *every* empty place in Heaven that you fill again with the eternal light you bring, shines now on you. The means of sinlessness can know no fear because they carry only love with them.

6. Child of peace, the light *has* come to you. The light you bring you do not recognize, and yet you will remember. Who can deny himself the vision that he brings to others? And who would fail to recognize a gift he let be laid in Heaven through himself? The gentle service that you give the Holy Spirit is service to yourself. You who are now His means must love all that He loves. And what you bring is your remembrance of everything that is eternal. No trace of anything in time can long remain in a mind that serves the timeless. And no illusion can disturb the peace of a relationship that has become the means of peace.

QUESTION 44. What's important to know about the power and the effects of your decision making?

Chapter 24. THE GOAL OF SPECIALNESS

I. Specialness as a Substitute for Love

1. Love is extension. To withhold the smallest gift is not to know love's purpose. Love offers everything forever. Hold back but one belief, one offering, and love is gone, because you asked a substitute to take its place. And now must war, the substitute for peace, come with the one alternative that you can choose for love. Your choosing it has given it all the reality it seems to have.

3. All that is ever cherished as a hidden belief, to be defended though unrecognized, is faith in specialness. This takes many forms, but always clashes with the reality of God's creation and with the grandeur that He gave His Son. What else could justify attack? For who could hate someone whose Self is his, and Whom he knows? Only the special could have enemies, for they are different and not the same. And difference of any kind imposes orders of reality, and a need to judge that cannot be escaped.

8. The fear of God and of your brother comes from each unrecognized belief in specialness. For you demand your brother bow to it against his will. And God Himself must honor it or suffer vengeance. Every twinge of malice, or stab of hate or wish to separate arises here. For here the purpose that you and your brother share becomes obscured from both of you. You would oppose this course because it teaches you you and your brother are alike. You have no purpose that is not the same, and none your Father does not share with you. For your relationship has been made clean of special goals. And would you now defeat the goal of holiness that Heaven gave it? What perspective can the special have that does not change with every seeming blow, each slight, or fancied judgment on themselves?

9. Those who are special must defend illusions against the truth. For what is specialness but an attack upon the Will of God? You love your brother not while it is this you would defend against him. This is what he attacks, and you protect. Here is the ground of battle which you wage against him. Here must he be your enemy and not your friend. Never can there be peace among the different. He is your friend *because* you are the same.

II. The Treachery of Specialness

1. Comparison must be an ego device, for love makes none. Specialness always makes comparisons. It is established by a lack

seen in another, and maintained by searching for, and keeping clear in sight, all lacks it can perceive. This does it seek, and this it looks upon. And always whom it thus diminishes would be your savior, had you not chosen to make of him a tiny measure of your specialness instead. Against the littleness you see in him you stand as tall and stately, clean and honest, pure and unsullied, by comparison with what you see. Nor do you understand it is yourself that you diminish thus.

III. The Forgiveness of Specialness

1.   Forgiveness is the end of specialness. Only illusions can be forgiven, and then they disappear. Forgiveness is release from all illusions, and that is why it is impossible but partly to forgive. No one who clings to one illusion can see himself as sinless, for he holds one error to himself as lovely still. And so he calls it "unforgivable," and makes it sin. How can he then give his forgiveness wholly, when he would not receive it for himself? For it is sure he would receive it wholly the instant that he gave it so. And thus his secret guilt would disappear, forgiven by himself.

IV. Specialness versus Sinlessness

2.   What could the purpose of the body be but specialness? And it is this that makes it frail and helpless in its own defense. It was conceived to make *you* frail and helpless. The goal of separation is its curse. Yet bodies have no goal. Purpose is of the mind. And minds can change as they desire. What they are, and all their attributes, they cannot change. But what they hold as purpose can be changed, and body states must shift accordingly. Of itself the body can do nothing. See it as means to hurt, and it is hurt. See it as means to heal, and it is healed.
3.   You can but hurt yourself. This has been oft repeated, but is difficult to grasp as yet. To minds intent on specialness it is impossible. Yet to those who wish to heal and not attack, it is quite obvious. The purpose of attack is in the mind, and its effects are felt but where it is. Nor is the mind limited; so must it be that harmful purpose hurts the mind as one. Nothing could make less sense to specialness. Nothing could make more sense to miracles. For miracles are merely change of purpose from hurt to healing. This shift in purpose does "endanger" specialness, but only in the sense that all illusions are "threatened" by the truth. They will not stand before it. Yet what

comfort has ever been in them, that you would keep the gift your Father asks from Him, and give it there instead? Given to Him, the universe is yours. Offered to them, no gifts can be returned. What you have given specialness has left you bankrupt and your treasure house barren and empty, with an open door inviting everything that would disturb your peace to enter and destroy.

4. Earlier I said consider not the means by which salvation is attained, nor how to reach it. But do consider, and consider well, whether it is your wish that you might see your brother sinless. To specialness the answer must be "no." A sinless brother *is* its enemy, while sin, if it were possible, would be its friend. Your brother's sin would justify itself, and give it meaning that the truth denies. All that is real proclaims his sinlessness. All that is false proclaims his sins as real. If he is sinful, then is your reality not real, but just a dream of specialness that lasts an instant, crumbling into dust.

V. The Christ in You

1. The Christ in you is very still. He looks on what He loves, and knows it as Himself. And thus does He rejoice at what He sees, because He knows that it is one with Him and with His Father. Specialness, too, takes joy in what it sees, although it is not true. Yet what you seek for is a source of joy as you conceive it. What you wish is true for you. Nor is it possible that you can wish for something and lack faith that it is so. Wishing makes real, as surely as does will create. The power of a wish upholds illusions as strongly as does love extend itself. Except that one deludes; the other heals.

2. There is no dream of specialness, however hidden or disguised the form, however lovely it may seem to be, however much it delicately offers the hope of peace and the escape from pain, in which you suffer not your condemnation. In dreams effect and cause are interchanged, for here the maker of the dream believes that what he made is happening to him. He does not realize he picked a thread from here, a scrap from there, and wove a picture out of nothing. For the parts do not belong together, and the whole contributes nothing to the parts to give them meaning.

3. Where could your peace arise *but* from forgiveness? The Christ in you looks only on the truth, and sees no condemnation that could need forgiveness. He is at peace *because* He sees no sin. Identify with Him, and what has He that you have not? He is your eyes, your ears, your hands, your feet. How gentle are the sights He sees, the sounds He hears. How beautiful His hand that holds His

brother's, and how lovingly He walks beside him, showing him what can be seen and heard, and where he will see nothing and there is no sound to hear.

6. The Christ in you is very still. He knows where you are going, and He leads you there in gentleness and blessing all the way. His Love for God replaces all the fear you thought you saw within yourself. His Holiness shows you Himself in him whose hand you hold, and whom you lead to Him. And what you see is like yourself. For what but Christ is there to see and hear and love and follow home? He looked upon you first, but recognized that you were not complete. And so He sought for your completion in each living thing that He beholds and loves. And seeks it still, that each might offer you the Love of God.

7. Yet is He quiet, for He knows that love is in you now, and safely held in you by that same hand that holds your brother's in your own. Christ's hand holds all His brothers in Himself. He gives them vision for their sightless eyes, and sings to them of Heaven, that their ears may hear no more the sound of battle and of death. He reaches through them, holding out His hand, that everyone may bless all living things, and see their holiness. And He rejoices that these sights are yours, to look upon with Him and share His joy. His perfect lack of specialness He offers you, that you may save all living things from death, receiving from each one the gift of life that your forgiveness offers to your Self. The sight of Christ is all there is to see. The song of Christ is all there is to hear. The hand of Christ is all there is to hold. There is no journey but to walk with Him.

8. You who would be content with specialness, and seek salvation in a war with love, consider this: The holy Lord of Heaven has Himself come down to you, to offer you your own completion. What is His is yours because in your completion is His Own. He Who willed not to be without His Son could never will that you be brotherless. And would He give a brother unto you except he be as perfect as yourself, and just as like to Him in holiness as you must be?

9. There must be doubt before there can be conflict. And every doubt must be about yourself. Christ has no doubt, and from His certainty His quiet comes. He will exchange His certainty for all your doubts, if you agree that He is One with you, and that this Oneness is endless, timeless, and within your grasp because your hands are His. He is within you, yet He walks beside you and before, leading the way that He must go to find Himself complete. His quietness becomes your certainty. And where is doubt when certainty has come?

VI. Salvation from Fear

2. Without you there would be a lack in God, a Heaven incomplete, a Son without a Father. There could be no universe and no reality. For what God wills is whole, and part of Him because His Will is One. Nothing alive that is not part of Him, and nothing is but is alive in Him. Your brother's holiness shows you that God is One with him and you; that what he has is yours because you are not separate from him nor from his Father.

3. Nothing is lost to you in all the universe. Nothing that God created has He failed to lay before you lovingly, as yours forever. And no Thought within His Mind is absent from your own. It is His Will you share His Love for you, and look upon yourself as lovingly as He conceived of you before the world began, and as He knows you still. God changes not His Mind about His Son with passing circumstance which has no meaning in eternity where He abides, and you with Him. Your brother *is* as He created him. And it is this that saves you from a world that He created not.

4. Forget not that the healing of God's Son is all the world is for. That is the only purpose the Holy Spirit sees in it, and thus the only one it has. Until you see the healing of the Son as all you wish to be accomplished by the world, by time and all appearances, you will not know the Father nor yourself. For you will use the world for what is not its purpose, and will not escape its laws of violence and death. Yet it is given you to be beyond its laws in all respects, in every way and every circumstance, in all temptation to perceive what is not there, and all belief God's Son can suffer pain because he sees himself as he is not.

5. Look on your brother, and behold in him the whole reversal of the laws that seem to rule this world. See in his freedom yours, for such it is. Let not his specialness obscure the truth in him, for not one law of death you bind him to will you escape. And not one sin you see in him but keeps you both in hell. Yet will his perfect sinlessness release you both, for holiness is quite impartial, with one judgment made for all it looks upon. And that is made, not of itself, but through the Voice that speaks for God in everything that lives and shares His Being.

6. It is His sinlessness that eyes that see can look upon. It is His loveliness they see in everything. And it is He they look for everywhere, and find no sight nor place nor time where He is not. Within your brother's holiness, the perfect frame for your salvation and the world's, is set the shining memory of Him in Whom your brother lives, and you along with him. Let not your eyes be blinded by the veil of specialness that hides the face of Christ from him, and you as well.

And let the fear of God no longer hold the vision you were meant to see from you. Your brother's body shows not Christ to you. He *is* set forth within his holiness.

7.   Choose, then, his body or his holiness as what you want to see, and which you choose is yours to look upon. Yet will you choose in countless situations, and through time that seems to have no end, until the truth be your decision. For eternity is not regained by still one more denial of Christ in him. And where is your salvation, if he is but a body? Where is your peace but in his holiness? And where is God Himself but in that part of Him He set forever in your brother's holiness, that you might see the truth about yourself, set forth at last in terms you recognized and understood?

QUESTION 45. What does forgiveness really forgive, and who walks with you on your path of forgiveness?

Chapter 25. THE JUSTICE OF GOD

Introduction

2. No one who carries Christ in him can fail to recognize Him everywhere. *Except* in bodies. And as long as he believes he is in a body, where he thinks he is He cannot be. And so he carries Him unknowingly, and does not make Him manifest. And thus he does not recognize Him where He is. The son of man is not the risen Christ. Yet does the Son of God abide exactly where he is, and walks with him within his holiness, as plain to see as is his specialness set forth within his body.

3. The body needs no healing. But the mind that thinks it is a body is sick indeed! And it is here that Christ sets forth the remedy. His purpose folds the body in His light, and fills it with the Holiness that shines from Him. And nothing that the body says or does but makes Him manifest. To those who know Him not it carries Him in gentleness and love, to heal their minds. Such is the mission that your brother has for you. And such it must be that your mission is for him.

I. The Link to Truth

1. It cannot be that it is hard to do the task that Christ appointed you to do, since it is He Who does it. And in the doing of it will you learn the body merely seems to be the means to do it. For the Mind is His. And so it must be yours. His Holiness directs the body through the mind at one with Him. And you are manifest unto your holy brother, as he to you. Here is the meeting of the holy Christ unto Himself; nor any differences perceived to stand between the aspects of His Holiness, which meet and join and raise Him to His Father, whole and pure and worthy of His everlasting Love.

4. *You* are the means for God; not separate, nor with a life apart from His. His life is manifest in you who are His Son. Each aspect of Himself is framed in holiness and perfect purity, in love celestial and so complete it wishes only that it may release all that it looks upon unto itself. Its radiance shines through each body that it looks upon, and brushes all its darkness into light merely by looking past it *to* the light. The veil is lifted through its gentleness, and nothing hides the face of Christ from its beholders. You and your brother stand before Him now, to let Him draw aside the veil that seems to keep you separate and apart.

5. Since you believe that you are separate, Heaven presents itself to you as separate, too. Not that it is in truth, but that the link that has been given you to join the truth may reach to you through what you understand. Father and Son and Holy Spirit are as One, as all your brothers join as one in truth. Christ and His Father never have been separate, and Christ abides within your understanding, in the part of you that shares His Father's Will. The Holy Spirit links the other part— the tiny, mad desire to be separate, different and special—to the Christ, to make the oneness clear to what is really one. In this world this is not understood, but can be taught.

6. The Holy Spirit serves Christ's purpose in your mind, so that the aim of specialness can be corrected where the error lies. Because His purpose still is one with both the Father and the Son, He knows the Will of God and what you really will. But this is understood by mind perceived as one, aware that it is one, and so experienced. It is the Holy Spirit's function to teach you how this oneness is experienced, what you must do that it can be experienced, and where you should go to do it.

7. All this takes note of time and place as if they were discrete, for while you think that part of you is separate, the concept of a Oneness joined as One is meaningless. It is apparent that a mind so split could never be the Teacher of a Oneness which unites all things within Itself. And so What is within this mind, and does unite all things together, must be its Teacher. Yet must It use the language that this mind can understand, in the condition in which it thinks it is. And It must use all learning to transfer illusions to the truth, taking all false ideas of what you are, and leading you beyond them to the truth that *is* beyond them. All this can very simply be reduced to this:

> *What is the same can not be different, and what is one can not have separate parts.*

III. Perception and Choice

3. Perception rests on choosing; knowledge does not. Knowledge has but one law because it has but one Creator. But this world has two who made it, and they do not see it as the same. To each it has a different purpose, and to each it is a perfect means to serve the goal for which it is perceived. For specialness, it is the perfect frame to set it off; the perfect battleground to wage its wars, the perfect shelter for illusions which it would make real. Not one but it upholds in its perception; not one but can be fully justified.

4. There is another Maker of the world, the simultaneous Corrector of the mad belief that anything could be established and maintained without some link that kept it still within the laws of God; not as the law itself upholds the universe as God created it, but in some form adapted to the need the Son of God believes he has. Corrected error is the error's end. And thus has God protected still His Son, even in error.

5. There is another purpose in the world that error made, because it has another Maker Who can reconcile its goal with His Creator's purpose. In His perception of the world, nothing is seen but justifies forgiveness and the sight of perfect sinlessness. Nothing arises but is met with instant and complete forgiveness. Nothing remains an instant, to obscure the sinlessness that shines unchanged, beyond the pitiful attempts of specialness to put it out of mind, where it must be, and light the body up instead of it. The lamps of Heaven are not for mind to choose to see them where it will. If it elects to see them elsewhere from their home, as if they lit a place where they could never be, then must the Maker of the world correct your error, lest you remain in darkness where the lamps are not.

6. Everyone here has entered darkness, yet no one has entered it alone. Nor need he stay more than an instant. For he has come with Heaven's Help within him, ready to lead him out of darkness into light at any time. The time he chooses can be any time, for help is there, awaiting but his choice. And when he chooses to avail himself of what is given him, then will he see each situation that he thought before was means to justify his anger turned to an event which justifies his love. He will hear plainly that the calls to war he heard before are really calls to peace. He will perceive that where he gave attack is but another altar where he can, with equal ease and far more happiness, bestow forgiveness. And he will reinterpret all temptation as just another chance to bring him joy.

7. How can a misperception be a sin? Let all your brother's errors be to you nothing except a chance for you to see the workings of the Helper given you to see the world He made instead of yours. What, then, *is* justified? What do you want? For these two questions are the same. And when you see them as the same, your choice is made. For it is seeing them as one that brings release from the belief there are two ways to see. This world has much to offer to your peace, and many chances to extend your own forgiveness. Such its purpose is, to those who want to see peace and forgiveness descend on them, and offer them the light.

world for them to fill; no place where they are needed, and no aim which only they can perfectly fulfill.

4. Such is the Holy Spirit's kind perception of specialness; His use of what you made, to heal instead of harm. To each He gives a special function in salvation he alone can fill; a part for only him. Nor is the plan complete until he finds his special function, and fulfills the part assigned to him, to make himself complete within a world where incompletion rules.

5. Here, where the laws of God do not prevail in perfect form, can he yet do *one* perfect thing and make *one* perfect choice. And by this act of special faithfulness to one perceived as other than himself, he learns the gift was given to himself, and so they must be one. Forgiveness is the only function meaningful in time. It is the means the Holy Spirit uses to translate specialness from sin into salvation. Forgiveness is for all. But when it rests on all it is complete, and every function of this world completed with it. Then is time no more. Yet while in time, there is still much to do. And each must do what is allotted him, for on his part does all the plan depend. He *has* a special part in time for so he chose, and choosing it, he made it for himself. His wish was not denied but changed in form, to let it serve his brother and himself, and thus become a means to save instead of lose.

7. The Holy Spirit needs your special function, that His may be fulfilled. Think not you lack a special value here. You wanted it, and it is given you. All that you made can serve salvation easily and well. The Son of God can make no choice the Holy Spirit cannot employ on his behalf, and not against himself. Only in darkness does your specialness appear to be attack. In light, you see it as your special function in the plan to save the Son of God from all attack, and let him understand that he is safe, as he has always been, and will remain in time and in eternity alike. This is the function given you for your brother. Take it gently, then, from your brother's hand, and let salvation be perfectly fulfilled in you. Do this *one* thing, that everything be given you.

VII. The Rock of Salvation

12. Salvation is rebirth of the idea no one can lose for anyone to gain. And everyone *must* gain, if anyone would be a gainer. Here is sanity restored. And on this single rock of truth can faith in God's eternal saneness rest in perfect confidence and perfect peace. Reason is satisfied, for all insane beliefs can be corrected here. And sin must be impossible, if this is true. This is the rock on which salvation rests, the

8. The Maker of the world of gentleness has perfect power to
the world of violence and hate that seems to stand between you
His gentleness. It is not there in His forgiving eyes. And theref(
need not be there in yours. Sin is the fixed belief perception ca
change. What has been damned is damned and damned for(
being forever unforgivable. If, then, it is forgiven, sin's perception
have been wrong. And thus is change made possible. The Holy S
too, sees what He sees as far beyond the chance of change. Bu
His vision sin cannot encroach, for sin has been corrected by
sight. And thus it must have been an error, not a sin. For wh(
claimed could never be, has been. Sin is attacked by punishm
and so preserved. But to forgive it is to change its state from error
truth.

9. The Son of God could never sin, but he can wish for what wo
hurt him. And he has the power to think he can be hurt. What co
this be except a misperception of himself? Is this a sin or a mista
forgivable or not? Does he need help or condemnation? Is it y(
purpose that he be saved or damned? Forgetting not that what h(
to you will make this choice your future? For you make it *now*,
instant when all time becomes a means to reach a goal. Make, th(
your choice. But recognize that in this choice the purpose of t
world you see is chosen, and will be justified.

VI. The Special Function

1. The grace of God rests gently on forgiving eyes, and everythin
they look on speaks of Him to the beholder. He can see no evi
nothing in the world to fear, and no one who is different fror
himself. And as he loves them, so he looks upon himself with lov
and gentleness. He would no more condemn himself for his mistake
than damn another. He is not an arbiter of vengeance, nor a punishe
of sin. The kindness of his sight rests on himself with all the tendernes;
it offers others. For he would only heal and only bless. And being in
accord with what God wills, he has the power to heal and bless all
those he looks on with the grace of God upon his sight.

3. The wish to see calls down the grace of God upon your eyes,
and brings the gift of light that makes sight possible. Would you
behold your brother? God is glad to have you look on him. He does
not will your savior be unrecognized by you. Nor does He will that he
remain without the function that He gave to him. Let him no more
be lonely, for the lonely ones are those who see no function in the

vantage point from which the Holy Spirit gives meaning and direction to the plan in which your special function has a part. For here your special function is made whole, because it shares the function of the whole.

VIII. Justice Returned to Love

1. The Holy Spirit can use all that you give to Him for your salvation. But He cannot use what you withhold, for He cannot take it from you without your willingness. For if He did, you would believe He wrested it from you against your will. And so you would not learn it *is* your will to be without it. You need not give it to Him wholly willingly, for if you could you had no need of Him. But this He needs; that you prefer He take it than that you keep it for yourself alone, and recognize that what brings loss to no one you would not know. This much is necessary to add to the idea no one can lose for you to gain. And nothing more.

14. You have the right to all the universe; to perfect peace, complete deliverance from all effects of sin, and to the life eternal, joyous and complete in every way, as God appointed for His holy Son. This is the only justice Heaven knows, and all the Holy Spirit brings to earth. Your special function shows you nothing else but perfect justice can prevail for you. And you are safe from vengeance in all forms. The world deceives, but it cannot replace God's justice with a version of its own. For only love is just, and can perceive what justice must accord the Son of God. Let love decide, and never fear that you, in your unfairness, will deprive yourself of what God's justice has allotted you.

IX. The Justice of Heaven

1. What can it be but arrogance to think your little errors cannot be undone by Heaven's justice? And what could this mean except that they are sins and not mistakes, forever uncorrectable, and to be met with vengeance, not with justice? Are you willing to be released from all effects of sin? You cannot answer this until you see all that the answer must entail. For if you answer "yes" it means you will forego all values of this world in favor of the peace of Heaven. Not one sin would you retain. And not one doubt that this is possible will you hold dear that sin be kept in place. You mean that truth has greater value now than all illusions. And you recognize that truth must be revealed to you, because you know not what it is.

3. Be certain any answer to a problem the Holy Spirit solves will always be one in which no one loses. And this must be true, because He asks no sacrifice of anyone. An answer which demands the slightest loss to anyone has not resolved the problem, but has added to it and made it greater, harder to resolve and more unfair. It is impossible the Holy Spirit could see unfairness as a resolution. To Him, what is unfair must be corrected *because* it is unfair. And *every* error is a perception in which one, at least, is seen unfairly. Thus is justice not accorded to the Son of God. When anyone is seen as losing, he has been condemned. And punishment becomes his due instead of justice.

10. The miracle that you receive, you give. Each one becomes an illustration of the law on which salvation rests; that justice must be done to all, if anyone is to be healed. No one can lose, and everyone must benefit. Each miracle is an example of what justice can accomplish when it is offered to everyone alike. It is received and given equally. It is awareness that giving and receiving are the same. Because it does not make the same unlike, it sees no differences where none exists. And thus it is the same for everyone, because it sees no differences in them. Its offering is universal, and it teaches but one message:

What is God's belongs to everyone, and is his due.

QUESTION 46. What's the importance of having two different makers of the world, and what is the importance of your special function?

Chapter 26. THE TRANSITION

II. Many Forms; One Correction

2. The Holy Spirit offers you release from every problem that you think you have. They are the same to Him because each one, regardless of the form it seems to take, is a demand that someone suffer loss and make a sacrifice that you might gain. And when the situation is worked out so no one loses is the problem gone, because it was an error in perception that now has been corrected. One mistake is not more difficult for Him to bring to truth than is another. For there *is* but one mistake; the whole idea that loss is possible, and could result in gain for anyone. If this were true, then God would be unfair; sin would be possible, attack be justified and vengeance fair.
3. This one mistake, in any form, has one correction. There is no loss; to think there is, is a mistake. You have no problems, though you think you have. And yet you could not think so if you saw them vanish one by one, without regard to size, complexity, or place and time, or any attribute which you perceive that makes each one seem different from the rest. Think not the limits you impose on what you *see* can limit God in any way.
7. Think, then, how great your own release will be when you are willing to receive correction for all your problems. You will not keep one, for pain in any form you will not want. And you will *see* each little hurt resolved before the Holy Spirit's gentle sight. For all of them *are* little in His sight, and worth no more than just a tiny sigh before they disappear, to be forever undone and unremembered. What seemed once to be a special problem, a mistake without a remedy, or an affliction without a cure, has been transformed into a universal blessing. Sacrifice is gone. And in its place the Love of God can be remembered, and will shine away all memory of sacrifice and loss.

III. The Borderland

2. There is a borderland of thought that stands between this world and Heaven. It is not a place, and when you reach it is apart from time. Here is the meeting place where thoughts are brought together; where conflicting values meet and all illusions are laid down beside the truth, where they are judged to be untrue. This borderland is just beyond the gate of Heaven. Here is *every* thought made pure and wholly simple. Here is sin denied, and everything that *is* received instead.

3. This is the journey's end. We have referred to it as the real world. And yet there is a contradiction here, in that the words imply a limited reality, a partial truth, a segment of the universe made true. This is because knowledge makes no attack upon perception. They are brought together, and only one continues past the gate where oneness is. Salvation is a borderland where place and time and choice have meaning still, and yet it can be seen that they are temporary, out of place, and every choice has been already made.

4. Nothing the Son of God believes can be destroyed. But what is truth to him must be brought to the last comparison that he will ever make; the last evaluation that will be possible, the final judgment upon this world. It is the judgment of the truth upon illusion, of knowledge on perception: "It has no meaning, and does not exist." This is not your decision. It is but a simple statement of a simple fact. But in this world there are no simple facts, because what is the same and what is different remain unclear. The one essential thing to make a choice at all is this distinction. And herein lies the difference between the worlds. In this one, choice is made impossible. In the real world is choosing simplified.

7. Is not this like your special function, where the separation is undone by change of purpose in what once was specialness, and now is union? All illusions are but one. And in the recognition this is so lies the ability to give up all attempts to choose between them, and to make them different. How simple is the choice between two things so clearly unalike. There is no conflict here. No sacrifice is possible in the relinquishment of an illusion recognized as such. Where all reality has been withdrawn from what was never true, can it be hard to give it up, and choose what *must* be true?

IV. Where Sin Has Left

2. Forgiveness turns the world of sin into a world of glory, wonderful to see. Each flower shines in light, and every bird sings of the joy of Heaven. There is no sadness and there is no parting here, for everything is totally forgiven. And what has been forgiven must join, for nothing stands between to keep them separate and apart. The sinless must perceive that they are one, for nothing stands between to push the other off. And in the space that sin left vacant do they join as one, in gladness recognizing what is part of them has not been kept apart and separate.

3. The holy place on which you stand is but the space that sin has left. And here you see the face of Christ, arising in its place. Who

could behold the face of Christ and not recall His Father as He really is? Who could fear love, and stand upon the ground where sin has left a place for Heaven's altar to rise and tower far above the world, and reach beyond the universe to touch the Heart of all creation? What is Heaven but a song of gratitude and love and praise by everything created to the Source of its creation? The holiest of altars is set where once sin was believed to be. And here does every light of Heaven come, to be rekindled and increased in joy. For here is what was lost restored to them, and all their radiance made whole again.

V. The Little Hindrance

3. God gave His Teacher to replace the one you made, not to conflict with it. And what He would replace has been replaced. Time lasted but an instant in your mind, with no effect upon eternity. And so is all time past, and everything exactly as it was before the way to nothingness was made. The tiny tick of time in which the first mistake was made, and all of them within that one mistake, held also the Correction for that one, and all of them that came within the first. And in that tiny instant time was gone, for that was all it ever was. What God gave answer to is answered and is gone.

4. To you who still believe you live in time and know not it is gone, the Holy Spirit still guides you through the infinitely small and senseless maze you still perceive in time, though it has long since gone. You think you live in what is past. Each thing you look upon you saw but for an instant, long ago, before its unreality gave way to truth. Not one illusion still remains unanswered in your mind. Uncertainty was brought to certainty so long ago that it is hard indeed to hold it to your heart, as if it were before you still.

5. The tiny instant you would keep and make eternal, passed away in Heaven too soon for anything to notice it had come. What disappeared too quickly to affect the simple knowledge of the Son of God can hardly still be there, for you to choose to be your teacher. Only in the past,— an ancient past, too short to make a world in answer to creation,—did this world appear to rise. So very long ago, for such a tiny interval of time, that not one note in Heaven's song was missed. Yet in each unforgiving act or thought, in every judgment and in all belief in sin, is that one instant still called back, as if it could be made again in time. You keep an ancient memory before your eyes. And he who lives in memories alone is unaware of where he is.

6. Forgiveness is the great release from time. It is the key to learning that the past is over. Madness speaks no more. There *is* no other

teacher and no other way. For what has been undone no longer is. And who can stand upon a distant shore, and dream himself across an ocean, to a place and time that have long since gone by? How real a hindrance can this dream be to where he really is? For this is fact, and does not change whatever dreams he has. Yet can he still imagine he is elsewhere, and in another time. In the extreme, he can delude himself that this is true, and pass from mere imagining into belief and into madness, quite convinced that where he would prefer to be, he *is*.

9. Forget the time of terror that has been so long ago corrected and undone. Can sin withstand the Will of God? Can it be up to you to *see* the past and put it in the present? You can *not* go back. And everything that points the way in the direction of the past but sets you on a mission whose accomplishment can only be unreal. Such is the justice your All-Loving Father has ensured must come to you. And from your own unfairness to yourself has He protected you. You cannot lose your way because there is no way but His, and nowhere can you go except to Him.

10. Would God allow His Son to lose his way along a road long since a memory of time gone by? This course will teach you only what is now. A dreadful instant in a distant past, now perfectly corrected, is of no concern nor value. Let the dead and gone be peacefully forgotten. Resurrection has come to take its place. And now you are a part of resurrection, not of death. No past illusions have the power to keep you in a place of death, a vault God's Son entered an instant, to be instantly restored unto his Father's perfect Love. And how can he be kept in chains long since removed and gone forever from his mind?

13. Each day, and *every* minute in each day, and *every* instant that each minute holds, you but relive the single instant when the time of terror took the place of love. And so you die each day to live again, until you cross the gap between the past and present, which is not a gap at all. Such is each life; a seeming interval from birth to death and on to life again, a repetition of an instant gone by long ago that cannot be relived. And all of time is but the mad belief that what is over is still here and now.

14. Forgive the past and let it go, for it *is* gone. You stand no longer on the ground that lies between the worlds. You have gone on, and reached the world that lies at Heaven's gate. There is no hindrance to the Will of God, nor any need that you repeat again a journey that was over long ago. Look gently on your brother, and behold the world in which perception of your hate has been transformed into a world of love.

VII. The Laws of Healing

2. All sickness comes from separation. When the separation is denied, it goes. For it is gone as soon as the idea that brought it has been healed, and been replaced by sanity. Sickness and sin are seen as consequence and cause, in a relationship kept hidden from awareness that it may be carefully preserved from reason's light.

3. Guilt asks for punishment, and its request is granted. Not in truth, but in the world of shadows and illusions built on sin. The Son of God perceived what he would see because perception is a wish fulfilled. Perception changes, made to take the place of changeless knowledge. Yet is truth unchanged. It cannot be perceived, but only known. What is perceived takes many forms, but none has meaning. Brought to truth, its senselessness is quite apparent. Kept apart from truth, it seems to have a meaning and be real.

6. It is impossible that one illusion be less amenable to truth than are the rest. But it is possible that some are given greater value, and less willingly offered to truth for healing and for help. No illusion has any truth in it. Yet it appears some are more true than others, although this clearly makes no sense at all. All that a hierarchy of illusions can show is preference, not reality. What relevance has preference to the truth? Illusions are illusions and are false. Your preference gives them no reality. Not one is true in any way, and all must yield with equal ease to what God gave as answer to them all. God's Will is One. And any wish that seems to go against His Will has no foundation in the truth.

9. Forgiveness takes away what stands between your brother and yourself. It is the wish that you be joined with him, and not apart. We call it "wish" because it still conceives of other choices, and has not yet reached beyond the world of choice entirely. Yet is this wish in line with Heaven's state, and not in opposition to God's Will. Although it falls far short of giving you your full inheritance, it does remove the obstacles that you have placed between the Heaven where you are, and recognition of where and what you are. Facts are unchanged. Yet facts can be denied and thus unknown, though they were known before they were denied.

10. Salvation, perfect and complete, asks but a little wish that what is true be true; a little willingness to overlook what is not there; a little sigh that speaks for Heaven as a preference to this world that death and desolation seem to rule. In joyous answer will creation rise within you, to replace the world you see with Heaven, wholly perfect and complete. What is forgiveness but a willingness that truth be true? What can remain unhealed and broken from a unity which holds all

things within itself? There is no sin. And every miracle is possible the instant that the Son of God perceives his wishes and the Will of God are one.

QUESTION 47. What can you do to let go of time—meaning let go of the past and future in order to accept the eternal now?

X. The End of Injustice

3. Unfairness and attack are one mistake, so firmly joined that where one is perceived the other must be seen. You cannot be unfairly treated. The belief you are is but another form of the idea you are deprived by someone not yourself. Projection of the cause of sacrifice is at the root of everything perceived to be unfair and not your just deserts. Yet it is you who ask this of yourself, in deep injustice to the Son of God. You have no enemy except yourself, and you are enemy indeed to him because you do not know him *as* yourself. What could be more unjust than that he be deprived of what he is, denied the right to be himself, and asked to sacrifice his Father's Love and yours as not his due?

4. Beware of the temptation to perceive yourself unfairly treated. In this view, you seek to find an innocence that is not Theirs but yours alone, and at the cost of someone else's guilt. Can innocence be purchased by the giving of your guilt to someone else? And *is* it innocence that your attack on him attempts to get? Is it not retribution for your own attack upon the Son of God you seek? Is it not safer to believe that you are innocent of this, and victimized despite your innocence? Whatever way the game of guilt is played, there must be loss. Someone must lose his innocence that someone else can take it from him, making it his own.

6. What this injustice does to you who judge unfairly, and who see as you have judged, you cannot calculate. The world grows dim and threatening, not a trace of all the happy sparkle that salvation brings can you perceive to lighten up your way. And so you see yourself deprived of light, abandoned to the dark, unfairly left without a purpose in a futile world. The world is fair because the Holy Spirit has brought injustice to the light within, and there has all unfairness been resolved and been replaced with justice and with love. If you perceive injustice anywhere, you need but say:

By this do I deny the Presence of the Father and the Son. And I would rather know of Them than see injustice, which Their Presence shines away.

Chapter 27. THE HEALING OF THE DREAM

II. The Fear of Healing

2. The unhealed cannot pardon. For they are the witnesses that pardon is unfair. They would retain the consequences of the guilt they overlook. Yet no one can forgive a sin that he believes is real. And what has consequences must be real, because what it has done is there to see. Forgiveness is not pity, which but seeks to pardon what it thinks to be the truth. Good cannot *be* returned for evil, for forgiveness does not first establish sin and then forgive it. Who can say and mean, "My brother, you have injured me, and yet, because I am the better of the two, I pardon you my hurt." His pardon and your hurt cannot exist together. One denies the other and must make it false.

3. To witness sin and yet forgive it is a paradox that reason cannot see. For it maintains what has been done to you deserves no pardon. And by giving it, you grant your brother mercy but retain the proof he is not really innocent. The sick remain accusers. They cannot forgive their brothers and themselves as well. For no one in whom true forgiveness rests can suffer. He holds not the proof of sin before his brother's eyes. And thus he must have overlooked it and removed it from his own. Forgiveness cannot be for one and not the other. Who forgives is healed. And in his healing lies the proof that he has truly pardoned, and retains no trace of condemnation that he still would hold against himself or any living thing.

4. Forgiveness is not real unless it brings a healing to your brother and yourself. You must attest his sins have no effect on you to demonstrate they are not real. How else could he be guiltless? And how could his innocence be justified unless his sins have no effect to warrant guilt? Sins are beyond forgiveness just because they would entail effects that cannot be undone and overlooked entirely. In their undoing lies the proof that they are merely errors. Let yourself be healed that you may be forgiving, offering salvation to your brother and yourself.

IV. The Quiet Answer

1. In quietness are all things answered, and is *every* problem quietly resolved. In conflict there can be no answer and no resolution, for its purpose is to make no resolution possible, and to ensure no answer will be plain. A problem set in conflict has no answer, for it is seen in

different ways. And what would be an answer from one point of view is not an answer in another light. You *are* in conflict. Thus it must be clear you cannot answer anything at all, for conflict has no limited effects. Yet if God gave an answer there must be a way in which your problems are resolved, for what He wills already has been done.

2. Thus it must be that time is not involved and every problem can be answered *now*. Yet it must also be that, in your state of mind, solution is impossible. Therefore, God must have given you a way of reaching to another state of mind in which the answer is already there. Such is the holy instant. It is here that all your problems should be brought and left. Here they belong, for here their answer is. And where its answer is, a problem must be simple and be easily resolved. It must be pointless to attempt to solve a problem where the answer cannot be. Yet just as surely it must be resolved, if it is brought to where the answer is.

V. The Healing Example

1. The only way to heal is to be healed. The miracle extends without your help, but you are needed that it can begin. Accept the miracle of healing, and it will go forth because of what it is. It is its nature to extend itself the instant it is born. And it is born the instant it is offered and received. No one can ask another to be healed. But he can let *himself* be healed, and thus offer the other what he has received. Who can bestow upon another what he does not have? And who can share what he denies himself? The Holy Spirit speaks to *you*. He does not speak to someone else. Yet by your listening His Voice extends, because you have accepted what He says.

2. Health is the witness unto health. As long as it is unattested, it remains without conviction. Only when it has been demonstrated is it proved, and must provide a witness that compels belief. No one is healed through double messages. If you wish only to be healed, you heal. Your single purpose makes this possible. But if you are afraid of healing, then it cannot come through you. The only thing that is required for a healing is a lack of fear. The fearful are not healed, and cannot heal. This does not mean the conflict must be gone forever from your mind to heal. For if it were, there were no need for healing then. But it does mean, if only for an instant, you love without attack. An instant is sufficient. Miracles wait not on time.

3. The holy instant is the miracle's abiding place. From there, each one is born into this world as witness to a state of mind that has transcended conflict, and has reached to peace. It carries comfort from

the place of peace into the battleground, and demonstrates that war has no effects. For all the hurt that war has sought to bring, the broken bodies and the shattered limbs, the screaming dying and the silent dead, are gently lifted up and comforted.

6. Come to the holy instant and be healed, for nothing that is there received is left behind on your returning to the world. And being blessed you will bring blessing. Life is given you to give the dying world. And suffering eyes no longer will accuse, but shine in thanks to you who blessing gave. The holy instant's radiance will light your eyes, and give them sight to see beyond all suffering and see Christ's face instead. Healing replaces suffering. Who looks on one cannot perceive the other, for they cannot both be there. And what you see the world will witness, and will witness to.

VI. The Witnesses to Sin

1. Pain demonstrates the body must be real. It is a loud, obscuring voice whose shrieks would silence what the Holy Spirit says, and keep His words from your awareness. Pain compels attention, drawing it away from Him and focusing upon itself. Its purpose is the same as pleasure, for they both are means to make the body real. What shares a common purpose is the same. This is the law of purpose, which unites all those who share in it within itself. Pleasure and pain are equally unreal, because their purpose cannot be achieved. Thus are they means for nothing, for they have a goal without a meaning. And they share the lack of meaning which their purpose has.

2. Sin shifts from pain to pleasure, and again to pain. For either witness is the same, and carries but one message: "You are here, within this body, and you can be hurt. You can have pleasure, too, but only at the cost of pain." These witnesses are joined by many more. Each one seems different because it has a different name, and so it seems to answer to a different sound. Except for this, the witnesses of sin are all alike. Call pleasure pain, and it will hurt. Call pain a pleasure, and the pain behind the pleasure will be felt no more. Sin's witnesses but shift from name to name, as one steps forward and another back. Yet which is foremost makes no difference. Sin's witnesses hear but the call of death.

5. The miracle makes no distinctions in the names by which sin's witnesses are called. It merely proves that what they represent has no effects. And this it proves because its own effects have come to take their place. It matters not the name by which you called your suffering. It is no longer there. The One Who brings the miracle

perceives them all as one, and called by name of fear. As fear is witness unto death, so is the miracle the witness unto life. It is a witness no one can deny, for it is the effects of life it brings. The dying live, the dead arise, and pain has vanished. Yet a miracle speaks not but for itself, but what it represents.

6. Love, too, has symbols in a world of sin. The miracle forgives because it stands for what is past forgiveness and is true. How foolish and insane it is to think a miracle is bound by laws that it came solely to undo! The laws of sin have different witnesses with different strengths. And they attest to different sufferings. Yet to the One Who sends forth miracles to bless the world, a tiny stab of pain, a little worldly pleasure, and the throes of death itself are but a single sound; a call for healing, and a plaintive cry for help within a world of misery. It is their sameness that the miracle attests. It is their sameness that it proves. The laws that call them different are dissolved, and shown as powerless. The purpose of a miracle is to accomplish this. And God Himself has guaranteed the strength of miracles for what they witness to.

7. Be you then witness to the miracle, and not the laws of sin. There is no need to suffer any more. But there *is* need that you be healed, because the suffering and sorrow of the world have made it deaf to its salvation and deliverance.

8. The resurrection of the world awaits your healing and your happiness, that you may demonstrate the healing of the world. The holy instant will replace all sin if you but carry its effects with you. And no one will elect to suffer more. What better function could you serve than this? Be healed that you may heal, and suffer not the laws of sin to be applied to you. And truth will be revealed to you who chose to let love's symbols take the place of sin.

VII. The Dreamer of the Dream

13. *You* are the dreamer of the world of dreams. No other cause it has, nor ever will. Nothing more fearful than an idle dream has terrified God's Son, and made him think that he has lost his innocence, denied his Father, and made war upon himself. So fearful is the dream, so seeming real, he could not waken to reality without the sweat of terror and a scream of mortal fear, unless a gentler dream preceded his awaking, and allowed his calmer mind to welcome, not to fear, the Voice that calls with love to waken him; a gentler dream, in which his suffering was healed and where his

brother was his friend. God willed he waken gently and with joy, and gave him means to waken without fear.

14. Accept the dream He gave instead of yours. It is not difficult to change a dream when once the dreamer has been recognized. Rest in the Holy Spirit, and allow His gentle dreams to take the place of those you dreamed in terror and in fear of death. He brings forgiving dreams, in which the choice is not who is the murderer and who shall be the victim. In the dreams He brings there is no murder and there is no death. The dream of guilt is fading from your sight, although your eyes are closed. A smile has come to lighten up your sleeping face. The sleep is peaceful now, for these are happy dreams.

15. Dream softly of your sinless brother, who unites with you in holy innocence. And from this dream the Lord of Heaven will Himself awaken His beloved Son. Dream of your brother's kindnesses instead of dwelling in your dreams on his mistakes. Select his thoughtfulness to dream about instead of counting up the hurts he gave. Forgive him his illusions, and give thanks to him for all the helpfulness he gave. And do not brush aside his many gifts because he is not perfect in your dreams. He represents his Father, Whom you see as offering both life and death to you.

16. Brother, He gives but life. Yet what you see as gifts your brother offers represent the gifts you dream your Father gives to you. Let all your brother's gifts be seen in light of charity and kindness offered you. And let no pain disturb your dream of deep appreciation for his gifts to you.

QUESTION 48. Why can't you forgive your brother while still believing he is guilty?

VIII. The "Hero" of the Dream

1. The body is the central figure in the dreaming of the world. There is no dream without it, nor does it exist without the dream in which it acts as if it were a person to be seen and be believed. It takes the central place in every dream, which tells the story of how it was made by other bodies, born into the world outside the body, lives a little while and dies, to be united in the dust with other bodies dying like itself. In the brief time allotted it to live, it seeks for other bodies as its friends and enemies. Its safety is its main concern. Its comfort is its guiding rule. It tries to look for pleasure, and avoid the things that would be hurtful. Above all, it tries to teach itself its pains and joys are different and can be told apart.

2.   The dreaming of the world takes many forms, because the body seeks in many ways to prove it is autonomous and real. It puts things on itself that it has bought with little metal discs or paper strips the world proclaims as valuable and real. It works to get them, doing senseless things, and tosses them away for senseless things it does not need and does not even want. It hires other bodies, that they may protect it and collect more senseless things that it can call its own. It looks about for special bodies that can share its dream. Sometimes it dreams it is a conqueror of bodies weaker than itself. But in some phases of the dream, it is the slave of bodies that would hurt and torture it.

3.   The body's serial adventures, from the time of birth to dying are the theme of every dream the world has ever had. The "hero" of this dream will never change, nor will its purpose. Though the dream itself takes many forms, and seems to show a great variety of places and events wherein its "hero" finds itself, the dream has but one purpose, taught in many ways. This single lesson does it try to teach again, and still again, and yet once more; that it is cause and not effect. And you are its effect, and cannot be its cause.

4.   Thus are you not the dreamer, but the dream. And so you wander idly in and out of places and events that it contrives. That this is all the body does is true, for it is but a figure in a dream. But who reacts to figures in a dream unless he sees them as if they were real? The instant that he sees them as they are they have no more effects on him, because he understands he gave them their effects by causing them and making them seem real.

5.   How willing are you to escape effects of all the dreams the world has ever had? Is it your wish to let no dream appear to be the cause of what it is you do? Then let us merely look upon the dream's beginning, for the part you see is but the second part, whose cause lies in the first. No one asleep and dreaming in the world remembers his attack upon himself. No one believes there really was a time when he knew nothing of a body, and could never have conceived this world as real. He would have seen at once that these ideas are one illusion, too ridiculous for anything but to be laughed away. How serious they now appear to be! And no one can remember when they would have met with laughter and with disbelief. We can remember this, if we but look directly at their cause. And we will see the grounds for laughter, not a cause for fear.

6.   Let us return the dream he gave away unto the dreamer, who perceives the dream as separate from himself and done to him. Into eternity, where all is one, there crept a tiny, mad idea, at which the

Son of God remembered not to laugh. In his forgetting did the thought become a serious idea, and possible of both accomplishment and real effects. Together, we can laugh them both away, and understand that time cannot intrude upon eternity. It is a joke to think that time can come to circumvent eternity, which *means* there is no time.

7.   A timelessness in which is time made real; a part of God that can attack itself; a separate brother as an enemy; a mind within a body all are forms of circularity whose ending starts at its beginning, ending at its cause. The world you see depicts exactly what you thought you did. Except that now you think that what you did is being done to you. The guilt for what you thought is being placed outside yourself, and on a guilty world that dreams your dreams and thinks your thoughts instead of you. It brings its vengeance, not your own. It keeps you narrowly confined within a body, which it punishes because of all the sinful things the body does within its dream. You have no power to make the body stop its evil deeds because you did not make it, and cannot control its actions nor its purpose nor its fate.

8.   The world but demonstrates an ancient truth; you will believe that others do to you exactly what you think you did to them. But once deluded into blaming them you will not see the cause of what they do, because you *want* the guilt to rest on them. How childish is the petulant device to keep your innocence by pushing guilt outside yourself, but never letting go! It is not easy to perceive the jest when all around you do your eyes behold its heavy consequences, but without their trifling cause. Without the cause do its effects seem serious and sad indeed. Yet they but follow. And it is their cause that follows nothing and is but a jest.

9.   In gentle laughter does the Holy Spirit perceive the cause, and looks not to effects. How else could He correct your error, who have overlooked the cause entirely? He bids you bring each terrible effect to Him that you may look together on its foolish cause and laugh with Him a while. *You* judge effects, but *He* has judged their cause. And by His judgment are effects removed. Perhaps you come in tears. But hear Him say, "My brother, holy Son of God, behold your idle dream, in which this could occur." And you will leave the holy instant with your laughter and your brother's joined with His.

10.   The secret of salvation is but this: that you are doing this unto yourself. No matter what the form of the attack, this still is true. Whoever takes the role of enemy and of attacker, still is this the truth. Whatever seems to be the cause of any pain and suffering you feel, this is still true. For you would not react at all to figures in a dream you knew that you were dreaming. Let them be as hateful and as

vicious as they may, they could have no effect on you unless you failed to recognize it is your dream.

11.   This single lesson learned will set you free from suffering, whatever form it takes. The Holy Spirit will repeat this one inclusive lesson of deliverance until it has been learned, regardless of the form of suffering that brings you pain. Whatever hurt you bring to Him He will make answer with this very simple truth. For this one answer takes away the cause of every form of sorrow and of pain. The form affects His answer not at all, for He would teach you but the single cause of all of them, no matter what their form. And you will understand that miracles reflect the simple statement, "*I* have done this thing, and it is this I would undo."

12.   Bring, then, all forms of suffering to Him Who knows that every one is like the rest. He sees no differences where none exists, and He will teach you how each one is caused. None has a different cause from all the rest, and all of them are easily undone by but a single lesson truly learned. Salvation is a secret you have kept but from yourself. The universe proclaims it so. Yet to its witnesses you pay no heed at all. For they attest the thing you do not want to know. They seem to keep it secret from you. Yet you need but learn you chose but not to listen, not to see.

13.   How differently will you perceive the world when this is recognized! When you forgive the world your guilt, you will be free of it. Its innocence does not demand your guilt, nor does your guiltlessness rest on its sins. This is the obvious; a secret kept from no one but yourself. And it is this that has maintained you separate from the world, and kept your brother separate from you. Now need you but to learn that both of you are innocent or guilty. The one thing that is impossible is that you be unlike each other; that they both be true. This is the only secret yet to learn. And it will be no secret you are healed.

Chapter 28. THE UNDOING OF FEAR

I. The Present Memory

4. The Holy Spirit can indeed make use of memory, for God Himself is there. Yet this is not a memory of past events, but only of a present state. You are so long accustomed to believe that memory holds only what is past, that it is hard for you to realize it is a skill that can remember *now*. The limitations on remembering the world imposes on it are as vast as those you let the world impose on you. There is no link of memory to the past. If you would have it there, then there it is. But only your desire made the link, and only you have held it to a part of time where guilt appears to linger still.

11. The miracle comes quietly into the mind that stops an instant and is still. It reaches gently from that quiet time, and from the mind it healed in quiet then, to other minds to share its quietness. And they will join in doing nothing to prevent its radiant extension back into the Mind which caused all minds to be. Born out of sharing, there can be no pause in time to cause the miracle delay in hastening to all unquiet minds, and bringing them an instant's stillness, when the memory of God returns to them. Their own remembering is quiet now, and what has come to take its place will not be wholly unremembered afterwards.

12. He to Whom time is given offers thanks for every quiet instant given Him. For in that instant is God's memory allowed to offer all its treasures to the Son of God, for whom they have been kept. How gladly does He offer them unto the one for whom He has been given them! And His Creator shares His thanks, because He would not be deprived of His Effects. The instant's silence that His Son accepts gives welcome to eternity and Him, and lets Them enter where They would abide. For in that instant does the Son of God do nothing that would make himself afraid.

II. Reversing Effect and Cause

12. This world is full of miracles. They stand in shining silence next to every dream of pain and suffering, of sin and guilt. They are the dream's alternative, the choice to be the dreamer, rather than deny the active role in making up the dream. They are the glad effects of taking back the consequence of sickness to its cause. The body is released because the mind acknowledges "this is not done to me, but

I am doing this." And thus the mind is free to make another choice instead. Beginning here, salvation will proceed to change the course of every step in the descent to separation, until all the steps have been retraced, the ladder gone, and all the dreaming of the world undone.

IV. The Greater Joining

1.   Accepting the Atonement for yourself means not to give support to someone's dream of sickness and of death. It means that you share not his wish to separate, and let him turn illusions on himself. Nor do you wish that they be turned, instead, on you. Thus have they no effects. And you are free of dreams of pain because you let him be. Unless you help him, you will suffer pain with him because that is your wish. And you become a figure in his dream of pain, as he in yours. So do you and your brother both become illusions, and without identity. You could be anyone or anything, depending on whose evil dream you share. You can be sure of just one thing; that you are evil, for you share in dreams of fear.

2.   There is a way of finding certainty right here and now. Refuse to be a part of fearful dreams whatever form they take, for you will lose identity in them. You find yourself by not accepting them as causing you, and giving you effects. You stand apart from them, but not apart from him who dreams them. Thus you separate the dreamer from the dream, and join in one, but let the other go. The dream is but illusion in the mind. And with the mind you would unite, but never with the dream. It is the dream you fear, and not the mind. You see them as the same, because you think that *you* are but a dream. And what is real and what is but illusion in yourself you do not know and cannot tell apart.

3.   Like you, your brother thinks he is a dream. Share not in his illusion of himself, for your Identity depends on his reality. Think, rather, of him as a mind in which illusions still persist, but as a mind which brother is to you. He is not brother made by what he dreams, nor is his body, "hero" of the dream, your brother. It is his reality that is your brother, as is yours to him. Your mind and his are joined in brotherhood. His body and his dreams but seem to make a little gap, where yours have joined with his.

7.   The Holy Spirit is in both your minds, and He is One because there is no gap that separates His Oneness from Itself. The gap between your bodies matters not, for what is joined in Him is always one. No one is sick if someone else accepts his union with him. His desire to be a sick and separated mind can not remain without a

witness or a cause. And both are gone if someone wills to be united with him. He has dreams that he was separated from his brother who, by sharing not his dream, has left the space between them vacant. And the Father comes to join His Son the Holy Spirit joined.

8. The Holy Spirit's function is to take the broken picture of the Son of God and put the pieces into place again. This holy picture, healed entirely, does He hold out to every separate piece that thinks it is a picture in itself. To each He offers his Identity, which the whole picture represents, instead of just a little, broken bit that he insisted was himself. And when he sees this picture he will recognize himself. If you share not your brother's evil dream, this is the picture that the miracle will place within the little gap, left clean of all the seeds of sickness and of sin. And here the Father will receive His Son, because His Son was gracious to himself.

9. I thank You, Father, knowing You will come to close each little gap that lies between the broken pieces of Your holy Son. Your Holiness, complete and perfect, lies in every one of them. And they are joined because what is in one is in them all. How holy is the smallest grain of sand, when it is recognized as being part of the completed picture of God's Son! The forms the broken pieces seem to take mean nothing. For the whole is in each one. And every aspect of the Son of God is just the same as every other part.

10. Join not your brother's dreams but join with him, and where you join His Son the Father is. Who seeks for substitutes when he perceives he has lost nothing? Who would want to have the "benefits" of sickness when he has received the simple happiness of health? What God has given cannot be a loss, and what is not of Him has no effects. What, then, would you perceive within the gap? The seeds of sickness come from the belief that there is joy in separation, and its giving up would be a sacrifice. But miracles are the result when you do not insist on seeing in the gap what is not there. Your willingness to let illusions go is all the Healer of God's Son requires. He will place the miracle of healing where the seeds of sickness were. And there will be no loss, but only gain.

QUESTION 49. What is the "central figure" playing the role of the "hero" of the dreaming of the world, and how is the "complete picture of the Son of God" described in Chapter 28 different from the "vision of the Son of God" and the "face of Christ" described in other chapters?

VI. The Secret Vows

4. The body represents the gap between the little bit of mind you call your own and all the rest of what is really yours. You hate it, yet you think it is your self, and that, without it, would your self be lost. This is the secret vow that you have made with every brother who would walk apart. This is the secret oath you take again, whenever you perceive yourself attacked. No one can suffer if he does not see himself attacked, and losing by attack. Unstated and unheard in consciousness is every pledge to sickness. Yet it is a promise to another to be hurt by him, and to attack him in return.

5. Sickness is anger taken out upon the body, so that it will suffer pain. It is the obvious effect of what was made in secret, in agreement with another's secret wish to be apart from you, as you would be apart from him. Unless you both agree that is your wish, it can have no effects. Whoever says, "There is no gap between my mind and yours" has kept God's promise, not his tiny oath to be forever faithful unto death. And by his healing is his brother healed.

6. Let this be your agreement with each one; that you be one with him and not apart. And he will keep the promise that you make with him, because it is the one that he has made to God, as God has made to him. God keeps His promises; His Son keeps his. In his creation did his Father say, "You are beloved of Me and I of you forever. Be you perfect as Myself, for you can never be apart from Me." His Son remembers not that he replied "I will," though in that promise he was born. Yet God reminds him of it every time he does not share a promise to be sick, but lets his mind be healed and unified. His secret vows are powerless before the Will of God, Whose promises he shares. And what he substitutes is not his will, who has made promise of himself to God.

VII. The Ark of Safety

2. The beautiful relationship you have with all your brothers is a part of you because it is a part of God Himself. Are you not sick, if you deny yourself your wholeness and your health, the Source of help, the Call to healing and the Call to heal? Your savior waits for healing, and the world waits with him. Nor are you apart from it. For healing will be one or not at all, its oneness being where the healing is. What could correct for separation but its opposite? There is no middle ground in any aspect of salvation. You accept it wholly or

accept it not. What is unseparated must be joined. And what is joined cannot be separate.

4. With *this* as purpose is the body healed. It is not used to witness to the dream of separation and disease. Nor is it idly blamed for what it did not do. It serves to help the healing of God's Son, and for this purpose it cannot be sick. It will not join a purpose not your own, and you have chosen that it not be sick. All miracles are based upon this choice, and given you the instant it is made. No forms of sickness are immune, because the choice cannot be made in terms of form. The choice of sickness seems to be of form, yet it is one, as is its opposite. And you are sick or well, accordingly.

7. Your home is built upon your brother's health, upon his happiness, his sinlessness, and everything his Father promised him. No secret promise you have made instead has shaken the Foundation of his home. The winds will blow upon it and the rain will beat against it, but with no effect. The world will wash away and yet this house will stand forever, for its strength lies not within itself alone. It is an ark of safety, resting on God's promise that His Son is safe forever in Himself. What gap can interpose itself between the safety of this shelter and its Source? From here the body can be seen as what it is, and neither less nor more in worth than the extent to which it can be used to liberate God's Son unto his home. And with this holy purpose is it made a home of holiness a little while, because it shares your Father's Will with you.

Chapter 29. THE AWAKENING

III. God's Witnesses

3. Within the dream of bodies and of death is yet one theme of truth; no more, perhaps, than just a tiny spark, a space of light created in the dark, where God still shines. You cannot wake yourself. Yet you can let yourself be wakened. You can overlook your brother's dreams. So perfectly can you forgive him his illusions he becomes your savior from your dreams. And as you see him shining in the space of light where God abides within the darkness, you will see that God Himself is where his body is. Before this light the body disappears, as heavy shadows must give way to light. The darkness cannot choose that it remain. The coming of the light means it is gone. In glory will you see your brother then, and understand what really fills the gap so long perceived as keeping you apart. There, in its place, God's witness has set forth the gentle way of kindness to God's Son. Whom you forgive is given power to forgive you your illusions. By your gift of freedom is it given unto you.

4. Make way for love, which you did not create, but which you can extend. On earth this means forgive your brother, that the darkness may be lifted from your mind. When light has come to him through your forgiveness, he will not forget his savior, leaving him unsaved. For it was in your face he saw the light that he would keep beside him, as he walks through darkness to the everlasting light.

5. How holy are you, that the Son of God can be your savior in the midst of dreams of desolation and disaster. See how eagerly he comes, and steps aside from heavy shadows that have hidden him, and shines on you in gratitude and love. He is himself, but not himself alone. And as his Father lost not part of him in your creation, so the light in him is brighter still because you gave your light to him, to save him from the dark. And now the light in you must be as bright as shines in him. This is the spark that shines within the dream; that you can help him waken, and be sure his waking eyes will rest on you. And in his glad salvation you are saved.

V. The Changeless Dwelling Place

1. There is a place in you where this whole world has been forgotten; where no memory of sin and of illusion lingers still. There is a place in

you which time has left, and echoes of eternity are heard. There is a resting place so still no sound except a hymn to Heaven rises up to gladden God the Father and the Son. Where Both abide are They remembered, Both. And where They are is Heaven and is peace.

2. Think not that you can change Their dwelling place. For your Identity abides in Them, and where They are, forever must you be. The changelessness of Heaven is in you, so deep within that nothing in this world but passes by, unnoticed and unseen. The still infinity of endless peace surrounds you gently in its soft embrace, so strong and quiet, tranquil in the might of its Creator, nothing can intrude upon the sacred Son of God within.

3. Here is the role the Holy Spirit gives to you who wait upon the Son of God, and would behold him waken and be glad. He is a part of you and you of him, because he is his Father's Son, and not for any purpose you may see in him. Nothing is asked of you but to accept the changeless and eternal that abide in him, for your Identity is there. The peace in you can but be found in him. And every thought of love you offer him but brings you nearer to your wakening to peace eternal and to endless joy.

4. This sacred Son of God is like yourself; the mirror of his Father's Love for you, the soft reminder of his Father's Love by which he was created and which still abides in him as it abides in you. Be very still and hear God's Voice in him, and let It tell you what his function is. He was created that you might be whole, for only the complete can be a part of God's completion, which created you.

5. There is no gift the Father asks of you but that you see in all creation but the shining glory of His gift to you. Behold His Son, His perfect gift, in whom his Father shines forever, and to whom is all creation given as his own. Because he has it is it given you, and where it lies in him behold your peace. The quiet that surrounds you dwells in him, and from this quiet come the happy dreams in which your hands are joined in innocence. These are not hands that grasp in dreams of pain. They hold no sword, for they have left their hold on every vain illusion of the world. And being empty they receive, instead, a brother's hand in which completion lies.

6. If you but knew the glorious goal that lies beyond forgiveness, you would not keep hold on any thought, however light the touch of evil on it may appear to be. For you would understand how great the cost of holding anything God did not give in minds that can direct the hand to bless, and lead God's Son unto his Father's house. Would you not want to be a friend to him, created by his Father as His

home? If God esteems him worthy of Himself, would you attack him with the hands of hate? Who would lay bloody hands on Heaven itself, and hope to find its peace? Your brother thinks he holds the hand of death. Believe him not. But learn, instead, how blessed are you who can release him, just by offering him yours.

7. A dream is given you in which he is your savior, not your enemy in hate. A dream is given you in which you have forgiven him for all his dreams of death; a dream of hope you share with him, instead of dreaming evil separate dreams of hate. Why does it seem so hard to share this dream? Because unless the Holy Spirit gives the dream its function, it was made for hate, and will continue in death's services. Each form it takes in some way calls for death. And those who serve the lord of death have come to worship in a separated world, each with his tiny spear and rusted sword, to keep his ancient promises to die.

8. Such is the core of fear in every dream that has been kept apart from use by Him Who sees a different function for a dream. When dreams are shared they lose the function of attack and separation, even though it was for this that every dream was made. Yet nothing in the world of dreams remains without the hope of change and betterment, for here is not where changelessness is found. Let us be glad indeed that this is so, and seek not the eternal in this world. Forgiving dreams are means to step aside from dreaming of a world outside yourself. And leading finally beyond all dreams, unto the peace of everlasting life.

VI. Forgiveness and the End of Time

1. How willing are you to forgive your brother? How much do you desire peace instead of endless strife and misery and pain? These questions are the same, in different form. Forgiveness is your peace, for herein lies the end of separation and the dream of danger and destruction, sin and death; of madness and of murder, grief and loss. This is the "sacrifice" salvation asks, and gladly offers peace instead of this.

6. How lovely is the world whose purpose is forgiveness of God's Son! How free from fear, how filled with blessing and with happiness! And what a joyous thing it is to dwell a little while in such a happy place! Nor can it be forgot, in such a world, it *is* a little while till timelessness comes quietly to take the place of time.

VII. Seek Not Outside Yourself

1. Seek not outside yourself. For it will fail, and you will weep each time an idol falls. Heaven cannot be found where it is not, and there can be no peace excepting there. Each idol that you worship when God calls will never answer in His place. There is no other answer you can substitute, and find the happiness His answer brings. Seek not outside yourself. For all your pain comes simply from a futile search for what you want, insisting where it must be found. What if it is not there? Do you prefer that you be right or happy? Be you glad that you are told where happiness abides, and seek no longer elsewhere. You will fail. But it is given you to know the truth, and not to seek for it outside yourself.

2. No one who comes here but must still have hope, some lingering illusion, or some dream that there is something outside of himself that will bring happiness and peace to him. If everything is in him this cannot be so. And therefore by his coming, he denies the truth about himself, and seeks for something more than everything, as if a part of it were separated off and found where all the rest of it is not. This is the purpose he bestows upon the body; that it seek for what he lacks, and give him what would make himself complete. And thus he wanders aimlessly about, in search of something that he cannot find, believing that he is what he is not.

4. Whenever you attempt to reach a goal in which the body's betterment is cast as major beneficiary, you try to bring about your death. For you believe that you can suffer lack, and lack *is* death. To sacrifice is to give up, and thus to be without and to have suffered loss. And by this giving up is life renounced. Seek not outside yourself. The search implies you are not whole within and fear to look upon your devastation, but prefer to seek outside yourself for what you are.

6. All idols of this world were made to keep the truth within from being known to you, and to maintain allegiance to the dream that you must find what is outside yourself to be complete and happy. It is vain to worship idols in the hope of peace. God dwells within, and your completion lies in Him. No idol takes His place. Look not to idols. Do not seek outside yourself.

7. Let us forget the purpose of the world the past has given it. For otherwise, the future will be like the past, and but a series of depressing dreams, in which all idols fail you, one by one, and you see death and disappointment everywhere.

QUESTION 50. In addition to Jesus, called your "elder brother" in the Course, who is your savior and why is this savior so important?

VIII. The Anti-Christ

1. What is an idol? Do you think you know? For idols are unrecognized as such, and never seen for what they really are. That is the only power that they have. Their purpose is obscure, and they are feared and worshipped, both, *because* you do not know what they are for, and why they have been made. An idol is an image of your brother that you would value more than what he is. Idols are made that he may be replaced, no matter what their form. And it is this that never is perceived and recognized. Be it a body or a thing, a place, a situation or a circumstance, an object owned or wanted, or a right demanded or achieved, it is the same.

2. Let not their form deceive you. Idols are but substitutes for your reality. In some way, you believe they will complete your little self, for safety in a world perceived as dangerous, with forces massed against your confidence and peace of mind. They have the power to supply your lacks, and add the value that you do not have. No one believes in idols who has not enslaved himself to littleness and loss. And thus must seek beyond his little self for strength to raise his head, and stand apart from all the misery the world reflects. This is the penalty for looking not within for certainty and quiet calm that liberates you from the world, and lets you stand apart, in quiet and in peace.

3. An idol is a false impression, or a false belief; some form of anti-Christ, that constitutes a gap between the Christ and what you see. An idol is a wish, made tangible and given form, and thus perceived as real and seen outside the mind. Yet it is still a thought, and cannot leave the mind that is its source. Nor is its form apart from the idea it represents. All forms of anti-Christ oppose the Christ. And fall before His face like a dark veil that seems to shut you off from Him, alone in darkness. Yet the light is there. A cloud does not put out the sun. No more a veil can banish what it seems to separate, nor darken by one whit the light itself.

4. This world of idols *is* a veil across the face of Christ, because its purpose is to separate your brother from yourself. A dark and fearful purpose, yet a thought without the power to change one blade of grass from something living to a sign of death. Its form is nowhere, for its source abides within your mind where God abideth not. Where is this place where what is everywhere has been excluded and been kept apart? What hand could be held up to block God's way? Whose voice could make demand He enter not? The "more-than-everything" is

not a thing to make you tremble and to quail in fear. Christ's enemy is nowhere. He can take no form in which he ever will be real.

5. What is an idol? Nothing! It must be believed before it seems to come to life, and given power that it may be feared. Its life and power are its believer's gift, and this is what the miracle restores to what *has* life and power worthy of the gift of Heaven and eternal peace. The miracle does not restore the truth, the light the veil between has not put out. It merely lifts the veil, and lets the truth shine unencumbered, being what it is. It does not need belief to be itself, for it has been created; so it *is*.

8. What purpose has an idol, then? What is it for? This is the only question that has many answers, each depending on the one of whom the question has been asked. The world believes in idols. No one comes unless he worshipped them, and still attempts to seek for one that yet might offer him a gift reality does not contain. Each worshipper of idols harbors hope his special deities will give him more than other men possess. It must be more. It does not really matter more of what; more beauty, more intelligence, more wealth, or even more affliction and more pain. But more of something is an idol for. And when one fails another takes its place, with hope of finding more of something else. Be not deceived by forms the "something" takes. An idol is a means for getting more. And it is this that is against God's Will.

9. God has not many Sons, but only One. Who can have more, and who be given less? In Heaven would the Son of God but laugh, if idols could intrude upon his peace. It is for him the Holy Spirit speaks, and tells you idols have no purpose here. For more than Heaven can you never have. If Heaven is within, why would you seek for idols that would make of Heaven less, to give you more than God bestowed upon your brother and on you, as one with Him? God gave you all there is. And to be sure you could not lose it, did He also give the same to every living thing as well. And thus is every living thing a part of you, as of Himself. No idol can establish you as more than God. But you will never be content with being less.

IX. The Forgiving Dream

1. The slave of idols is a willing slave. For willing he must be to let himself bow down in worship to what has no life, and seek for power in the powerless. What happened to the holy Son of God that this could be his wish; to let himself fall lower than the stones upon the ground, and look to idols that they raise him up? Hear, then, your

story in the dream you made, and ask yourself if it be not the truth that you believe that it is not a dream.

2. A dream of judgment came into the mind that God created perfect as Himself. And in that dream was Heaven changed to hell, and God made enemy unto His Son. How can God's Son awaken from the dream? It is a dream of judgment. So must he judge not, and he will waken. For the dream will seem to last while he is part of it. Judge not, for he who judges will have need of idols, which will hold the judgment off from resting on himself. Nor can he know the Self he has condemned. Judge not, because you make yourself a part of evil dreams, where idols are your "true" identity, and your salvation from the judgment laid in terror and in guilt upon yourself.

7. The real world still is but a dream. Except the figures have been changed. They are not seen as idols which betray. It is a dream in which no one is used to substitute for something else, nor interposed between the thoughts the mind conceives and what it sees. No one is used for something he is not, for childish things have all been put away. And what was once a dream of judgment now has changed into a dream where all is joy, because that is the purpose that it has. Only forgiving dreams can enter here, for time is almost over. And the forms that enter in the dream are now perceived as brothers, not in judgment, but in love.

8. Forgiving dreams have little need to last. They are not made to separate the mind from what it thinks. They do not seek to prove the dream is being dreamed by someone else. And in these dreams a melody is heard that everyone remembers, though he has not heard it since before all time began. Forgiveness, once complete, brings timelessness so close the song of Heaven can be heard, not with the ears, but with the holiness that never left the altar that abides forever deep within the Son of God. And when he hears this song again, he knows he never heard it not. And where is time, when dreams of judgment have been put away?

10. Forgiving dreams remind you that you live in safety and have not attacked yourself. So do your childish terrors melt away, and dreams become a sign that you have made a new beginning, not another try to worship idols and to keep attack. Forgiving dreams are kind to everyone who figures in the dream. And so they bring the dreamer full release from dreams of fear. He does not fear his judgment for he has judged no one, nor has sought to be released through judgment from what judgment must impose. And all the while he is remembering what he forgot, when judgment seemed to be the way to save him from its penalty.

Chapter 30. THE NEW BEGINNING

III. Beyond All Idols

1. Idols are quite specific. But your will is universal, being limitless. And so it has no form, nor is content for its expression in the terms of form. Idols are limits. They are the belief that there are forms that will bring happiness, and that, by limiting, is all attained. It is as if you said, "I have no need of everything. This little thing I want, and it will be as everything to me." And this must fail to satisfy, because it is your will that everything be yours. Decide for idols and you ask for loss. Decide for truth and everything is yours.

2. It is not form you seek. What form can be a substitute for God the Father's Love? What form can take the place of all the love in the Divinity of God the Son? What idol can make two of what is one? And can the limitless be limited? You do not want an idol. It is not your will to have one. It will not bestow on you the gift you seek. When you decide upon the form of what you want, you lose the understanding of its purpose. So you see your will within the idol, thus reducing it to a specific form. Yet this could never be your will, because what shares in all creation cannot be content with small ideas and little things.

3. Behind the search for every idol lies the yearning for completion. Wholeness has no form because it is unlimited. To seek a special person or a thing to add to you to make yourself complete, can only mean that you believe some form is missing. And by finding this, you will achieve completion in a form you like. This is the purpose of an idol; that you will not look beyond it, to the source of the belief that you are incomplete. Only if you had sinned could this be so. For sin is the idea you are alone and separated off from what is whole. And thus it would be necessary for the search for wholeness to be made beyond the boundaries of limits on yourself.

5. Completion is the *function* of God's Son. He has no need to seek for it at all. Beyond all idols stands his holy will to be but what he is. For more than whole is meaningless. If there were change in him, if he could be reduced to any form and limited to what is not in him, he would not be as God created him. What idol can he need to be himself? For can he give a part of him away? What is not whole cannot make whole. But what is really asked for cannot be denied. Your will *is* granted. Not in any form that would content you not, but in the whole completely lovely Thought God holds of you.

6. Nothing that God knows not exists. And what He knows exists forever, changelessly. For thoughts endure as long as does the mind that thought of them. And in the Mind of God there is no ending, nor a time in which His Thoughts were absent or could suffer change. Thoughts are not born and cannot die. They share the attributes of their creator, nor have they a separate life apart from his. The thoughts you think are in your mind, as you are in the Mind which thought of you. And so there are no separate parts in what exists within God's Mind. It is forever One, eternally united and at peace.

7. Thoughts seem to come and go. Yet all this means is that you are sometimes aware of them, and sometimes not. An unremembered thought is born again to you when it returns to your awareness. Yet it did not die when you forgot it. It was always there, but you were unaware of it. The Thought God holds of you is perfectly unchanged by your forgetting. It will always be exactly as it was before the time when you forgot, and will be just the same when you remember. And it is the same within the interval when you forgot.

8. The Thoughts of God are far beyond all change, and shine forever. They await not birth. They wait for welcome and remembering. The Thought God holds of you is like a star, unchangeable in an eternal sky. So high in Heaven is it set that those outside of Heaven know not it is there. Yet still and white and lovely will it shine through all eternity. There was no time it was not there; no instant when its light grew dimmer or less perfect ever was.

9. Who knows the Father knows this light, for He is the eternal sky that holds it safe, forever lifted up and anchored sure. Its perfect purity does not depend on whether it is seen on earth or not. The sky embraces it and softly holds it in its perfect place, which is as far from earth as earth from Heaven. It is not the distance nor the time that keeps this star invisible to earth. But those who seek for idols cannot know the star is there.

10. Beyond all idols is the Thought God holds of you. Completely unaffected by the turmoil and the terror of the world, the dreams of birth and death that here are dreamed, the myriad of forms that fear can take; quite undisturbed, the Thought God holds of you remains exactly as it always was. Surrounded by a stillness so complete no sound of battle comes remotely near, it rests in certainty and perfect peace. Here is your one reality kept safe, completely unaware of all the world that worships idols, and that knows not God. In perfect sureness of its changelessness and of its rest in its eternal home, the Thought God holds of you has never left the Mind of its Creator Whom it knows, as its Creator knows that it is there.

QUESTION 51. What is an idol, and how do idols affect you and your relationships with others?

V. The Only Purpose

1. The real world is the state of mind in which the only purpose of the world is seen to be forgiveness. Fear is not its goal, for the escape from guilt becomes its aim. The value of forgiveness is perceived and takes the place of idols, which are sought no longer, for their "gifts" are not held dear. No rules are idly set, and no demands are made of anyone or anything to twist and fit into the dream of fear. Instead, there is a wish to understand all things created as they really are. And it is recognized that all things must be first forgiven, and *then* understood.

2. Here, it is thought that understanding is acquired by attack. There, it is clear that by attack is understanding lost. The folly of pursuing guilt as goal is fully recognized. And idols are not wanted there, for guilt is understood as the sole cause of pain in any form. No one is tempted by its vain appeal, for suffering and death have been perceived as things not wanted and not striven for. The possibility of freedom has been grasped and welcomed, and the means by which it can be gained can now be understood. The world becomes a place of hope, because its only purpose is to be a place where hope of happiness can be fulfilled. And no one stands outside this hope, because the world has been united in belief the purpose of the world is one which all must share, if hope be more than just a dream.

3. Not yet is Heaven quite remembered, for the purpose of forgiveness still remains. Yet everyone is certain he will go beyond forgiveness, and he but remains until it is made perfect in himself. He has no wish for anything but this. And fear has dropped away, because he is united in his purpose with himself. There is a hope of happiness in him so sure and constant he can barely stay and wait a little longer, with his feet still touching earth. Yet is he glad to wait till every hand is joined, and every heart made ready to arise and go with him. For thus is he made ready for the step in which is all forgiveness left behind.

4. The final step is God's, because it is but God Who could create a perfect Son and share His Fatherhood with him. No one outside of Heaven knows how this can be, for understanding this is Heaven itself. Even the real world has a purpose still beneath creation and eternity. But fear is gone because its purpose is forgiveness, not idolatry. And so is Heaven's Son prepared to be himself, and to remember that the

Son of God knows everything his Father understands, and understands it perfectly with Him.

5. The real world still falls short of this, for this is God's Own purpose; only His, and yet completely shared and perfectly fulfilled. The real world is a state in which the mind has learned how easily do idols go when they are still perceived but wanted not. How willingly the mind can let them go when it has understood that idols are nothing and nowhere, and are purposeless. For only then can guilt and sin be seen without a purpose, and as meaningless.

6. Thus is the real world's purpose gently brought into awareness, to replace the goal of sin and guilt. And all that stood between your image of yourself and what you are, forgiveness washes joyfully away. Yet God need not create His Son again, that what is his be given back to him. The gap between your brother and yourself was never there. And what the Son of God knew in creation he must know again.

7. When brothers join in purpose in the world of fear, they stand already at the edge of the real world. Perhaps they still look back, and think they see an idol that they want. Yet has their path been surely set away from idols toward reality. For when they joined their hands it was Christ's hand they took, and they will look on Him Whose hand they hold. The face of Christ is looked upon before the Father is remembered. For He must be unremembered till His Son has reached beyond forgiveness to the Love of God. Yet is the Love of Christ accepted first. And then will come the knowledge They are One.

8. How light and easy is the step across the narrow boundaries of the world of fear when you have recognized Whose hand you hold! Within your hand is everything you need to walk with perfect confidence away from fear forever, and to go straight on, and quickly reach the gate of Heaven itself. For He Whose hand you hold was waiting but for you to join Him. Now that you have come, would He delay in showing you the way that He must walk with you? His blessing lies on you as surely as His Father's Love rests upon Him. His gratitude to you is past your understanding, for you have enabled Him to rise from chains and go with you, together, to His Father's house.

11. The Will of God forever lies in those whose hands are joined. Until they joined, they thought He was their enemy. But when they joined and shared a purpose, they were free to learn their will is one. And thus the Will of God must reach to their awareness. Nor can they forget for long that it is but their own.

VI. The Justification for Forgiveness

1. Anger is *never* justified. Attack has *no* foundation. It is here escape from fear begins, and will be made complete. Here is the real world given in exchange for dreams of terror. For it is on this forgiveness rests, and is but natural. You are not asked to offer pardon where attack is due, and would be justified. For that would mean that you forgive a sin by overlooking what is really there. This is not pardon. For it would assume that, by responding in a way which is not justified, your pardon will become the answer to attack that has been made. And thus is pardon inappropriate, by being granted where it is not due.

2. Pardon is *always* justified. It has a sure foundation. You do not forgive the unforgivable, nor overlook a real attack that calls for punishment. Salvation does not lie in being asked to make unnatural responses which are inappropriate to what is real. Instead, it merely asks that you respond appropriately to what is not real by not perceiving what has not occurred. If pardon were unjustified, you would be asked to sacrifice your rights when you return forgiveness for attack. But you are merely asked to see forgiveness as the natural reaction to distress that rests on error, and thus calls for help. Forgiveness is the only sane response. It *keeps* your rights from being sacrificed.

3. This understanding is the only change that lets the real world rise to take the place of dreams of terror. Fear cannot arise unless attack is justified, and if it had a real foundation pardon would have none. The real world is achieved when you perceive the basis of forgiveness is quite real and fully justified. While you regard it as a gift unwarranted, it must uphold the guilt you would "forgive." Unjustified forgiveness is attack. And this is all the world can ever give. It pardons "sinners" sometimes, but remains aware that they have sinned. And so they do not merit the forgiveness that it gives.

4. This is the false forgiveness which the world employs to keep the sense of sin alive. And recognizing God is just, it seems impossible His pardon could be real. Thus is the fear of God the sure result of seeing pardon as unmerited. No one who sees himself as guilty can avoid the fear of God. But he is saved from this dilemma if he can forgive. The mind must think of its Creator as it looks upon itself. If you can see your brother merits pardon, you have learned forgiveness is your right as much as his. Nor will you think that God intends for you a fearful judgment that your brother does not merit. For it is the truth that you can merit neither more nor less than he.

5. Forgiveness recognized as merited will heal. It gives the miracle its strength to overlook illusions. This is how you learn that you must be forgiven too. There can be no appearance that can not be overlooked. For if there were, it would be necessary first there be some sin that stands beyond forgiveness. There would be an error that is more than a mistake; a special form of error that remains unchangeable, eternal, and beyond correction or escape. There would be one mistake that had the power to undo creation, and to make a world that could replace it and destroy the Will of God. Only if this were possible could there be some appearances that could withstand the miracle, and not be healed by it.

6. There is no surer proof idolatry is what you wish than a belief there are some forms of sickness and of joylessness forgiveness cannot heal. This means that you prefer to keep some idols, and are not prepared, as yet, to let all idols go. And thus you think that some appearances are real and not appearances at all. Be not deceived about the meaning of a fixed belief that some appearances are harder to look past than others are. It always means you think forgiveness must be limited. And you have set a goal of partial pardon and a limited escape from guilt for you. What can this be except a false forgiveness of yourself, and everyone who seems apart from you?

7. It must be true the miracle can heal all forms of sickness, or it cannot heal. Its purpose cannot be to judge which forms are real, and which appearances are true. If one appearance must remain apart from healing, one illusion must be part of truth. And you could not escape all guilt, but only some of it. You must forgive God's Son entirely. Or you will keep an image of yourself that is not whole, and will remain afraid to look within and find escape from every idol there. Salvation rests on faith there cannot be some forms of guilt that you cannot forgive. And so there cannot be appearances that have replaced the truth about God's Son.

8. Look on your brother with the willingness to see him as he is. And do not keep a part of him outside your willingness that he be healed. To heal is to make whole. And what is whole can have no missing parts that have been kept outside. Forgiveness rests on recognizing this, and being glad there cannot be some forms of sickness which the miracle must lack the power to heal.

VII. The New Interpretation

3. Only a constant purpose can endow events with stable meaning. But it must accord *one* meaning to them all. If they are given

different meanings, it must be that they reflect but different purposes. And this is all the meaning that they have. Can this be meaning? Can confusion be what meaning means? Perception cannot be in constant flux, and make allowance for stability of meaning anywhere. Fear is a judgment never justified. Its presence has no meaning but to show you wrote a fearful script, and are afraid accordingly. But not because the thing you fear has fearful meaning in itself.

4. A common purpose is the only means whereby perception can be stabilized, and one interpretation given to the world and all experiences here. In this shared purpose is one judgment shared by everyone and everything you see. You do not have to judge, for you have learned one meaning has been given everything, and you are glad to see it everywhere. It cannot change *because* you would perceive it everywhere, unchanged by circumstance. And so you offer it to all events, and let them offer you stability.

5. Escape from judgment simply lies in this; all things have but one purpose, which you share with all the world. And nothing in the world can be opposed to it, for it belongs to everything, as it belongs to you. In single purpose is the end of all ideas of sacrifice, which must assume a different purpose for the one who gains and him who loses. There could be no thought of sacrifice apart from this idea. And it is this idea of different goals that makes perception shift and meaning change. In one united goal does this become impossible, for your agreement makes interpretation stabilize and last.

VIII. Changeless Reality

5. *Because* reality is changeless is a miracle already there to heal all things that change, and offer them to you to see in happy form, devoid of fear. It will be given you to look upon your brother thus. But not while you would have it otherwise in some respects. For this but means you would not have him healed and whole. The Christ in him is perfect. Is it this that you would look upon? Then let there be no dreams about him that you would prefer to seeing this. And you will see the Christ in him because you let Him come to you. And when He has appeared to you, you will be certain you are like Him, for He is the changeless in your brother and in you.

6. This will you look upon when you decide there is not one appearance you would hold in place of what your brother really is. Let no temptation to prefer a dream allow uncertainty to enter here. Be not made guilty and afraid when you are tempted by a dream of what he is. But do not give it power to replace the changeless in him

in your sight of him. There is no false appearance but will fade, if you request a miracle instead. There is no pain from which he is not free, if you would have him be but what he is. Why should you fear to see the Christ in him? You but behold yourself in what you see. As he is healed are you made free of guilt, for his appearance is your own to you.

QUESTION 52. When you join your brother in the one purpose of forgiveness, whose hand do you hold and whose face will you see, and why is anger never justified and forgiveness always justified?

Chapter 31. THE FINAL VISION

I. The Simplicity of Salvation

9.   There is no living thing that does not share the universal Will that it be whole, and that you do not leave its call unheard. Without your answer is it left to die, as it is saved from death when you have heard its calling as the ancient call to life, and understood that it is but your own. The Christ in you remembers God with all the certainty with which He knows His Love. But only if His Son is innocent can He be Love. For God were fear indeed if he whom He created innocent could be a slave to guilt. God's perfect Son remembers his creation. But in guilt he has forgotten what he really is.

10.   The fear of God results as surely from the lesson that His Son is guilty as God's Love must be remembered when he learns his innocence. For hate must father fear, and look upon its father as itself. How wrong are you who fail to hear the call that echoes past each seeming call to death, that sings behind each murderous attack and pleads that love restore the dying world. You do not understand Who calls to you beyond each form of hate; each call to war. Yet you will recognize Him as you give Him answer in the language that He calls. He will appear when you have answered Him, and you will know in Him that God is Love.

12.   Let us be still an instant, and forget all things we ever learned, all thoughts we had, and every preconception that we hold of what things mean and what their purpose is. Let us remember not our own ideas of what the world is for. We do not know. Let every image held of everyone be loosened from our minds and swept away.

13.   Be innocent of judgment, unaware of any thoughts of evil or of good that ever crossed your mind of anyone. Now do you know him not. But you are free to learn of him, and learn of him anew. Now is he born again to you, and you are born again to him, without the past that sentenced him to die, and you with him. Now is he free to live as you are free, because an ancient learning passed away, and left a place for truth to be reborn.

II. Walking with Christ

8.   Be very still an instant. Come without all thought of what you ever learned before, and put aside all images you made. The old

will fall away before the new without your opposition or intent. There will be no attack upon the things you thought were precious and in need of care. There will be no assault upon your wish to hear a call that never has been made. Nothing will hurt you in this holy place, to which you come to listen silently and learn the truth of what you really want. No more than this will you be asked to learn. But as you hear it, you will understand you need but come away without the thoughts you did not want, and that were never true.

9. Forgive your brother all appearances, that are but ancient lessons you have taught yourself about the sinfulness in you. Hear but his call for mercy and release from all the fearful images he holds of what he is and of what you must be. He is afraid to walk with you, and thinks perhaps a bit behind, a bit ahead would be a safer place for him to be. Can you make progress if you think the same, advancing only when he would step back, and falling back when he would go ahead? For so do you forget the journey's goal, which is but to decide to walk with him, so neither leads nor follows. Thus it is a way you go together, not alone. And in this choice is learning's outcome changed, for Christ has been reborn to both of you.

10. An instant spent without your old ideas of who your great companion is and what he should be asking for, will be enough to let this happen. And you will perceive his purpose is the same as yours. He asks for what you want, and needs the same as you. It takes, perhaps, a different form in him, but it is not the form you answer to. He asks and you receive, for you have come with but one purpose; that you learn you love your brother with a brother's love. And as a brother, must his Father be the same as yours, as he is like yourself in truth.

11. Together is your joint inheritance remembered and accepted by you both. Alone it is denied to both of you. Is it not clear that while you still insist on leading or on following, you think you walk alone, with no one by your side? This is the road to nowhere, for the light cannot be given while you walk alone, and so you cannot see which way you go. And thus there is confusion, and a sense of endless doubting as you stagger back and forward in the darkness and alone. Yet these are but appearances of what the journey is, and how it must be made. For next to you is One Who holds the light before you, so that every step is made in certainty and sureness of the road. A blindfold can indeed obscure your sight, but cannot make the way itself grow dark. And He Who travels with you *has* the light.

V. Self-Concept versus Self

2.   A concept of the self is made by you. It bears no likeness to yourself at all. It is an idol, made to take the place of your reality as Son of God. The concept of the self the world would teach is not the thing that it appears to be. For it is made to serve two purposes, but one of which the mind can recognize. The first presents the face of innocence, the aspect acted on. It is this face that smiles and charms and even seems to love. It searches for companions and it looks, at times with pity, on the suffering, and sometimes offers solace. It believes that it is good within an evil world.

3.   This aspect can grow angry, for the world is wicked and unable to provide the love and shelter innocence deserves. And so this face is often wet with tears at the injustices the world accords to those who would be generous and good. This aspect never makes the first attack. But every day a hundred little things make small assaults upon its innocence, provoking it to irritation, and at last to open insult and abuse.

4.   The face of innocence the concept of the self so proudly wears can tolerate attack in self-defense, for is it not a well-known fact the world deals harshly with defenseless innocence? No one who makes a picture of himself omits this face, for he has need of it. The other side he does not want to see. Yet it is here the learning of the world has set its sights, for it is here the world's "reality" is set, to see to it the idol lasts.

5.   Beneath the face of innocence there is a lesson that the concept of the self was made to teach. It is a lesson in a terrible displacement, and a fear so devastating that the face that smiles above it must forever look away, lest it perceive the treachery it hides. The lesson teaches this: "I am the thing you made of me, and as you look on me, you stand condemned because of what I am." On this conception of the self the world smiles with approval, for it guarantees the pathways of the world are safely kept, and those who walk on them will not escape.

7.   Concepts are learned. They are not natural. Apart from learning they do not exist. They are not given, so they must be made. Not one of them is true, and many come from feverish imaginations, hot with hatred and distortions born of fear. What is a concept but a thought to which its maker gives a meaning of his own? Concepts maintain the world. But they can not be used to demonstrate the world is real. For all of them are made within the world, born in its

shadow, growing in its ways and finally "maturing" in its thought. They are ideas of idols, painted with the brushes of the world, which cannot make a single picture representing truth.

8. A concept of the self is meaningless, for no one here can see what it is for, and therefore cannot picture what it is. Yet is all learning that the world directs begun and ended with the single aim of teaching you this concept of yourself, that you will choose to follow this world's laws, and never seek to go beyond its roads nor realize the way you see yourself. Now must the Holy Spirit find a way to help you see this concept of the self must be undone, if any peace of mind is to be given you. Nor can it be unlearned except by lessons aimed to teach that you are something else. For otherwise, you would be asked to make exchange of what you now believe for total loss of self, and greater terror would arise in you.

14. The concept of the self has always been the great preoccupation of the world. And everyone believes that he must find the answer to the riddle of himself. Salvation can be seen as nothing more than the escape from concepts. It does not concern itself with content of the mind, but with the simple statement that it thinks. And what can think has choice, and can be shown that different thoughts have different consequence. So it can learn that everything it thinks reflects the deep confusion that it feels about how it was made and what it is. And vaguely does the concept of the self appear to answer what it does not know.

15. Seek not your Self in symbols. There can be no concept that can stand for what you are. What matters it which concept you accept while you perceive a self that interacts with evil, and reacts to wicked things? Your concept of yourself will still remain quite meaningless. And you will not perceive that you can interact but with yourself. To see a guilty world is but the sign your learning has been guided by the world, and you behold it as you see yourself. The concept of the self embraces all you look upon, and nothing is outside of this perception. If you can be hurt by anything, you see a picture of your secret wishes. Nothing more than this. And in your suffering of any kind you see your own concealed desire to kill.

16. You will make many concepts of the self as learning goes along. Each one will show the changes in your own relationships, as your perception of yourself is changed. There will be some confusion every time there is a shift, but be you thankful that the learning of the world is loosening its grasp upon your mind. And be you sure and happy in the confidence that it will go at last, and leave your mind at peace. The role of the accuser will appear in many places

and in many forms. And each will seem to be accusing you. Yet have no fear it will not be undone.

17. The world can teach no images of you unless you want to learn them. There will come a time when images have all gone by, and you will see you know not what you are. It is to this unsealed and open mind that truth returns, unhindered and unbound. Where concepts of the self have been laid by is truth revealed exactly as it is. When every concept has been raised to doubt and question, and been recognized as made on no assumptions that would stand the light, then is the truth left free to enter in its sanctuary, clean and free of guilt. There is no statement that the world is more afraid to hear than this:

> I do not know the thing I am, and therefore do not know what I am doing, where I am, or how to look upon the world or on myself.

Yet in this learning is salvation born. And What you are will tell you of Itself.

VI. Recognizing the Spirit

1. You see the flesh or recognize the spirit. There is no compromise between the two. If one is real the other must be false, for what is real denies its opposite. There is no choice in vision but this one. What you decide in this determines all you see and think is real and hold as true. On this one choice does all your world depend, for here have you established what you are, as flesh or spirit in your own belief. If you choose flesh, you never will escape the body as your own reality, for you have chosen that you want it so. But choose the spirit, and all Heaven bends to touch your eyes and bless your holy sight, that you may see the world of flesh no more except to heal and comfort and to bless.

2. Salvation is undoing. If you choose to see the body, you behold a world of separation, unrelated things, and happenings that make no sense at all. This one appears and disappears in death; that one is doomed to suffering and loss. And no one is exactly as he was an instant previous, nor will he be the same as he is now an instant hence. Who could have trust where so much change is seen, for who is worthy if he be but dust? Salvation is undoing of all this. For constancy arises in the sight of those whose eyes salvation has released from looking at the cost of keeping guilt, because they chose to let it go instead.

3. Salvation does not ask that you behold the spirit and perceive the body not. It merely asks that this should be your choice. For you can see the body without help, but do not understand how to behold a world apart from it. It is your world salvation will undo, and let you see another world your eyes could never find. Be not concerned how this could ever be. You do not understand how what you see arose to meet your sight. For if you did, it would be gone. The veil of ignorance is drawn across the evil and the good, and must be passed that both may disappear, so that perception finds no hiding place. How is this done? It is not done at all. What could there be within the universe that God created that must still be done?

5. You who believe that you can choose to see the Son of God as you would have him be, forget not that no concept of yourself will stand against the truth of what you are. Undoing truth would be impossible. But concepts are not difficult to change. One vision, clearly seen, that does not fit the picture as it was perceived before will change the world for eyes that learn to see, because the concept of the self has changed.

6. Are you invulnerable? Then the world is harmless in your sight. Do you forgive? Then is the world forgiving, for you have forgiven it its trespasses, and so it looks on you with eyes that see as yours. Are you a body? So is all the world perceived as treacherous, and out to kill. Are you a spirit, deathless, and without the promise of corruption and the stain of sin upon you? So the world is seen as stable, fully worthy of your trust; a happy place to rest in for a while, where nothing need be feared, but only loved. Who is unwelcome to the kind in heart? And what could hurt the truly innocent?

7. Your will be done, you holy child of God. It does not matter if you think you are in earth or Heaven. What your Father wills of you can never change. The truth in you remains as radiant as a star, as pure as light, as innocent as love itself. And you *are* worthy that your will be done!

QUESTION 53. What self-concept masks do you wear, and what is the benefit of admitting that your concept of yourself is mistaken?

VII. The Savior's Vision

5. Have faith in him who walks with you, so that your fearful concept of yourself may change. And look upon the good in him, that you may not be frightened by your "evil" thoughts because they do not cloud your view of him. And all this shift requires is that you

be willing that this happy change occur. No more than this is asked. On its behalf, remember what the concept of yourself that now you hold has brought you in its wake, and welcome the glad contrast offered you. Hold out your hand, that you may have the gift of kind forgiveness which you offer one whose need for it is just the same as yours. And let the cruel concept of yourself be changed to one that brings the peace of God.

6. The concept of yourself that now you hold would guarantee your function here remain forever unaccomplished and undone. And thus it dooms you to a bitter sense of deep depression and futility. Yet it need not be fixed, unless you choose to hold it past the hope of change and keep it static and concealed within your mind. Give it instead to Him Who understands the changes that it needs to let it serve the function given you to bring you peace, that you may offer peace to have it yours. Alternatives are in your mind to use, and you can see yourself another way. Would you not rather look upon yourself as needed for salvation of the world, instead of as salvation's enemy?

7. The concept of the self stands like a shield, a silent barricade before the truth, and hides it from your sight. All things you see are images, because you look on them as through a barrier that dims your sight and warps your vision, so that you behold nothing with clarity. The light is kept from everything you see. At most, you glimpse a shadow of what lies beyond. At least, you merely look on darkness, and perceive the terrified imaginings that come from guilty thoughts and concepts born of fear. And what you see is hell, for fear *is* hell. All that is given you is for release; the sight, the vision and the inner Guide all lead you out of hell with those you love beside you, and the universe with them.

8. Behold your role within the universe! To every part of true creation has the Lord of Love and life entrusted all salvation from the misery of hell. And to each one has He allowed the grace to be a savior to the holy ones especially entrusted to his care. And this he learns when first he looks upon one brother as he looks upon himself, and sees the mirror of himself in him. Thus is the concept of himself laid by, for nothing stands between his sight and what he looks upon, to judge what he beholds. And in this single vision does he see the face of Christ, and understands he looks on *everyone* as he beholds this one. For there is light where darkness was before, and now the veil is lifted from his sight.

9. The veil across the face of Christ, the fear of God and of salvation, and the love of guilt and death, they all are different names for just

one error; that there is a space between you and your brother, kept apart by an illusion of yourself that holds him off from you, and you away from him. The sword of judgment is the weapon that you give to the illusion of yourself, that it may fight to keep the space that holds your brother off unoccupied by love. Yet while you hold this sword, you must perceive the body as yourself, for you are bound to separation from the sight of him who holds the mirror to another view of what he is, and thus what you must be.

10. What is temptation but the wish to stay in hell and misery? And what could this give rise to but an image of yourself that can be miserable, and remain in hell and torment? Who has learned to see his brother not as this has saved himself, and thus is he a savior to the rest. To everyone has God entrusted all, because a partial savior would be one who is but partly saved. The holy ones whom God has given you to save are but everyone you meet or look upon, not knowing who they are; all those you saw an instant and forgot, and those you knew a long while since, and those you will yet meet; the unremembered and the not yet born. For God has given you His Son to save from *every* concept that he ever held.

11. Yet while you wish to stay in hell, how could you be the savior of the Son of God? How would you know his holiness while you see him apart from yours? For holiness is seen through holy eyes that look upon the innocence within, and thus expect to see it everywhere. And so they call it forth in everyone they look upon, that he may be what they expect of him. This is the savior's vision; that he see his innocence in all he looks upon, and see his own salvation everywhere. He holds no concept of himself between his calm and open eyes and what he sees. He brings the light to what he looks upon, that he may see it as it really is.

12. Whatever form temptation seems to take, it always but reflects a wish to be a self that you are not. And from that wish a concept rises, teaching that you are the thing you wish to be. It will remain your concept of yourself until the wish that fathered it no longer is held dear. But while you cherish it, you will behold your brother in the likeness of the self whose image has the wish begot of you. For seeing can but represent a wish, because it has no power to create. Yet it can look with love or look with hate, depending only on the simple choice of whether you would join with what you see, or keep yourself apart and separate.

13. The savior's vision is as innocent of what your brother is as it is free of any judgment made upon yourself. It sees no past in anyone at all. And thus it serves a wholly open mind, unclouded by

old concepts, and prepared to look on only what the present holds. It cannot judge because it does not know. And recognizing this, it merely asks, "What is the meaning of what I behold?" Then is the answer given. And the door held open for the face of Christ to shine upon the one who asks, in innocence, to see beyond the veil of old ideas and ancient concepts held so long and dear against the vision of the Christ in you.

14. Be vigilant against temptation, then, remembering that it is but a wish, insane and meaningless, to make yourself a thing that you are not. And think as well upon the thing that you would be instead. It is a thing of madness, pain and death; a thing of treachery and black despair, of failing dreams and no remaining hope except to die, and end the dream of fear. *This* is temptation; nothing more than this. Can this be difficult to choose *against*? Consider what temptation is, and see the real alternatives you choose between. There are but two. Be not deceived by what appears as many choices. There is hell or Heaven, and of these you choose but one.

15. Let not the world's light, given unto you, be hidden from the world. It needs the light, for it is dark indeed, and men despair because the savior's vision is withheld and what they see is death. Their savior stands, unknowing and unknown, beholding them with eyes unopened. And they cannot see until he looks on them with seeing eyes, and offers them forgiveness with his own. Can you to whom God says, "Release My Son!" be tempted not to listen, when you learn that it is you for whom He asks release? And what but this is what this course would teach? And what but this is there for you to learn?

VIII. Choose Once Again

1. Temptation has one lesson it would teach, in all its forms, wherever it occurs. It would persuade the holy Son of God he is a body, born in what must die, unable to escape its frailty, and bound by what it orders him to feel. It sets the limits on what he can do; its power is the only strength he has; his grasp cannot exceed its tiny reach. Would you be this, if Christ appeared to you in all His glory, asking you but this:

> *Choose once again if you would take your place among the saviors of the world, or would remain in hell, and hold your brothers there.*

For He *has* come, and He *is* asking this.

2. How do you make the choice? How easily is this explained! You always choose between your weakness and the strength of Christ in you. And what you choose is what you think is real. Simply by never using weakness to direct your actions, you have given it no power. And the light of Christ in you is given charge of everything you do. For you have brought your weakness unto Him, and He has given you His strength instead.

3. Trials are but lessons that you failed to learn presented once again, so where you made a faulty choice before you now can make a better one, and thus escape all pain that what you chose before has brought to you. In every difficulty, all distress, and each perplexity Christ calls to you and gently says, "My brother, choose again." He would not leave one source of pain unhealed, nor any image left to veil the truth. He would remove all misery from you whom God created altar unto joy. He would not leave you comfortless, alone in dreams of hell, but would release your mind from everything that hides His face from you. His Holiness is yours because He is the only power that is real in you. His strength is yours because He is the Self that God created as His only Son.

4. The images you make cannot prevail against what God Himself would have you be. Be never fearful of temptation, then, but see it as it is; another chance to choose again, and let Christ's strength prevail in every circumstance and every place you raised an image of yourself before. For what appears to hide the face of Christ is powerless before His majesty, and disappears before His holy sight. The saviors of the world, who see like Him, are merely those who choose His strength instead of their own weakness, seen apart from Him. They will redeem the world, for they are joined in all the power of the Will of God. And what they will is only what He wills.

5. Learn, then, the happy habit of response to all temptation to perceive yourself as weak and miserable with these words:

> I am as God created me. His Son can suffer nothing. And
> I am His Son.

Thus is Christ's strength invited to prevail, replacing all your weakness with the strength that comes from God and that can never fail. And thus are miracles as natural as fear and agony appeared to be before the choice for holiness was made. For in that choice are false distinctions gone, illusory alternatives laid by, and nothing left to interfere with truth.

6. You *are* as God created you, and so is *every* living thing you look upon, regardless of the images you see. What you behold as sickness and as pain, as weakness and as suffering and loss, is but temptation to perceive yourself defenseless and in hell. Yield not to this, and you will see all pain, in every form, wherever it occurs, but disappear as mists before the sun. A miracle has come to heal God's Son, and close the door upon his dreams of weakness, opening the way to his salvation and release. Choose once again what you would have him be, remembering that every choice you make establishes your own identity as you will see it and believe it is.

7. Deny me not the little gift I ask, when in exchange I lay before your feet the peace of God, and power to bring this peace to everyone who wanders in the world uncertain, lonely, and in constant fear. For it is given you to join with him, and through the Christ in you unveil his eyes, and let him look upon the Christ in him.

8. My brothers in salvation, do not fail to hear my voice and listen to my words. I ask for nothing but your own release. There is no place for hell within a world whose loveliness can yet be so intense and so inclusive it is but a step from there to Heaven. To your tired eyes I bring a vision of a different world, so new and clean and fresh you will forget the pain and sorrow that you saw before. Yet this a vision is which you must share with everyone you see, for otherwise you will behold it not. To give this gift is how to make it yours. And God ordained, in loving kindness, that it be for you.

9. Let us be glad that we can walk the world, and find so many chances to perceive another situation where God's gift can once again be recognized as ours! And thus will all the vestiges of hell, the secret sins and hidden hates be gone. And all the loveliness which they concealed appear like lawns of Heaven to our sight, to lift us high above the thorny roads we travelled on before the Christ appeared. Hear me, my brothers, hear and join with me. God has ordained I cannot call in vain, and in His certainty I rest content. For you *will* hear, and you *will* choose again. And in this choice is everyone made free.

10. I thank You, Father, for these holy ones who are my brothers as they are Your Sons. My faith in them is Yours. I am as sure that they will come to me as You are sure of what they are, and will forever be. They will accept the gift I offer them, because You gave it me on their behalf. And as I would but do Your holy Will, so will they choose. And I give thanks for them. Salvation's song will echo through the world with every choice they make. For we are one in purpose, and the end of hell is near.

11. In joyous welcome is my hand outstretched to every brother who would join with me in reaching past temptation, and who looks with fixed determination toward the light that shines beyond in perfect constancy. Give me my own, for they belong to You. And can You fail in what is but Your Will? I give You thanks for what my brothers are. And as each one elects to join with me, the song of thanks from earth to Heaven grows from tiny scattered threads of melody to one inclusive chorus from a world redeemed from hell, and giving thanks to You.

12. And now we say "Amen." For Christ has come to dwell in the abode You set for Him before time was, in calm eternity. The journey closes, ending at the place where it began. No trace of it remains. Not one illusion is accorded faith, and not one spot of darkness still remains to hide the face of Christ from anyone. Thy Will is done, complete and perfectly, and all creation recognizes You, and knows You as the only Source it has. Clear in Your likeness does the light shine forth from everything that lives and moves in You. For we have reached where all of us are one, and we are home, where You would have us be.

QUESTION 54. What choice does Jesus ask you to make, and what temptations need to be avoided?

\

MANUAL FOR TEACHERS

≈ ◦ ≈

INTRODUCTION

1. The role of teaching and learning is actually reversed in the thinking of the world. The reversal is characteristic. It seems as if the teacher and the learner are separated, the teacher giving something to the learner rather than to himself. Further, the act of teaching is regarded as a special activity, in which one engages only a relatively small proportion of one's time. The course, on the other hand, emphasizes that to teach is to learn, so that teacher and learner are the same. It also emphasizes that teaching is a constant process; it goes on every moment of the day, and continues into sleeping thoughts as well.

2. To teach is to demonstrate. There are only two thought systems, and you demonstrate that you believe one or the other is true all the time. From your demonstration others learn, and so do you. The question is not whether you will teach, for in that there is no choice. The purpose of the course might be said to provide you with a means of choosing what you want to teach on the basis of what you want to learn. You cannot give to someone else, but only to yourself, and this you learn through teaching. Teaching is but a call to witnesses to attest to what you believe. It is a method of conversion. This is not done by words alone. Any situation must be to you a chance to teach others what you are, and what they are to you. No more than that, but also never less.

1. WHO ARE GOD'S TEACHERS?

1. A teacher of God is anyone who chooses to be one. His qualifications consist solely in this; somehow, somewhere he has made a deliberate choice in which he did not see his interests as apart from someone else's. Once he has done that, his road is established and his direction is sure. A light has entered the darkness. It may be a single light, but that is enough. He has entered an agreement with God even if he does not yet believe in Him. He has become a bringer of salvation. He has become a teacher of God.

3. There is a course for every teacher of God. The form of the course varies greatly. So do the particular teaching aids involved. But the content of the course never changes. Its central theme is always, "God's Son is guiltless, and in his innocence is his salvation." It can be taught by actions or thoughts; in words or soundlessly; in any language or in no language; in any place or time or manner. It does not matter who the teacher was before he heard the Call. He has become a savior by his answering. He has seen someone else as himself. He has therefore found his own salvation and the salvation of the world. In his rebirth is the world reborn.

2. WHO ARE THEIR PUPILS?

1. Certain pupils have been assigned to each of God's teachers, and they will begin to look for him as soon as he has answered the Call. They were chosen for him because the form of the universal curriculum that he will teach is best for them in view of their level of understanding. His pupils have been waiting for him, for his coming is certain. Again, it is only a matter of time. Once he has chosen to fulfill his role, they are ready to fulfill theirs. Time waits on his choice, but not on whom he will serve. When he is ready to learn, the opportunities to teach will be provided for him.
5. When pupil and teacher come together, a teaching-learning situation begins. For the teacher is not really the one who does the teaching. God's Teacher speaks to any two who join together for learning purposes. The relationship is holy because of that purpose, and God has promised to send His Spirit into any holy relationship. In the teaching-learning situation, each one learns that giving and receiving are the same. The demarcations they have drawn between their roles, their minds, their bodies, their needs, their interests, and all the differences they thought separated them from one another, fade and grow dim and disappear. Those who would learn the same course share one interest and one goal. And thus he who was the learner becomes a teacher of God himself, for he has made the one decision that gave his teacher to him. He has seen in another person the same interests as his own.

3. WHAT ARE THE LEVELS OF TEACHING?

2. The simplest level of teaching appears to be quite superficial. It consists of what seem to be very casual encounters; a "chance" meeting of two apparent strangers in an elevator, a child who is not looking where he is going running into an adult "by chance,"

two students "happening" to walk home together. These are not chance encounters. Each of them has the potential for becoming a teaching-learning situation. Perhaps the seeming strangers in the elevator will smile to one another; perhaps the adult will not scold the child for bumping into him; perhaps the students will become friends. Even at the level of the most casual encounter, it is possible for two people to lose sight of separate interests, if only for a moment. That moment will be enough. Salvation has come.

4. Each teaching-learning situation is maximal in the sense that each person involved will learn the most that he can from the other person at that time. In this sense, and in this sense only, we can speak of levels of teaching. Using the term in this way, the second level of teaching is a more sustained relationship, in which, for a time, two people enter into a fairly intense teaching-learning situation and then appear to separate. As with the first level, these meetings are not accidental, nor is what appears to be the end of the relationship a real end. Again, each has learned the most he can at the time. Yet all who meet will someday meet again, for it is the destiny of all relationships to become holy. God is not mistaken in His Son.

5. The third level of teaching occurs in relationships which, once they are formed, are lifelong. These are teaching-learning situations in which each person is given a chosen learning partner who presents him with unlimited opportunities for learning. These relationships are generally few, because their existence implies that those involved have reached a stage simultaneously in which the teaching-learning balance is actually perfect. This does not mean that they necessarily recognize this; in fact, they generally do not. They may even be quite hostile to each other for some time, and perhaps for life. Yet should they decide to learn it, the perfect lesson is before them and can be learned. And if they decide to learn that lesson, they become the saviors of the teachers who falter and may even seem to fail. No teacher of God can fail to find the Help he needs.

4. WHAT ARE THE CHARACTERISTICS OF GOD'S TEACHERS?

1. The surface traits of God's teachers are not at all alike. They do not look alike to the body's eyes, they come from vastly different backgrounds, their experiences of the world vary greatly, and their superficial "personalities" are quite distinct. Nor, at the beginning stages of their functioning as teachers of God, have they as yet acquired the deeper characteristics that will establish them as what

they are. God gives special gifts to His teachers, because they have a special role in His plan for Atonement. Their specialness is, of course, only temporary; set in time as a means of leading out of time. These special gifts, born in the holy relationship toward which the teaching-learning situation is geared, become characteristic of all teachers of God who have advanced in their own learning. In this respect they are all alike.

2. All differences among the Sons of God are temporary. Nevertheless, in time it can be said that the advanced teachers of God have the following characteristics:

I. Trust

1. This is the foundation on which their ability to fulfill their function rests. Perception is the result of learning. In fact, perception *is* learning, because cause and effect are never separated. The teachers of God have trust in the world, because they have learned it is not governed by the laws the world made up. It is governed by a power that is *in* them but not *of* them. It is this power that keeps all things safe. It is through this power that the teachers of God look on a forgiven world.

2. When this power has once been experienced, it is impossible to trust one's own petty strength again. Who would attempt to fly with the tiny wings of a sparrow when the mighty power of an eagle has been given him? And who would place his faith in the shabby offerings of the ego when the gifts of God are laid before him? And who would place his faith in the shabby offerings of the ego when the gifts of God are laid before him? What is it that induces them to make the shift?

A. Development of Trust

3. First, they must go through what might be called "a period of undoing." This need not be painful, but it usually is so experienced. It seems as if things are being taken away, and it is rarely understood initially that their lack of value is merely being recognized. How can lack of value be perceived unless the perceiver is in a position where he must see things in a different light? He is not yet at a point at which he can make the shift entirely internally. And so the plan will sometimes call for changes in what seem to be external circumstances. These changes are always helpful. When the teacher of God has learned that much, he goes on to the second stage.

4. Next, the teacher of God must go through "a period of sorting out." This is always somewhat difficult because, having learned that the changes in his life are always helpful, he must now decide all things on the basis of whether they increase the helpfulness or hamper it.

He will find that many, if not most of the things he valued before will merely hinder his ability to transfer what he has learned to new situations as they arise. Because he has valued what is really valueless, he will not generalize the lesson for fear of loss and sacrifice. It takes great learning to understand that all things, events, encounters and circumstances are helpful. It is only to the extent to which they are helpful that any degree of reality should be accorded them in this world of illusion. The word "value" can apply to nothing else.

5. The third stage through which the teacher of God must go can be called "a period of relinquishment." If this is interpreted as giving up the desirable, it will engender enormous conflict. Few teachers of God escape this distress entirely. There is, however, no point in sorting out the valuable from the valueless unless the next obvious step is taken. Therefore, the period of overlap is apt to be one in which the teacher of God feels called upon to sacrifice his own best interests on behalf of truth. He has not realized as yet how wholly impossible such a demand would be. He can learn this only as he actually does give up the valueless. Through this, he learns that where he anticipated grief, he finds a happy lightheartedness instead; where he thought something was asked of him, he finds a gift bestowed on him.

6. Now comes "a period of settling down." This is a quiet time, in which the teacher of God rests a while in reasonable peace. Now he consolidates his learning. Now he begins to see the transfer value of what he has learned. Its potential is literally staggering, and the teacher of God is now at the point in his progress at which he sees in it his whole way out. "Give up what you do not want, and keep what you do." How simple is the obvious! And how easy to do! The teacher of God needs this period of respite. He has not yet come as far as he thinks. Yet when he is ready to go on, he goes with mighty companions beside him. Now he rests a while, and gathers them before going on. He will not go on from here alone.

7. The next stage is indeed "a period of unsettling." Now must the teacher of God understand that he did not really know what was valuable and what was valueless. All that he really learned so far was that he did not want the valueless, and that he did want the valuable. Yet his own sorting out was meaningless in teaching him the difference. The idea of sacrifice, so central to his own thought system, had made it impossible for him to judge. He thought he learned willingness, but now he sees that he does not know what the willingness is for. And now he must attain a state that may remain impossible to reach for a long, long time. He must learn

to lay all judgment aside, and ask only what he really wants in every circumstance. Were not each step in this direction so heavily reinforced, it would be hard indeed!

8. And finally, there is "a period of achievement." It is here that learning is consolidated. Now what was seen as merely shadows before become solid gains, to be counted on in all "emergencies" as well as tranquil times. Indeed, the tranquility is their result; the outcome of honest learning, consistency of thought and full transfer. This is the stage of real peace, for here is Heaven's state fully reflected. From here, the way to Heaven is open and easy. In fact, it is here. Who would "go" anywhere, if peace of mind is already complete? And who would seek to change tranquility for something more desirable? What could be more desirable than this?

II. Honesty

1. All other traits of God's teachers rest on trust. Once that has been achieved, the others cannot fail to follow. Only the trusting can afford honesty, for only they can see its value. Honesty does not apply only to what you say. The term actually means consistency. There is nothing you say that contradicts what you think or do; no thought opposes any other thought; no act belies your word; and no word lacks agreement with another. Such are the truly honest. At no level are they in conflict with themselves. Therefore it is impossible for them to be in conflict with anyone or anything.

III. Tolerance

1. God's teachers do not judge. To judge is to be dishonest, for to judge is to assume a position you do not have. Judgment without self-deception is impossible. Judgment implies that you have been deceived in your brothers. How, then, could you not have been deceived in yourself? Judgment implies a lack of trust, and trust remains the bedrock of the teacher of God's whole thought system. Let this be lost, and all his learning goes. Without judgment are all things equally acceptable, for who could judge otherwise? Without judgment are all men brothers, for who is there who stands apart? Judgment destroys honesty and shatters trust. No teacher of God can judge and hope to learn.

IV. Gentleness

2. Therefore, God's teachers are wholly gentle. They need the strength of gentleness, for it is in this that the function of salvation

becomes easy. To those who would do harm, it is impossible. To those to whom harm has no meaning, it is merely natural. What choice but this has meaning to the sane? Who chooses hell when he perceives a way to Heaven? And who would choose the weakness that must come from harm in place of the unfailing, all-encompassing and limitless strength of gentleness? The might of God's teachers lies in their gentleness, for they have understood their evil thoughts came neither from God's Son nor his Creator. Thus did they join their thoughts with Him Who is their Source. And so their will, which always was His Own, is free to be itself.

V. Joy

1. Joy is the inevitable result of gentleness. Gentleness means that fear is now impossible, and what could come to interfere with joy? The open hands of gentleness are always filled. The gentle have no pain. They cannot suffer. Why would they not be joyous? They are sure they are beloved and must be safe. Joy goes with gentleness as surely as grief attends attack. God's teachers trust in Him. And they are sure His Teacher goes before them, making sure no harm can come to them. They hold His gifts and follow in His way, because God's Voice directs them in all things. Joy is their song of thanks. And Christ looks down on them in thanks as well. His need of them is just as great as theirs of Him. How joyous it is to share the purpose of salvation!

VI. Defenselessness

1. God's teachers have learned how to be simple. They have no dreams that need defense against the truth. They do not try to make themselves. Their joy comes from their understanding Who created them. And does what God created need defense? No one can become an advanced teacher of God until he fully understands that defenses are but foolish guardians of mad illusions. The more grotesque the dream, the fiercer and more powerful its defenses seem to be. Yet when the teacher of God finally agrees to look past them, he finds that nothing was there. Slowly at first he lets himself be undeceived. But he learns faster as his trust increases. It is not danger that comes when defenses are laid down. It is safety. It is peace. It is joy. And it is God.

QUESTION 55. Who is a teacher of God, and what are his stages of learning trust?

VII. Generosity

2. The teacher of God is generous out of Self interest. This does not refer, however, to the self of which the world speaks. The teacher of God does not want anything he cannot give away, because he realizes it would be valueless to him by definition. What would he want it *for*? He could only lose because of it. He could not gain. Therefore he does not seek what only he could keep, because that is a guarantee of loss. He does not want to suffer. Why should he ensure himself pain? But he does want to keep for himself all things that are of God, and therefore for His Son. These are the things that belong to him. These he can give away in true generosity, protecting them forever for himself.

VIII. Patience

1. Those who are certain of the outcome can afford to wait, and wait without anxiety. Patience is natural to the teacher of God. All he sees is certain outcome, at a time perhaps unknown to him as yet, but not in doubt. The time will be as right as is the answer. And this is true for everything that happens now or in the future. The past as well held no mistakes; nothing that did not serve to benefit the world, as well as him to whom it seemed to happen. Perhaps it was not understood at the time. Even so, the teacher of God is willing to reconsider all his past decisions, if they are causing pain to anyone. Patience is natural to those who trust. Sure of the ultimate interpretation of all things in time, no outcome already seen or yet to come can cause them fear.

IX. Faithfulness

1. The extent of the teacher of God's faithfulness is the measure of his advancement in the curriculum. Does he still select some aspects of his life to bring to his learning, while keeping others apart? If so, his advancement is limited, and his trust not yet firmly established. Faithfulness is the teacher of God's trust in the Word of God to set all things right; not some, but all. Generally, his faithfulness begins by resting on just some problems, remaining carefully limited for a time. To give up all problems to one Answer is to reverse the thinking of the world entirely. And that alone is faithfulness. Nothing but that really deserves the name. Yet each degree, however small, is worth achieving. Readiness, as the text notes, is not mastery.

X. Open-Mindedness

1. The centrality of open-mindedness, perhaps the last of the attributes the teacher of God acquires, is easily understood when its relation to forgiveness is recognized. Open-mindedness comes with lack of judgment. As judgment shuts the mind against God's Teacher, so open-mindedness invites Him to come in. As condemnation judges the Son of God as evil, so open-mindedness permits him to be judged by the Voice for God on His behalf. As the projection of guilt upon him would send him to hell, so open-mindedness lets Christ's image be extended to him. Only the open-minded can be at peace, for they alone see reason for it.

2. How do the open-minded forgive? They have let go all things that would prevent forgiveness. They have in truth abandoned the world, and let it be restored to them in newness and in joy so glorious they could never have conceived of such a change. Nothing is now as it was formerly. Nothing but sparkles now which seemed so dull and lifeless before. And above all are all things welcoming, for threat is gone. No clouds remain to hide the face of Christ. Now is the goal achieved. Forgiveness is the final goal of the curriculum. It paves the way for what goes far beyond all learning. The curriculum makes no effort to exceed its legitimate goal. Forgiveness is its single aim, at which all learning ultimately converges. It is indeed enough.

5. HOW IS HEALING ACCOMPLISHED?

1. Healing involves an understanding of what the illusion of sickness is for. Healing is impossible without this.

I. The Perceived Purpose of Sickness

1. Healing is accomplished the instant the sufferer no longer sees any value in pain. Who would choose suffering unless he thought it brought him something, and something of value to him? He must think it is a small price to pay for something of greater worth. For sickness is an election; a decision. It is the choice of weakness, in the mistaken conviction that it is strength. When this occurs, real strength is seen as threat and health as danger. Sickness is a method, conceived in madness, for placing God's Son on his Father's throne. God is seen as outside, fierce and powerful, eager to keep all power for Himself. Only by His death can He be conquered by His Son.

II. The Shift in Perception

2. The acceptance of sickness as a decision of the mind, for a purpose for which it would use the body, is the basis of healing. And this is so for healing in all forms. A patient decides that this is so, and he recovers. If he decides against recovery, he will not be healed. Who is the physician? Only the mind of the patient himself. The outcome is what he decides that it is. Special agents seem to be ministering to him, yet they but give form to his own choice. He chooses them in order to bring tangible form to his desires. And it is this they do, and nothing else. They are not actually needed at all. The patient could merely rise up without their aid and say, "I have no use for this." There is no form of sickness that would not be cured at once.

3. What is the single requisite for this shift in perception? It is simply this; the recognition that sickness is of the mind, and has nothing to do with the body. What does this recognition "cost"? It costs the whole world you see, for the world will never again appear to rule the mind. For with this recognition is responsibility placed where it belongs; not with the world, but on him who looks on the world and sees it as it is not. He looks on what he chooses to see. No more and no less. The world does nothing to him. He only thought it did. Nor does he do anything to the world, because he was mistaken about what it is. Herein is the release from guilt and sickness both, for they are one. Yet to accept this release, the insignificance of the body must be an acceptable idea.

III. The Function of the Teacher of God

1. If the patient must change his mind in order to be healed, what does the teacher of God do? Can he change the patient's mind for him? Certainly not. For those already willing to change their minds he has no function except to rejoice with them, for they have become teachers of God with him. He has, however, a more specific function for those who do not understand what healing is. These patients do not realize they have chosen sickness. On the contrary, they believe that sickness has chosen them. Nor are they open-minded on this point. The body tells them what to do and they obey. They have no idea how insane this concept is. If they even suspected it, they would be healed. Yet they suspect nothing. To them the separation is quite real.

3. Not once do the advanced teachers of God consider the forms of sickness in which their brother believes. To do this is to forget that all of them have the same purpose, and therefore are not really different. They seek for God's Voice in this brother who would so deceive himself as to believe God's Son can suffer. And they remind him that he did not make himself, and must remain as God created him. They recognize illusions can have no effect. The truth in their minds reaches out to the truth in the minds of their brothers, so that illusions are not reinforced. They are thus brought to truth; truth is not brought to them. So are they dispelled, not by the will of another, but by the union of the one Will with itself. And this is the function of God's teachers; to see no will as separate from their own, nor theirs as separate from God's.

6. IS HEALING CERTAIN?

1. Healing is always certain. It is impossible to let illusions be brought to truth and keep the illusions. Truth demonstrates illusions have no value. The teacher of God has seen the correction of his errors in the mind of the patient, recognizing it for what it is. Having accepted the Atonement for himself, he has also accepted it for the patient. Yet what if the patient uses sickness as a way of life, believing healing is the way to death? When this is so, a sudden healing might precipitate intense depression, and a sense of loss so deep that the patient might even try to destroy himself. Having nothing to live for, he may ask for death. Healing must wait, for his protection.

3. It is not the function of God's teachers to evaluate the outcome of their gifts. It is merely their function to give them. Once they have done that they have also given the outcome, for that is part of the gift. No one can give if he is concerned with the result of giving. That is a limitation on the giving itself, and neither the giver nor the receiver would have the gift. Trust is an essential part of giving; in fact, it is the part that makes sharing possible, the part that guarantees the giver will not lose, but only gain. Who gives a gift and then remains with it, to be sure it is used as the giver deems appropriate? Such is not giving but imprisoning.

4. It is the relinquishing of all concern about the gift that makes it truly given. And it is trust that makes true giving possible. Healing is the change of mind that the Holy Spirit in the patient's mind is

seeking for him. And it is the Holy Spirit in the mind of the giver Who gives the gift to him. How can it be lost? How can it be ineffectual? How can it be wasted? God's treasure house can never be empty. And if one gift is missing, it would not be full. Yet is its fullness guaranteed by God. What concern, then, can a teacher of God have about what becomes of his gifts? Given by God to God, who in this holy exchange can receive less than everything?

7. SHOULD HEALING BE REPEATED?

1. This question really answers itself. Healing cannot be repeated. If the patient is healed, what remains to heal him from? And if the healing is certain, as we have already said it is, what is there to repeat? For a teacher of God to remain concerned about the result of healing is to limit the healing. It is now the teacher of God himself whose mind needs to be healed. And it is this he must facilitate. He is now the patient, and he must so regard himself. He has made a mistake, and must be willing to change his mind about it. He lacked the trust that makes for giving truly, and so he has not received the benefit of his gift.

2. Whenever a teacher of God has tried to be a channel for healing he has succeeded. Should he be tempted to doubt this, he should not repeat his previous effort. That was already maximal, because the Holy Spirit so accepted it and so used it. Now the teacher of God has only one course to follow. He must use his reason to tell himself that he has given the problem to One Who cannot fail, and must recognize that his own uncertainty is not love but fear, and therefore hate. His position has thus become untenable, for he is offering hate to one to whom he offered love. This is impossible. Having offered love, only love can be received.

4. One of the most difficult temptations to recognize is that to doubt a healing because of the appearance of continuing symptoms is a mistake in the form of lack of trust. As such it is an attack. Usually it seems to be just the opposite. It does appear unreasonable at first to be told that continued concern is attack. It has all the appearances of love. Yet love without trust is impossible, and doubt and trust cannot coexist. And hate must be the opposite of love, regardless of the form it takes. Doubt not the gift and it is impossible to doubt its result. This is the certainty that gives God's teachers the power to be miracle workers, for they have put their trust in Him.

8. HOW CAN PERCEPTION OF ORDER OF DIFFICULTIES BE AVOIDED?

5. There can be no order of difficulty in healing merely because all sickness is illusion. Is it harder to dispel the belief of the insane in a larger hallucination as opposed to a smaller one? Will he agree more quickly to the unreality of a louder voice he hears than to that of a softer one? Will he dismiss more easily a whispered demand to kill than a shout? And do the number of pitchforks the devils he sees carrying affect their credibility in his perception? His mind has categorized them all as real, and so they are all real to him. When he realizes they are all illusions they will disappear. And so it is with healing. The properties of illusions which seem to make them different are really irrelevant, for their properties are as illusory as they are.

6. The body's eyes will continue to see differences. But the mind that has let itself be healed will no longer acknowledge them. There will be those who seem to be "sicker" than others, and the body's eyes will report their changed appearances as before. But the healed mind will put them all in one category; they are unreal. This is the gift of its Teacher; the understanding that only two categories are meaningful in sorting out the messages the mind receives from what appears to be the outside world. And of these two, but one is real. Just as reality is wholly real, apart from size and shape and time and place— for differences cannot exist within it—so too are illusions without distinctions. The one answer to sickness of any kind is healing. The one answer to all illusions is truth.

9. ARE CHANGES REQUIRED IN THE LIFE SITUATION OF GOD'S TEACHERS?

1. Changes are required in the *minds* of God's teachers. This may or may not involve changes in the external situation. Remember that no one is where he is by accident, and chance plays no part in God's plan. It is most unlikely that changes in attitudes would not be the first step in the newly made teacher of God's training. There is, however, no set pattern, since training is always highly individualized. There are those who are called upon to change their life situation almost immediately, but these are generally special cases. By far the majority are given a slowly evolving training program, in which as many previous mistakes as possible are corrected. Relationships in particular must be properly perceived,

and all dark cornerstones of unforgiveness removed. Otherwise the old thought system still has a basis for return.

2. As the teacher of God advances in his training, he learns one lesson with increasing thoroughness. He does not make his own decisions; he asks his Teacher for His answer, and it is this he follows as his guide for action. This becomes easier and easier, as the teacher of God learns to give up his own judgment. The giving up of judgment, the obvious prerequisite for hearing God's Voice, is usually a fairly slow process, not because it is difficult, but because it is apt to be perceived as personally insulting. The world's training is directed toward achieving a goal in direct opposition to that of our curriculum. The world trains for reliance on one's judgment as the criterion for maturity and strength. Our curriculum trains for the relinquishment of judgment as the necessary condition of salvation.

QUESTION 56. How is the face of Christ completely revealed, and how does a teacher of God improve his ability to make decisions?

10. HOW IS JUDGMENT RELINQUISHED?

2. It is necessary for the teacher of God to realize, not that he should not judge, but that he cannot. In giving up judgment, he is merely giving up what he did not have. He gives up an illusion; or better, he has an illusion of giving up. He has actually merely become more honest. Recognizing that judgment was always impossible for him, he no longer attempts it. This is no sacrifice. On the contrary, he puts himself in a position where judgment *through* him rather than *by* him can occur. And this judgment is neither "good" nor "bad." It is the only judgment there is, and it is only one: "God's Son is guiltless, and sin does not exist."

3. The aim of our curriculum, unlike the goal of the world's learning, is the recognition that judgment in the usual sense is impossible. This is not an opinion but a fact. In order to judge anything rightly, one would have to be fully aware of an inconceivably wide range of things; past, present and to come. One would have to recognize in advance all the effects of his judgments on everyone and everything involved in them in any way. And one would have to be certain there is no distortion in his perception, so that his judgment would be wholly fair to everyone on whom it rests now and in the future. Who is in a position to do this? Who except in grandiose fantasies would claim this for himself?

4. Remember how many times you thought you knew all the "facts" you needed for judgment, and how wrong you were! Is there anyone

who has not had this experience? Would you know how many times you merely thought you were right, without ever realizing you were wrong? Why would you choose such an arbitrary basis for decision making? Wisdom is not judgment; it is the relinquishment of judgment. Make then but one more judgment. It is this: There is Someone with you Whose judgment is perfect. He does know all the facts; past, present and to come. He does know all the effects of His judgment on everyone and everything involved in any way. And He is wholly fair to everyone, for there is no distortion in His perception.

6. It is not difficult to relinquish judgment. But it is difficult indeed to try to keep it. The teacher of God lays it down happily the instant he recognizes its cost. All of the ugliness he sees about him is its outcome. All of the pain he looks upon is its result. All of the loneliness and sense of loss; of passing time and growing hopelessness; of sickening despair and fear of death; all these have come of it. And now he knows that these things need not be. Not one is true. For he has given up their cause, and they, which never were but the effects of his mistaken choice, have fallen from him. Teacher of God, this step will bring you peace. Can it be difficult to want but this?

11. HOW IS PEACE POSSIBLE IN THIS WORLD?

3. The text explains that the Holy Spirit is the Answer to all problems you have made. These problems are not real, but that is meaningless to those who believe in them. And everyone believes in what he made, for it was made by his believing it. Into this strange and paradoxical situation,—one without meaning and devoid of sense, yet out of which no way seems possible,—God has sent His Judgment to answer yours. Gently His Judgment substitutes for yours. And through this substitution is the un-understandable made understandable. How is peace possible in this world? In your judgment it is not possible, and can never be possible. But in the Judgment of God what is reflected here is only peace.

4. Peace is impossible to those who look on war. Peace is inevitable to those who offer peace. How easily, then, is your judgment of the world escaped! It is not the world that makes peace seem impossible. It is the world you see that is impossible. Yet has God's Judgment on this distorted world redeemed it and made it fit to welcome peace. And peace descends on it in joyous answer. Peace now belongs here, because a Thought of God has entered. What else but a Thought of God turns hell to Heaven merely by being what it is? The earth bows down before its gracious Presence, and it leans down in answer, to

raise it up again. Now is the question different. It is no longer, "Can peace be possible in this world?" but instead, "Is it not impossible that peace be absent here?"

12. HOW MANY TEACHERS OF GOD ARE NEEDED TO SAVE THE WORLD?

1. The answer to this question is—one. One wholly perfect teacher, whose learning is complete, suffices. This one, sanctified and redeemed, becomes the Self Who is the Son of God. He who was always wholly spirit now no longer sees himself as a body, or even as in a body. Therefore he is limitless. And being limitless, his thoughts are joined with God's forever and ever. His perception of himself is based upon God's Judgment, not his own. Thus does he share God's Will, and bring His Thoughts to still deluded minds. He is forever one, because he is as God created him. He has accepted Christ, and he is saved.

2. Thus does the son of man become the Son of God. It is not really a change; it is a change of mind. Nothing external alters, but everything internal now reflects only the Love of God. God can no longer be feared, for the mind sees no cause for punishment. God's teachers appear to be many, for that is what is the world's need. Yet being joined in one purpose, and one they share with God, how could they be separate from each other? What does it matter if they then appear in many forms? Their minds are one; their joining is complete. And God works through them now as one, for that is what they are.

5. The central lesson is always this; that what you use the body for it will become to you. Use it for sin or for attack, which is the same as sin, and you will see it as sinful. Because it is sinful it is weak, and being weak, it suffers and it dies. Use it to bring the Word of God to those who have it not, and the body becomes holy. Because it is holy it cannot be sick, nor can it die. When its usefulness is done it is laid by, and that is all. The mind makes this decision, as it makes all decisions that are responsible for the body's condition. Yet the teacher of God does not make this decision alone. To do that would be to give the body another purpose from the one that keeps it holy. God's Voice will tell him when he has fulfilled his role, just as It tells him what his function is. He does not suffer either in going or remaining. Sickness is now impossible to him.

6. Oneness and sickness cannot coexist. God's teachers choose to look on dreams a while. It is a conscious choice. For they have

learned that all choices are made consciously, with full awareness of their consequences. The dream says otherwise, but who would put his faith in dreams once they are recognized for what they are? Awareness of dreaming is the real function of God's teachers. They watch the dream figures come and go, shift and change, suffer and die. Yet they are not deceived by what they see. They recognize that to behold a dream figure as sick and separate is no more real than to regard it as healthy and beautiful. Unity alone is not a thing of dreams. And it is this God's teachers acknowledge as behind the dream, beyond all seeming and yet surely theirs.

13. WHAT IS THE REAL MEANING OF SACRIFICE?

2. It takes great learning both to realize and to accept the fact that the world has nothing to give. What can the sacrifice of nothing mean? It cannot mean that you have less because of it. There is no sacrifice in the world's terms that does not involve the body. Think a while about what the world calls sacrifice. Power, fame, money, physical pleasure; who is the "hero" to whom all these things belong? Could they mean anything except to a body? Yet a body cannot evaluate. By seeking after such things the mind associates itself with the body, obscuring its Identity and losing sight of what it really is.

6. You may believe this course requires sacrifice of all you really hold dear. In one sense this is true, for you hold dear the things that crucify God's Son, and it is the course's aim to set him free. But do not be mistaken about what sacrifice means. It always means the giving up of what you want. And what, O teacher of God, is it that you want? You have been called by God, and you have answered. Would you now sacrifice that Call? Few have heard it as yet, and they can but turn to you. There is no other hope in all the world that they can trust. There is no other voice in all the world that echoes God's. If you would sacrifice the truth, they stay in hell. And if they stay, you will remain with them.

7. Do not forget that sacrifice is total. There are no half sacrifices. You cannot give up Heaven partially. You cannot be a little bit in hell. The Word of God has no exceptions. It is this that makes it holy and beyond the world. It is its holiness that points to God. It is its holiness that makes you safe. It is denied if you attack any brother for anything. For it is here the split with God occurs. A split that is impossible. A split that cannot happen. Yet a split in which you surely will believe, because you have set up a situation that is

impossible. And in this situation the impossible can seem to happen. It seems to happen at the "sacrifice" of truth.

8. Teacher of God, do not forget the meaning of sacrifice, and remember what each decision you make must mean in terms of cost. Decide for God, and everything is given you at no cost at all. Decide against Him, and you choose nothing, at the expense of the awareness of everything. What would you teach? Remember only what you would learn. For it is here that your concern should be. Atonement is for you. Your learning claims it and your learning gives it. The world contains it not. But learn this course and it is yours. God holds out His Word to you, for He has need of teachers. What other way is there to save His Son?

14. HOW WILL THE WORLD END?

1. Can what has no beginning really end? The world will end in an illusion, as it began. Yet will its ending be an illusion of mercy. The illusion of forgiveness, complete, excluding no one, limitless in gentleness, will cover it, hiding all evil, concealing all sin and ending guilt forever. So ends the world that guilt had made, for now it has no purpose and is gone. The father of illusions is the belief that they have a purpose; that they serve a need or gratify a want. Perceived as purposeless, they are no longer seen. Their uselessness is recognized, and they are gone. How but in this way are all illusions ended? They have been brought to truth, and truth saw them not. It merely overlooked the meaningless.

2. Until forgiveness is complete, the world does have a purpose. It becomes the home in which forgiveness is born, and where it grows and becomes stronger and more all-embracing. Here is it nourished, for here it is needed. A gentle Savior, born where sin was made and guilt seemed real. Here is His home, for here there is need of Him indeed. He brings the ending of the world with Him. It is His Call God's teachers answer, turning to Him in silence to receive His Word. The world will end when all things in it have been rightly judged by His judgment. The world will end with the benediction of holiness upon it. When not one thought of sin remains, the world is over. It will not be destroyed nor attacked nor even touched. It will merely cease to seem to be.

15. IS EACH ONE TO BE JUDGED IN THE END?

1. Indeed, yes! No one can escape God's Final Judgment. Who could flee forever from the truth? But the Final Judgment will not

come until it is no longer associated with fear. One day each one will welcome it, and on that very day it will be given him. He will hear his sinlessness proclaimed around and around the world, setting it free as God's Final Judgment on him is received. This is the Judgment in which salvation lies. This is the Judgment that will set him free. This is the Judgment in which all things are freed with him. Time pauses as eternity comes near, and silence lies across the world that everyone may hear this Judgment of the Son of God:

> Holy are you, eternal, free and whole, at
> peace forever in the Heart of God. Where
> is the world, and where is sorrow now?

2. Is this your judgment on yourself, teacher of God? Do you believe that this is wholly true? No; not yet, not yet. But this is still your goal; why you are here. It is your function to prepare yourself to hear this Judgment and to recognize that it is true. One instant of complete belief in this, and you will go beyond belief to Certainty. One instant out of time can bring time's end. Judge not, for you but judge yourself, and thus delay this Final Judgment. What is your judgment of the world, teacher of God? Have you yet learned to stand aside and hear the Voice of Judgment in yourself? Or do you still attempt to take His role from Him? Learn to be quiet, for His Voice is heard in stillness. And His Judgment comes to all who stand aside in quiet listening, and wait for Him.

QUESTION 57. What does the teacher of God need to know about judgment?

16. HOW SHOULD THE TEACHER OF GOD SPEND HIS DAY?

1. To the advanced teacher of God this question is meaningless. There is no program, for the lessons change each day. Yet the teacher of God is sure of but one thing; they do not change at random. Seeing this and understanding that it is true, he rests content. He will be told all that his role should be, this day and every day. And those who share that role with him will find him, so they can learn the lessons for the day together. Not one is absent whom he needs; not one is sent without a learning goal already set, and one which can be learned that very day. For the advanced teacher of God, then, this question is superfluous. It has been asked and answered, and he

keeps in constant contact with the Answer. He is set, and sees the road on which he walks stretch surely and smoothly before him.

3. At the beginning, it is wise to think in terms of time. This is by no means the ultimate criterion, but at the outset it is probably the simplest to observe. The saving of time is an essential early emphasis which, although it remains important throughout the learning process, becomes less and less emphasized. At the outset, we can safely say that time devoted to starting the day right does indeed save time. How much time should be so spent? This must depend on the teacher of God himself. He cannot claim that title until he has gone through the workbook, since we are learning within the framework of our course. After completion of the more structured practice periods, which the workbook contains, individual need becomes the chief consideration.

4. This course is always practical. It may be that the teacher of God is not in a situation that fosters quiet thought as he awakes. If this is so, let him but remember that he chooses to spend time with God as soon as possible, and let him do so. Duration is not the major concern. One can easily sit still an hour with closed eyes and accomplish nothing. One can as easily give God only an instant, and in that instant join with Him completely. Perhaps the one generalization that can be made is this; as soon as possible after waking take your quiet time, continuing a minute or two after you begin to find it difficult. You may find that the difficulty will diminish and drop away. If not, that is the time to stop.

7. How simply and how easily does time slip by for the teacher of God who has accepted His protection! All that he did before in the name of safety no longer interests him. For he is safe, and knows it to be so. He has a Guide Who will not fail. He need make no distinctions among the problems he perceives, for He to Whom he turns with all of them recognizes no order of difficulty in resolving them. He is as safe in the present as he was before illusions were accepted into his mind, and as he will be when he has let them go. There is no difference in his state at different times and different places, because they are all one to God. This is his safety. And he has no need for more than this.

9. The avoidance of magic is the avoidance of temptation. For all temptation is nothing more than the attempt to substitute another will for God's. These attempts may indeed seem frightening, but they are merely pathetic. They can have no effects; neither good nor bad, neither rewarding nor demanding sacrifice, healing nor destructive, quieting nor fearful. When all magic is recognized as

merely nothing, the teacher of God has reached the most advanced state. All intermediate lessons will but lead to this, and bring this goal nearer to recognition. For magic of any kind, in all its forms, simply does nothing. Its powerlessness is the reason it can be so easily escaped. What has no effects can hardly terrify.

10. There is no substitute for the Will of God. In simple statement, it is to this fact that the teacher of God devotes his day. Each substitute he may accept as real can but deceive him. But he is safe from all deception if he so decides. Perhaps he needs to remember, "God is with me. I cannot be deceived." Perhaps he prefers other words, or only one, or none at all. Yet each temptation to accept magic as true must be abandoned through his recognition, not that it is fearful, not that it is sinful, not that it is dangerous, but merely that it is meaningless. Rooted in sacrifice and separation, two aspects of one error and no more, he merely chooses to give up all that he never had. And for this "sacrifice" is Heaven restored to his awareness.

17. HOW DO GOD'S TEACHERS DEAL WITH MAGIC THOUGHTS?

1. This is a crucial question both for teacher and pupil. If this issue is mishandled, the teacher of God has hurt himself and has also attacked his pupil. This strengthens fear, and makes the magic seem quite real to both of them. How to deal with magic thus becomes a major lesson for the teacher of God to master. His first responsibility in this is not to attack it. If a magic thought arouses anger in any form, God's teacher can be sure that he is strengthening his own belief in sin and has condemned himself. He can be sure as well that he has asked for depression, pain, fear and disaster to come to him. Let him remember, then, it is not this that he would teach, because it is not this that he would learn.

2. There is, however, a temptation to respond to magic in a way that reinforces it. Nor is this always obvious. It can, in fact, be easily concealed beneath a wish to help. It is this double wish that makes the help of little value, and must lead to undesired outcomes. Nor should it be forgotten that the outcome that results will always come to teacher and to pupil alike. How many times has it been emphasized that you give but to yourself? And where could this be better shown than in the kinds of help the teacher of God gives to those who need his aid? Here is his gift most clearly given him. For he will give only what he has chosen for himself. And in this gift is his judgment upon the holy Son of God.

3. It is easiest to let error be corrected where it is most apparent, and errors can be recognized by their results. A lesson truly taught can lead to nothing but release for teacher and pupil, who have shared in one intent. Attack can enter only if perception of separate goals has entered. And this must indeed have been the case if the result is anything but joy. The single aim of the teacher turns the divided goal of the pupil into one direction, with the call for help becoming his one appeal. This then is easily responded to with just one answer, and this answer will enter the teacher's mind unfailingly. From there it shines into his pupil's mind, making it one with his.

4. Perhaps it will be helpful to remember that no one can be angry at a fact. It is always an interpretation that gives rise to negative emotions, regardless of their seeming justification by what *appears* as facts. Regardless, too, of the intensity of the anger that is aroused. It may be merely slight irritation, perhaps too mild to be even clearly recognized. Or it may also take the form of intense rage, accompanied by thoughts of violence, fantasied or apparently acted out. It does not matter. All of these reactions are the same. They obscure the truth, and this can never be a matter of degree. Either truth is apparent, or it is not. It cannot be partially recognized. Who is unaware of truth must look upon illusions.

8. Into this hopeless situation God sends His teachers. They bring the light of hope from God Himself. There is a way in which escape is possible. It can be learned and taught, but it requires patience and abundant willingness. Given that, the lesson's manifest simplicity stands out like an intense white light against a black horizon, for such it is. If anger comes from an interpretation and not a fact, it is never justified. Once this is even dimly grasped, the way is open. Now it is possible to take the next step. The interpretation can be changed at last. Magic thoughts need not lead to condemnation, for they do not really have the power to give rise to guilt. And so they can be overlooked, and thus forgotten in the truest sense.

18. HOW IS CORRECTION MADE?

1. Correction of a lasting nature,—and only this is true correction,— cannot be made until the teacher of God has ceased to confuse interpretation with fact, or illusion with truth. If he argues with his pupil about a magic thought, attacks it, tries to establish its error or demonstrate its falsity, he is but witnessing to its reality. Depression is then inevitable, for he has "proved," both to his pupil and himself, that it is their task to escape from what is real. And this can only

be impossible. Reality is changeless. Magic thoughts are but illusions. Otherwise salvation would be only the same age-old impossible dream in but another form. Yet the dream of salvation has new content. It is not the form alone in which the difference lies.

2. God's teachers' major lesson is to learn how to react to magic thoughts wholly without anger. Only in this way can they proclaim the truth about themselves. Through them, the Holy Spirit can now speak of the reality of the Son of God. Now He can remind the world of sinlessness, the one unchanged, unchangeable condition of all that God created. Now He can speak the Word of God to listening ears, and bring Christ's vision to eyes that see. Now is He free to teach all minds the truth of what they are, so they will gladly be returned to Him. And now is guilt forgiven, overlooked completely in His sight and in God's Word.

3. Anger but screeches, "Guilt is real!" Reality is blotted out as this insane belief is taken as replacement for God's Word. The body's eyes now "see"; its ears alone can "hear." Its little space and tiny breath become the measure of reality. And truth becomes diminutive and meaningless. Correction has one answer to all this, and to the world that rests on this:

You but mistake interpretation for the truth. And you are wrong. But a mistake is not a sin, nor has reality been taken from its throne by your mistakes. God reigns forever, and His laws alone prevail upon you and upon the world. His Love remains the only thing there is. Fear is illusion, for you are like Him.

4. In order to heal, it thus becomes essential for the teacher of God to let all his own mistakes be corrected. If he senses even the faintest hint of irritation in himself as he responds to anyone, let him instantly realize that he has made an interpretation that is not true. Then let him turn within to his eternal Guide, and let Him judge what the response should be. So is he healed, and in his healing is his pupil healed with him. The sole responsibility of God's teacher is to accept the Atonement for himself. Atonement means correction, or the undoing of errors. When this has been accomplished, the teacher of God becomes a miracle worker by definition. His sins have been forgiven him, and he no longer condemns himself. How can he then condemn anyone? And who is there whom his forgiveness can fail to heal?

19. WHAT IS JUSTICE?

1. Justice is the divine correction for injustice. Injustice is the basis for all the judgments of the world. Justice corrects the interpretations to which injustice gives rise, and cancels them out. Neither justice nor injustice exists in Heaven, for error is impossible and correction meaningless. In this world, however, forgiveness depends on justice, since all attack can only be unjust. Justice is the Holy Spirit's verdict upon the world. Except in His judgment justice is impossible, for no one in the world is capable of making only just interpretations and laying all injustices aside. If God's Son were fairly judged, there would be no need for salvation. The thought of separation would have been forever inconceivable.

4. Salvation is God's justice. It restores to your awareness the wholeness of the fragments you perceive as broken off and separate. And it is this that overcomes the fear of death. For separate fragments must decay and die, but wholeness is immortal. It remains forever and forever like its Creator, being one with Him. God's Judgment is His justice. Onto this,—a Judgment wholly lacking in condemnation; an evaluation based entirely on love,—you have projected your injustice, giving God the lens of warped perception through which you look. Now it belongs to Him and not to you. You are afraid of Him, and do not see you hate and fear your Self as enemy.

5. Pray for God's justice, and do not confuse His mercy with your own insanity. Perception can make whatever picture the mind desires to see. Remember this. In this lies either Heaven or hell, as you elect. God's justice points to Heaven just because it is entirely impartial. It accepts all evidence that is brought before it, omitting nothing and assessing nothing as separate and apart from all the rest. From this one standpoint does it judge, and this alone. Here all attack and condemnation becomes meaningless and indefensible. Perception rests, the mind is still, and light returns again. Vision is now restored. What had been lost has now been found. The peace of God descends on all the world, and we can see. And we can see!

20. WHAT IS THE PEACE OF GOD?

1. It has been said that there is a kind of peace that is not of this world. How is it recognized? How is it found? And being found, how can it be retained? Let us consider each of these questions separately, for each reflects a different step along the way.

2. First, how can the peace of God be recognized? God's peace is recognized at first by just one thing; in every way it is totally unlike

all previous experiences. It calls to mind nothing that went before. It brings with it no past associations. It is a new thing entirely. There is a contrast, yes, between this thing and all the past. But strangely, it is not a contrast of true differences. The past just slips away, and in its place is everlasting quiet. Only that. The contrast first perceived has merely gone. Quiet has reached to cover everything.

3. How is this quiet found? No one can fail to find it who but seeks out its conditions. God's peace can never come where anger is, for anger must deny that peace exists. Who sees anger as justified in any way or any circumstance proclaims that peace is meaningless, and must believe that it cannot exist. In this condition, peace cannot be found. Therefore, forgiveness is the necessary condition for finding the peace of God. More than this, given forgiveness there *must* be peace. For what except attack will lead to war? And what but peace is opposite to war? Here the initial contrast stands out clear and apparent. Yet when peace is found, the war is meaningless. And it is conflict now that is perceived as nonexistent and unreal.

4. How is the peace of God retained, once it is found? Returning anger, in whatever form, will drop the heavy curtain once again, and the belief that peace cannot exist will certainly return. War is again accepted as the one reality. Now must you once again lay down your sword, although you do not recognize that you have picked it up again. But you will learn, as you remember even faintly now what happiness was yours without it, that you must have taken it again as your defense. Stop for a moment now and think of this: Is conflict what you want, or is God's peace the better choice? Which gives you more? A tranquil mind is not a little gift. Would you not rather live than choose to die?

5. Living is joy, but death can only weep. You see in death escape from what you made. But this you do not see; that you made death, and it is but illusion of an end. Death cannot be escape, because it is not life in which the problem lies. Life has no opposite, for it is God. Life and death seem to be opposites because you have decided death ends life. Forgive the world, and you will understand that everything that God created cannot have an end, and nothing He did not create is real. In this one sentence is our course explained. In this one sentence is our practicing given its one direction. And in this one sentence is the Holy Spirit's whole curriculum specified exactly as it is.

6. What is the peace of God? No more than this; the simple understanding that His Will is wholly without opposite. There is no thought that contradicts His Will, yet can be true. The contrast

between His Will and yours but seemed to be reality. In truth there was no conflict, for His Will is yours. Now is the mighty Will of God Himself His gift to you. He does not seek to keep it for Himself. Why would you seek to keep your tiny frail imaginings apart from Him? The Will of God is One and all there is. This is your heritage. The universe beyond the sun and stars, and all the thoughts of which you can conceive, belongs to you. God's peace is the condition for His Will. Attain His peace, and you remember Him.

QUESTION 58. How do teachers of God spend their time, and what must the teacher of God do to be able to let healing happen through him?

21. WHAT IS THE ROLE OF WORDS IN HEALING?

1. Strictly speaking, words play no part at all in healing. The motivating factor is prayer, or asking. What you ask for you receive. But this refers to the prayer of the heart, not to the words you use in praying. Sometimes the words and the prayer are contradictory; sometimes they agree. It does not matter. God does not understand words, for they were made by separated minds to keep them in the illusion of separation. Words can be helpful, particularly for the beginner, in helping concentration and facilitating the exclusion, or at least the control, of extraneous thoughts. Let us not forget, however, that words are but symbols of symbols. They are thus twice removed from reality.

2. As symbols, words have quite specific references. Even when they seem most abstract, the picture that comes to mind is apt to be very concrete. Unless a specific referent does occur to the mind in conjunction with the word, the word has little or no practical meaning, and thus cannot help the healing process. The prayer of the heart does not really ask for concrete things. It always requests some kind of experience, the specific things asked for being the bringers of the desired experience in the opinion of the asker. The words, then, are symbols for the things asked for, but the things themselves but stand for the experiences that are hoped for.

3. The prayer for things of this world will bring experiences of this world. If the prayer of the heart asks for this, this will be given because this will be received. It is impossible that the prayer of the heart remain unanswered in the perception of the one who asks. If he asks for the impossible, if he wants what does not exist or seeks for illusions in his heart, all this becomes his own. The power of his

decision offers it to him as he requests. Herein lie hell and Heaven. The sleeping Son of God has but this power left to him. It is enough. His words do not matter. Only the Word of God has any meaning, because it symbolizes that which has no human symbols at all. The Holy Spirit alone understands what this Word stands for. And this, too, is enough.

22. HOW ARE HEALING AND ATONEMENT RELATED?

1. Healing and Atonement are not related; they are identical. There is no order of difficulty in miracles because there are no degrees of Atonement. It is the one complete concept possible in this world, because it is the source of a wholly unified perception. Partial Atonement is a meaningless idea, just as special areas of hell in Heaven are inconceivable. Accept Atonement and you are healed. Atonement is the Word of God. Accept His Word and what remains to make sickness possible? Accept His Word and every miracle has been accomplished. To forgive is to heal. The teacher of God has taken accepting the Atonement for himself as his only function. What is there, then, he cannot heal? What miracle can be withheld from him?

2. The progress of the teacher of God may be slow or rapid, depending on whether he recognizes the Atonement's inclusiveness, or for a time excludes some problem areas from it. In some cases, there is a sudden and complete awareness of the perfect applicability of the lesson of the Atonement to all situations, but this is comparatively rare. The teacher of God may have accepted the function God has given him long before he has learned all that his acceptance holds out to him. It is only the end that is certain. Anywhere along the way, the necessary realization of inclusiveness may reach him. If the way seems long, let him be content. He has decided on the direction he wants to take. What more was asked of him? And having done what was required, would God withhold the rest?

3. That forgiveness is healing needs to be understood, if the teacher of God is to make progress. The idea that a body can be sick is a central concept in the ego's thought system. This thought gives the body autonomy, separates it from the mind, and keeps the idea of attack inviolate. If the body could be sick Atonement would be impossible. A body that can order a mind to do as it sees fit could merely take the place of God and prove salvation is impossible.

What, then, is left to heal? The body has become lord of the mind. How could the mind be returned to the Holy Spirit unless the body is killed? And who would want salvation at such a price?

4. Certainly sickness does not appear to be a decision. Nor would anyone actually believe he wants to be sick. Perhaps he can accept the idea in theory, but it is rarely if ever consistently applied to all specific forms of sickness, both in the individual's perception of himself and of all others as well. Nor is it at this level that the teacher of God calls forth the miracle of healing. He overlooks the mind *and* body, seeing only the face of Christ shining in front of him, correcting all mistakes and healing all perception. Healing is the result of the recognition, by God's teacher, of who it is that is in need of healing. This recognition has no special reference. It is true of all things that God created. In it are all illusions healed.

6. The offer of Atonement is universal. It is equally applicable to all individuals in all circumstances. And in it is the power to heal all individuals of all forms of sickness. Not to believe this is to be unfair to God, and thus unfaithful to Him. A sick person perceives himself as separate from God. Would you see him as separate from you? It is your task to heal the sense of separation that has made him sick. It is your function to recognize for him that what he believes about himself is not the truth. It is your forgiveness that must show him this. Healing is very simple. Atonement is received and offered. Having been received, it must be accepted. It is in the receiving, then, that healing lies. All else must follow from this single purpose.

23. DOES JESUS HAVE A SPECIAL PLACE IN HEALING?

1. God's gifts can rarely be received directly. Even the most advanced of God's teachers will give way to temptation in this world. Would it be fair if their pupils were denied healing because of this? The Bible says, "Ask in the name of Jesus Christ." Is this merely an appeal to magic? A name does not heal, nor does an invocation call forth any special power. What does it mean to call on Jesus Christ? What does calling on his name confer? Why is the appeal to him part of healing?

2. We have repeatedly said that one who has perfectly accepted the Atonement for himself can heal the world. Indeed, he has already done so. Temptation may recur to others, but never to this One. He has become the risen Son of God. He has overcome death because he has accepted life. He has recognized himself as God created him,

and in so doing he has recognized all living things as part of him. There is now no limit on his power, because it is the power of God. So has his name become the Name of God, for he no longer sees himself as separate from Him.

3. What does this mean for you? It means that in remembering Jesus you are remembering God. The whole relationship of the Son to the Father lies in him. His part in the Sonship is also yours, and his completed learning guarantees your own success. Is he still available for help? What did he say about this? Remember his promises, and ask yourself honestly whether it is likely that he will fail to keep them. Can God fail His Son? And can one who is one with God be unlike Him? Who transcends the body has transcended limitation. Would the greatest teacher be unavailable to those who follow him?

4. The name of Jesus Christ as such is but a symbol. But it stands for love that is not of this world. It is a symbol that is safely used as a replacement for the many names of all the gods to which you pray. It becomes the shining symbol for the Word of God, so close to what it stands for that the little space between the two is lost, the moment that the name is called to mind. Remembering the name of Jesus Christ is to give thanks for all the gifts that God has given you. And gratitude to God becomes the way in which He is remembered, for love cannot be far behind a grateful heart and thankful mind. God enters easily, for these are the true conditions for your homecoming.

5. Jesus has led the way. Why would you not be grateful to him? He has asked for love, but only that he might give it to you. You do not love yourself. But in his eyes your loveliness is so complete and flawless that he sees in it an image of his Father. You become the symbol of his Father here on earth. To you he looks for hope, because in you he sees no limit and no stain to mar your beautiful perfection. In his eyes Christ's vision shines in perfect constancy. He has remained with you. Would you not learn the lesson of salvation through his learning? Why would you choose to start again, when he has made the journey for you?

6. No one on earth can grasp what Heaven is, or what its one Creator really means. Yet we have witnesses. It is to them that wisdom should appeal. There have been those whose learning far exceeds what we can learn. Nor would we teach the limitations we have laid on us. No one who has become a true and dedicated teacher of God forgets his brothers. Yet what he can offer them is limited by what he learns himself. Then turn to one who laid all limits by, and went

beyond the farthest reach of learning. He will take you with him, for he did not go alone. And you were with him then, as you are now. 7. This course has come from him because his words have reached you in a language you can love and understand. Are other teachers possible, to lead the way to those who speak in different tongues and appeal to different symbols? Certainly there are. Would God leave anyone without a very present help in time of trouble; a savior who can symbolize Himself? Yet do we need a many-faceted curriculum, not because of content differences, but because symbols must shift and change to suit the need. Jesus has come to answer yours. In him you find God's Answer. Do you, then, teach with him, for he is with you; he is always here.

24. IS REINCARNATION SO?

1. In the ultimate sense, reincarnation is impossible. There is no past or future, and the idea of birth into a body has no meaning either once or many times. Reincarnation cannot, then, be true in any real sense. Our only question should be, "Is the concept helpful?" And that depends, of course, on what it is used for. If it is used to strengthen the recognition of the eternal nature of life, it is helpful indeed. Is any other question about it really useful in lighting up the way? Like many other beliefs, it can be bitterly misused. At least, such misuse offers preoccupation and perhaps pride in the past. At worst, it induces inertia in the present. In between, many kinds of folly are possible.

2. Reincarnation would not, under any circumstances, be the problem to be dealt with *now*. If it were responsible for some of the difficulties the individual faces now, his task would still be only to escape from them now. If he is laying the groundwork for a future life, he can still work out his salvation only now. To some, there may be comfort in the concept, and if it heartens them its value is self-evident. It is certain, however, that the way to salvation can be found by those who believe in reincarnation and by those who do not. The idea cannot, therefore, be regarded as essential to the curriculum. There is always some risk in seeing the present in terms of the past. There is always some good in any thought which strengthens the idea that life and the body are not the same.

3. For our purposes, it would not be helpful to take any definite stand on reincarnation. A teacher of God should be as helpful to those who believe in it as to those who do not. If a definite stand were required of him, it would merely limit his usefulness, as well as his own decision making. Our course is not concerned with any

concept that is not acceptable to anyone, regardless of his formal beliefs. His ego will be enough for him to cope with, and it is not the part of wisdom to add sectarian controversies to his burdens. Nor would there be an advantage in his premature acceptance of the course merely because it advocates a long-held belief of his own.

4. It cannot be too strongly emphasized that this course aims at a complete reversal of thought. When this is finally accomplished, issues such as the validity of reincarnation become meaningless. Until then, they are likely to be merely controversial. The teacher of God is, therefore, wise to step away from all such questions, for he has much to teach and learn apart from them. He should both learn and teach that theoretical issues but waste time, draining it away from its appointed purpose. If there are aspects to any concept or belief that will be helpful, he will be told about it. He will also be told how to use it. What more need he know?

5. Does this mean that the teacher of God should not believe in reincarnation himself, or discuss it with others who do? The answer is, certainly not! If he does believe in reincarnation, it would be a mistake for him to renounce the belief unless his internal Teacher so advised. And this is most unlikely. He might be advised that he is misusing the belief in some way that is detrimental to his pupil's advance or his own. Reinterpretation would then be recommended, because it is necessary. All that must be recognized, however, is that birth was not the beginning, and death is not the end. Yet even this much is not required of the beginner. He need merely accept the idea that what he knows is not necessarily all there is to learn. His journey has begun.

6. The emphasis of this course always remains the same;—it is at this moment that complete salvation is offered you, and it is at this moment that you can accept it. This is still your one responsibility. Atonement might be equated with total escape from the past and total lack of interest in the future. Heaven is here. There is nowhere else. Heaven is now. There is no other time. No teaching that does not lead to this is of concern to God's teachers. All beliefs will point to this if properly interpreted. In this sense, it can be said that their truth lies in their usefulness. All beliefs that lead to progress should be honored. This is the sole criterion this course requires. No more than this is necessary.

QUESTION 59. What does the teacher of God need to learn to make progress and to heal others, and why is it helpful to call on the name of Jesus Christ as a part of healing?

25. ARE "PSYCHIC" POWERS DESIRABLE?

2. Certainly there are many "psychic" powers that are clearly in line with this course. Communication is not limited to the small range of channels the world recognizes. If it were, there would be little point in trying to teach salvation. It would be impossible to do so. The limits the world places on communication are the chief barriers to direct experience of the Holy Spirit, Whose Presence is always there and Whose Voice is available but for the hearing. These limits are placed out of fear, for without them the walls that surround all the separate places of the world would fall at the holy sound of His Voice. Who transcends these limits in any way is merely becoming more natural. He is doing nothing special, and there is no magic in his accomplishments.

3. The seemingly new abilities that may be gathered on the way can be very helpful. Given to the Holy Spirit, and used under His direction, they are valuable teaching aids. To this, the question of how they arise is irrelevant. The only important consideration is how they are used. Taking them as ends in themselves, no matter how this is done, will delay progress. Nor does their value lie in proving anything; achievements from the past, unusual attunement with the "unseen," or "special" favors from God. God gives no special favors, and no one has any powers that are not available to everyone. Only by tricks of magic are special powers "demonstrated."

5. Even those who no longer value the material things of the world may still be deceived by "psychic" powers. As investment has been withdrawn from the world's material gifts, the ego has been seriously threatened. It may still be strong enough to rally under this new temptation to win back strength by guile. Many have not seen through the ego's defenses here, although they are not particularly subtle. Yet, given a remaining wish to be deceived, deception is made easy. Now the "power" is no longer a genuine ability, and cannot be used dependably. It is almost inevitable that, unless the individual changes his mind about its purpose, he will bolster his "power's" uncertainties with increasing deception.

6. Any ability that anyone develops has the potentiality for good. To this there is no exception. And the more unusual and unexpected the power, the greater its potential usefulness. Salvation has need of all abilities, for what the world would destroy the Holy Spirit would restore. "Psychic" abilities have been used to call upon the devil, which merely means to strengthen the ego. Yet here is also a great channel of hope and healing in the Holy Spirit's service. Those who have developed "psychic" powers have simply let some of the

limitations they laid upon their minds be lifted. It can be but further limitations they lay upon themselves if they utilize their increased freedom for greater imprisonment. The Holy Spirit needs these gifts, and those who offer them to Him and Him alone go with Christ's gratitude upon their hearts, and His holy sight not far behind.

26. CAN GOD BE REACHED DIRECTLY?

1. God indeed can be reached directly, for there is no distance between Him and His Son. His awareness is in everyone's memory, and His Word is written on everyone's heart. Yet this awareness and this memory can arise across the threshold of recognition only where all barriers to truth have been removed. In how many is this the case? Here, then, is the role of God's teachers. They, too, have not attained the necessary understanding as yet, but they have joined with others. This is what sets them apart from the world. And it is this that enables others to leave the world with them. Alone they are nothing. But in their joining is the power of God.

3. Sometimes a teacher of God may have a brief experience of direct union with God. In this world, it is almost impossible that this endure. It can, perhaps, be won after much devotion and dedication, and then be maintained for much of the time on earth. But this is so rare that it cannot be considered a realistic goal. If it happens, so be it. If it does not happen, so be it as well. All worldly states must be illusory. If God were reached directly in sustained awareness, the body would not be long maintained. Those who have laid the body down merely to extend their helpfulness to those remaining behind are few indeed. And they need helpers who are still in bondage and still asleep, so that by their awakening can God's Voice be heard.

27. WHAT IS DEATH?

1. Death is the central dream from which all illusions stem. Is it not madness to think of life as being born, aging, losing vitality, and dying in the end? We have asked this question before, but now we need to consider it more carefully. It is the one fixed, unchangeable belief of the world that all things in it are born only to die. This is regarded as "the way of nature," not to be raised to question, but to be accepted as the "natural" law of life. The cyclical, the changing and unsure; the undependable and the unsteady, waxing and waning in a certain way upon a certain path,—all this is taken as the Will of God. And no one asks if a benign Creator could will this.

4. The curious belief that there is part of dying things that may go on apart from what will die, does not proclaim a loving God nor

re-establish any grounds for trust. If death is real for anything, there is no life. Death denies life. But if there is reality in life, death is denied. No compromise in this is possible. There is either a god of fear or One of Love. The world attempts a thousand compromises, and will attempt a thousand more. Not one can be acceptable to God's teachers, because not one could be acceptable to God. He did not make death because He did not make fear. Both are equally meaningless to Him.

7. Teacher of God, your one assignment could be stated thus: Accept no compromise in which death plays a part. Do not believe in cruelty, nor let attack conceal the truth from you. What seems to die has but been misperceived and carried to illusion. Now it becomes your task to let the illusion be carried to the truth. Be steadfast but in this; be not deceived by the "reality" of any changing form. Truth neither moves nor wavers nor sinks down to death and dissolution. And what is the end of death? Nothing but this; the realization that the Son of God is guiltless now and forever. Nothing but this. But do not let yourself forget it is not less than this.

28. WHAT IS THE RESURRECTION?

1. Very simply, the resurrection is the overcoming or surmounting of death. It is a reawakening or a rebirth; a change of mind about the meaning of the world. It is the acceptance of the Holy Spirit's interpretation of the world's purpose; the acceptance of the Atonement for oneself. It is the end of dreams of misery, and the glad awareness of the Holy Spirit's final dream. It is the recognition of the gifts of God. It is the dream in which the body functions perfectly, having no function except communication. It is the lesson in which learning ends, for it is consummated and surpassed with this. It is the invitation to God to take His final step. It is the relinquishment of all other purposes, all other interests, all other wishes and all other concerns. It is the single desire of the Son for the Father.

2. The resurrection is the denial of death, being the assertion of life. Thus is all the thinking of the world reversed entirely. Life is now recognized as salvation, and pain and misery of any kind perceived as hell. Love is no longer feared, but gladly welcomed. Idols have disappeared, and the remembrance of God shines unimpeded across the world. Christ's face is seen in every living thing, and nothing is held in darkness, apart from the light of forgiveness. There is no sorrow still upon the earth. The joy of Heaven has come upon it.

3. Here the curriculum ends. From here on, no directions are needed. Vision is wholly corrected and all mistakes undone. Attack

is meaningless and peace has come. The goal of the curriculum has been achieved. Thoughts turn to Heaven and away from hell. All longings are satisfied, for what remains unanswered or incomplete? The last illusion spreads across the world, forgiving all things and replacing all attack. The whole reversal is accomplished. Nothing is left to contradict the Word of God. There is no opposition to the truth. And now the truth can come at last. How quickly will it come as it is asked to enter and envelop such a world!

4. All living hearts are tranquil with a stir of deep anticipation, for the time of everlasting things is now at hand. There is no death. The Son of God is free. And in his freedom is the end of fear. No hidden places now remain on earth to shelter sick illusions, dreams of fear and misperceptions of the universe. All things are seen in light, and in the light their purpose is transformed and understood. And we, God's children, rise up from the dust and look upon our perfect sinlessness. The song of Heaven sounds around the world, as it is lifted up and brought to truth.

5. Now there are no distinctions. Differences have disappeared and Love looks on Itself. What further sight is needed? What remains that vision could accomplish? We have seen the face of Christ, His sinlessness, His Love behind all forms, beyond all purposes. Holy are we because His Holiness has set us free indeed! And we accept His Holiness as ours; as it is. As God created us so will we be forever and forever, and we wish for nothing but His Will to be our own. Illusions of another will are lost, for unity of purpose has been found.

6. These things await us all, but we are not prepared as yet to welcome them with joy. As long as any mind remains possessed of evil dreams, the thought of hell is real. God's teachers have the goal of wakening the minds of those asleep, and seeing there the vision of Christ's face to take the place of what they dream. The thought of murder is replaced with blessing. Judgment is laid by, and given Him Whose function judgment is. And in His Final Judgment is restored the truth about the holy Son of God. He is redeemed, for he has heard God's Word and understood its meaning. He is free because he let God's Voice proclaim the truth. And all he sought before to crucify are resurrected with him, by his side, as he prepares with them to meet his God.

29. AS FOR THE REST...

1. This manual is not intended to answer all questions that both teacher and pupil may raise. In fact, it covers only a few of the more obvious ones, in terms of a brief summary of some of the major

concepts in the text and workbook. It is not a substitute for either, but merely a supplement. While it is called a manual for teachers, it must be remembered that only time divides teacher and pupil, so that the difference is temporary by definition. In some cases, it may be helpful for the pupil to read the manual first. Others might do better to begin with the workbook. Still others may need to start at the more abstract level of the text.

2. Which is for which? Who would profit more from prayers alone? Who needs but a smile, being as yet unready for more? No one should attempt to answer these questions alone. Surely no teacher of God has come this far without realizing that. The curriculum is highly individualized, and all aspects are under the Holy Spirit's particular care and guidance. Ask and He will answer. The responsibility is His, and He alone is fit to assume it. To do so is His function. To refer the questions to Him is yours. Would you want to be responsible for decisions about which you understand so little? Be glad you have a Teacher Who cannot make a mistake. His answers are always right. Would you say that of yours?

3. There is another advantage,—and a very important one,—in referring decisions to the Holy Spirit with increasing frequency. Perhaps you have not thought of this aspect, but its centrality is obvious. To follow the Holy Spirit's guidance is to let yourself be absolved of guilt. It is the essence of the Atonement. It is the core of the curriculum. The imagined usurping of functions not your own is the basis of fear. The whole world you see reflects the illusion that you have done so, making fear inevitable. To return the function to the One to Whom it belongs is thus the escape from fear. And it is this that lets the memory of love return to you. Do not, then, think that following the Holy Spirit's guidance is necessary merely because of your own inadequacies. It is the way out of hell for you.

5. Who assumes a power that he does not possess is deceiving himself. Yet to accept the power given him by God is but to acknowledge his Creator and accept His gifts. And His gifts have no limit. To ask the Holy Spirit to decide for you is simply to accept your true inheritance. Does this mean that you cannot say anything without consulting Him? No, indeed! That would hardly be practical, and it is the practical with which this course is most concerned. If you have made it a habit to ask for help when and where you can, you can be confident that wisdom will be given you when you need it. Prepare for this each morning, remember God when you can throughout the day, ask the Holy Spirit's help when it is feasible

to do so, and thank Him for His guidance at night. And your confidence will be well founded indeed.

6. Never forget that the Holy Spirit does not depend on your words. He understands the requests of your heart, and answers them. Does this mean that, while attack remains attractive to you, He will respond with evil? Hardly! For God has given Him the power to translate your prayers of the heart into His language. He understands that an attack is a call for help. And He responds with help accordingly. God would be cruel if He let your words replace His Own. A loving father does not let his child harm himself, or choose his own destruction. He may ask for injury, but his father will protect him still. And how much more than this does your Father love His Son?

7. Remember you are His completion and His Love. Remember your weakness is His strength. But do not read this hastily or wrongly. If His strength is in you, what you perceive as your weakness is but illusion. And He has given you the means to prove it so. Ask all things of His Teacher, and all things are given you. Not in the future but immediately; now. God does not wait, for waiting implies time and He is timeless. Forget your foolish images, your sense of frailty and your fear of harm, your dreams of danger and selected "wrongs." God knows but His Son, and as he was created so he is. In confidence I place you in His Hands, and I give thanks for you that this is so.

8. And now in all your doings be you blessed.
God turns to you for help to save the world.
Teacher of God, His thanks He offers you,
And all the world stands silent in the grace
You bring from Him. You are the Son He loves,
And it is given you to be the means
Through which His Voice is heard around the world,
To close all things of time; to end the sight
Of all things visible; and to undo
All things that change. Through you is ushered in
A world unseen, unheard, yet truly there.
Holy are you, and in your light the world
Reflects your holiness, for you are not
Alone and friendless. I give thanks for you,
And join your efforts on behalf of God,
Knowing they are on my behalf as well,
And for all those who walk to God with me.

　　　AMEN

QUESTION 60. Where is the Course curriculum leading you?

INSTRUCTIONS FOR THE SECOND MONTH

~ • ~

This condensed version of the Course includes 30 Workbook lessons, which ideally can be completed in the second month of the Two-Month Bridge. Only one exercise is to be undertaken in any one day. Doing the exercises in 30 consecutive days is certainly recommended, but not absolutely necessary. After all, this is your learning experience. Therefore, you can set your own schedule of how long it will take for you to complete all 30 exercises. For example, you may want to repeat the same lesson twice on two different days if you think it would be helpful for you. Or you may want to skip a day here and there, which is fine as long as you eventually complete all 30 exercises and don't mind extending the Two-Month Bridge beyond its intended length of time.

You can do the exercises anywhere. You need no preparation. The exercises are simple and do not require a great deal of time. The beginning exercises are designed to help you undo the way you perceive now, and later Workbook lessons are geared toward acquiring a new way of perceiving based on true perception.

The exercises for each day focus on one central concept. This central idea is stated first and is followed by instructions describing how to put the idea into practical application. What if you find that you make mistakes in your application of the instructions? Simply do the best that you can. Remember to have a forgiving attitude toward yourself so you avoid any temptation toward indulging in self-condemnation.

The following section provides the Course Introduction to the Workbook for Students. Because the Two-Month Bridge includes only 30 exercises, two paragraphs containing references to the full 365 exercises have been omitted from the Introduction. Before beginning the second month of the Two-Month Bridge, please carefully read the following Workbook Introduction:

THIRTY WORKBOOK LESSONS

≈ • ≈

INTRODUCTION

1. A theoretical foundation such as the text provides is necessary as a framework to make the exercises in this workbook meaningful. Yet it is doing the exercises that will make the goal of the course possible. An untrained mind can accomplish nothing. It is the purpose of this workbook to train your mind to think along the lines the text sets forth.

4. The purpose of the workbook is to train your mind in a systematic way to a different perception of everyone and everything in the world. The exercises are planned to help you generalize the lessons, so that you will understand that each of them is equally applicable to everyone and everything you see.

5. Transfer of training in true perception does not proceed as does transfer of the training of the world. If true perception has been achieved in connection with any person, situation or event, total transfer to everyone and everything is certain. On the other hand, one exception held apart from true perception makes its accomplishments anywhere impossible.

6. The only general rules to be observed throughout, then, are: First, that the exercises be practiced with great specificity, as will be indicated. This will help you to generalize the ideas involved to every situation in which you find yourself, and to everyone and everything in it. Second, be sure that you do not decide for yourself that there are some people, situations or things to which the ideas are inapplicable. This will interfere with transfer of training. The very nature of true perception is that it has no limits. It is the opposite of the way you see now.

7. The overall aim of the exercises is to increase your ability to extend the ideas you will be practicing to include everything. This

will require no effort on your part. The exercises themselves meet the conditions necessary for this kind of transfer.

8. Some of the ideas the workbook presents you will find hard to believe, and others may seem to be quite startling. This does not matter. You are merely asked to apply the ideas as you are directed to do. You are not asked to judge them at all. You are asked only to use them. It is their use that will give them meaning to you, and will show you that they are true.

9. Remember only this; you need not believe the ideas, you need not accept them, and you need not even welcome them. Some of them you may actively resist. None of this will matter, or decrease their efficacy. But do not allow yourself to make exceptions in applying the ideas the workbook contains, and whatever your reactions to the ideas may be, use them. Nothing more than that is required.

DAY 1 — LESSON 15

My thoughts are images that I have made.

1. It is because the thoughts you think you think appear as images that you do not recognize them as nothing. You think you think them, and so you think you see them. This is how your "seeing" was made. This is the function you have given your body's eyes. It is not seeing. It is image making. It takes the place of seeing, replacing vision with illusions.

2. This introductory idea to the process of image making that you call seeing will not have much meaning for you. You will begin to understand it when you have seen little edges of light around the same familiar objects which you see now. That is the beginning of real vision. You can be certain that real vision will come quickly when this has occurred.

3. As we go along, you may have many "light episodes." They may take many different forms, some of them quite unexpected. Do not be afraid of them. They are signs that you are opening your eyes at last. They will not persist, because they merely symbolize true perception, and they are not related to knowledge. These exercises will not reveal knowledge to you. But they will prepare the way to it.

4. In practicing the idea for today, repeat it first to yourself, and then apply it to whatever you see around you, using its name and letting your eyes rest on it as you say:

> *This _____ is an image that I have made.*
> *That _____ is an image that I have made.*

It is not necessary to include a large number of specific subjects for the application of today's idea. It is necessary, however, to continue to look at each subject while you repeat the idea to yourself. The idea should be repeated quite slowly each time.

5. Although you will obviously not be able to apply the idea to very many things during the minute or so of practice that is recommended, try to make the selection as random as possible. Less than a minute will do for the practice periods, if you begin to feel uneasy. Do not have more than three application periods for today's idea unless you feel completely comfortable with it, and do not exceed four. However, the idea can be applied as needed throughout the day.

DAY 2 — LESSSON 28

Above all else I want to see things differently.

1. Today we are really giving specific application to the idea for yesterday. In these practice periods, you will be making a series of definite commitments. The question of whether you will keep them in the future is not our concern here. If you are willing at least to make them now, you have started on the way to keeping them. And we are still at the beginning.

2. You may wonder why it is important to say, for example, "Above all else I want to see this table differently." In itself it is not important at all. Yet what is by itself? And what does "in itself" mean? You see a lot of separate things about you, which really means you are not seeing at all. You either see or not. When you have seen one thing differently, you will see all things differently. The light you will see in any one of them is the same light you will see in them all.

3. When you say, "Above all else I want to see this table differently," you are making a commitment to withdraw your preconceived ideas about the table, and open your mind to what it is, and what it is for. You are not defining it in past terms. You are asking what it is, rather than telling it what it is. You are not binding its meaning to your tiny experience of tables, nor are you limiting its purpose to your little personal thoughts.

4. You will not question what you have already defined. And the purpose of these exercises is to ask questions and receive the answers. In saying, "Above all else I want to see this table differently," you are committing yourself to seeing. It is not an exclusive commitment. It is a commitment that applies to the table just as much as to anything else, neither more nor less.

5. You could, in fact, gain vision from just that table, if you would withdraw all your own ideas from it, and look upon it with a completely open mind. It has something to show you; something beautiful and clean and of infinite value, full of happiness and hope. Hidden under all your ideas about it is its real purpose, the purpose it shares with all the universe.

6. In using the table as a subject for applying the idea for today, you are therefore really asking to see the purpose of the universe. You will be making this same request of each subject that you use in the

practice periods. And you are making a commitment to each of them to let its purpose be revealed to you, instead of placing your own judgment upon it.

7. We will have six two-minute practice periods today, in which the idea for the day is stated first, and then applied to whatever you see about you. Not only should the subjects be chosen randomly, but each one should be accorded equal sincerity as today's idea is applied to it, in an attempt to acknowledge the equal value of them all in their contribution to your seeing.

8. As usual, the applications should include the name of the subject your eyes happen to light on, and you should rest your eyes on it while saying:

Above all else I want to see this _____ differently.

Each application should be made quite slowly, and as thoughtfully as possible. There is no hurry.

DAY 3 — LESSON 36

My holiness envelops everything I see.

1. Today's idea extends the idea for yesterday from the perceiver to the perceived. You are holy because your mind is part of God's. And because you are holy, your sight must be holy as well. "Sinless" means without sin. You cannot be without sin a little. You are sinless or not. If your mind is part of God's you must be sinless, or a part of His Mind would be sinful. Your sight is related to His Holiness, not to your ego, and therefore not to your body.

2. Four three-to-five-minute practice periods are required for today. Try to distribute them fairly evenly, and make the shorter applications frequently, to protect your protection throughout the day. The longer practice periods should take this form:

3. First, close your eyes and repeat the idea for today several times, slowly. Then open your eyes and look quite slowly about you, applying the idea specifically to whatever you note in your casual survey. Say, for example:

> *My holiness envelops that rug.*
> *My holiness envelops that wall.*
> *My holiness envelops these fingers.*
> *My holiness envelops that chair.*
> *My holiness envelops that body.*
> *My holiness envelops this pen.*

Several times during these practice periods, close your eyes and repeat the idea to yourself. Then open your eyes, and continue as before.

4. For the shorter exercise periods, close your eyes and repeat the idea; look about you as you repeat it again; and conclude with one more repetition with your eyes closed. All applications should, of course, be made quite slowly, as effortlessly and unhurriedly as possible.

DAY 4 — LESSON 41

God goes with me wherever I go.

1. Today's idea will eventually overcome completely the sense of loneliness and abandonment all the separated ones experience. Depression is an inevitable consequence of separation. So are anxiety, worry, a deep sense of helplessness, misery, suffering and intense fear of loss.

2. The separated ones have invented many "cures" for what they believe to be "the ills of the world." But the one thing they do not do is to question the reality of the problem. Yet its effects cannot be cured because the problem is not real. The idea for today has the power to end all this foolishness forever. And foolishness it is, despite the serious and tragic forms it may take.

3. Deep within you is everything that is perfect, ready to radiate through you and out into the world. It will cure all sorrow and pain and fear and loss because it will heal the mind that thought these things were real, and suffered out of its allegiance to them.

4. You can never be deprived of your perfect holiness because its Source goes with you wherever you go. You can never suffer because the Source of all joy goes with you wherever you go. You can never be alone because the Source of all life goes with you wherever you go. Nothing can destroy your peace of mind because God goes with you wherever you go.

5. We understand that you do not believe all this. How could you, when the truth is hidden deep within, under a heavy cloud of insane thoughts, dense and obscuring, yet representing all you see? Today we will make our first real attempt to get past this dark and heavy cloud, and to go through it to the light beyond.

6. There will be only one long practice period today. In the morning, as soon as you get up if possible, sit quietly for some three to five minutes, with your eyes closed. At the beginning of the practice period, repeat today's idea very slowly. Then make no effort to think of anything. Try, instead, to get a sense of turning inward, past all the idle thoughts of the world. Try to enter very deeply into your own mind, keeping it clear of any thoughts that might divert your attention.

7. From time to time, you may repeat the idea if you find it helpful. But most of all, try to sink down and inward, away from the world

and all the foolish thoughts of the world. You are trying to reach past all these things. You are trying to leave appearances and approach reality.

8. It is quite possible to reach God. In fact it is very easy, because it is the most natural thing in the world. You might even say it is the only natural thing in the world. The way will open, if you believe that it is possible. This exercise can bring very startling results even the first time it is attempted, and sooner or later it is always successful. We will go into more detail about this kind of practice as we go along. But it will never fail completely, and instant success is possible.

9. Throughout the day use today's idea often, repeating it very slowly, preferably with eyes closed. Think of what you are saying; what the words mean. Concentrate on the holiness that they imply about you; on the unfailing companionship that is yours; on the complete protection that surrounds you.

10. You can indeed afford to laugh at fear thoughts, remembering that God goes with you wherever you go.

DAY 5 — LESSON 44

God is the light in which I see.

1. Today we are continuing the idea for yesterday, adding another dimension to it. You cannot see in darkness, and you cannot make light. You can make darkness and then think you see in it, but light reflects life, and is therefore an aspect of creation. Creation and darkness cannot coexist, but light and life must go together, being but different aspects of creation.

2. In order to see, you must recognize that light is within, not without. You do not see outside yourself, nor is the equipment for seeing outside you. An essential part of this equipment is the light that makes seeing possible. It is with you always, making vision possible in every circumstance.

3. Today we are going to attempt to reach that light. For this purpose, we will use a form of exercise which has been suggested before, and which we will utilize increasingly. It is a particularly difficult form for the undisciplined mind, and represents a major goal of mind training. It requires precisely what the untrained mind lacks. Yet this training must be accomplished if you are to see.

4. Have at least three practice periods today, each lasting three to five minutes. A longer time is highly recommended, but only if you find the time slipping by with little or no sense of strain. The form of practice we will use today is the most natural and easy one in the world for the trained mind, just as it seems to be the most unnatural and difficult for the untrained mind.

5. Your mind is no longer wholly untrained. You are quite ready to learn the form of exercise we will use today, but you may find that you will encounter strong resistance. The reason is very simple. While you practice in this way, you leave behind everything that you now believe, and all the thoughts that you have made up. Properly speaking, this is the release from hell. Yet perceived through the ego's eyes, it is loss of identity and a descent into hell.

6. If you can stand aside from the ego by ever so little, you will have no difficulty in recognizing that its opposition and its fears are meaningless. You might find it helpful to remind yourself, from time to time, that to reach light is to escape from darkness, whatever you may believe to the contrary. God is the light in which you see. You are attempting to reach Him.

7. Begin the practice period by repeating today's idea with your eyes open, and close them slowly, repeating the idea several times more. Then try to sink into your mind, letting go every kind of interference and intrusion by quietly sinking past them. Your mind cannot be stopped in this unless you choose to stop it. It is merely taking its natural course. Try to observe your passing thoughts without involvement, and slip quietly by them.

8. While no particular approach is advocated for this form of exercise, what is needful is a sense of the importance of what you are doing; its inestimable value to you, and an awareness that you are attempting something very holy. Salvation is your happiest accomplishment. It is also the only one that has any meaning, because it is the only one that has any real use to you at all.

9. If resistance rises in any form, pause long enough to repeat today's idea, keeping your eyes closed unless you are aware of fear. In that case, you will probably find it more reassuring to open your eyes briefly. Try, however, to return to the exercises with eyes closed as soon as possible.

10. If you are doing the exercises correctly, you should experience some sense of relaxation, and even a feeling that you are approaching, if not actually entering into light. Try to think of light, formless and without limit, as you pass by the thoughts of this world. And do not forget that they cannot hold you to the world unless you give them the power to do so.

11. Throughout the day repeat the idea often, with eyes open or closed as seems better to you at the time. But do not forget. Above all, be determined not to forget today.

DAY 6 — LESSON 46

God is the Love in which I forgive.

1. God does not forgive because He has never condemned. And there must be condemnation before forgiveness is necessary. Forgiveness is the great need of this world, but that is because it is a world of illusions. Those who forgive are thus releasing themselves from illusions, while those who withhold forgiveness are binding themselves to them. As you condemn only yourself, so do you forgive only yourself.

2. Yet although God does not forgive, His Love is nevertheless the basis of forgiveness. Fear condemns and love forgives. Forgiveness thus undoes what fear has produced, returning the mind to the awareness of God. For this reason, forgiveness can truly be called salvation. It is the means by which illusions disappear.

3. Today's exercises require at least three full five-minute practice periods, and as many shorter ones as possible. Begin the longer practice periods by repeating today's idea to yourself, as usual. Close your eyes as you do so, and spend a minute or two in searching your mind for those whom you have not forgiven. It does not matter "how much" you have not forgiven them. You have forgiven them entirely or not at all.

4. If you are doing the exercises well you should have no difficulty in finding a number of people you have not forgiven. It is a safe rule that anyone you do not like is a suitable subject. Mention each one by name, and say:

> *God is the Love in which I forgive you, [name].*

5. The purpose of the first phase of today's practice periods is to put you in a position to forgive yourself. After you have applied the idea to all those who have come to mind, tell yourself:

> *God is the Love in which I forgive myself.*

Then devote the remainder of the practice period to adding related ideas such as:

> *God is the Love with which I love myself.*
> *God is the Love in which I am blessed.*

6. The form of the application may vary considerably, but the central idea should not be lost sight of. You might say, for example:

> *I cannot be guilty because I am a Son of God.*
> *I have already been forgiven.*
> *No fear is possible in a mind beloved of God.*
> *There is no need to attack because love has forgiven me.*

The practice period should end, however, with a repetition of today's idea as originally stated.

7. The shorter practice periods may consist either of a repetition of the idea for today in the original or in a related form, as you prefer. Be sure, however, to make more specific applications if they are needed. They will be needed at any time during the day when you become aware of any kind of negative reaction to anyone, present or not. In that event, tell him silently:

> *God is the Love in which I forgive you.*

DAY 7 — LESSON 50

I am sustained by the Love of God.

1. Here is the answer to every problem that will confront you, today and tomorrow and throughout time. In this world, you believe you are sustained by everything but God. Your faith is placed in the most trivial and insane symbols; pills, money, "protective" clothing, influence, prestige, being liked, knowing the "right" people, and an endless list of forms of nothingness that you endow with magical powers.

2. All these things are your replacements for the Love of God. All these things are cherished to ensure a body identification. They are songs of praise to the ego. Do not put your faith in the worthless. It will not sustain you.

3. Only the Love of God will protect you in all circumstances. It will lift you out of every trial, and raise you high above all the perceived dangers of this world into a climate of perfect peace and safety. It will transport you into a state of mind that nothing can threaten, nothing can disturb, and where nothing can intrude upon the eternal calm of the Son of God.

4. Put not your faith in illusions. They will fail you. Put all your faith in the Love of God within you; eternal, changeless and forever unfailing. This is the answer to whatever confronts you today. Through the Love of God within you, you can resolve all seeming difficulties without effort and in sure confidence. Tell yourself this often today. It is a declaration of release from the belief in idols. It is your acknowledgment of the truth about yourself.

5. For ten minutes, twice today, morning and evening, let the idea for today sink deep into your consciousness. Repeat it, think about it, let related thoughts come to help you recognize its truth, and allow peace to flow over you like a blanket of protection and surety. Let no idle and foolish thoughts enter to disturb the holy mind of the Son of God. Such is the Kingdom of Heaven. Such is the resting place where your Father has placed you forever.

DAY 8 — LESSON 62

Forgiveness is my function as the light of the world.

1. It is your forgiveness that will bring the world of darkness to the light. It is your forgiveness that lets you recognize the light in which you see. Forgiveness is the demonstration that you are the light of the world. Through your forgiveness does the truth about yourself return to your memory. Therefore, in your forgiveness lies your salvation.

2. Illusions about yourself and the world are one. That is why all forgiveness is a gift to yourself. Your goal is to find out who you are, having denied your Identity by attacking creation and its Creator. Now you are learning how to remember the truth. For this attack must be replaced by forgiveness, so that thoughts of life may replace thoughts of death.

3. Remember that in every attack you call upon your own weakness, while each time you forgive you call upon the strength of Christ in you. Do you not then begin to understand what forgiveness will do for you? It will remove all sense of weakness, strain and fatigue from your mind. It will take away all fear and guilt and pain. It will restore the invulnerability and power God gave His Son to your awareness.

4. Let us be glad to begin and end this day by practicing today's idea, and to use it as frequently as possible throughout the day. It will help to make the day as happy for you as God wants you to be. And it will help those around you, as well as those who seem to be far away in space and time, to share this happiness with you.

5. As often as you can, closing your eyes if possible, say to yourself today:

> *Forgiveness is my function as the light of the world.*
> *I would fulfill my function that I may be happy.*

Then devote a minute or two to considering your function and the happiness and release it will bring you. Let related thoughts come freely, for your heart will recognize these words, and in your mind is the awareness they are true. Should your attention wander, repeat the idea and add:

> *I would remember this because I want to be happy.*

DAY 9 — LESSON 67

Love created me like itself.

1. Today's idea is a complete and accurate statement of what you are. This is why you are the light of the world. This is why God appointed you as the world's savior. This is why the Son of God looks to you for his salvation. He is saved by what you are. We will make every effort today to reach this truth about you, and to realize fully, if only for a moment, that it is the truth.

2. In the longer practice period, we will think about your reality and its wholly unchanged and unchangeable nature. We will begin by repeating this truth about you, and then spend a few minutes adding some relevant thoughts, such as:

> *Holiness created me holy.*
> *Kindness created me kind.*
> *Helpfulness created me helpful.*
> *Perfection created me perfect.*

Any attribute which is in accord with God as He defines Himself is appropriate for use. We are trying today to undo your definition of God and replace it with His Own. We are also trying to emphasize that you are part of His definition of Himself.

3. After you have gone over several such related thoughts, try to let all thoughts drop away for a brief preparatory interval, and then try to reach past all your images and preconceptions about yourself to the truth in you. If love created you like itself, this Self must be in you. And somewhere in your mind It is there for you to find.

4. You may find it necessary to repeat the idea for today from time to time to replace distracting thoughts. You may also find that this is not sufficient, and that you need to continue adding other thoughts related to the truth about yourself. Yet perhaps you will succeed in going past that, and through the interval of thoughtlessness to the awareness of a blazing light in which you recognize yourself as love created you. Be confident that you will do much today to bring that awareness nearer, whether you feel you have succeeded or not.

5. It will be particularly helpful today to practice the idea for the day as often as you can. You need to hear the truth about yourself as frequently as possible, because your mind is so preoccupied with false

self-images. Four or five times an hour, and perhaps even more, it would be most beneficial to remind yourself that love created you like itself. Hear the truth about yourself in this.

6. Try to realize in the shorter practice periods that this is not your tiny, solitary voice that tells you this. This is the Voice for God, reminding you of your Father and of your Self. This is the Voice of truth, replacing everything that the ego tells you about yourself with the simple truth about the Son of God. You were created by love like itself.

DAY 10 — LESSON 68

Love holds no grievances.

1. You who were created by love like itself can hold no grievances and know your Self. To hold a grievance is to forget who you are. To hold a grievance is to see yourself as a body. To hold a grievance is to let the ego rule your mind and to condemn the body to death. Perhaps you do not yet fully realize just what holding grievances does to your mind. It seems to split you off from your Source and make you unlike Him. It makes you believe that He is like what you think you have become, for no one can conceive of his Creator as unlike himself.

2. Shut off from your Self, which remains aware of Its likeness to Its Creator, your Self seems to sleep, while the part of your mind that weaves illusions in its sleep appears to be awake. Can all this arise from holding grievances? Oh, yes! For he who holds grievances denies he was created by love, and his Creator has become fearful to him in his dream of hate. Who can dream of hatred and not fear God?

3. It is as sure that those who hold grievances will redefine God in their own image, as it is certain that God created them like Himself, and defined them as part of Him. It is as sure that those who hold grievances will suffer guilt, as it is certain that those who forgive will find peace. It is as sure that those who hold grievances will forget who they are, as it is certain that those who forgive will remember.

4. Would you not be willing to relinquish your grievances if you believed all this were so? Perhaps you do not think you can let your grievances go. That, however, is simply a matter of motivation. Today we will try to find out how you would feel without them. If you succeed even by ever so little, there will never be a problem in motivation ever again.

5. Begin today's extended practice period by searching your mind for those against whom you hold what you regard as major grievances. Some of these will be quite easy to find. Then think of the seemingly minor grievances you hold against those you like and even think you love. It will quickly become apparent that there is no one against whom you do not cherish grievances of some sort. This has left you alone in all the universe in your perception of yourself.

6. Determine now to see all these people as friends. Say to them all, thinking of each one in turn as you do so:

> *I would see you as my friend, that I may remember*
> *you are part of me and come to know myself.*

Spend the remainder of the practice period trying to think of yourself as completely at peace with everyone and everything, safe in a world that protects you and loves you, and that you love in return. Try to feel safety surrounding you, hovering over you and holding you up. Try to believe, however briefly, that nothing can harm you in any way. At the end of the practice period tell yourself:

> *Love holds no grievances. When I let all grievances*
> *go I will know I am perfectly safe.*

7. The short practice periods should include a quick application of today's idea in this form, whenever any thought of grievance arises against anyone, physically present or not:

> *Love holds no grievances. Let me not betray my Self.*

In addition, repeat the idea several times an hour in this form:

> *Love holds no grievances. I would wake to my Self*
> *by laying all my grievances aside and wakening in*
> *Him.*

DAY 11 — LESSON 69

My grievances hide the light of the world in me.

1. No one can look upon what your grievances conceal. Because your grievances are hiding the light of the world in you, everyone stands in darkness, and you beside him. But as the veil of your grievances is lifted, you are released with him. Share your salvation now with him who stood beside you when you were in hell. He is your brother in the light of the world that saves you both.

2. Today let us make another real attempt to reach the light in you. Before we undertake this in our more extended practice period, let us devote several minutes to thinking about what we are trying to do. We are literally attempting to get in touch with the salvation of the world. We are trying to see past the veil of darkness that keeps it concealed. We are trying to let the veil be lifted, and to see the tears of God's Son disappear in the sunlight.

3. Let us begin our longer practice period today with the full realization that this is so, and with real determination to reach what is dearer to us than all else. Salvation is our only need. There is no other purpose here, and no other function to fulfill. Learning salvation is our only goal. Let us end the ancient search today by finding the light in us, and holding it up for everyone who searches with us to look upon and rejoice.

4. Very quietly now, with your eyes closed, try to let go of all the content that generally occupies your consciousness. Think of your mind as a vast circle, surrounded by a layer of heavy, dark clouds. You can see only the clouds because you seem to be standing outside the circle and quite apart from it.

5. From where you stand, you can see no reason to believe there is a brilliant light hidden by the clouds. The clouds seem to be the only reality. They seem to be all there is to see. Therefore, you do not attempt to go through them and past them, which is the only way in which you would be really convinced of their lack of substance. We will make this attempt today.

6. After you have thought about the importance of what you are trying to do for yourself and the world, try to settle down in perfect stillness, remembering only how much you want to reach the light in you today,—now! Determine to go past the clouds. Reach out and touch them in your mind. Brush them aside with your hand; feel them

resting on your cheeks and forehead and eyelids as you go through them. Go on; clouds cannot stop you.

7. If you are doing the exercises properly, you will begin to feel a sense of being lifted up and carried ahead. Your little effort and small determination call on the power of the universe to help you, and God Himself will raise you from darkness into light. You are in accord with His Will. You cannot fail because your will is His.

8. Have confidence in your Father today, and be certain that He has heard you and answered you. You may not recognize His answer yet, but you can indeed be sure that it is given you and you will yet receive it. Try, as you attempt to go through the clouds to the light, to hold this confidence in your mind. Try to remember that you are at last joining your will to God's. Try to keep the thought clearly in mind that what you undertake with God must succeed. Then let the power of God work in you and through you, that His Will and yours be done.

9. In the shorter practice periods, which you will want to do as often as possible in view of the importance of today's idea to you and your happiness, remind yourself that your grievances are hiding the light of the world from your awareness. Remind yourself also that you are not searching for it alone, and that you do know where to look for it. Say, then:

> *My grievances hide the light of the world in me. I cannot see what I have hidden. Yet I want to let it be revealed to me, for my salvation and the salvation of the world.*

Also, be sure to tell yourself:

> *If I hold this grievance the light of the world will be hidden from me,*

if you are tempted to hold anything against anyone today.

DAY 12 — LESSON 74

There is no will but God's.

1. The idea for today can be regarded as the central thought toward which all our exercises are directed. God's is the only Will. When you have recognized this, you have recognized that your will is His. The belief that conflict is possible has gone. Peace has replaced the strange idea that you are torn by conflicting goals. As an expression of the Will of God, you have no goal but His.

2. There is great peace in today's idea, and the exercises for today are directed towards finding it. The idea itself is wholly true. Therefore it cannot give rise to illusions. Without illusions conflict is impossible. Let us try to recognize this today, and experience the peace this recognition brings.

3. Begin the longer practice periods by repeating these thoughts several times, slowly and with firm determination to understand what they mean, and to hold them in mind:

> *There is no will but God's. I cannot be in conflict.*

Then spend several minutes in adding some related thoughts, such as:

> *I am at peace.*
> *Nothing can disturb me. My will is God's.*
> *My will and God's are one.*
> *God wills peace for His Son.*

During this introductory phase, be sure to deal quickly with any conflict thoughts that may cross your mind. Tell yourself immediately:

> *There is no will but God's.*
> *These conflict thoughts are meaningless.*

4. If there is one conflict area that seems particularly difficult to resolve, single it out for special consideration. Think about it briefly but very specifically, identify the particular person or persons and the situation or situations involved, and tell yourself:

There is no will but God's. I share it with Him.
My conflicts about _____ cannot be real.

5. After you have cleared your mind in this way, close your eyes and try to experience the peace to which your reality entitles you. Sink into it and feel it closing around you. There may be some temptation to mistake these attempts for withdrawal, but the difference is easily detected. If you are succeeding, you will feel a deep sense of joy and an increased alertness, rather than a feeling of drowsiness and enervation.

6. Joy characterizes peace. By this experience will you recognize that you have reached it. If you feel yourself slipping off into withdrawal, quickly repeat the idea for today and try again. Do this as often as necessary. There is definite gain in refusing to allow retreat into withdrawal, even if you do not experience the peace you seek.

7. In the shorter periods, which should be undertaken at regular and predetermined intervals today, say to yourself:

There is no will but God's. I seek His peace today.

Then try to find what you are seeking. A minute or two every half an hour, with eyes closed if possible, would be well spent on this today.

DAY 13 — LESSON 78

Let miracles replace all grievances.

1. Perhaps it is not yet quite clear to you that each decision that you make is one between a grievance and a miracle. Each grievance stands like a dark shield of hate before the miracle it would conceal. And as you raise it up before your eyes, you will not see the miracle beyond. Yet all the while it waits for you in light, but you behold your grievances instead.

2. Today we go beyond the grievances, to look upon the miracle instead. We will reverse the way you see by not allowing sight to stop before it sees. We will not wait before the shield of hate, but lay it down and gently lift our eyes in silence to behold the Son of God.

3. He waits for you behind your grievances, and as you lay them down he will appear in shining light where each one stood before. For every grievance is a block to sight, and as it lifts you see the Son of God where he has always been. He stands in light, but you were in the dark. Each grievance made the darkness deeper, and you could not see.

4. Today we will attempt to see God's Son. We will not let ourselves be blind to him; we will not look upon our grievances. So is the seeing of the world reversed, as we look out toward truth, away from fear. We will select one person you have used as target for your grievances, and lay the grievances aside and look at him. Someone, perhaps, you fear and even hate; someone you think you love who angered you; someone you call a friend, but whom you see as difficult at times or hard to please, demanding, irritating or untrue to the ideal he should accept as his, according to the role you set for him.

5. You know the one to choose; his name has crossed your mind already. He will be the one of whom we ask God's Son be shown to you. Through seeing him behind the grievances that you have held against him, you will learn that what lay hidden while you saw him not is there in everyone, and can be seen. He who was enemy is more than friend when he is freed to take the holy role the Holy Spirit has assigned to him. Let him be savior unto you today. Such is his role in God your Father's plan.

6. Our longer practice periods today will see him in this role. You will attempt to hold him in your mind, first as you now consider him. You

will review his faults, the difficulties you have had with him, the pain he caused you, his neglect, and all the little and the larger hurts he gave. You will regard his body with its flaws and better points as well, and you will think of his mistakes and even of his "sins."

7. Then let us ask of Him Who knows this Son of God in his reality and truth, that we may look on him a different way, and see our savior shining in the light of true forgiveness, given unto us. We ask Him in the holy Name of God and of His Son, as holy as Himself:

> *Let me behold my savior in this one You have appointed as the one for me to ask to lead me to the holy light in which he stands, that I may join with him.*

The body's eyes are closed, and as you think of him who grieved you, let your mind be shown the light in him beyond your grievances.

8. What you have asked for cannot be denied. Your savior has been waiting long for this. He would be free, and make his freedom yours. The Holy Spirit leans from him to you, seeing no separation in God's Son. And what you see through Him will free you both. Be very quiet now, and look upon your shining savior. No dark grievances obscure the sight of him. You have allowed the Holy Spirit to express through him the role God gave Him that you might be saved.

9. God thanks you for these quiet times today in which you laid your images aside, and looked upon the miracle of love the Holy Spirit showed you in their place. The world and Heaven join in thanking you, for not one Thought of God but must rejoice as you are saved, and all the world with you.

10. We will remember this throughout the day, and take the role assigned to us as part of God's salvation plan, and not our own. Temptation falls away when we allow each one we meet to save us, and refuse to hide his light behind our grievances. To everyone you meet, and to the ones you think of or remember from the past, allow the role of savior to be given, that you may share it with him. For you both, and all the sightless ones as well, we pray:

> *Let miracles replace all grievances.*

DAY 14 — LESSON 94

I am as God created me.

1. Today we continue with the one idea which brings complete salvation; the one statement which makes all forms of temptation powerless; the one thought which renders the ego silent and entirely undone. You are as God created you. The sounds of this world are still, the sights of this world disappear, and all the thoughts that this world ever held are wiped away forever by this one idea. Here is salvation accomplished. Here is sanity restored.

2. True light is strength, and strength is sinlessness. If you remain as God created you, you must be strong and light must be in you. He Who ensured your sinlessness must be the guarantee of strength and light as well. You are as God created you. Darkness cannot obscure the glory of God's Son. You stand in light, strong in the sinlessness in which you were created, and in which you will remain throughout eternity.

3. Today we will again devote the first five minutes of each waking hour to the attempt to feel the truth in you. Begin these times of searching with these words:

I am as God created me.
I am His Son eternally.

Now try to reach the Son of God in you. This is the Self that never sinned, nor made an image to replace reality. This is the Self that never left Its home in God to walk the world uncertainly. This is the Self that knows no fear, nor could conceive of loss or suffering or death.

4. Nothing is required of you to reach this goal except to lay all idols and self-images aside; go past the list of attributes, both good and bad, you have ascribed to yourself; and wait in silent expectancy for the truth. God has Himself promised that it will be revealed to all who ask for it. You are asking now. You cannot fail because He cannot fail.

5. If you do not meet the requirement of practicing for the first five minutes of every hour, at least remind yourself hourly:

I am as God created me.
I am His Son eternally.

Tell yourself frequently today that you are as God created you. And be sure to respond to anyone who seems to irritate you with these words:

> *You are as God created you.*
> *You are His Son eternally.*

Make every effort to do the hourly exercises today. Each one you do will be a giant stride toward your release, and a milestone in learning the thought system which this course sets forth.

DAY 15 — LESSON 108

To give and to receive are one in truth.

1. Vision depends upon today's idea. The light is in it, for it reconciles all seeming opposites. And what is light except the resolution, born of peace, of all your conflicts and mistaken thoughts into one concept which is wholly true? Even that one will disappear, because the Thought behind it will appear instead to take its place. And now you are at peace forever, for the dream is over then.

2. True light that makes true vision possible is not the light the body's eyes behold. It is a state of mind that has become so unified that darkness cannot be perceived at all. And thus what is the same is seen as one, while what is not the same remains unnoticed, for it is not there.

3. This is the light that shows no opposites, and vision, being healed, has power to heal. This is the light that brings your peace of mind to other minds, to share it and be glad that they are one with you and with themselves. This is the light that heals because it brings single perception, based upon one frame of reference, from which one meaning comes.

4. Here are both giving and receiving seen as different aspects of one Thought whose truth does not depend on which is seen as first, nor which appears to be in second place. Here it is understood that both occur together, that the Thought remain complete. And in this understanding is the base on which all opposites are reconciled, because they are perceived from the same frame of reference which unifies this Thought.

5. One thought, completely unified, will serve to unify all thought. This is the same as saying one correction will suffice for all correction, or that to forgive one brother wholly is enough to bring salvation to all minds. For these are but some special cases of one law which holds for every kind of learning, if it be directed by the One Who knows the truth.

6. To learn that giving and receiving are the same has special usefulness, because it can be tried so easily and seen as true. And when this special case has proved it always works, in every circumstance where it is tried, the thought behind it can be generalized to other areas of doubt and double vision. And from there it will extend, and finally arrive at the one Thought which underlies them all.

7. Today we practice with the special case of giving and receiving. We will use this simple lesson in the obvious because it has results we cannot miss. To give is to receive. Today we will attempt to offer peace to everyone, and see how quickly peace returns to us. Light is tranquility, and in that peace is vision given us, and we can see.
8. So we begin the practice periods with the instruction for today, and say:

> *To give and to receive are one in truth.*
> *I will receive what I am giving now.*

Then close your eyes, and for five minutes think of what you would hold out to everyone, to have it yours. You might, for instance, say:

> *To everyone I offer quietness.*
> *To everyone I offer peace of mind.*
> *To everyone I offer gentleness.*

9. Say each one slowly and then pause a while, expecting to receive the gift you gave. And it will come to you in the amount in which you gave it. You will find you have exact return, for that is what you asked. It might be helpful, too, to think of one to whom to give your gifts. He represents the others, and through him you give to all.
10. Our very simple lesson for today will teach you much. Effect and cause will be far better understood from this time on, and we will make much faster progress now. Think of the exercises for today as quick advances in your learning, made still faster and more sure each time you say, "To give and to receive are one in truth."

DAY 16 — LESSON 109

I rest in God.

1. We ask for rest today, and quietness unshaken by the world's appearances. We ask for peace and stillness, in the midst of all the turmoil born of clashing dreams. We ask for safety and for happiness, although we seem to look on danger and on sorrow. And we have the thought that will answer our asking with what we request.

2. "I rest in God." This thought will bring to you the rest and quiet, peace and stillness, and the safety and the happiness you seek. "I rest in God." This thought has power to wake the sleeping truth in you, whose vision sees beyond appearances to that same truth in everyone and everything there is. Here is the end of suffering for all the world, and everyone who ever came and yet will come to linger for a while. Here is the thought in which the Son of God is born again, to recognize himself.

3. "I rest in God." Completely undismayed, this thought will carry you through storms and strife, past misery and pain, past loss and death, and onward to the certainty of God. There is no suffering it cannot heal. There is no problem that it cannot solve. And no appearance but will turn to truth before the eyes of you who rest in God.

4. This is the day of peace. You rest in God, and while the world is torn by winds of hate your rest remains completely undisturbed. Yours is the rest of truth. Appearances cannot intrude on you. You call to all to join you in your rest, and they will hear and come to you because you rest in God. They will not hear another voice than yours because you gave your voice to God, and now you rest in Him and let Him speak through you.

5. In Him you have no cares and no concerns, no burdens, no anxiety, no pain, no fear of future and no past regrets. In timelessness you rest, while time goes by without its touch upon you, for your rest can never change in any way at all. You rest today. And as you close your eyes, sink into stillness. Let these periods of rest and respite reassure your mind that all its frantic fantasies were but the dreams of fever that has passed away. Let it be still and thankfully accept its healing. No more fearful dreams will come, now that you rest in God. Take time today to slip away from dreams and into peace.

6. Each hour that you take your rest today, a tired mind is suddenly made glad, a bird with broken wings begins to sing, a stream long dry

begins to flow again. The world is born again each time you rest, and hourly remember that you came to bring the peace of God into the world, that it might take its rest along with you.

7. With each five minutes that you rest today, the world is nearer waking. And the time when rest will be the only thing there is comes closer to all worn and tired minds, too weary now to go their way alone. And they will hear the bird begin to sing and see the stream begin to flow again, with hope reborn and energy restored to walk with lightened steps along the road that suddenly seems easy as they go.

8. You rest within the peace of God today, and call upon your brothers from your rest to draw them to their rest, along with you. You will be faithful to your trust today, forgetting no one, bringing everyone into the boundless circle of your peace, the holy sanctuary where you rest. Open the temple doors and let them come from far across the world, and near as well; your distant brothers and your closest friends; bid them all enter here and rest with you.

9. You rest within the peace of God today, quiet and unafraid. Each brother comes to take his rest, and offer it to you. We rest together here, for thus our rest is made complete, and what we give today we have received already. Time is not the guardian of what we give today. We give to those unborn and those passed by, to every Thought of God, and to the Mind in which these Thoughts were born and where they rest. And we remind them of their resting place each time we tell ourselves, "I rest in God."

DAY 17 — LESSON 121

Forgiveness is the key to happiness.

1. Here is the answer to your search for peace. Here is the key to meaning in a world that seems to make no sense. Here is the way to safety in apparent dangers that appear to threaten you at every turn, and bring uncertainty to all your hopes of ever finding quietness and peace. Here are all questions answered; here the end of all uncertainty ensured at last.

2. The unforgiving mind is full of fear, and offers love no room to be itself; no place where it can spread its wings in peace and soar above the turmoil of the world. The unforgiving mind is sad, without the hope of respite and release from pain. It suffers and abides in misery, peering about in darkness, seeing not, yet certain of the danger lurking there.

3. The unforgiving mind is torn with doubt, confused about itself and all it sees; afraid and angry, weak and blustering, afraid to go ahead, afraid to stay, afraid to waken or to go to sleep, afraid of every sound, yet more afraid of stillness; terrified of darkness, yet more terrified at the approach of light. What can the unforgiving mind perceive but its damnation? What can it behold except the proof that all its sins are real?

4. The unforgiving mind sees no mistakes, but only sins. It looks upon the world with sightless eyes, and shrieks as it beholds its own projections rising to attack its miserable parody of life. It wants to live, yet wishes it were dead. It wants forgiveness, yet it sees no hope. It wants escape, yet can conceive of none because it sees the sinful everywhere.

5. The unforgiving mind is in despair, without the prospect of a future which can offer anything but more despair. Yet it regards its judgment of the world as irreversible, and does not see it has condemned itself to this despair. It thinks it cannot change, for what it sees bears witness that its judgment is correct. It does not ask, because it thinks it knows. It does not question, certain it is right.

6. Forgiveness is acquired. It is not inherent in the mind, which cannot sin. As sin is an idea you taught yourself, forgiveness must be learned by you as well, but from a Teacher other than yourself, Who represents the other Self in you. Through Him you learn how to forgive the self you think you made, and let it disappear. Thus

you return your mind as one to Him Who is your Self, and Who can never sin.

7. Each unforgiving mind presents you with an opportunity to teach your own how to forgive itself. Each one awaits release from hell through you, and turns to you imploringly for Heaven here and now. It has no hope, but you become its hope. And as its hope, do you become your own. The unforgiving mind must learn through your forgiveness that it has been saved from hell. And as you teach salvation, you will learn. Yet all your teaching and your learning will be not of you, but of the Teacher Who was given you to show the way to you.

8. Today we practice learning to forgive. If you are willing, you can learn today to take the key to happiness, and use it on your own behalf. We will devote ten minutes in the morning, and at night another ten, to learning how to give forgiveness and receive forgiveness, too.

9. The unforgiving mind does not believe that giving and receiving are the same. Yet we will try to learn today that they are one through practicing forgiveness toward one whom you think of as an enemy, and one whom you consider as a friend. And as you learn to see them both as one, we will extend the lesson to yourself, and see that their escape included yours.

10. Begin the longer practice periods by thinking of someone you do not like, who seems to irritate you, or to cause regret in you if you should meet him; one you actively despise, or merely try to overlook. It does not matter what the form your anger takes. You probably have chosen him already. He will do.

11. Now close your eyes and see him in your mind, and look at him a while. Try to perceive some light in him somewhere; a little gleam which you had never noticed. Try to find some little spark of brightness shining through the ugly picture that you hold of him. Look at this picture till you see a light somewhere within it, and then try to let this light extend until it covers him, and makes the picture beautiful and good.

12. Look at this changed perception for a while, and turn your mind to one you call a friend. Try to transfer the light you learned to see around your former "enemy" to him. Perceive him now as more than friend to you, for in that light his holiness shows you your savior, saved and saving, healed and whole.

13. Then let him offer you the light you see in him, and let your "enemy" and friend unite in blessing you with what you gave. Now are you one with them, and they with you. Now have you been

forgiven by yourself. Do not forget, throughout the day, the role forgiveness plays in bringing happiness to every unforgiving mind, with yours among them. Every hour tell yourself:

Forgiveness is the key to happiness. I will awaken from the dream that I am mortal, fallible and full of sin, and know I am the perfect Son of God.

DAY 18 — LESSON 122

Forgiveness offers everything I want.

1. What could you want forgiveness cannot give? Do you want peace? Forgiveness offers it. Do you want happiness, a quiet mind, a certainty of purpose, and a sense of worth and beauty that transcends the world? Do you want care and safety, and the warmth of sure protection always? Do you want a quietness that cannot be disturbed, a gentleness that never can be hurt, a deep abiding comfort, and a rest so perfect it can never be upset?

2. All this forgiveness offers you, and more. It sparkles on your eyes as you awake, and gives you joy with which to meet the day. It soothes your forehead while you sleep, and rests upon your eyelids so you see no dreams of fear and evil, malice and attack. And when you wake again, it offers you another day of happiness and peace. All this forgiveness offers you, and more.

3. Forgiveness lets the veil be lifted up that hides the face of Christ from those who look with unforgiving eyes upon the world. It lets you recognize the Son of God, and clears your memory of all dead thoughts so that remembrance of your Father can arise across the threshold of your mind. What would you want forgiveness cannot give? What gifts but these are worthy to be sought? What fancied value, trivial effect or transient promise, never to be kept, can hold more hope than what forgiveness brings?

4. Why would you seek an answer other than the answer that will answer everything? Here is the perfect answer, given to imperfect questions, meaningless requests, halfhearted willingness to hear, and less than halfway diligence and partial trust. Here is the answer! Seek for it no more. You will not find another one instead.

5. God's plan for your salvation cannot change, nor can it fail. Be thankful it remains exactly as He planned it. Changelessly it stands before you like an open door, with warmth and welcome calling from beyond the doorway, bidding you to enter in and make yourself at home, where you belong.

6. Here is the answer! Would you stand outside while all of Heaven waits for you within? Forgive and be forgiven. As you give you will receive. There is no plan but this for the salvation of the Son of God. Let us today rejoice that this is so, for here we have an answer, clear

and plain, beyond deceit in its simplicity. All the complexities the world has spun of fragile cobwebs disappear before the power and the majesty of this extremely simple statement of the truth.

7. Here is the answer! Do not turn away in aimless wandering again. Accept salvation now. It is the gift of God, and not the world. The world can give no gifts of any value to a mind that has received what God has given as its own. God wills salvation be received today, and that the intricacies of your dreams no longer hide their nothingness from you.

8. Open your eyes today and look upon a happy world of safety and of peace. Forgiveness is the means by which it comes to take the place of hell. In quietness it rises up to greet your open eyes, and fill your heart with deep tranquility as ancient truths, forever newly born, arise in your awareness. What you will remember then can never be described. Yet your forgiveness offers it to you.

9. Remembering the gifts forgiveness gives, we undertake our practicing today with hope and faith that this will be the day salvation will be ours. Earnestly and gladly will we seek for it today, aware we hold the key within our hands, accepting Heaven's answer to the hell we made, but where we would remain no more.

10. Morning and evening do we gladly give a quarter of an hour to the search in which the end of hell is guaranteed. Begin in hopefulness, for we have reached the turning point at which the road becomes far easier. And now the way is short that yet we travel. We are close indeed to the appointed ending of the dream.

11. Sink into happiness as you begin these practice periods, for they hold out the sure rewards of questions answered and what your acceptance of the answer brings. Today it will be given you to feel the peace forgiveness offers, and the joy the lifting of the veil holds out to you.

12. Before the light you will receive today the world will fade until it disappears, and you will see another world arise you have no words to picture. Now we walk directly into light, and we receive the gifts that have been held in store for us since time began, kept waiting for today.

13. Forgiveness offers everything you want. Today all things you want are given you. Let not your gifts recede throughout the day, as you return again to meet a world of shifting change and bleak appearances. Retain your gifts in clear awareness as you see the changeless in the heart of change; the light of truth behind appearances.

14. Be tempted not to let your gifts slip by and drift into forgetfulness, but hold them firmly in your mind by your attempts to think of them at least a minute as each quarter of an hour passes by. Remind yourself how precious are these gifts with this reminder, which has power to hold your gifts in your awareness through the day:

> *Forgiveness offers everything I want.*
> *Today I have accepted this as true.*
> *Today I have received the gifts of God.*

DAY 19— LESSON 124

Let me remember I am one with God.

1. Today we will again give thanks for our Identity in God. Our home is safe, protection guaranteed in all we do, power and strength available to us in all our undertakings. We can fail in nothing. Everything we touch takes on a shining light that blesses and that heals. At one with God and with the universe we go our way rejoicing, with the thought that God Himself goes everywhere with us.

2. How holy are our minds! And everything we see reflects the holiness within the mind at one with God and with itself. How easily do errors disappear, and death give place to everlasting life. Our shining footprints point the way to truth, for God is our Companion as we walk the world a little while. And those who come to follow us will recognize the way because the light we carry stays behind, yet still remains with us as we walk on.

3. What we receive is our eternal gift to those who follow after, and to those who went before or stayed with us a while. And God, Who loves us with the equal love in which we were created, smiles on us and offers us the happiness we gave.

4. Today we will not doubt His Love for us, nor question His protection and His care. No meaningless anxieties can come between our faith and our awareness of His Presence. We are one with Him today in recognition and remembrance. We feel Him in our hearts. Our minds contain His Thoughts; our eyes behold His loveliness in all we look upon. Today we see only the loving and the lovable.

5. We see it in appearances of pain, and pain gives way to peace. We see it in the frantic, in the sad and the distressed, the lonely and afraid, who are restored to the tranquility and peace of mind in which they were created. And we see it in the dying and the dead as well, restoring them to life. All this we see because we saw it first within ourselves.

6. No miracle can ever be denied to those who know that they are one with God. No thought of theirs but has the power to heal all forms of suffering in anyone, in times gone by and times as yet to come, as easily as in the ones who walk beside them now. Their thoughts are timeless, and apart from distance as apart from time.

7. We join in this awareness as we say that we are one with God. For in these words we say as well that we are saved and healed;

that we can save and heal accordingly. We have accepted, and we now would give. For we would keep the gifts our Father gave. Today we would experience ourselves at one with Him, so that the world may share our recognition of reality. In our experience the world is freed. As we deny our separation from our Father, it is healed along with us.

8. Peace be to you today. Secure your peace by practicing awareness you are one with your Creator, as He is with you. Sometime today, whenever it seems best, devote a half an hour to the thought that you are one with God. This is our first attempt at an extended period for which we give no rules nor special words to guide your meditation. We will trust God's Voice to speak as He sees fit today, certain He will not fail. Abide with Him this half an hour. He will do the rest.

9. Your benefit will not be less if you believe that nothing happens. You may not be ready to accept the gain today. Yet sometime, somewhere, it will come to you, nor will you fail to recognize it when it dawns with certainty upon your mind. This half an hour will be framed in gold, with every minute like a diamond set around the mirror that this exercise will offer you. And you will see Christ's face upon it, in reflection of your own.

10. Perhaps today, perhaps tomorrow, you will see your own trans-figuration in the glass this holy half an hour will hold out to you, to look upon yourself. When you are ready you will find it there, within your mind and waiting to be found. You will remember then the thought to which you gave this half an hour, thankfully aware no time was ever better spent.

11. Perhaps today, perhaps tomorrow, you will look into this glass, and understand the sinless light you see belongs to you; the loveliness you look on is your own. Count this half hour as your gift to God, in certainty that His return will be a sense of love you cannot understand, a joy too deep for you to comprehend, a sight too holy for the body's eyes to see. And yet you can be sure someday, perhaps today, perhaps tomorrow, you will understand and comprehend and see.

12. Add further jewels to the golden frame that holds the mirror offered you today, by hourly repeating to yourself:

> *Let me remember I am one with God, at one with*
> *all my brothers and my Self, in everlasting holiness*
> *and peace.*

DAY 20— LESSON 126

All that I give is given to myself.

1. Today's idea, completely alien to the ego and the thinking of the world, is crucial to the thought reversal that this course will bring about. If you believed this statement, there would be no problem in complete forgiveness, certainty of goal, and sure direction. You would understand the means by which salvation comes to you, and would not hesitate to use it now.

2. Let us consider what you do believe, in place of this idea. It seems to you that other people are apart from you, and able to behave in ways which have no bearing on your thoughts, nor yours on theirs. Therefore, your attitudes have no effect on them, and their appeals for help are not in any way related to your own. You further think that they can sin without affecting your perception of yourself, while you can judge their sin, and yet remain apart from condemnation and at peace.

3. When you "forgive" a sin, there is no gain to you directly. You give charity to one unworthy, merely to point out that you are better, on a higher plane than he whom you forgive. He has not earned your charitable tolerance, which you bestow on one unworthy of the gift, because his sins have lowered him beneath a true equality with you. He has no claim on your forgiveness. It holds out a gift to him, but hardly to yourself.

4. Thus is forgiveness basically unsound; a charitable whim, benevolent yet undeserved, a gift bestowed at times, at other times withheld. Unmerited, withholding it is just, nor is it fair that you should suffer when it is withheld. The sin that you forgive is not your own. Someone apart from you committed it. And if you then are gracious unto him by giving him what he does not deserve, the gift is no more yours than was his sin.

5. If this be true, forgiveness has no grounds on which to rest dependably and sure. It is an eccentricity, in which you sometimes choose to give indulgently an undeserved reprieve. Yet it remains your right to let the sinner not escape the justified repayment for his sin. Think you the Lord of Heaven would allow the world's salvation to depend on this? Would not His care for you be small indeed, if your salvation rested on a whim?

6. You do not understand forgiveness. As you see it, it is but a check upon overt attack, without requiring correction in your mind. It cannot

give you peace as you perceive it. It is not a means for your release from what you see in someone other than yourself. It has no power to restore your unity with him to your awareness. It is not what God intended it to be for you.

7. Not having given Him the gift He asks of you, you cannot recognize His gifts, and think He has not given them to you. Yet would He ask you for a gift unless it was for you? Could He be satisfied with empty gestures, and evaluate such petty gifts as worthy of His Son? Salvation is a better gift than this. And true forgiveness, as the means by which it is attained, must heal the mind that gives, for giving is receiving. What remains as unreceived has not been given, but what has been given must have been received.

8. Today we try to understand the truth that giver and receiver are the same. You will need help to make this meaningful, because it is so alien to the thoughts to which you are accustomed. But the Help you need is there. Give Him your faith today, and ask Him that He share your practicing in truth today. And if you only catch a tiny glimpse of the release that lies in the idea we practice for today, this is a day of glory for the world.

9. Give fifteen minutes twice today to the attempt to understand today's idea. It is the thought by which forgiveness takes its proper place in your priorities. It is the thought that will release your mind from every bar to what forgiveness means, and let you realize its worth to you.

10. In silence, close your eyes upon the world that does not understand forgiveness, and seek sanctuary in the quiet place where thoughts are changed and false beliefs laid by. Repeat today's idea, and ask for help in understanding what it really means. Be willing to be taught. Be glad to hear the Voice of truth and healing speak to you, and you will understand the words He speaks, and recognize He speaks your words to you.

11. As often as you can, remind yourself you have a goal today; an aim which makes this day of special value to yourself and all your brothers. Do not let your mind forget this goal for long, but tell yourself:

> *All that I give is given to myself. The Help I need to*
> *learn that this is true is with me now. And I will trust*
> *in Him.*

Then spend a quiet moment, opening your mind to His correction and His Love. And what you hear of Him you will believe, for what He gives will be received by you.

DAY 21— LESSON 127

There is no love but God's.

1. Perhaps you think that different kinds of love are possible. Perhaps you think there is a kind of love for this, a kind for that; a way of loving one, another way of loving still another. Love is one. It has no separate parts and no degrees; no kinds nor levels, no divergencies and no distinctions. It is like itself, unchanged throughout. It never alters with a person or a circumstance. It is the Heart of God, and also of His Son.

2. Love's meaning is obscure to anyone who thinks that love can change. He does not see that changing love must be impossible. And thus he thinks that he can love at times, and hate at other times. He also thinks that love can be bestowed on one, and yet remain itself although it is withheld from others. To believe these things of love is not to understand it. If it could make such distinctions, it would have to judge between the righteous and the sinner, and perceive the Son of God in separate parts.

3. Love cannot judge. As it is one itself, it looks on all as one. Its meaning lies in oneness. And it must elude the mind that thinks of it as partial or in part. There is no love but God's, and all of love is His. There is no other principle that rules where love is not. Love is a law without an opposite. Its wholeness is the power holding everything as one, the link between the Father and the Son which holds Them both forever as the same.

4. No course whose purpose is to teach you to remember what you really are could fail to emphasize that there can never be a difference in what you really are and what love is. Love's meaning is your own, and shared by God Himself. For what you are is what He is. There is no love but His, and what He is, is everything there is. There is no limit placed upon Himself, and so are you unlimited as well.

5. No law the world obeys can help you grasp love's meaning. What the world believes was made to hide love's meaning, and to keep it dark and secret. There is not one principle the world upholds but violates the truth of what love is, and what you are as well.

6. Seek not within the world to find your Self. Love is not found in darkness and in death. Yet it is perfectly apparent to the eyes that see and ears that hear love's Voice. Today we practice making free your mind of all the laws you think you must obey; of all the limits under

which you live, and all the changes that you think are part of human destiny. Today we take the largest single step this course requests in your advance towards its established goal.

7. If you achieve the faintest glimmering of what love means today, you have advanced in distance without measure and in time beyond the count of years to your release. Let us together, then, be glad to give some time to God today, and understand there is no better use for time than this.

8. For fifteen minutes twice today escape from every law in which you now believe. Open your mind and rest. The world that seems to hold you prisoner can be escaped by anyone who does not hold it dear. Withdraw all value you have placed upon its meager offerings and senseless gifts, and let the gift of God replace them all.

9. Call to your Father, certain that His Voice will answer. He Himself has promised this. And He Himself will place a spark of truth within your mind wherever you give up a false belief, a dark illusion of your own reality and what love means. He will shine through your idle thoughts today, and help you understand the truth of love. In loving gentleness He will abide with you, as you allow His Voice to teach love's meaning to your clean and open mind. And He will bless the lesson with His Love.

10. Today the legion of the future years of waiting for salvation disappears before the timelessness of what you learn. Let us give thanks today that we are spared a future like the past. Today we leave the past behind us, nevermore to be remembered. And we raise our eyes upon a different present, where a future dawns unlike the past in every attribute.

11. The world in infancy is newly born. And we will watch it grow in health and strength, to shed its blessing upon all who come to learn to cast aside the world they thought was made in hate to be love's enemy. Now are they all made free, along with us. Now are they all our brothers in God's Love.

12. We will remember them throughout the day, because we cannot leave a part of us outside our love if we would know our Self. At least three times an hour think of one who makes the journey with you, and who came to learn what you must learn. And as he comes to mind, give him this message from your Self:

> *I bless you, brother, with the Love of God, which I would share with you. For I would learn the joyous lesson that there is no love but God's and yours and mine and everyone's.*

DAY 22— LESSON 134

Let me perceive forgiveness as it is.

1. Let us review the meaning of "forgive," for it is apt to be distorted and to be perceived as something that entails an unfair sacrifice of righteous wrath, a gift unjustified and undeserved, and a complete denial of the truth. In such a view, forgiveness must be seen as mere eccentric folly, and this course appear to rest salvation on a whim.

2. This twisted view of what forgiveness means is easily corrected, when you can accept the fact that pardon is not asked for what is true. It must be limited to what is false. It is irrelevant to everything except illusions. Truth is God's creation, and to pardon that is meaningless. All truth belongs to Him, reflects His laws and radiates His Love. Does this need pardon? How can you forgive the sinless and eternally benign?

3. The major difficulty that you find in genuine forgiveness on your part is that you still believe you must forgive the truth, and not illusions. You conceive of pardon as a vain attempt to look past what is there; to overlook the truth, in an unfounded effort to deceive yourself by making an illusion true. This twisted viewpoint but reflects the hold that the idea of sin retains as yet upon your mind, as you regard yourself.

4. Because you think your sins are real, you look on pardon as deception. For it is impossible to think of sin as true and not believe forgiveness is a lie. Thus is forgiveness really but a sin, like all the rest. It says the truth is false, and smiles on the corrupt as if they were as blameless as the grass; as white as snow. It is delusional in what it thinks it can accomplish. It would see as right the plainly wrong; the loathsome as the good.

5. Pardon is no escape in such a view. It merely is a further sign that sin is unforgivable, at best to be concealed, denied or called another name, for pardon is a treachery to truth. Guilt cannot be forgiven. If you sin, your guilt is everlasting. Those who are forgiven from the view their sins are real are pitifully mocked and twice condemned; first, by themselves for what they think they did, and once again by those who pardon them.

6. It is sin's unreality that makes forgiveness natural and wholly sane, a deep relief to those who offer it; a quiet blessing where it is received. It does not countenance illusions, but collects them lightly,

with a little laugh, and gently lays them at the feet of truth. And there they disappear entirely.

7. Forgiveness is the only thing that stands for truth in the illusions of the world. It sees their nothingness, and looks straight through the thousand forms in which they may appear. It looks on lies, but it is not deceived. It does not heed the self-accusing shrieks of sinners mad with guilt. It looks on them with quiet eyes, and merely says to them, "My brother, what you think is not the truth."

8. The strength of pardon is its honesty, which is so uncorrupted that it sees illusions as illusions, not as truth. It is because of this that it becomes the undeceiver in the face of lies; the great restorer of the simple truth. By its ability to overlook what is not there, it opens up the way to truth, which has been blocked by dreams of guilt. Now are you free to follow in the way your true forgiveness opens up to you. For if one brother has received this gift of you, the door is open to yourself.

9. There is a very simple way to find the door to true forgiveness, and perceive it open wide in welcome. When you feel that you are tempted to accuse someone of sin in any form, do not allow your mind to dwell on what you think he did, for that is self-deception. Ask instead, "Would I accuse myself of doing this?"

10. Thus will you see alternatives for choice in terms that render choosing meaningful, and keep your mind as free of guilt and pain as God Himself intended it to be, and as it is in truth. It is but lies that would condemn. In truth is innocence the only thing there is. Forgiveness stands between illusions and the truth; between the world you see and that which lies beyond; between the hell of guilt and Heaven's gate.

11. Across this bridge, as powerful as love which laid its blessing on it, are all dreams of evil and of hatred and attack brought silently to truth. They are not kept to swell and bluster, and to terrify the foolish dreamer who believes in them. He has been gently wakened from his dream by understanding what he thought he saw was never there. And now he cannot feel that all escape has been denied to him.

12. He does not have to fight to save himself. He does not have to kill the dragons which he thought pursued him. Nor need he erect the heavy walls of stone and iron doors he thought would make him safe. He can remove the ponderous and useless armor made to chain his mind to fear and misery. His step is light, and as he lifts his foot to stride ahead a star is left behind, to point the way to those who follow him.

13. Forgiveness must be practiced, for the world cannot perceive its meaning, nor provide a guide to teach you its beneficence. There is no thought in all the world that leads to any understanding of the laws it follows, nor the Thought that it reflects. It is as alien to the world as is your own reality. And yet it joins your mind with the reality in you.

14. Today we practice true forgiveness, that the time of joining be no more delayed. For we would meet with our reality in freedom and in peace. Our practicing becomes the footsteps lighting up the way for all our brothers, who will follow us to the reality we share with them. That this may be accomplished, let us give a quarter of an hour twice today, and spend it with the Guide Who understands the meaning of forgiveness, and was sent to us to teach it. Let us ask of Him:

Let me perceive forgiveness as it is.

15. Then choose one brother as He will direct, and catalogue his "sins," as one by one they cross your mind. Be certain not to dwell on any one of them, but realize that you are using his "offenses" but to save the world from all ideas of sin. Briefly consider all the evil things you thought of him, and each time ask yourself, "Would I condemn myself for doing this?"

16. Let him be freed from all the thoughts you had of sin in him. And now you are prepared for freedom. If you have been practicing thus far in willingness and honesty, you will begin to sense a lifting up, a lightening of weight across your chest, a deep and certain feeling of relief. The time remaining should be given to experiencing the escape from all the heavy chains you sought to lay upon your brother, but were laid upon yourself.

17. Forgiveness should be practiced through the day, for there will still be many times when you forget its meaning and attack yourself. When this occurs, allow your mind to see through this illusion as you tell yourself:

Let me perceive forgiveness as it is. Would I accuse myself of doing this? I will not lay this chain upon myself.

In everything you do remember this:

No one is crucified alone, and yet no one can enter Heaven by himself.

DAY 23 — LESSON 139

I will accept Atonement for myself.

1. Here is the end of choice. For here we come to a decision to accept ourselves as God created us. And what is choice except uncertainty of what we are? There is no doubt that is not rooted here. There is no question but reflects this one. There is no conflict that does not entail the single, simple question, "What am I?"

2. Yet who could ask this question except one who has refused to recognize himself? Only refusal to accept yourself could make the question seem to be sincere. The only thing that can be surely known by any living thing is what it is. From this one point of certainty, it looks on other things as certain as itself.

3. Uncertainty about what you must be is self-deception on a scale so vast, its magnitude can hardly be conceived. To be alive and not to know yourself is to believe that you are really dead. For what is life except to be yourself, and what but you can be alive instead? Who is the doubter? What is it he doubts? Whom does he question? Who can answer him?

4. He merely states that he is not himself, and therefore, being something else, becomes a questioner of what that something is. Yet he could never be alive at all unless he knew the answer. If he asks as if he does not know, it merely shows he does not want to be the thing he is. He has accepted it because he lives; has judged against it and denied its worth, and has decided that he does not know the only certainty by which he lives.

5. Thus he becomes uncertain of his life, for what it is has been denied by him. It is for this denial that you need Atonement. Your denial made no change in what you are. But you have split your mind into what knows and does not know the truth. You are yourself. There is no doubt of this. And yet you doubt it. But you do not ask what part of you can really doubt yourself. It cannot really be a part of you that asks this question. For it asks of one who knows the answer. Were it part of you, then certainty would be impossible.

6. Atonement remedies the strange idea that it is possible to doubt yourself, and be unsure of what you really are. This is the depth of madness. Yet it is the universal question of the world. What does this

mean except the world is mad? Why share its madness in the sad belief that what is universal here is true?

7. Nothing the world believes is true. It is a place whose purpose is to be a home where those who claim they do not know themselves can come to question what it is they are. And they will come again until the time Atonement is accepted, and they learn it is impossible to doubt yourself, and not to be aware of what you are.

8. Only acceptance can be asked of you, for what you are is certain. It is set forever in the holy Mind of God, and in your own. It is so far beyond all doubt and question that to ask what it must be is all the proof you need to show that you believe the contradiction that you know not what you cannot fail to know. Is this a question, or a statement which denies itself in statement? Let us not allow our holy minds to occupy themselves with senseless musings such as this.

9. We have a mission here. We did not come to reinforce the madness that we once believed in. Let us not forget the goal that we accepted. It is more than just our happiness alone we came to gain. What we accept as what we are proclaims what everyone must be, along with us. Fail not your brothers, or you fail yourself. Look lovingly on them, that they may know that they are part of you, and you of them.

10. This does Atonement teach, and demonstrates the Oneness of God's Son is unassailed by his belief he knows not what he is. Today accept Atonement, not to change reality, but merely to accept the truth about yourself, and go your way rejoicing in the endless Love of God. It is but this that we are asked to do. It is but this that we will do today.

11. Five minutes in the morning and at night we will devote to dedicate our minds to our assignment for today. We start with this review of what our mission is:

> *I will accept Atonement for myself,*
> *for I remain as God created me.*

We have not lost the knowledge that God gave to us when He created us like Him. We can remember it for everyone, for in creation are all minds as one. And in our memory is the recall how dear our brothers are to us in truth, how much a part of us is every mind, how faithful they have really been to us, and how our Father's Love contains them all.

12. In thanks for all creation, in the Name of its Creator and His Oneness with all aspects of creation, we repeat our dedication to our cause today each hour, as we lay aside all thoughts that would distract us from our holy aim. For several minutes let your mind be cleared of all the foolish cobwebs which the world would weave around the holy Son of God. And learn the fragile nature of the chains that seem to keep the knowledge of yourself apart from your awareness, as you say:

> *I will accept Atonement for myself,*
> *for I remain as God created me.*

DAY 24 — LESSON 155

I will step back and let Him lead the way.

1. There is a way of living in the world that is not here, although it seems to be. You do not change appearance, though you smile more frequently. Your forehead is serene; your eyes are quiet. And the ones who walk the world as you do recognize their own. Yet those who have not yet perceived the way will recognize you also, and believe that you are like them, as you were before.

2. The world is an illusion. Those who choose to come to it are seeking for a place where they can be illusions, and avoid their own reality. Yet when they find their own reality is even here, then they step back and let it lead the way. What other choice is really theirs to make? To let illusions walk ahead of truth is madness. But to let illusion sink behind the truth and let the truth stand forth as what it is, is merely sanity.

3. This is the simple choice we make today. The mad illusion will remain awhile in evidence, for those to look upon who chose to come, and have not yet rejoiced to find they were mistaken in their choice. They cannot learn directly from the truth, because they have denied that it is so. And so they need a Teacher Who perceives their madness, but Who still can look beyond illusion to the simple truth in them.

4. If truth demanded they give up the world, it would appear to them as if it asked the sacrifice of something that is real. Many have chosen to renounce the world while still believing its reality. And they have suffered from a sense of loss, and have not been released accordingly. Others have chosen nothing but the world, and they have suffered from a sense of loss still deeper, which they did not understand.

5. Between these paths there is another road that leads away from loss of every kind, for sacrifice and deprivation both are quickly left behind. This is the way appointed for you now. You walk this path as others walk, nor do you seem to be distinct from them, although you are indeed. Thus can you serve them while you serve yourself, and set their footsteps on the way that God has opened up to you, and them through you.

6. Illusion still appears to cling to you, that you may reach them. Yet it has stepped back. And it is not illusion that they hear you speak of, nor illusion that you bring their eyes to look on and their minds to grasp. Nor can the truth, which walks ahead of you, speak to them

through illusions, for the road leads past illusion now, while on the way you call to them, that they may follow you.

7. All roads will lead to this one in the end. For sacrifice and deprivation are paths that lead nowhere, choices for defeat, and aims that will remain impossible. All this steps back as truth comes forth in you, to lead your brothers from the ways of death, and set them on the way to happiness. Their suffering is but illusion. Yet they need a guide to lead them out of it, for they mistake illusion for the truth.

8. Such is salvation's call, and nothing more. It asks that you accept the truth, and let it go before you, lighting up the path of ransom from illusion. It is not a ransom with a price. There is no cost, but only gain. Illusion can but seem to hold in chains the holy Son of God. It is but from illusions he is saved. As they step back, he finds himself again.

9. Walk safely now, yet carefully, because this path is new to you. And you may find that you are tempted still to walk ahead of truth, and let illusions be your guide. Your holy brothers have been given you, to follow in your footsteps as you walk with certainty of purpose to the truth. It goes before you now, that they may see something with which they can identify; something they understand to lead the way.

10. Yet at the journey's ending there will be no gap, no distance between truth and you. And all illusions walking in the way you travelled will be gone from you as well, with nothing left to keep the truth apart from God's completion, holy as Himself. Step back in faith and let truth lead the way. You know not where you go. But One Who knows goes with you. Let Him lead you with the rest.

11. When dreams are over, time has closed the door on all the things that pass and miracles are purposeless, the holy Son of God will make no journeys. There will be no wish to be illusion rather than the truth. And we step forth toward this, as we progress along the way that truth points out to us. This is our final journey, which we make for everyone. We must not lose our way. For as truth goes before us, so it goes before our brothers who will follow us.

12. We walk to God. Pause and reflect on this. Could any way be holier, or more deserving of your effort, of your love and of your full intent? What way could give you more than everything, or offer less and still content the holy Son of God? We walk to God. The truth that walks before us now is one with Him, and leads us to where He has always been. What way but this could be a path that you would choose instead?

13. Your feet are safely set upon the road that leads the world to God. Look not to ways that seem to lead you elsewhere. Dreams are not a worthy guide for you who are God's Son. Forget not He has placed His Hand in yours, and given you your brothers in His trust that you are worthy of His trust in you. He cannot be deceived. His trust has made your pathway certain and your goal secure. You will not fail your brothers nor your Self.

14. And now He asks but that you think of Him a while each day, that He may speak to you and tell you of His Love, reminding you how great His trust; how limitless His Love. In your Name and His Own, which are the same, we practice gladly with this thought today:

> *I will step back and let Him lead the way,*
> *for I would walk along the road to Him.*

DAY 25 — LESSON 157

Into His Presence would I enter now.

1. This is a day of silence and of trust. It is a special time of promise in your calendar of days. It is a time Heaven has set apart to shine upon, and cast a timeless light upon this day, when echoes of eternity are heard. This day is holy, for it ushers in a new experience; a different kind of feeling and awareness. You have spent long days and nights in celebrating death. Today you learn to feel the joy of life.

2. This is another crucial turning point in the curriculum. We add a new dimension now; a fresh experience that sheds a light on all that we have learned already, and prepares us for what we have yet to learn. It brings us to the door where learning ceases, and we catch a glimpse of what lies past the highest reaches it can possibly attain. It leaves us here an instant, and we go beyond it, sure of our direction and our only goal.

3. Today it will be given you to feel a touch of Heaven, though you will return to paths of learning. Yet you have come far enough along the way to alter time sufficiently to rise above its laws, and walk into eternity a while. This you will learn to do increasingly, as every lesson, faithfully rehearsed, brings you more swiftly to this holy place and leaves you, for a moment, to your Self.

4. He will direct your practicing today, for what you ask for now is what He wills. And having joined your will with His this day, what you are asking must be given you. Nothing is needed but today's idea to light your mind, and let it rest in still anticipation and in quiet joy, wherein you quickly leave the world behind.

5. From this day forth, your ministry takes on a genuine devotion, and a glow that travels from your fingertips to those you touch, and blesses those you look upon. A vision reaches everyone you meet, and everyone you think of, or who thinks of you. For your experience today will so transform your mind that it becomes the touchstone for the holy Thoughts of God.

6. Your body will be sanctified today, its only purpose being now to bring the vision of what you experience this day to light the world. We cannot give experience like this directly. Yet it leaves a vision in our eyes which we can offer everyone, that he may come the sooner

to the same experience in which the world is quietly forgot, and Heaven is remembered for a while.

7. As this experience increases and all goals but this become of little worth, the world to which you will return becomes a little closer to the end of time; a little more like Heaven in its ways; a little nearer its deliverance. And you who bring it light will come to see the light more sure; the vision more distinct. The time will come when you will not return in the same form in which you now appear, for you will have no need of it. Yet now it has a purpose, and will serve it well.

8. Today we will embark upon a course you have not dreamed of. But the Holy One, the Giver of the happy dreams of life, Translator of perception into truth, the holy Guide to Heaven given you, has dreamed for you this journey which you make and start today, with the experience this day holds out to you to be your own.

9. Into Christ's Presence will we enter now, serenely unaware of everything except His shining face and perfect Love. The vision of His face will stay with you, but there will be an instant which transcends all vision, even this, the holiest. This you will never teach, for you attained it not through learning. Yet the vision speaks of your rememberance of what you knew that instant, and will surely know again.

DAY 26 — LESSON 158

Today I learn to give as I receive.

1. What has been given you? The knowledge that you are a mind, in Mind and purely mind, sinless forever, wholly unafraid, because you were created out of love. Nor have you left your Source, remaining as you were created. This was given you as knowledge which you cannot lose. It was given as well to every living thing, for by that knowledge only does it live.

2. You have received all this. No one who walks the world but has received it. It is not this knowledge which you give, for that is what creation gave. All this cannot be learned. What, then, are you to learn to give today? Our lesson yesterday evoked a theme found early in the text. Experience cannot be shared directly, in the way that vision can. The revelation that the Father and the Son are one will come in time to every mind. Yet is that time determined by the mind itself, not taught.

3. The time is set already. It appears to be quite arbitrary. Yet there is no step along the road that anyone takes but by chance. It has already been taken by him, although he has not yet embarked on it. For time but seems to go in one direction. We but undertake a journey that is over. Yet it seems to have a future still unknown to us.

4. Time is a trick, a sleight of hand, a vast illusion in which figures come and go as if by magic. Yet there is a plan behind appearances that does not change. The script is written. When experience will come to end your doubting has been set. For we but see the journey from the point at which it ended, looking back on it, imagining we make it once again; reviewing mentally what has gone by.

5. A teacher does not give experience, because he did not learn it. It revealed itself to him at its appointed time. But vision is his gift. This he can give directly, for Christ's knowledge is not lost, because He has a vision He can give to anyone who asks. The Father's Will and His are joined in knowledge. Yet there is a vision which the Holy Spirit sees because the Mind of Christ beholds it too.

6. Here is the joining of the world of doubt and shadows made with the intangible. Here is a quiet place within the world made holy by forgiveness and by love. Here are all contradictions reconciled, for

here the journey ends. Experience—unlearned, untaught, unseen— is merely there. This is beyond our goal, for it transcends what needs to be accomplished. Our concern is with Christ's vision. This we can attain.

7. Christ's vision has one law. It does not look upon a body, and mistake it for the Son whom God created. It beholds a light beyond the body; an idea beyond what can be touched, a purity undimmed by errors, pitiful mistakes, and fearful thoughts of guilt from dreams of sin. It sees no separation. And it looks on everyone, on every circumstance, all happenings and all events, without the slightest fading of the light it sees.

8. This can be taught; and must be taught by all who would achieve it. It requires but the recognition that the world can not give anything that faintly can compare with this in value; nor set up a goal that does not merely disappear when this has been perceived. And this you give today: See no one as a body. Greet him as the Son of God he is, acknowledging that he is one with you in holiness.

9. Thus are his sins forgiven him, for Christ has vision that has power to overlook them all. In His forgiveness are they gone. Unseen by One they merely disappear, because a vision of the holiness that lies beyond them comes to take their place. It matters not what form they took, nor how enormous they appeared to be, nor who seemed to be hurt by them. They are no more. And all effects they seemed to have are gone with them, undone and never to be done.

10. Thus do you learn to give as you receive. And thus Christ's vision looks on you as well. This lesson is not difficult to learn, if you remember in your brother you but see yourself. If he be lost in sin, so must you be; if you see light in him, your sins have been forgiven by yourself. Each brother whom you meet today provides another chance to let Christ's vision shine on you, and offer you the peace of God.

11. It matters not when revelation comes, for that is not of time. Yet time has still one gift to give, in which true knowledge is reflected in a way so accurate its image shares its unseen holiness; its likeness shines with its immortal love. We practice seeing with the eyes of Christ today. And by the holy gifts we give, Christ's vision looks upon ourselves as well.

DAY 27 — LESSON 159

I give the miracles I have received.

1. No one can give what he has not received. To give a thing requires first you have it in your own possession. Here the laws of Heaven and the world agree. But here they also separate. The world believes that to possess a thing, it must be kept. Salvation teaches otherwise. To give is how to recognize you have received. It is the proof that what you have is yours.

2. You understand that you are healed when you give healing. You accept forgiveness as accomplished in yourself when you forgive. You recognize your brother as yourself, and thus do you perceive that you are whole. There is no miracle you cannot give, for all are given you. Receive them now by opening the storehouse of your mind where they are laid, and giving them away.

3. Christ's vision is a miracle. It comes from far beyond itself, for it reflects eternal love and the rebirth of love which never dies, but has been kept obscure. Christ's vision pictures Heaven, for it sees a world so like to Heaven that what God created perfect can be mirrored there. The darkened glass the world presents can show but twisted images in broken parts. The real world pictures Heaven's innocence.

4. Christ's vision is the miracle in which all miracles are born. It is their source, remaining with each miracle you give, and yet remaining yours. It is the bond by which the giver and receiver are united in extension here on earth, as they are one in Heaven. Christ beholds no sin in anyone. And in His sight the sinless are as one. Their holiness was given by His Father and Himself.

5. Christ's vision is the bridge between the worlds. And in its power can you safely trust to carry you from this world into one made holy by forgiveness. Things which seem quite solid here are merely shadows there; transparent, faintly seen, at times forgot, and never able to obscure the light that shines beyond them. Holiness has been restored to vision, and the blind can see.

6. This is the Holy Spirit's single gift; the treasure house to which you can appeal with perfect certainty for all the things that can contribute to your happiness. All are laid here already. All can be received but for the asking. Here the door is never locked, and no one is denied his least

request or his most urgent need. There is no sickness not already healed, no lack unsatisfied, no need unmet within this golden treasury of Christ.

7. Here does the world remember what was lost when it was made. For here it is repaired, made new again, but in a different light. What was to be the home of sin becomes the center of redemption and the hearth of mercy, where the suffering are healed and welcome. No one will be turned away from this new home, where his salvation waits. No one is stranger to him. No one asks for anything of him except the gift of his acceptance of his welcoming.

8. Christ's vision is the holy ground in which the lilies of forgiveness set their roots. This is their home. They can be brought from here back to the world, but they can never grow in its unnourishing and shallow soil. They need the light and warmth and kindly care Christ's charity provides. They need the love with which He looks on them. And they become His messengers, who give as they received.

9. Take from His storehouse, that its treasures may increase. His lilies do not leave their home when they are carried back into the world. Their roots remain. They do not leave their source, but carry its beneficence with them, and turn the world into a garden like the one they came from, and to which they go again with added fragrance. Now are they twice blessed. The messages they brought from Christ have been delivered, and returned to them. And they return them gladly unto Him.

10. Behold the store of miracles set out for you to give. Are you not worth the gift, when God appointed it be given you? Judge not God's Son, but follow in the way He has established. Christ has dreamed the dream of a forgiven world. It is His gift, whereby a sweet transition can be made from death to life; from hopelessness to hope. Let us an instant dream with Him. His dream awakens us to truth. His vision gives the means for a return to our unlost and everlasting sanctity in God.

DAY 28 — LESSON 161

Give me your blessing, holy Son of God.

1. Today we practice differently, and take a stand against our anger, that our fears may disappear and offer room to love. Here is salvation in the simple words in which we practice with today's idea. Here is the answer to temptation which can never fail to welcome in the Christ where fear and anger had prevailed before. Here is Atonement made complete, the world passed safely by and Heaven now restored. Here is the answer of the Voice for God.

2. Complete abstraction is the natural condition of the mind. But part of it is now unnatural. It does not look on everything as one. It sees instead but fragments of the whole, for only thus could it invent the partial world you see. The purpose of all seeing is to show you what you wish to see. All hearing but brings to your mind the sounds it wants to hear.

3. Thus were specifics made. And now it is specifics we must use in practicing. We give them to the Holy Spirit, that He may employ them for a purpose which is different from the one we gave to them. Yet He can use but what we made, to teach us from a different point of view, so we can see a different use in everything.

4. One brother is all brothers. Every mind contains all minds, for every mind is one. Such is the truth. Yet do these thoughts make clear the meaning of creation? Do these words bring perfect clarity with them to you? What can they seem to be but empty sounds; pretty, perhaps, correct in sentiment, yet fundamentally not understood nor understandable. The mind that taught itself to think specifically can no longer grasp abstraction in the sense that it is all-encompassing. We need to see a little, that we learn a lot.

5. It seems to be the body that we feel limits our freedom, makes us suffer, and at last puts out our life. Yet bodies are but symbols for a concrete form of fear. Fear without symbols calls for no response, for symbols can stand for the meaningless. Love needs no symbols, being true. But fear attaches to specifics, being false.

6. Bodies attack, but minds do not. This thought is surely reminiscent of our text, where it is often emphasized. This is the reason bodies easily become fear's symbols. You have many times been urged to look beyond the body, for its sight presents the symbol of love's

"enemy" Christ's vision does not see. The body is the target for attack, for no one thinks he hates a mind. Yet what but mind directs the body to attack? What else could be the seat of fear except what thinks of fear?

7. Hate is specific. There must be a thing to be attacked. An enemy must be perceived in such a form he can be touched and seen and heard, and ultimately killed. When hatred rests upon a thing, it calls for death as surely as God's Voice proclaims there is no death. Fear is insatiable, consuming everything its eyes behold, seeing itself in everything, compelled to turn upon itself and to destroy.

8. Who sees a brother as a body sees him as fear's symbol. And he will attack, because what he beholds is his own fear external to himself, poised to attack, and howling to unite with him again. Mistake not the intensity of rage projected fear must spawn. It shrieks in wrath, and claws the air in frantic hope it can reach to its maker and devour him.

9. This do the body's eyes behold in one whom Heaven cherishes, the angels love and God created perfect. This is his reality. And in Christ's vision is his loveliness reflected in a form so holy and so beautiful that you could scarce refrain from kneeling at his feet. Yet you will take his hand instead, for you are like him in the sight that sees him thus. Attack on him is enemy to you, for you will not perceive that in his hands is your salvation. Ask him but for this, and he will give it to you. Ask him not to symbolize your fear. Would you request that love destroy itself? Or would you have it be revealed to you and set you free?

10. Today we practice in a form we have attempted earlier. Your readiness is closer now, and you will come today nearer Christ's vision. If you are intent on reaching it, you will succeed today. And once you have succeeded, you will not be willing to accept the witnesses your body's eyes call forth. What you will see will sing to you of ancient melodies you will remember. You are not forgot in Heaven. Would you not remember it?

11. Select one brother, symbol of the rest, and ask salvation of him. See him first as clearly as you can, in that same form to which you are accustomed. See his face, his hands and feet, his clothing. Watch him smile, and see familiar gestures which he makes so frequently. Then think of this: What you are seeing now conceals from you the sight of one who can forgive you all your sins; whose sacred hands can take away the nails which pierce your own, and lift the crown of thorns which you have placed upon your bleeding head. Ask this of him, that he may set you free:

Give me your blessing, holy Son of God. I
would behold you with the eyes of Christ,
and see my perfect sinlessness in you.

12. And He will answer Whom you called upon. For He will hear the Voice for God in you, and answer in your own. Behold him now, whom you have seen as merely flesh and bone, and recognize that Christ has come to you. Today's idea is your safe escape from anger and from fear. Be sure you use it instantly, should you be tempted to attack a brother and perceive in him the symbol of your fear. And you will see him suddenly transformed from enemy to savior; from the devil into Christ.

DAY 29 — LESSON 183

I call upon God's Name and on my own.

1. God's Name is holy, but no holier than yours. To call upon His Name is but to call upon your own. A father gives his son his name, and thus identifies the son with him. His brothers share his name, and thus are they united in a bond to which they turn for their identity. Your Father's Name reminds you who you are, even within a world that does not know; even though you have not remembered it.

2. God's Name can not be heard without response, nor said without an echo in the mind that calls you to remember. Say His Name, and you invite the angels to surround the ground on which you stand, and sing to you as they spread out their wings to keep you safe, and shelter you from every worldly thought that would intrude upon your holiness.

3. Repeat God's Name, and all the world responds by laying down illusions. Every dream the world holds dear has suddenly gone by, and where it seemed to stand you find a star; a miracle of grace. The sick arise, healed of their sickly thoughts. The blind can see; the deaf can hear. The sorrowful cast off their mourning, and the tears of pain are dried as happy laughter comes to bless the world.

4. Repeat the Name of God, and little names have lost their meaning. No temptation but becomes a nameless and unwanted thing before God's Name. Repeat His Name, and see how easily you will forget the names of all the gods you valued. They have lost the name of god you gave them. They become anonymous and valueless to you, although before you let the Name of God replace their little names, you stood before them worshipfully, naming them as gods.

5. Repeat the Name of God, and call upon your Self, Whose Name is His. Repeat His Name, and all the tiny, nameless things on earth slip into right perspective. Those who call upon the Name of God can not mistake the nameless for the Name, nor sin for grace, nor bodies for the holy Son of God. And should you join a brother as you sit with him in silence, and repeat God's Name along with him within your quiet mind, you have established there an altar which reaches to God Himself and to His Son.

6. Practice but this today; repeat God's Name slowly again and still again. Become oblivious to every name but His. Hear nothing else. Let all your thoughts become anchored on this. No other word we use

except at the beginning, when we say today's idea but once. And then God's Name becomes our only thought, our only word, the only thing that occupies our minds, the only wish we have, the only sound with any meaning, and the only Name of everything that we desire to see; of everything that we would call our own.

7. Thus do we give an invitation which can never be refused. And God will come, and answer it Himself. Think not He hears the little prayers of those who call on Him with names of idols cherished by the world. They cannot reach Him thus. He cannot hear requests that He be not Himself, or that His Son receive another name than His.

8. Repeat God's Name, and you acknowledge Him as sole Creator of reality. And you acknowledge also that His Son is part of Him, creating in His Name. Sit silently, and let His Name become the all-encompassing idea that holds your mind completely. Let all thoughts be still except this one. And to all other thoughts respond with this, and see God's Name replace the thousand little names you gave your thoughts, not realizing that there is one Name for all there is, and all that there will be.

9. Today you can achieve a state in which you will experience the gift of grace. You can escape all bondage of the world, and give the world the same release you found. You can remember what the world forgot, and offer it your own remembering. You can accept today the part you play in its salvation, and your own as well. And both can be accomplished perfectly.

10. Turn to the Name of God for your release, and it is given you. No prayer but this is necessary, for it holds them all within it. Words are insignificant, and all requests unneeded when God's Son calls on his Father's Name. His Father's Thoughts become his own. He makes his claim to all his Father gave, is giving still, and will forever give. He calls on Him to let all things he thought he made be nameless now, and in their place the holy Name of God becomes his judgment of their worthlessness.

11. All little things are silent. Little sounds are soundless now. The little things of earth have disappeared. The universe consists of nothing but the Son of God, who calls upon his Father. And his Father's Voice gives answer in his Father's holy Name. In this eternal, still relationship, in which communication far transcends all words, and yet exceeds in depth and height whatever words could possibly convey, is peace eternal. In our Father's Name, we would experience this peace today. And in His Name, it shall be given us.

DAY 30 — LESSON 189

I feel the Love of God within me now.

1. There is a light in you the world can not perceive. And with its eyes you will not see this light, for you are blinded by the world. Yet you have eyes to see it. It is there for you to look upon. It was not placed in you to be kept hidden from your sight. This light is a reflection of the thought we practice now. To feel the Love of God within you is to see the world anew, shining in innocence, alive with hope, and blessed with perfect charity and love.

2. Who could feel fear in such a world as this? It welcomes you, rejoices that you came, and sings your praises as it keeps you safe from every form of danger and of pain. It offers you a warm and gentle home in which to stay a while. It blesses you throughout the day, and watches through the night as silent guardian of your holy sleep. It sees salvation in you, and protects the light in you, in which it sees its own. It offers you its flowers and its snow, in thankfulness for your benevolence.

3. This is the world the Love of God reveals. It is so different from the world you see through darkened eyes of malice and of fear, that one belies the other. Only one can be perceived at all. The other one is wholly meaningless. A world in which forgiveness shines on everything, and peace offers its gentle light to everyone, is inconceivable to those who see a world of hatred rising from attack, poised to avenge, to murder and destroy.

4. Yet is the world of hatred equally unseen and inconceivable to those who feel God's Love in them. Their world reflects the quietness and peace that shines in them; the gentleness and innocence they see surrounding them; the joy with which they look out from the endless wells of joy within. What they have felt in them they look upon, and see its sure reflection everywhere.

5. What would you see? The choice is given you. But learn and do not let your mind forget this law of seeing: You will look upon that which you feel within. If hatred finds a place within your heart, you will perceive a fearful world, held cruelly in death's sharp-pointed, bony fingers. If you feel the Love of God within you, you will look out on a world of mercy and of love.

6. Today we pass illusions, as we seek to reach to what is true in us, and feel its all-embracing tenderness, its Love which knows us perfect as itself, its sight which is the gift its Love bestows on us. We learn the way today. It is as sure as Love itself, to which it carries us. For its simplicity avoids the snares the foolish convolutions of the world's apparent reasoning but serve to hide.

7. Simply do this: Be still, and lay aside all thoughts of what you are and what God is; all concepts you have learned about the world; all images you hold about yourself. Empty your mind of everything it thinks is either true or false, or good or bad, of every thought it judges worthy, and all the ideas of which it is ashamed. Hold onto nothing. Do not bring with you one thought the past has taught, nor one belief you ever learned before from anything. Forget this world, forget this course, and come with wholly empty hands unto your God.

8. Is it not He Who knows the way to you? You need not know the way to Him. Your part is simply to allow all obstacles that you have interposed between the Son and God the Father to be quietly removed forever. God will do His part in joyful and immediate response. Ask and receive. But do not make demands, nor point the road to God by which He should appear to you. The way to reach Him is merely to let Him be. For in that way is your reality proclaimed as well.

9. And so today we do not choose the way in which we go to Him. But we do choose to let Him come. And with this choice we rest. And in our quiet hearts and open minds, His Love will blaze its pathway of itself. What has not been denied is surely there, if it be true and can be surely reached. God knows His Son, and knows the way to him. He does not need His Son to show Him how to find His way. Through every opened door His Love shines outward from its home within, and lightens up the world in innocence.

10. *Father, we do not know the way to You. But we have called, and You have answered us. We will not interfere. Salvation's ways are not our own, for they belong to You. And it is unto You we look for them. Our hands are open to receive Your gifts. We have no thoughts we think apart from You, and cherish no beliefs of what we are, or Who created us. Yours is the way that we would find and follow. And we ask but that Your Will, which is our own as well, be done in us and in the world, that it become a part of Heaven now. Amen.*

SIXTY ANSWERS

~ ∘ ~

This section contains sixty questions, although many of these are actually two-part questions. These questions will help you review your understanding of the condensed version of the Course in this book. The answers given here to these questions are very brief to introduce the correct answers to you. The same exact questions are identified in the book *"A Course in Miracles" Seven Keys to Heaven.* In that book, the answers are elaborated upon to build upon what you have learned in the Two-Month Bridge.

QUESTION 1. Why is the Course summarized by these two lines: "Nothing real can be threatened. Nothing unreal exists," and what is a miracle and who benefits from the expression of a miracle?

ANSWER 1. The whole Course is a course in discriminating between reality and illusions. The line "Nothing real can be threatened" means your reality in God can never be lost. The line "Nothing unreal exists" means the blocks to your awareness of your reality are all only illusions of reality that do not exist.

A miracle is an expression of love. A miracle always benefits the giver and receiver, who both experience an increase of love.

QUESTION 2. How would you compare miracles with revelation?

ANSWER 2. Revelation is a direct transcendental experience of God initiated by God in contrast to miracles, which induce interpersonal sharing with your brother. Revelation brings about only experience. Miracles facilitate action, which is more useful for you now because miracles help you overcome fear and produce healing in interpersonal relationships.

QUESTION 3. What is "the only lack you really need" to correct?

ANSWER 3. The only lack you really need to heal is your false perception that you are separate from God. This illusion of separation needs to be corrected so you can recognize your union with God that was never lost.

QUESTION 4. What is the Holy Spirit's plan called the "Atonement" and what will be the end result of this plan?

ANSWER 4. The Atonement is the Holy Spirit's remedy of love that corrects all errors at every level of consciousness and results in healing the split mind thus restoring the mind to its wholeness in Heaven.

QUESTION 5. What is your only responsibility in order to be a miracle worker, and what is your responsibility in relation to fear?

ANSWER 5. The only responsibility required of you as a miracle worker is to accept the Atonement for yourself. Then through the Holy Spirit, your healed mind can bring healing to other minds.
   Controlling and correcting fear is your responsibility, and you must accept this as your responsibility.

QUESTION 6. How is perception different than knowledge?

ANSWER 6. Perception is a temporary form of partial and unstable awareness that is part of the experience of time and space. Knowledge is a stable form of complete awareness that is experienced in Heaven and provides total certainty.

QUESTION 7. What is the authority problem?

ANSWER 7. The authority problem is the false perception that God is not your Author, and therefore you must be the author of yourself. This false belief in self-creation causes confusion, fear, and discontent due to losing the awareness of the peace of God.

QUESTION 8. What are "your greatest strengths now"?

ANSWER 8. Your greatest strengths now are teaching and learning, which gives you the power to change your mind and bring changes to the minds of others. These changes in perception that bring healing are miracles.

QUESTION 9. What is the ego?

ANSWER 9. The ego is simply the false idea of being alone and separate from others and from God. The ego came about because of the separation, and it will persist only as long as you believe in the idea of separation.

QUESTION 10. What is "the question that *you* must learn to ask in connection with everything"?

ANSWER 10. You must learn to ask, "What is it for?" in relation to everything. Your recognition of your purpose is a way of setting your goal so that your actions will automatically lead you toward that goal.

QUESTION 11. What is the nature and role of the Holy Spirit, and how is the Holy Spirit related to the Atonement?

ANSWER 11. God the Father created the Holy Spirit as His Answer to the separation. The Holy Spirit's job is to return the split minds of God's Sons back to Onemindedness, the wholeness of Heaven. The Holy Spirit is the Mind of the Atonement that will bring healing by correcting all errors in perception and will facilitate awakening in Heaven.

QUESTION 12. What is the significance of sharing, and what is the opposite of sharing?

ANSWER 12. Sharing is the means in which love is expressed as healing in the world and as creating in the oneness of Heaven. The opposite of sharing is the ego's expression of division that separates, producing conflicting thoughts that cannot be shared.

QUESTION 13. How are the ego and guilt related and will the ego eventually be destroyed?

ANSWER 13. The ego itself is a fearful thought of guilt. Responding in any way by identifying with the ego will bring guilt and the fear of punishment associated with guilt.

The ego cannot be destroyed because it is a part of your mind. But the ego will eventually be undone, meaning it will be reinterpreted so love and sharing will replace all guilt and fear.

QUESTION 14. What four false perceptions support the illusion that anger is justified, and what is the message of the crucifixion?

ANSWER 14. Anger is based on believing four false premises: You have been attacked. Your attack in return is justified. You are in no way responsible for your attack in return. Your brother is worthy of attack rather than of love.

The message of the crucifixion is that the body can be attacked, but you are not a body. Your reality is beyond destruction. You are invulnerable because you *are* love and so you must teach only love.

QUESTION 15. The ego functions using the projection of guilt and separation, but what is the alternative to projection?

ANSWER 15. In contrast to the ego's use of the projection of guilt and separation, the Holy Spirit uses extension to bring healing, wholeness, and peace to the sleeping Sons of God. The Holy Spirit extends love to you, but you must extend it to others in order to recognize that it is within you.

QUESTION 16. What is the significance of light in relation to your mind and in relation to your brothers and sisters in the Sonship?

ANSWER 16. Light is significant to you because God's light is what your mind is. Light is significant in your relationships because the light that God has extended to you can then be extended by you to your brothers and sisters, who in turn extend light back to you in the miracle of mutual healing.

QUESTION 17. You made the ego, but what does the Course say about letting go of your identification with the ego?

ANSWER 17. The ego is an unloving illusion claiming that you are a separate being. By seeing the ego as unbelievable in everyone, you can easily give up this illusion about your identity. Letting go of the ego is achieved by accepting the Atonement, an act of sharing, which reveals you cannot be alone. Learning that you cannot be alone brings the awareness that the ego idea of separation is not true.

QUESTION 18. Can you find the divine only by looking within yourself, and what must you do to find your place in God's Kingdom?

ANSWER 18. You can experience the divine within yourself, but you cannot find your true nature by looking within yourself *alone*. You can find your place in God's Kingdom only by acknowledging and appreciating your brother's place with you in the Sonship.

QUESTION 19. What is the best way to utilize the body?

ANSWER 19. The Holy Spirit teaches you that the best way to use the body is as a communication device for healing and for joining with your brother. Using the body lovelessly will produce sickness as a by-product.

QUESTION 20. What are errors, and what is the best attitude to have about errors of others and about correcting your own errors?

ANSWER 20. Errors are mistakes of the ego that can be corrected. Your best attitude toward errors of others is to not react to them at all. Errors, sometimes mistakenly called "sins," are merely a lack of love. Giving errors to the Holy Spirit for correction and accepting the Atonement provide perfect love that supplies the love that had been lacking.

QUESTION 21. How would you compare the Holy Spirit's forgiveness through overlooking errors with the ego's plan of forgiveness?

ANSWER 21. The ego's plan of forgiveness is to clearly examine errors and then overlook them, which makes errors seem real so they cannot be overlooked. The Holy Spirit's plan of forgiveness is to overlook errors immediately in order to keep them unreal for you. Instead of looking at errors even just to examine them, the Holy Spirit wants you to look at your brother's reality in Christ because doing so reminds you of your own reality in Christ.

QUESTION 22. What do bedtime dreams have in common with the dream of this world in apparent banishment from God, and is it helpful for you to sympathize with your brother by agreeing with his belief in his sickness?

ANSWER 22. The dreams that seem real while sleeping in your bed instantly disappear when you wake up in the morning. Similarly, this world appears real to you, while in fact you are sleeping in Heaven right now. It seems natural for your dream self and dream world to be replaced by your everyday self and everyday world. Likewise, you will think it is perfectly natural to see your earthly self and earthly world disappear, replaced by your true Self in Christ when you wake up in Heaven.

It is not helpful for you to sympathize with your brother in his belief in sickness because your sympathy for him will encourage him to continue to deny the Love of God that is within him. Instead, it is very helpful to see his reality, which is his invulnerability as a holy Son of God.

QUESTION 23. What does light mean to God and to you, and what is the relationship between God's Will and your will?

ANSWER 23. God created you by giving Himself to you through extending His Light into you, making you an eternal part of His Light. Your mind is light, which you can extend to others just as God has extended His Mind and His Light to you.

You are afraid of God's Will because you imagine your will is different than His, but your spiritual growth depends on recognizing the truth that your will is exactly the same as God's Will.

QUESTION 24. What are the characteristics of your perceptions of the real world, and why do these perceptions lead to awakening in Heaven?

ANSWER 24. In contrast to the everyday world that contains both unloving false perceptions and loving true perceptions, the real world consists of only loving true perceptions. All loving thoughts are eternal so perceiving the real world leads to awakening in Heaven because the content of pure love is so much like God the Father.

QUESTION 25. Is the world outside your mind or inside your mind?

ANSWER 25. The world you see around you is entirely within you mind. The world is a dream image you have projected outside your mind and your body is a dream image which you have mistakenly identified as your self in your dream world. There are two worlds in your mind: One is the real world of only loving thoughts. The other is your everyday world of both loving and unloving thoughts, which you have projected outwardly.

QUESTION 26. What enables you to see the real world of loving thoughts, and what are the various results of having the vision of the real world?

ANSWER 26. You must accept Christ's vision given to you by Christ and the Holy Spirit to enable you to perceive the real world of only loving thoughts that reflect Heaven. But you must accept His vision as yours, and not rely on the vision shown to you by your physical eyes.

When you see the real world of loving thoughts, you will begin to identify with your true nature of love. Seeing the real world will lead to seeing the face of Christ and bringing back the memory of God.

QUESTION 27. Why are you attracted to love and yet afraid of both love and redemption, and what happened the first time you requested "special favor" (special love) from God?

ANSWER 27. God is Love, and you are love as an expression of God. You are naturally attracted to love since love is attracted to love with an irresistible power. Ironically you are afraid of love and redemption because you want to hold on to the illusions you have made rather than accept the reality of God's Love. You are afraid of yourself— meaning your Self—and would rather cling to an imaginary self that has no reality.

Some parts of the Sonship, who were in Heaven before the separation, asked God for "special favor." They wanted God to give them special love, meaning they wanted more love than God gave every part of the Sonship. God could not agree to unequal love, and so parts of the Sonship made the separation. They closed off communication with God and fell asleep in Heaven while dreaming of the illusory world of time and space.

QUESTION 28. How are light, vision, and Christ related?

ANSWER 28. Christ is light and love, and He gives His vision through the medium of light and love. Christ's vision shows you the real world of only light and love. To receive Christ's vision requires that you receive His light that enables you to perceive the face of Christ in the real world. There are only two emotions: fear and love. You made the illusion of fear. God created love as the extension of His Reality. Christ's vision enables you to choose the reality of love instead of the illusion of fear.

QUESTION 29. How would you compare partial awareness with the awareness of wholeness, and if you love everyone except one person whom you see as guilty, what will the result be?

ANSWER 29. Perception is partial awareness of this world. Knowledge is total awareness of wholeness that exists in Heaven. There are parts in the knowledge of Heaven, but the parts are not limited. Each part or aspect in Heaven contains the whole, meaning each part has the total awareness of knowledge and no part is separate from any other part. You are a part of Christ and are simultaneously the whole of Christ.

Excluding anyone from your love by perceiving guilt will prevent you from understanding or experiencing the true nature of love. You cannot look upon some parts of the Sonship as more worthy of love than other parts without fostering specialness and guilt within your own mind, which will darken your awareness of God's Love within you.

QUESTION 30. What is the importance of your power of decision?

ANSWER 30. Your power of decision directs your path. You have only two alternatives: You can choose either the ego or the Holy Spirit. Choosing the ego fosters guilt, illusion, and unhappiness. Choosing the Holy Spirit opens you to holiness, truth, and happiness. Letting the Holy Spirit decide for you allows the Atonement to undo your errors and leads to awakening in Heaven.

QUESTION 31. Who is called to enter the circle of Atonement, and what does the Holy Spirit ask of you?

ANSWER 31. You are called to enter the circle of Atonement and so is *every* Son of God. When you accept the Atonement, you accept your own holiness in this circle of purity where Jesus stands beside you. If you see any brother outside as guilty, you will join him outside the circle. If you see your brother as holy, he will join you within the circle of Atonement where you can give him your embrace of love.

The Holy Spirit asks you to give Him *every* bit of pain and *every* unloving thought you have hidden in darkness. When you join your perception with the Holy Spirit's, your dark illusions will dissolve in the light of truth. Yet the Holy Spirit cannot heal what you do not give to Him.

QUESTION 32. Holiness is yours, but what can you do with your mind to help others with your holiness, and what are the two categories of thought you need to adopt as your way of perceiving your brother and yourself?

ANSWER 32. The best way to let your holiness help others is to clean your mind so it becomes a pure reflection of the Holiness coming from God that shines through you to the world. When the mirror of your mind only reflects holiness, you become a vehicle for healing others and yourself.

The Holy Spirit teaches you that there are only two categories for correctly evaluating your brother's behavior and your own behavior. Your brother and you can only express love or call for love. If you see a brother call for love, you can supply the love he is calling for and bring healing.

QUESTION 33. What are the features of the holy instant?

ANSWER 33. The holy instant is an experience of giving and receiving in perfect communication with the entire Sonship. The holy instant is the Holy Spirit's gift given to you as you give it to your brother in an experience of sharing in the present moment without any reference to the past or future. The holy instant is the suspension of all judgment. It is a recognition of union with God the Father, the Holy Spirit, and the Sonship joined in Christ. The holy instant opens you to the limitless nature of love because it extends to eternity and to the Mind of God, the Home of Love.

QUESTION 34. What is the link between the special relationship and guilt, and do you need to understand miracles in order to perform them?

ANSWER 34. In the special relationship, each partner's ego wants to get specialness from the other. The ego offers an illusion of love to attract each partner, while hiding the fact that getting specialness must foster guilt and not love. When special love relationships fail, the love is revealed as an illusion and partners are angry. This anger is a projection of guilt, which denies each partner's original goal of taking specialness from the partner.

Miracles do not require your understanding in order to perform them. In fact, the transcendental nature of miracles is so radically different than your everyday experience in the world that you do not understand them. But it is very helpful to know you can rely on the Holy Spirit and can perform miracles as expressions of love by letting them happen *through* you.

QUESTION 35. What is the nature of love in the special love relationship, and what is traded in the bargain of a special love relationship?

ANSWER 35. Love in a special relationship is not love it all; it is merely an illusion of love. Love in a special relationship is really special love, which pretends to offer union, while it only fosters separateness based on specialness. The special relationship is a rejection of God's Love based on union and instead embraces the acquisition of specialness.

In the special relationship, each partner attempts to trade his unworthy "self" for the more worthy "self" of the other and thereby acquire the other person's specialness for himself. This relationship is about taking without giving and results in guilt, not the union of true love.

QUESTION 36. What will forgiveness show you in the real world, and what happens when two people join in a holy relationship?

ANSWER 36. Practicing forgiveness will show you the beauty and holiness of the real world of all loving thoughts. You will see the true divine holiness of your brothers and sisters in Christ.

When two people join in the holy relationship, a holy instant occurs and the Holy Spirit enters the relationship. The partners join for a common purpose with common interests, but the Holy Spirit replaces the partners' goals with His goal of holiness.

QUESTION 37. When you are uncertain about a situation, what do you need to consider and clarify in order to be led by the Holy Spirit?

ANSWER 37. When you are involved in any situation, you need to clearly identify the goal by asking yourself, "What outcome do I want?" Setting the goal will enable you to perceive the situation as a means of accomplishing the goal. Therefore, you will disregard everything in the situation that interferes with reaching the goal and will focus all your efforts toward whatever aspects of the situation that will help to accomplish the goal. The Course recommends making truth your goal of every situation because that is the Holy Spirit's purpose and will result in peace of mind.

QUESTION 38. What is required of you to manifest the miracle of the holy instant?

ANSWER 38. Having the experience of the holy instant requires most of all your willingness to let it be the miracle that it is. In order to give your willingness to the holy instant, you must give up your false belief that you are not worthy of it. You do not have to remove all your fear, hate, and guilt before you open yourself to the holy instant or before you call upon the Holy Spirit. After all, the holy instant and the

Holy Spirit have been given to you as your means of releasing you from your inner blocks if you only give your little willingness to be healed.

QUESTION 39. What is it like to go beyond the limitations imposed by the body, and what is the Course really recommending when it says "you need do nothing"?

ANSWER 39. The feeling of releasing your body awareness involves experiencing a state of union with something or someone beyond the limitations of your small self. You let go of fear and accept love as union by joining with anything and transcending the ordinarily accepted "laws" of time and space that govern the body and limit you. In this holy instant you remember your true nature is love.

The Course phrase "you need do nothing" refers to doing nothing with the body so you can rest and find peace within. The Workbook advocates a variety of meditation practices as long as these quiet times do not reinforce the false belief in sinfulness and unworthiness. Finding your "quiet center within" brings communion with the Holy Spirit.

QUESTION 40. What is the body's relationship to the ego, to love, to your Self, and to God?

ANSWER 40. The body is intended to be a limitation. It limits your awareness of love, of your Self, and of God. The ego relies on the body to prove to you that you are limited and you are separate. The ego tells you that you are the body. Through this false identification with the body, the ego replaces the Reality of Heaven, your true Home, with the apparent reality of this world of form, the home of the body. The way to open your mind to the belief in limitlessness is to give your little willingness to welcoming the holy instant that will reveal aspects of your true nature beyond limitations.

QUESTION 41. What is the truth about sin and its effects?

ANSWER 41. The idea of sin is that your reality, your true nature created by God, can be violated. If you believe that your reality can be violated or changed in any way, then the ramifications of that belief are that you will invite a whole series of other false beliefs. These additional false beliefs are the beliefs that God made a mistake when He created you, that you have offended God, that you should feel guilty, and that you are now separate from God, which is the foundation of your belief in the ego. If sins violate reality, they cannot be corrected. But sins are merely mistakes that represent a lack of love. They are corrected by supplying the love that was lacking.

QUESTION 42. What role does love play and what role does your brother play in lifting the veil that separates you from your Home in Heaven?

ANSWER 42. God's Love calls you to awaken. Also, you love God, Who created you out of Love. You are irresistibly drawn by the attraction of love, which overcomes every obstacle on your path to awakening. Love Itself will awaken you with the realization that you are love just as God created you.

Your brother whom you have forgiven becomes your savior who joins with you in your awakening. Your forgiveness reveals to you that your brother is holy as part of the one Christ and reminds you that you are just as holy and just as much a part of the one Christ as he is.

QUESTION 43. What will the Holy Spirit do for you when you accept His plan as your one function, and what is the vision that carries "the memory of what you are"?

ANSWER 43. When you accept God's plan as your most important function, you give the Holy Spirit permission to arrange everything about your life to facilitate your accomplishment of your part in God's plan.

The "vision of the Son of God" holds the "memory of what you are." This vision of the Son of God can also be called the "face of Christ." It is a vision of a great expanding circle of blazing light. It will remind you of your intense love for God, and you will leap into God's Arms as He takes the final step of lifting your mind back to the Mind of Christ in Heaven.

QUESTION 44. What's important to know about the power and the effects of your decision making?

ANSWER 44. The most important thing to know about the power of your decision making is that all your experiences are the result of your own decisions. Accepting responsibility for experiencing exactly what you have asked for in every situation means you can never be a victim.

Since your decision making is so powerful in the effects it brings to you, you must be very careful about what goal you decide you want to achieve. You can safely let the Holy Spirit decide for you because He will choose the goal of holiness and will decide for God for you. The goal of holiness will help you see holiness in your brother, and your brother will become your savior, enabling you to see your own holiness.

QUESTION 45. What does forgiveness really forgive, and who walks with you on your path of forgiveness?

ANSWER 45. Forgiveness always forgives only illusions. Since illusions are nothing and not real, they did not happen in reality and therefore did not happen at all. Thus forgiveness merely forgives what never happened. Forgiveness is looking past illusions and looking for what is real. If you think what you are forgiving is real, you will not be able to forgive wholeheartedly without resentment. But if you understand you forgive only illusions, you will have no reason to withhold your forgiveness.

Practicing forgiveness reveals that Christ walks with you on your path. Christ's vision will show you the holiness in your brother. You will gladly take your brother's hand, and he will just as gladly take your hand. You become saviors for each other as you both take the hand of Christ.

QUESTION 46. What's the importance of having two different makers of the world, and what is the importance of your special function?

ANSWER 46. The sleeping Sons of God made the illusory world of form. Yet there is another Maker of the world Who is the Holy Spirit. God assigned the Holy Spirit the task of bringing reflections of God's laws into the world of form. This Maker manifested the real world, the face of Christ, and the Atonement. Because there are two makers of the world, you have two choices: You can choose the darkness made to proclaim specialness or you can choose forgiveness that reflects Heaven.

You made specialness as a means of separating yourself from your brother. However, the Holy Spirit uses the idea of specialness positively by assigning a special function to you alone. Your special function is always a specific expression of forgiveness that only you can accomplish.

QUESTION 47. What can you do to let go of time—meaning let go of the past and future in order to accept the eternal now?

ANSWER 47. Before you can let go of the idea of time, you must first recognize that it is entirely an illusion. According to the Course, the "tiny tick of time" called the "separation" was healed immediately by God when He created the Holy Spirit as His Answer. This instant of separation is now gone, yet this one instant appears to you as the illusion of the passage of millions and millions of years of time.

Forgiveness is your means of releasing the illusion of time because it always replaces illusions with reality. Forgiveness teaches you to let go of the fear of the past and future and replaces it with the eternal now.

QUESTION 48. Why can't you forgive your brother while still believing he is guilty?

ANSWER 48. If you believe your brother is really guilty, you cannot overlook the reality of that guilt because you will feel you are hiding the truth about him by this kind of false forgiveness that must be seen as self-deception. Fortunately, true forgiveness can overlook guilt because of the simple truth that your brother is just as holy now as when God created him. True forgiveness sees sin as merely an illusion, and illusions are easy to overlook because they are not real.

QUESTION 49. What is the "central figure" playing the role of the "hero" of the dreaming of the world, and how is the "complete picture of the Son of God" described in Chapter 28 different from the "vision of the Son of God" and the "face of Christ" described in other chapters?

ANSWER 49. "The body is the central figure in the dreaming of the world." This quote is saying that the "hero" of your dream of separation is the body. Awakening, when it finally comes, will be a release from the illusion of the body and an acceptance of your true spiritual nature.

The function of Holy Spirit is to show the "whole picture" of the Son of God to each seeker, who thought he was only a broken and separate part. When the seeker sees the "complete picture of the Son of God," he will see exactly the same image described elsewhere in the Course as the "vision of the Son of God" and the "face of Christ." This picture of his Identity is only an image, but it is the "place where the Father receives His Son"—where God takes the final step of awakening His Son.

QUESTION 50. In addition to Jesus, called your "elder brother" in the Course, who is your savior and why is this savior so important?

ANSWER 50. You do not have the power to awaken yourself. You do have the power to heal your brother's mind, which helps him to awaken. Your brother blesses you for your forgiveness and becomes your savior by empowering you to forgive yourself. By helping your brother to heal his mind, you can heal your own mind, leading to your awakening. Your primary means of healing others and in turn healing yourself is forgiveness, which heals the perception of separation. When you forgive your brother, you join with him and overcome the sense of separation manufactured by dreams of space and time. You are your brother's savior and your brother is your savior because forgiveness is mutually beneficial.

QUESTION 51. What is an idol, and how do idols affect you and your relationships with others?

ANSWER 51. An idol is a substitute for God or Heaven or any other aspect of the divine presence. An idol is always a belief in something that does not exist, but which seems more desirable than reality. Idols are the currency of self-deception. Idols represent the desire for more of something—anything unreal—to fulfill the manufactured need for specialness. Letting go of idols requires releasing your striving for specialness and accepting your true equality with your brother. If you decide you want to see the face of Christ and wake up in Heaven, you will have to let go of the idols that blind you to the divine presence underlying all of life.

QUESTION 52. When you join your brother in the one purpose of forgiveness, whose hand do you hold and whose face will you see, and why is anger never justified and forgiveness always justified?

ANSWER 52. When you take your brother's hand by joining in the purpose of forgiveness, you are likewise taking the hand of Christ. As you look upon your brother's face, you can see the divine light shining through him to reveal the face of Christ.

You are not an ego or a body that can be attacked. In your true nature you are invulnerable. Every Son of God always deserves only love so anger is never justified. Anger is merely a projection of guilt and failure to perceive holiness. Forgiveness is always justified because what you pardon are only illusions. Thus forgiveness is merely the giving up of the false judgments of separation. Forgiveness is always warranted because every Son of God deserves the healing that forgiveness brings.

QUESTION 53. What self-concept masks do you wear, and what is the benefit of admitting that your concept of yourself is mistaken?

ANSWER 53. The face of innocence is the outer mask that you want to present to others. This mask says, "I am a good person in an evil world and would not hurt anyone. But if someone attacked me first, I would have to attack back to protect myself from being unfairly treated. I am innocent because my anger is justified since I am being forced to act in self-defense."

Below the face of innocence is the victim mask and victimizer mask that hide fear, hate, condemnation, and self-condemnation. These concepts of yourself are not your true Self. Taking off these masks will bring the benefit of allowing you to truly admit you really do not know who or what you are. Opening your mind will make room for the Truth to present Itself.

QUESTION 54. What choice does Jesus ask you to make, and what temptations need to be avoided?

ANSWER 54. Christ asks you to choose between being a savior for others and save yourself as well or instead to remain lost in the illusion that says you are a body and not the holy Son of God. If you think Christ is what is real in you, you will choose to follow Christ and rely on His strength.

The major temptation you need to avoid is investing in the idea that you are the body and not the holy Son of God. This false belief will make you think your weakness is your reality. Each time you give in to the illusion of being a body, you have a new opportunity to choose again for the Christ in you that will strengthen you.

QUESTION 55. Who is a teacher of God, and what are his stages of learning trust?

ANSWER 55. A teacher of God is anyone who chooses to be one. His choice implies he has studied the Text, completed the Workbook, and demonstrated his learning by making a deliberate choice to join with another in a holy relationship. His stages of learning trust are listed below:

1. A Period of Undoing — He learns changes are always helpful.

2. A Period of Sorting Out — The teacher of God makes difficult choices based on whether they increase helpfulness or hinder it.

3. A Period of Relinquishment — He feels conflicted about making sacrifices, but later sees his sacrifices were actually blessings in disguise.

4. A Period of Settling Down — He consolidates his learning during a peaceful time and generalizes his learning to many new situations.

5. A Period of Unsettling — He reassesses what is really valuable and valueless. He wants only what is truly valuable and gives up judgment.

6. A Period of Achievement — His peace of mind reflects Heaven since learning has been consolidated and generalized to all situations.

QUESTION 56. How is the face of Christ completely revealed, and how does a teacher of God improve his ability to make decisions?

ANSWER 56. The face of Christ with all of its blazing light can only be seen after all that covers it has been removed. Every covering of the face of Christ is merely an illusion of fear based on a false perception. Forgiveness is the only aim of the Course because it removes every obstructing illusion, every false perception to reveal the spotless face of Christ. Although the face of Christ is an image in the world of form, it is the one form that leads to formlessness because it perfectly reflects Heaven.

The teacher of God improves his ability to make decisions by giving up judgment. The teacher of God turns to the Holy Spirit and asks Him to decide for God for him, and trusts in His answer to every question.

QUESTION 57. What does the teacher of God need to know about judgment?

ANSWER 57. The teacher of God needs to know accurate judgment is impossible for him and only the Holy Spirit is qualified to make totally accurate judgments. Thus he lets judgment happen *through* him by listening to the guidance of the Holy Spirit and acting on His judgment. The judgment happening through the Holy Spirit is that false beliefs in sin and guilt have never changed the perfect holiness of the Son of God.

QUESTION 58. How do teachers of God spend their time, and what must the teacher of God do to be able to let healing happen through him?

ANSWER 58. Becoming a teacher of God requires completing the one year of daily workbook lessons as a foundation for future less structured daily practice. The teacher of God is encouraged to set aside "quiet times" of meditation for every morning and evening to connect with God.

In order to be a healer, a miracle worker, the teacher of God has the one responsibility of accepting the Atonement for himself. This enables his own mind to be healed as his mistakes are forgiven and he releases self-condemnation. His healing is passed along to his pupil through the action of the Holy Spirit, Who unites all the minds of the Sons of God.

QUESTION 59. What does the teacher of God need to learn to make progress and to heal others, and why is it helpful to call on the name of Jesus Christ as a part of healing?

ANSWER 59. The Atonement and healing are identical. The teacher of God makes progress by applying the acceptance of Atonement for himself to more and more situations. Finally he will generalize his learning to apply his acceptance of the Atonement to all situations. Also, the teacher of God needs to learn that forgiveness is healing in which he overlooks the ego and looks for the Son of God in each seeker.

Calling on the name of Jesus, who has perfectly accepted the Atonement, opens you to likewise accept the Atonement for correcting errors and healing perception. Any name is only a symbol, but since the name of Jesus has become the name of God, it calls upon the perfect love that is the Atonement. Calling the name of Jesus brings the divine love it represents and brings gratitude for God's many gifts.

QUESTION 60. Where is the Course curriculum leading you?

ANSWER 60. The Course is leading you to release all your dark illusions and to accept the Holy Spirit's final dream. The one last illusion the Holy Spirit shows you is the face of Christ that brings back the memory of God. This is the same as fully accepting the Atonement, having your mind completely healed by forgiveness, and accepting God's Will as your own will. By giving up your judgment and accepting the judgment of the Holy Spirit, you prepare yourself for God's Final Judgment, which is an acknowledgment that you are His holy Son and that you have never been separate from His eternal Love. In this last stage of your redemption, God takes the final step of welcoming you to the oneness of Heaven, which is merely the release of your illusions of separation.

WHAT'S NEXT?

~ • ~

The book you have just read with its condensed version of the Course can stand on its own as a preparation for studying the full edition of the Course. But actually it is the second of three books that can be used in sequence to provide a thoroughly solid foundation for understanding and applying the Course principles. These three books were already mentioned at the beginning of this book in the "Instructions for the First Month." However, for emphasis, all three books are listed below in their recommended sequence:

1. *An Overview of "A Course in Miracles": Introduction to the Course—What Beginners Need to Know* provides an easy-to-follow outline of your journey through the entire Course from beginning to end. In less than one hundred pages, it introduces the spiritual principles of the Course and helps you decide if you want to deepen your understanding of this path.

2. *The Two-Month Bridge to "A Course in Miracles": A Condensed Edition of "A Course in Miracles"* gives you direct experience of the Course itself for two months. During the first month, you read one fourth of the 1249 pages of the Course. As a learning device, sixty questions are asked and concisely answered. For the second month, you do thirty of the 365 Workbook lessons. This direct experience helps you decide if you want to complete your journey through the entire Course.

3. *"A Course in Miracles" Seven Keys to Heaven* clarifies the significance of the seven tools of the Holy Spirit that are your means of transformation. It also identifies the interrelationships between these seven instruments showing how they all work together and eventually lead toward spiritual awakening. The same sixty questions raised in *The Two-Month Bridge to "A Course in Miracles"* are presented again, and this time answered in a much more complete way to review and to build on what you have previously learned.

Ideally all three books will be read in this sequence. However, these are companion books that can be read in any sequence, and also each book stands on its own as a preparation for the Course. These books are in no way a replacement for completing all three parts of the Course. You are encouraged to read and study the entire *Text* and *Manual for Teachers* and do all of the 365 lessons in the *Workbook for Students*. If you have already walked a long way along the spiritual path, you may not need to read these three books as a preparation for the Course. If you are now fully open to the guidance of the Holy Spirit, He will teach you everything you need to know about the Course. On the other hand, if you are a beginner, these three books will prepare you by opening your mind to the teachings the Holy Spirit wants you to learn and put into practice. The Course requires only that you have the "little willingness" to make the transition from an old way of thinking to a new perception of the world, others, and yourself. These three books make that transition smoother, and then a full study of the Course itself will enable you to complete this transition. Then the Holy Spirit Himself will guide you:

> And if I need a word to help me, He will give it to me. If I need a thought, that will He also give. And if I need but stillness and a tranquil, open mind, these are the gifts I will receive of Him. He is in charge by my request. And He will hear and answer me, because He speaks for God my Father and His holy Son.[1]

---

1. W-361 to 365.1:1-5, p. 486

THE MISSING BLESSING

~ ๐ ~

You will learn a great deal through completing the Two-Month Bridge. Afterwards you may decide to continue with further study of the Course, or you may go in a different direction with your spiritual studies and experiences. In either case, you will learn much more in your journey through life. But what is the most significant lesson for you to learn? The answer is subjective, yet consider the following:

> *Only you can deprive yourself of anything.* Do not oppose this realization, for it is truly the beginning of the dawn of light. Remember also that the denial of this simple fact takes many forms, and these you must learn to recognize and to oppose steadfastly, without exception. This is a crucial step in the reawakening. The beginning phases of this reversal are often quite painful, for as blame is withdrawn from without, there is a strong tendency to harbor it within. It is difficult at first to realize that this is exactly the same thing, for there is no distinction between within and without.[1]

If your spiritual growth is successful, you will learn how to remove all of your tendencies to project any negativity onto your brothers and sisters. Thus you will learn the most important lesson the Course emphasizes—forgiveness of everyone. You are enabled to forgive by realizing God has forgiven you for everything, so it will become quite natural for you to forgive everyone. Yet the greatest blessing you will ever receive is not God's blessing of you since God has already given you all of His love and blessing. The most important blessing you will ever receive is the one you give to yourself. It is the blessing of totally forgiving yourself. Guilt is an illusion of self-punishment. God does not believe in guilt, but you do. The only blessing you are missing is the one you have denied to yourself. God has totally absolved you of all your imaginings of guilt, even the guilt of leaving Heaven, but when will you absolve yourself of all your illusions of guilt by realizing they have no reality? In all of your spiritual lessons, you are merely learning to forgive yourself. There is nothing else you need to learn. When you give yourself this most important blessing, you will leap into Heaven and realize you have never left your Father's Embrace.

---

1. T-11.IV.4:1-6, p. 201

Lightning Source UK Ltd.
Milton Keynes UK
UKHW021433260321
381037UK00006B/1564